Sustaining a Culture of Process Control and Continuous Improvement

The Roadmap for Efficiency and Operational Excellence

Sustaining a Culture of Process Control and Continuous Improvement

The Roadmap for Efficiency and Operational Excellence

By

Philip Gisi

Routledge
Taylor & Francis Group
A PRODUCTIVITY PRESS BOOK

Routledge
Taylor & Francis Group
711 Third Avenue, New York, NY 10017

Productivity Press is an imprint of Taylor & Francis Group, an Informa business

Printed on acid-free paper

International Standard Book Number-13: 978-1-138-54557-1 (Hardback)
International Standard Book Number-13: 978-1-138-29733-3 (Paperback)
International Standard Book Number-13: 978-1-315-09936-1 (eBook)

Library of Congress Cataloging-in-Publication Data

Names: Gisi, Philip, author.
Title: Sustaining a culture of process control and continuous improvement : the roadmap for efficiency and operational excellence / Philip Gisi.
Description: New York : Taylor & Francis, [2018] | Includes bibliographical references and index.
Identifiers: LCCN 2017060755 (print) | LCCN 2018009671 (ebook) | ISBN 9781315099361 (eBook) | ISBN 9781138297333 (pbk. : alk. paper) | ISBN 9781138545571 (hardback : alk. paper)
Subjects: LCSH: Process control. | Corporate culture.
Classification: LCC TS156.8 (ebook) | LCC TS156.8 .G55 2018 (print) | DDC 658.5/62--dc23
LC record available at https://lccn.loc.gov/2017060755

Visit the Taylor & Francis Web site at
http://www.taylorandfrancis.com

and the Productivity Press site at
http://www.ProductivityPress.com

Contents

Foreword

All outcomes are the consequence of a process. It is nearly impossible for even good people to consistently produce ideal results with a poor process both inside and outside the organization. There is a natural tendency to blame the people involved when something goes wrong or is less than ideal, when in reality the vast majority of the time the issue is rooted in an imperfect process, not the people.

The Shingo Institute
Shingo Model Basics, 2016 Utah State University

In the world of continuous improvement, there has been a significant emphasis on lean or lean manufacturing. Perhaps lean is not the right term. Manufacturing is never really lean, since lean implies an end result, destination or goal. Lean, in reality, is a journey. It's a journey of continuous process improvement that starts with understanding a process's current state followed by incrementally working toward a more efficient, desired state. As with any journey, steps must be taken to prepare for the long road ahead. Becoming a leaner organization involves a focus on quality, followed by an ongoing effort to build a more robust, efficient and sustainable process. The purpose of this book is to take you on this lean journey to realize a more efficient operation by ensuring a stable and capable (reliable) process. Stability and capability are prerequisites for sustainable improvements in process efficiency and flow as well as critical to remaining competitive in a constantly expanding global market.

This journey will occur in three parts. Part I focuses on quality improvements with the objective of establishing process stability and capability as the foundation for Part II. Our focus in Part II turns toward implementing efficiency improvements rooted in waste reduction and continuous process flow. Part III explores the culture, principles, systems and behaviors required to achieve a higher level of process performance and the organizational structure, discipline and accountability necessary to build a sustainable lean enterprise.

This journey also explores key topics such as the influence of variation on process performance, the importance of standards for process stability, the impact of variation on process capability, lean tools and techniques for enhancing process efficiency and the mindset required for operation excellence.

As we move ahead, keep in mind, process capability can't be established without process stability and efficiency improvements are meaningless without a stable and capable process. Efficiency is driven through the elimination of waste, rapid problem-solving and the application of just-in-time principles to achieve a more continuous process flow. While pursuing these objectives, we must ensure process control and performance improvements are maintained by reinforcing the behavior necessary for long-term sustainability. Thus, *sustaining a culture of process control and continuous improvement* requires:

Process stability and capability before efficiency
Efficiency through waste elimination and flow improvement
Sustainability through structure, discipline and accountability

The Roadmap for Efficiency and Operational Excellence is built on a solid foundation of stability, capability and control, improved through waste elimination and flow while sustained through organizational structure, discipline and accountability.

These ideas establish the context, slogan and mantra of our operational excellence journey. To visualize this journey, Figure F.1 outlines the building blocks for process quality, efficiency and operational excellence while Figure F.2 presents a high-level roadmap for operational excellence that can be customized and detailed to meet the needs of an enterprise.

Figure F.1 Operational Excellence Maturity.

Quality and Efficiency Improvements → Operational Excellence

	Focus	Goal	Objective	Tools and methods	Benefit
	Process standardization				
Quality improvement	Process stability ⇩	Process predictable over time	Eliminate defects	• Pareto chart • Run and control charts • Problem-solving	Process control
	Process capability ⇩	Process consistently meets customer requirements	Reduce variation	• Histogram • Cause and Effect analysis • SOV studies • Standard work	
Efficiency improvement	Eliminate waste ⇩	Reduce cycle time	Reduce waste	• Value stream and process maps • 5S / visual controls • Changeover • Mistake proofing	Process optimization
	Continuous flow	Smooth, Steady, and continuous (one-piece) flow	Continuous process flow	• JIT / Pull system • Kanban • Work leveling / TPM • Supermarkets / FIFO • VSM / VSD	Value stream optimization

Figure F.2 Operational Excellence Roadmap.

Acknowledgment

Few manuscripts have been as well traveled as this one, the contents of which have been documented and scripted at 30,000 feet in the air, in major cities throughout the world and at some of the busiest airports in the United States, Europe and Asia. This work has been a career passion that has been inspired by years of reading, observing, talking, listening and doing. Inspiration to write about process comes from industry giants such as Liker, Rother, Shook, Womack, Shingo, and so many others I have never met but, who I owe a debt of gratitude for providing me with the knowledge, insight and understanding required to prepare this manuscript. May their impact on humanity be everlasting and may others see this work as a reflection of that reality.

I would like to thank those who have freely shared their knowledge and understanding of process through their books, articles, training, blogs, conversations and the Internet, so that I could see the world from many different perspectives and document a view of process improvement that I hope you will find value-added and insightful. In particular, I would like to thank my wife Kathleen Holloway, for being my listener, editor, supporter and key advisor. I would also like to recognize many of my former colleagues and current associates who have kindly shared their knowledge and understanding of process through training and in-depth conversations on many topics covered in this book. Finally, I would like to thank those who have embraced my counsel and support over the years because their questions, comments and conversations have formulated my thoughts, allowing me to articulate a roadmap for operational excellence presented in this publication.

This text was prepared to present a holistic approach or methodology for continuous process improvement, with each chapter building on the next, unfolding a logical, sequential, sustainable journey toward operational excellence. Although one chapter complements the next, they were also written in a way that each can stand alone, independent of the others. In writing the chapters in this way, you may sense repetitive ideas and themes being revisited throughout this book. This was intentional to maintain chapter autonym, while reinforcing key points essential to understanding the fundamental concepts behind continuous efficiency improvement.

As you read this book, I hope that each chapter enhances your knowledge and understanding and serves to further ignite your passion for the pursuit of operational excellence. In this spirit, I welcome the opportunity to hear and learn from you. If you would like to offer any comments, suggestions or opportunities for improvement concerning this book, please feel free to contact me at gisi.opexcellence@gmail.com.

Introduction

> The four goals of improvement must be to make things easier, better, faster and cheaper. Particular emphasis is placed on a quicker, more flexible response throughout the system.
>
> **The Shingo Model for Operational Excellence**

Overview

When we are hired into a manufacturing or process-orientated company, we are being hired for two primary objectives: first, to maintain process control and second to continuously improve the process. It does not matter if you are hired in logistics, purchasing, maintenance or human resources, you are there to serve the process by ensuring the process or service operators have what they need (e.g. materials and information) to make goods or provide services that satisfy customers and generate revenue for the company.

Engineering designs are expected to produce processes that are stable and capable of delivering products and services that consistently meet customer requirements while all other functions work to support and maintain process control and efficiency improvements. In reality, everything done by the direct or indirect support of operations should ensure that the process continues to satisfy key stakeholders. A process that can't reliably meet customer requirements ends up producing waste, challenging a company's ability to generate capital for its continued growth, profitability and competitiveness.

Process Control

Process control is about maintaining a stable and capable process so that production consistently and reliably delivers the results needed to satisfy customers. Unfortunately, many of the processes we struggle to maintain and improve today, performed well at their inception. Over time, with all running well, other priorities draw our attention elsewhere, leading us to ignore the periodic monitoring and control required for process maintenance. This loss of focus and often unclear process ownership develop into roadblocks for people working with these processes. These unresolved roadblocks lead to the creation of workarounds in order to simply get the job done! Problems continue as new concerns arise, all of which are being overlooked due to a lack of clear process ownership, discipline and accountability. As the number of workarounds increases, process efficiency decreases, impacting the stability and capability of a process to continually meet stakeholder expectations.

Eventually, we come to realize that our processes have broken down and are no longer performing to expectation due to little or no upkeep or maintenance. As with any process or system, if we do not take the time to look for and correct deviations from standard, a process will slowly deteriorate, leaving in its wake defective products, inadequate services, frustrated employees and dissatisfied customers. Complicating the situation further, many organizations embark on efficiency improvements without

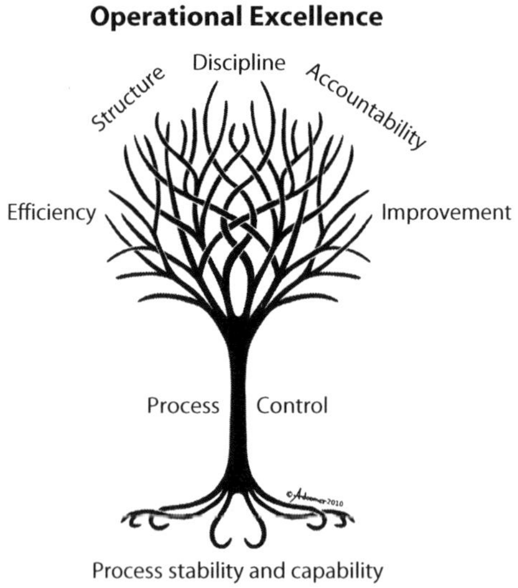

Figure I.1 Operational excellence tree.

first evaluating the integrity of their existing processes. This oversight often jeopardizes the sustainability of subsequent improvements since unstable processes are unlikely to hold up over time. Figure I.1 shows that process control forms the base or foundation upon which efficiency improvements are achieved, which leads to a culture of operational excellence supported by organizational structure, discipline and accountability.

If a company believes the implementation of lean is vital to its future growth and competitiveness, it must first confirm that its core processes such as sales and marketing, design and development and manufacturing have a sound foundation upon which efficiency improvements can be rooted. This foundation is forged by ensuring stable and capable processes are in place along with the discipline necessary to maintain and sustain their intended state over a process's life cycle. Once reliability and control are confirmed, the building blocks are firmly in place and ready to support a more efficient and sustainable operating environment of process improvement.

Continuous Improvement

Continuous improvement is a mindset, it's a competitive advantage, it's a business imperative necessary to grow and develop a more efficient and effective operation. More specifically, continuous improvement is an ongoing effort within an organization to improve products, processes and standards. Often, these efforts are "incremental" in nature but, can also be "breakthrough", focused activities pursued by individuals or teams.

Continuous improvement often involves using the Deming cycle of plan-do-check-act (PDCA). This simple but, effective method can facilitate continuous improvements when approached with structure and discipline as demonstrated later in this text. The following is a brief description of the PDCA cycle.

- *Plan*: The act of stopping to think about differences between the current and desired state while identifying actions required to eliminate causes for the gap.
- *Do*: Executing action(s) intended to remove issues or obstacles, one by one, which are contributing to the gap. This results in incremental improvement toward a more desired state.
- *Check (study)*: Involves reviewing the results, assessing the impact, considering additional options and determining next actions for improvement. It includes stopping to think about what was learned.

- *Act*: Requires follow-up action to drive improvements based on lessons learned and decisions made from data and information acquired in previous do and check cycles.

The fundamental goal of continuous improvement is to reduce variation. Variation is inherent in all processes and is characterized by differences in individual process outputs. Variation is considered a process "evil" and must be managed to realize a reliable process. Variation can be classified as either common cause or special cause variation. Total variation is the combination of special cause and common cause variation acting on a process. Special cause variation affects a process in intermittent, irregular and unpredictable ways, causing process instability. This instability is the result of process defects that manifest themselves as special cause variation. By identifying, targeting and eliminating process defects, these sources of variation can be reduced and controlled to achieve process stability.

Common cause variation affects all individual values of the process output and is indicative of a stable process. It's the result of many sources of variation, consistently acting on the process in predictable ways, and can be reduced through process improvement activities focused on identifying and minimizing the factors contributing to its cause in order to achieve a more reliable output. All products, services and processes experience some degree of variation. By understanding variation's influence on process performance, we begin to see how it affects process stability and capability, which are two characteristics essential to process control and sustainable efficiency improvements.

An organization can manage variation in two ways: they can make their products and processes more robust to variation using methods like Design for Six Sigma (DFSS) or proven tools and techniques such as Six Sigma and total quality management to identify and minimize factors contributing to variation. Since making products more robust against variation is outside the scope of this discussion, we will concentrate our attention on special and common cause variation by understanding their impact on current process performance and how we can use this knowledge to manage it.

The more stable and capable a process is, the better its overall performance. True performance improvement starts at the point where process control is demonstrated because process control is about maintaining a process at its current level of expected performance. Thus, any activity engaged in maintaining an accepted level of performance is not an improvement but simply process maintenance. On the other hand, activities that augment process performance, above the current standard, fall within the realm of continuous improvement. Figure I.2 visualizes the relationship of quality and efficiency improvement under the umbrella of continuous process improvement.

Two major phases within the process improvement journey are quality and efficiency improvement. Quality can be viewed in terms of achieving and maintaining process stability and capability as the foundation for process control. Process control is concerned with the management of deviations from existing standards. Efficiency improvement can be approached from the perspective of waste elimination and continuous flow, which occur when changes are made to elevate existing standards to higher levels of performance. This is the continuous improvement journey that we will be exploring.

Part I: Quality Improvement

This book begins with a discussion of quality improvement and explores the role of variation on process stability. The objective of any process improvement effort is to first ensure a solid foundation is in place upon which to build sustainable efficiency improvements. Process sustainability starts with a stable and capable process. To build and maintain a desirable process, we must understand variation and its impact on resulting outputs. Standardized work will also be discussed as a way to minimize and control process variation. Part I continues with an in-depth discussion of process stability and capability and their roles in continuous efficiency

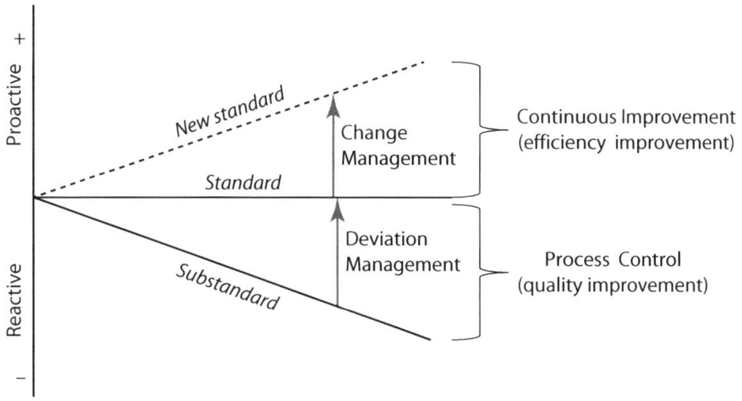

Figure I.2 Continuous process improvement.

improvement. This part ends with the fundamental activity of process control as a way to maintain stability and capability before turning our attention to efficiency improvements. The following is a brief overview of each chapter in Part I.

Chapter 1: Process Variation

In the world of manufacturing and many other disciplines, variation is considered the enemy. Reflect on air travel, for example; it would be great if every plane arrived and left on time. Although this is an ideal state, all too often, variables like severe weather and equipment malfunctions contribute to the unpredictable outcomes we often experience while utilizing airline travel. A quality process or service starts with the elimination of special cause variation, which is a prime contributor to process instability, followed by a reduction of common cause variation, when a stable process is not capable of consistently meeting customer requirements. The very essence of continuous improvement is rooted in variation reduction, reflected in our drive to eliminate defects and waste as we journey to reduce cycle time and improve process flow. This chapter explores how significant quality improvements can be made through the effective reduction and management of variation as we set the stage for sustainable efficiency improvement.

Chapter 2: Process Standardization

Without a defined or documented standard process to follow, it's difficult to accurately predict a process's outcome due to uncontrolled variation. One of the most effective ways to minimize the impact of variation on a process is to standardize it through procedures and work instructions. The first logical step in most process improvement efforts, especially where repetitive work is encountered, is to ensure an unambiguous set of work activities has been documented and is being implemented to minimize the negative impact of variation on process output. Standardized work can establish a baseline from which process monitoring and control occur and continuous improvements are initiated, measured and sustained. The simple act of defining and performing work to a standard routine can significantly improve process stability.

Chapter 2 focuses on the importance of establishing, maintaining and controlling work standards as a key contributor to process stability and to continuously enhancing existing standards through experimentation, problem analysis, obstacle eradication and lessons learned.

Chapter 3: Process Stability

The application of a proven method can provide a structured and disciplined approach to achieving certain objectives in a timely and efficient manner. This is no different for process stability. After standardizing a process, the second step on the road to continuous process improvement is to focus on identifying and eliminating defects that are causing process instability. To do so, we must first evaluate the current state of stability in our existing process through data collection and analysis. This data, when transformed into information, will allow us to visualize the degree of fluctuation and predictability in process output and point the direction for the next improvement steps. If stability is elusive, we must analyze the process to understand the causes of all significant deviations in output and identify countermeasures to minimize their impact or eliminate them. Process output stability starts with understanding and controlling key inputs and process activities that influence outputs of interest. Thus, improvements to process stability are primarily driven by standardization and defect elimination. Chapter 3 focuses on process stability and explores ways to assess, achieve and maintain process stability as part of our continuous improvement journey.

Chapter 4: Process Capability

Process output must be consistent (stable) before capability can be effectively assessed. A capable process is one that consistently produces products and provides services that meet customer requirements. If your process is not consistently making and delivering goods and services that meet customer expectations, then you are generating waste that is negatively impacting customer satisfaction, process efficiency and the company's bottom line. If defect elimination to remove special cause variation does not lead to a capable process, the next step along the road to continuous improvement is to reduce common cause variation until process output is consistently within customer-defined specification limits.

Chapter 4 looks to provide an understanding and approach to assess, achieve and maintain a capable process as we move to reinforce the foundation upon which efficiency improvements will take root.

Chapter 5: Process Control

If a stable and capable process is the foundation for efficiency improvements, how can we ensure this foundation is maintained so lean improvements can become part of an operational norm? As with any stable and capable process, long-term sustainability is the result of a structured and disciplined approach to process control. However, process control must be preceded by robust design and development activities. If all goes well during process and product inception, the results should yield a stable and capable process that only requires periodic monitoring and control to maintain a consistent and predictable output. Although we will not venture into the topic of robust design and development, it's an important part of ensuring a capable process can be realized.

Chapter 5 focuses on assessing, establishing and maintaining process control as a prerequisite to exploring and implementing the benefits of lean efficiency improvements. The objective is not to introduce you to new methods, tools or techniques for process control since there are plenty of materials and information available on this topic. The intent is to present a structured and proven approach to using existing tools and techniques to maintain the process at an acceptable state of performance. What's important to remember is that both stability and capability are requirements for process control and process control is a prerequisite for implementing many of the lean (efficiency) improvements that will be discussed in Part II.

Part II: Process Efficiency (Lean) Improvement

Changing one's process focus from a quality to an efficiency improvement perspective must start with an understanding of variation's contribution to process waste and its impact on process flow. Waste is reduced through the identification and elimination of non-value-added process activities and is often reflected in process cycle time. However, process flow improvements present a greater challenge to an organization striving to achieve a smooth, steady, uninterrupted flow of material and information that aligns with a customer's take rate. Variation has a significant influence on process efficiency since it impacts many factors contributing to process waste and flow. Efficiency improvement is at the center of the continuous improvement journey with change management as the engine for elevating process standards to a new level of performance once process control is demonstrated. The topic of efficiency improvement is explored in Part II.

Common tools and techniques within the lean portfolio are also discussed within context as a way to better understand and achieve the maximum benefit each can offer. More specifically, this section highlights simple, logical and clear approaches to eliminating waste and improving flow. Although a lot of information exists on the various methods available to support lean, less exists on the best ways to apply them in a logical, practical and sustainable manner.

Part II separates waste elimination and continuous flow improvements into two different chapters because organizations often focus on one or both. Non-manufacturing operations typically focus on activities that eliminate waste while manufacturing facilities tend to focus on both objectives of waste elimination and improving process flow within a value stream. As we discuss the topics of waste elimination and process flow separately, there is no question as to the clear connection between them. Focusing on one of these topics means that you are working toward the same objective, the achievement of more efficient processes with the common, never-ending aim of continuous improvement and process optimization through variation (waste) reduction.

Chapter 6: A Lean Mindset

Living lean requires more than the application of lean tools and methods. Lean requires that we move beyond simply focusing on results and turn our attention to the process activities generating those results. A lean mindset is about understanding process inputs and activities that drive desired outputs. Lean is about identifying, analyzing and optimizing the integrated work activities that comprise the value streams, leading to customer value. Lean is about proactively identifying and eliminating problems, obstacles and flow disruptors before they negatively impact process outputs.

A truly lean mind is never satisfied and always strives to make things better. It's the pursuit of perfection, knowing it can never be achieved. It's realizing everything can always be improved and learning from mistakes is a powerful conduit for continuous improvement and core to operational excellence. Chapter 6 explores these ideas and more as we work to change the way we think, act, behave and react on our never-ending journey of continuous improvement.

Chapter 7: Lean Preparation

Lean offers many tools and techniques for eliminating waste and improving flow. At a more fundamental level, tools like 5S can be used to establish a disciplined approach to operational cleanliness, visualization and deviation management, in addition to serving as a bellwether for assessing an organization's ability to implement standard work practices. At the other end of the spectrum is the application of value stream mapping (VSM) as a way to initiate and drive a structured and incremental approach to reducing waste with a particular emphasis on enhancing information and material flow through the process. Before moving toward a leaner operation, where focus on the value stream becomes a primary means for driving improvements, there must be an understanding, acceptance and adherence to several basic principles. These guiding principles act as the foundation upon which waste reduction and flow improvements are based. One of these principles is the concept of just-in-time (JIT), the object of which is to produce and deliver the right parts, in the correct quantity, at their expected time with minimum resources. Doing so is a challenge and requires a finely tuned system supported by a mindset of stopping to fix problems, production leveling, enhancing equipment reliability and implementing pull systems and other relevant tools and techniques. Chapter 7 covers key concepts required to support a lean initiative and reviews essential methods that Toyota and others have identified and refined to facilitate progression toward operational excellence.

Chapter 8: Waste Elimination

Once process control is evident, we start to increase our focus on waste to improve process efficiency through waste elimination and process flow optimization. Waste reduction is a broad or "lighter" approach to lean that involves a concentrated scope of activities that do not require as deep an understanding in applying some of the lean tools and concepts necessary for improving flow. This approach leverages concepts such as process mapping, Jishuken workshops and Yamazumi charts to acquire a detailed overview and understanding of a process and highlight areas where significant waste reduction opportunities exist. In this situation, we use process analysis to decompose work activities into categories of value-added and non-value added. A Pareto chart can be employed to highlight the most significant non-value-added activities or waste and Kaizen events scheduled to implement focused improvements. This is a relatively simple, easy and straightforward way to engage in the practice of lean with a realistic objective of making incremental efficiency improvements.

Chapter 9: Process Flow

Eliminating waste clearly benefits continuous process flow since many forms of waste interrupt the movement of materials and information through a facility's value stream. When focused specifically on improving flow, more sophisticated practices, tools and techniques are employed to stress the process in ways that reveal obstacles disrupting flow. As we move closer to a more ideal flow pattern, we increasingly stress our systems, revealing weaknesses that must be addressed to continuously advance and sustain newly enhanced levels of operational performance. VSM is a proven technique to reveal obstacles and opportunities for incremental flow improvement by mapping a process's current as well as desired state followed by identifying actions to remove barriers to achieving a more optimized flow. Once a current and future state map have been prepared, an improvement plan can be developed to transition from one state to the next in a structured, disciplined and incremental manner, moving the enterprise closer to realizing a more continuous material and information flow pattern.

Chapter 9 explores the concepts of material, information and product flow by reviewing the factors that affect flow. This information is then used to understand and create sustainable efficiency improvements within the context of operational excellence.

Part III: Sustainable Improvements

Part III explores an area that traditionally has not received much consideration but is gaining more attention as organizations move toward a "lean thinking" state of mind and improved operational performance. Creating a lean culture for operational excellence requires that we look beyond simply focusing on results and broaden our perspective by giving more attention to the process that generates those results. This is a difficult transition for many of us who have traditionally been rewarded for results, not time and effort spent on monitoring, controlling and improving the process that produces those results. Thinking more about process (vs. results) will require a discussion on changing the mindset and culture of an organization in addition to setting the framework for this endeavor. We explore the benefits of establishing structure, discipline and accountability as part of this framework and the need to embrace guiding principles as a basis for establishing systems that drive behaviors that lead to desired results. In essence, the objective of this section is to explore the idea of organizational culture and to understand the influences that drive it so that a deliberate effort can be made to steer its evolution in an intentional and meaningful way toward excellence.

Chapter 10: Creating a Culture of Operational Excellence

Organizational culture is defined by many things. It is a reflection of the attitudes and behaviors of people belonging to a common group or enterprise. Group behaviors develop from principles that govern process outcomes. These principles create the foundation upon which a culture is built, and drive systems that influence behaviors from which results are realized. Chapter 10 explores the links between organizational culture, guiding principles, systems, behaviors and results as well as the transformation required to align these elements with an organization's strategic direction consistent with sustaining improvements while striving for perfection.

Chapter 11: Daily Shop Floor Management

Chapter 11 on daily shop floor management is the bedrock for sustaining improvements and supporting an environment of operational excellence including *structure*, *discipline* and *accountability*. These three components are vital to maintaining process control and building a culture of continuous improvement. Organizational *structure* provides a clear framework for application of quality and efficiency practices, tools and techniques essential for productivity improvements and process optimization. *Discipline* is an attitude required for effective deployment of process control and improvement routines. It's a behavior that's difficult to maintain and even more challenging to sustain. The survival and growth of an organization depends on its ability to do what it does best, correctly and consistently over time.

Accountability is rooted in the expectation that people will follow through with their commitments. In the process world, expectations are often defined through work routines intended to maintain process control and change management to facilitate continuous improvements. Accountability encompasses how people choose to perform their tasks. As important is the formation of good work habits to follow up on critical issues and ensure implemented actions are completed and confirmed effective. The challenge of accountability lies in the discipline to do what's required to get the job done in a timely and efficient manner, at the lowest cost, without compromising quality or safety.

Effective daily shop floor management maintains process stability and capability and ensures that structure, discipline and accountability are in place to prevent processes from reverting to a state of underperformance while facilitating continuous process improvements. In this chapter, we will spend time exploring the topics of structure, discipline and accountability as the basis for sustainable process control and efficiency improvements, in addition to reviewing how the fundamental disciplines of daily shop floor management can play a key role in creating a sustainable environment for operational excellence.

Chapter 12: Building a Sustainable Lean Enterprise

Building a sustainable lean enterprise takes time and patience. Different work areas and functions exhibit different levels of maturity, each of which will likely require a unique approach to align people, practices and systems with the fundamental principles behind a stable, capable and efficient operation. A lean management system must be customized and integrated into the DNA or core of an organization's operations, with the support of leadership and a community of people who understand, believe and are willing to exercise their beliefs and commitment through their words and actions. Chapter 12 examines the elements behind a lean enterprise and the importance of creating a lean management system to control and continuously improve processes, procedures, systems and behaviors needed to realize operational excellence.

It's important to remember, lean is a journey. Don't think about lean in terms of what you want the organization to be, think about how you want the organization to get there and then plan accordingly. Very few people would undertake a cross-country road trip without ensuring that their vehicle is prepared for the adventure by plotting a route that aligns with their interests. And so it goes with lean and a commitment to operational excellence, one must be ready and willing to take on the challenges ahead before embarking on a journey of continuous, yet never-ending, improvement.

In closure, I would like to leave this introduction with a guideline to help navigate your way along the continuous improvement journey. The following activities, when performed sequentially, establish a framework or roadmap for the journey from process control through efficiency improvement to operational excellence. These guiding principles are not definitive or unique, but provide a logical and practical approach for the road ahead.

Guiding Principles for Efficiency and Operational Excellence

- *Process standardization*: Establish consistency
- *Process stabilization*: Demonstrate consistency over time
- *Process capability*: Demonstrate consistent conformance to requirements
- *Process control*: Maintain a stable and capable performance baseline
- *Process efficiency*: Reduce process cycle time
- *Process flow*: Deliver what's needed, in the amount needed, when needed
- *Operational excellence*: Continuous sustainable improvements that deliver expected results

To visualize what has been presented, Figure I.3 outlines the principles for sustaining a culture of process control and continuous improvement. It's a roadmap for operational success that will take time and a commitment by the entire organization to realize.

Why Is This Book Different?

This text presents a methodology for continuous process improvement in a structured, logical and easily understandable framework based on industry-accepted tools, techniques and practices. It starts from the inception of

Figure I.3 Principles for sustaining a culture of process control and continuous improvement.

a process by highlighting and explaining the conditions necessary to establish a stable and capable process and actions necessary to maintain process control while setting the stage for sustainable efficiency improvements driven by waste elimination and process flow enhancement.

This structured approach to continuous process improvement makes a clear connection between the need for a quality process to serve as the foundation for incremental efficiency improvements. The expectation of this work is to move beyond simply talking about the value contribution of applying the tools and techniques of continuous improvement and focus more on applying these methods at strategic points within a process life cycle with consideration of the systems and behaviors needed for successful deployment.

This text starts the discussion of continuous process improvement with an understanding of variation and its impact on processes. It continues by stressing the importance of standardizing a process before stabilizing it. Once the process output is predictable, attention can turn to ensuring it's capable of meeting customer expectations. This series of activities sets the foundation for efficiency improvements.

The section on efficiency improvement focuses on eliminating waste while improving process flow using existing tools, techniques and methods to do so. The book wraps up by exploring the systems and behaviors required to sustain incremental improvements achieved on the journey to operational excellence.

QUALITY IMPROVEMENT: BUILDING A FOUNDATION FOR LEAN EFFICIENCY IMPROVEMENTS

I

Overview

Processes exhibit a life cycle. They start with a design concept, move into development and are verified against product and process requirements before manufacturing starts. During the development stage, process stability and capability must be demonstrated before the product and supporting process are released into production since both contribute to a foundation upon which all other improvements take hold. Unfortunately, many organizations embark on efficiency improvements without considering the current quality (e.g. stability and capability) of their existing processes validated during the development phase. This oversight may jeopardize the integrity of subsequent improvement efforts since process enhancements built on an unstable process are not likely to be sustainable over time.

In our quest for continuous improvement, we often rush to implement changes without due consideration of current process conditions. When we recognize processes have not been performing to expectation, we must first "fix" what's broken before making enhancements. Unfortunately, many of the processes that we struggle to improve today were likely efficient and effective at their inception. In fact, most of these processes were designed to be stable and capable of consistently meeting customer requirements. Regrettably, with all running well, other priorities started drawing our attention elsewhere, leading us to ignore the periodic monitoring and control necessary to prevent these processes from slowly deteriorating into a state of instability and underperformance over time. With loss of attention and often unclear process ownership, people working with these core processes encounter problems that become roadblocks. These unresolved roadblocks lead to creation of workarounds in order to simply *get the job done!*

Problems continue to mount as new obstacles occur, all of which are being overlooked due to lack of clear ownership and accountability. As the number of workarounds increases, process efficiency decreases, impacting the overall performance of resulting outputs. Consequently, we eventually come to realize our processes have broken down due to a lack of attention and control. As with any process or system, if we do not take time to look for deviations and react appropriately to maintain proper control, a process will slowly deteriorate, leaving in its wake defective products, inadequate services, frustrated employees and unsatisfied customers.

Quality improvement starts with the identification and elimination of defects (or special cause variation) preventing continuous conformance to requirements. Defects cause process instability. Special cause variation must be eliminated in order for a process to achieve stability. A stable process exhibits only common cause variation. This is where the process is behaving in a systematic and predictable manner. It's statistically stable. Variation is consistent and "normal" for the way the process is expected to operate. One must have a stable process before process improvements can be meaningfully pursued.

Several methods have been introduced over the years focused on improving quality, including the plan-do-check-act (PDCA) cycle discussed previously, ISO 9000, total quality management (TQM) and Six Sigma, to name a few. These approaches to improvement have had some level of prominence in manufacturing and transactional domains for the past 30–40 years due to their focus on the elimination of process defects. While many of these methods continue to be used for quality improvement today, others like lean concepts have been included or even used to replace them. Regardless of the method or combination of methods used for process improvement, the fundamental approach remains the same … *process stability and capability before efficiency; efficiency through waste elimination and flow improvement; sustainability through structure, discipline and accountability.*

As discussed previously, the first part of this book will explore process quality, which is rooted in stability and conformance to requirements. A process must be stable and capable before meaningful efficiency improvements can be pursued. If a process is not stable, the first course of action is to achieve stability. If stable, process capability is the next priority to create a solid foundation for efficiency improvements, which is covered in more detail in the second part of this book.

TQM and Six Sigma

The American Society for Quality (asq.org) describes ISO 9000 as a set of international standards on quality management and quality assurance developed to help companies effectively document their quality practices in order to maintain an efficient quality system. According to *i Six Sigma* (isixsigma.com), "Total Quality Management (TQM) is a management approach that originated in the 1950s and has steadily become more popular since the early 1980s. Total quality is a description of the culture, attitude and organization of a company that strives to provide customers with products and services that satisfy their needs. The culture requires quality in all aspects of the company's operations, with processes being done right the first time and defects and waste eradicated from operations". Although there is no widely agreed-upon approach to TQM, it leverages many of the existing quality tools and techniques used to establish and maintain process control.

Another method that grew in prominence during the 1980s was Six Sigma. Contrary to TQM, Six Sigma brought a very specific methodology, called define, measure, analyze, improve and control (DMAIC), to process improvement. Six Sigma is a disciplined, data-driven approach for improving the quality and efficiency of an organization's operational and transactional processes. It's a data-based methodology that is used to address product and service problems through reducing product variation, optimizing processes and developing robust new products and services. This is accomplished through the deployment of statistical- and analytical-based tools proven effective for problem-solving and decision-making.

The ultimate goal of any quality initiative is to achieve and maintain product and service conformance to requirements. Once consistency has been demonstrated, improvement activities can shift their focus from eliminating special cause variation to reducing common cause variation in cases where product or service reliability requires further enhancement. Once stability and capability have been confirmed, process efforts can focus on efficiency (productivity) improvements.

Key Points

- Quality improvements focus on individual processes to ensure conformance to requirements.
- A stable and capable process is a prerequisite for implementing efficiency (lean) improvements.
- A process must be stable before capability can be assessed, established and controlled.
- All processes must be continuously monitored and controlled to ensure stability and maintain reliability over time.
- Process control sustains quality improvements.

Chapter 1

Process Variation

Variation in behavior leads to variation in results.

The Shingo Model for Operational Excellence

Understanding Process Variation

Process variation is the root of many quality problems. The ability of a process to produce results that conform to requirements is an indicator of its capability. Conformance is often assessed by the degree to which a process is performed within its control parameters or a product meets the form, fit or functional requirements specified by engineering or customer. Process capability can be evaluated by comparing output results to a process target (mean), data variation (standard deviation) or proportions (e.g. percent good vs. bad). Figure 1.1 visualizes the benefit of shifting a process output to better align with its desired target value (mean) and reducing process variation to within specification limits to achieve a more capable process. Stability is reflected in consistent demonstration of process output capability.

The known characteristics associated with variation that should be understood when working to manage it include:

- Variation exists in everything we do; it's always present
- Variation is caused, can be predicted and quantified
- Sources of variation are additive

- Process output variation is affected by input and process activities
- Quality can be affected by significant process variation
- Process variation is a combination of part and measurement system variation

Variation observed in process outputs can be correlated with variation observed in process inputs and activities, which include machines, methods, materials, people and the environment involved in executing a process. Variation from many of these sources and their interactions can be controlled through product design as well as daily shop floor management routines.

Special and Common Cause Variation

Variation can be classified as either common cause or special cause variation. Total process variation is the combination of common cause and special cause variation observed in manufacturing of parts and measurement

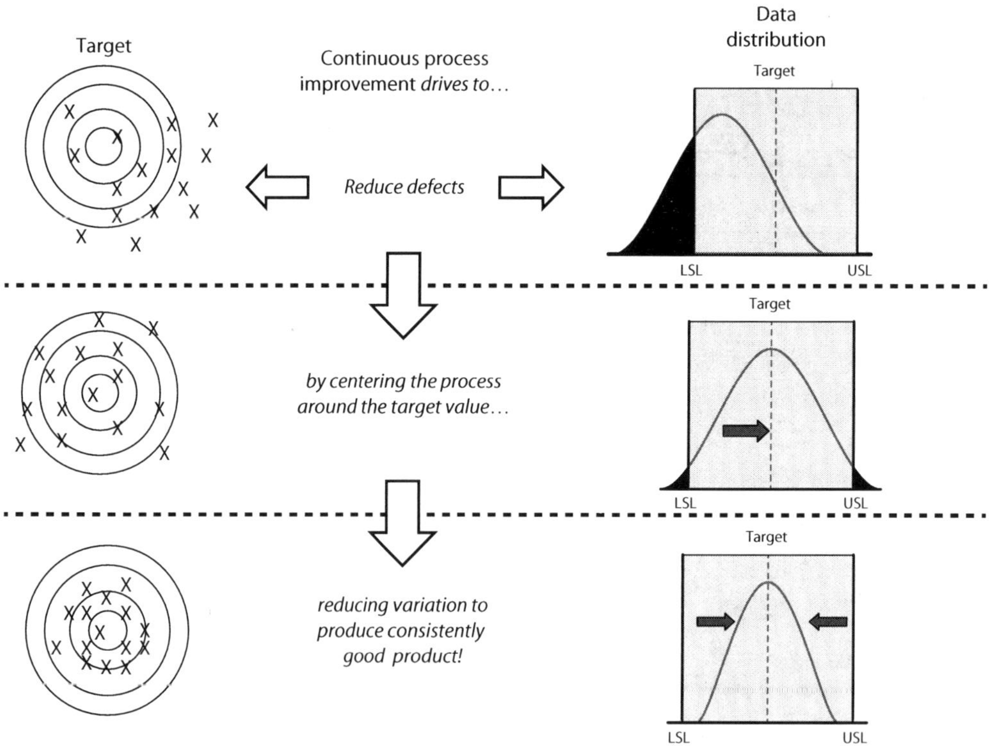

Figure 1.1 Reducing process variation. (Source unknown – Reproduced.)

systems data used to assess output performance. Special cause variation affects a process in intermittent, irregular and unpredictable ways, causing process instability. By identifying, targeting and eliminating process defects, special cause variation can be removed to achieve a more consistent and predictable process output. On the other hand, common cause variation affects all individual values of a process output and is characteristic of a stable process. It's the result of many sources of variation, consistently acting on a process in predictable ways, and can be reduced through process improvement activities focused on identifying and minimizing known and controllable factors contributing to its cause. A reduction in common cause variation can reduce process variation and improve process reliability. Figure 1.2 provides different terms for and examples of common and special cause variation.

Total Process Variation

Process improvement efforts can typically be pursued from two perspectives: (1) design and development of products or services for manufacturing; and (2) data used to measure, monitor and control process performance. Although design and development can significantly contribute to product and process variation, this text will primarily focus on influences within manufacturing on variation. To understand total process variation, we must explore the sources of variation affecting the

	Special cause	Common cause
Terms →	➢ Random ➢ Irregular ➢ Intermittent ➢ Unpredictable ➢ Assignable ➢ Uncontrolled	➢ Systematic ➢ Natural ➢ Consistent ➢ Predictable
Process examples: Baking 	➢ Dead batch of yeast ➢ Sour batch of cream ➢ Different style of oven ➢ Forgot an ingredient ➢ Forgot to grease pan ➢ Different pan material	➢ Different batch of yeast ➢ Different brand of cream ➢ Same style / different oven ➢ Amounts of each ingredient ➢ Different grease used on pan ➢ Same material / different pan
Process examples: Commuting to work 	➢ Road construction ➢ Severe weather ➢ Traffic accidents ➢ Freight train crossing	➢ Traffic lights ➢ Weather ➢ Time of day ➢ Commuter train crossings

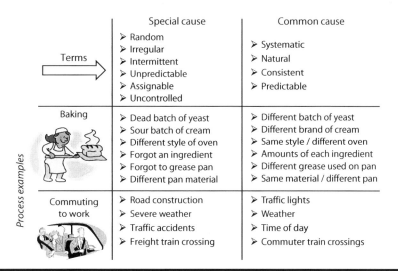

Figure 1.2 Special versus common cause variation.

manufacturing process producing the parts and the measurement devices used to verify part conformance to specifications. A source of variation (SOV) study can be employed to assess the type of variation and the effect that variation has on a process and corresponding measurement systems. Cause and effect (C&E) analysis and multi-vari analysis (MVA) are two tools used for this purpose. Let's explore each contributor to process variation with the understanding that

$$\text{Total Process Variation} = \text{Part Variation} + \text{Measurement System Variation.}$$

Measurement System Variation

The quality of data can be affected by the degree of variation exhibited in the measurement systems used to acquire it. Measurement system variation considers all variation related to the measurement process. The sources of variation within a measurement system include gages, standards, sampling and test procedures, software and environmental factors, among others. For example, a steel rod of known height that is measured several times may generate various results that are different from the known value due to measurement system variation. If several parts, measured from the same manufacturing line, produce different results, variation is likely to reflect a combination of measurement system and process variation. It's important that measurement system variation be considerably smaller than part-to-part variation so that meaningful measurements can be obtained. As with all processes, a measurement system is also subjected to special and common cause variation. Gage repeatability and reproducibility studies can be employed to determine how much total process variation is due to measurement system variation. Typically, measurement system variation within most manufacturing operations should not exceed 30% of overall process variation with 15% or less being more widely accepted.

Precision and Accuracy

We often use the precision and accuracy of process data to assess the impact of total process variation. A process that exhibits good precision and accuracy over time, relative to a known reference or specification, can be considered a process in control. However, a process can exhibit precision without being accurate and accuracy without being precise. In either case,

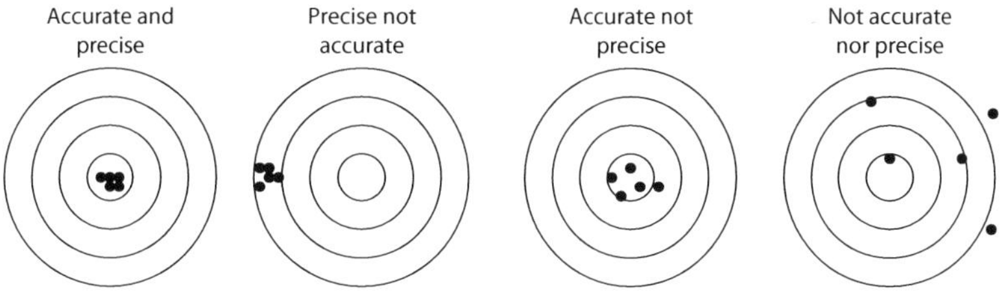

Figure 1.3 Measurement accuracy versus precision. (Reproduced from Minitab Help Menu.)

this may identify opportunities for reducing process variation, if variation is found to be excessive. Figure 1.3 visually displays the differences in process accuracy and precision.

Accuracy can typically be improved by adjusting process inputs and activities to better align with a process's target value or by reducing process variation about the mean. Unfortunately, the latter can be a more challenging endeavor since reducing common cause variation is not always inherently obvious.

Part Variation

Part variation is apparent and disruptive when expected outputs can't be consistently reproduced within the desired tolerance each time a process is performed. Every process has variation that negatively impacts cost when parts (and services) deviate from requirements, leading to rework and scrap. Variation can be used as a measure of process performance, while reducing variation can lead to defect reduction, cost savings and increased customer satisfaction. Part variation is often influenced by product design, equipment settings (including tools and fixtures), set-up procedures, work instructions and environmental conditions such as humidity, temperature and cleanliness. The following tools (MVA, C&E analysis and Control Charts) can be used to manage variation.

Multi-Vari Analysis (MVA)

We can use MVA to understanding part variation. MVA is a graphical technique that is used to display sources of variation within major categories of process variation. Most sources of manufacturing part variation can be classified into three categories: positional (within

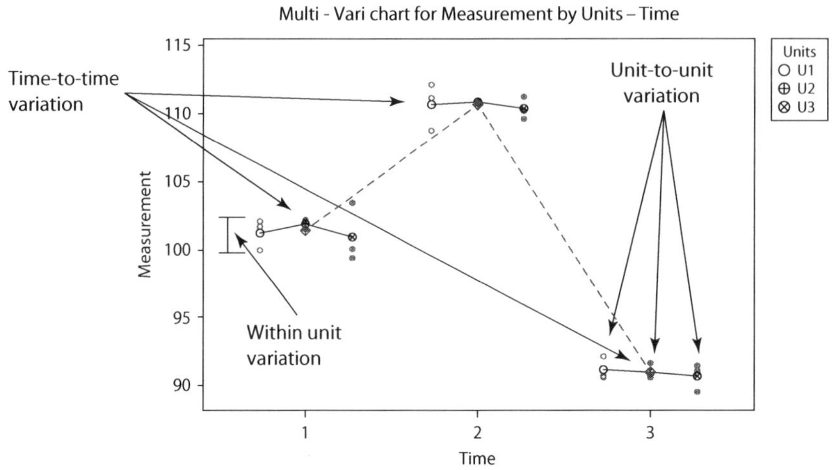

Figure 1.4 Multi-vari analysis output (using Minitab® Statistical Software).

part variation), part-to-part (variation among parts) and temporal (part variation over time), the causes of which will vary due to differences in people executing the process, methods used to perform the work, equipment wear, material variations and environmental conditions. Figure 1.4 is an MVA used to evaluate the magnitude of a part's sources of process variation.

Performing MVA requires observing the process over time to determine contributions to variation due to

- Output measurements
- Measurement frequency
- Categories of variation
- Sample size

A table can be prepared to record data over time, which is plotted using a multi-vari chart to analyze and interpret results. If variation is not graphically evident within parts, between sequential parts or among parts over time, consider collecting more data or evaluating the capability of your measurement system to satisfactorily provide a measurement resolution sufficient to meet your needs. If required, perform a C&E (fishbone) analysis to identify *common cause variation* within the largest category of variation and take action to reduce variation impacting critical measurement parameters.

Some sampling rules for MVA include:

- *Positional assessment*: Choose a minimum of two positions per part expected to have the same value.
- *Part-to-part assessment*: Choose a minimum of three consecutive parts per batch or time period.
- *Temporal assessment*: Choose a minimum of 20 pre-selected time periods.

Guidelines for MVA:

- Avoid random sampling unless it's an inherent part of the process.
- Structure sample gathering (e.g. shift to shift and; day to day).
- Obtain a sample that reflects about 70%–80% of process variation.
- Strive to acquire new versus historical data for analysis.

The objective of MVA is to determine which categories contribute greatest to part variation; helping to identify, reduce and control these influences in production.

Cause and Effect Analysis

Process mapping in concert with a C&E (fishbone) diagram and matrix are good tools for targeting key sources of variation for reduction. Process mapping can be used to visualize key steps within a process of interest followed by use of a C&E diagram to highlight input variables that drive corresponding process outputs within each process step. Sources of variation fall into two primary categories: controlled and uncontrolled. Controlled sources generally include process input factors, while uncontrolled sources can vary considerably and typically fall within the following groups:

- Part to part
- Change over time
- External environment
- System interaction
- Customer usage

The C&E tool can be employed to reveal the most sensitive input variables affecting a particular process output. Appropriate actions can then be

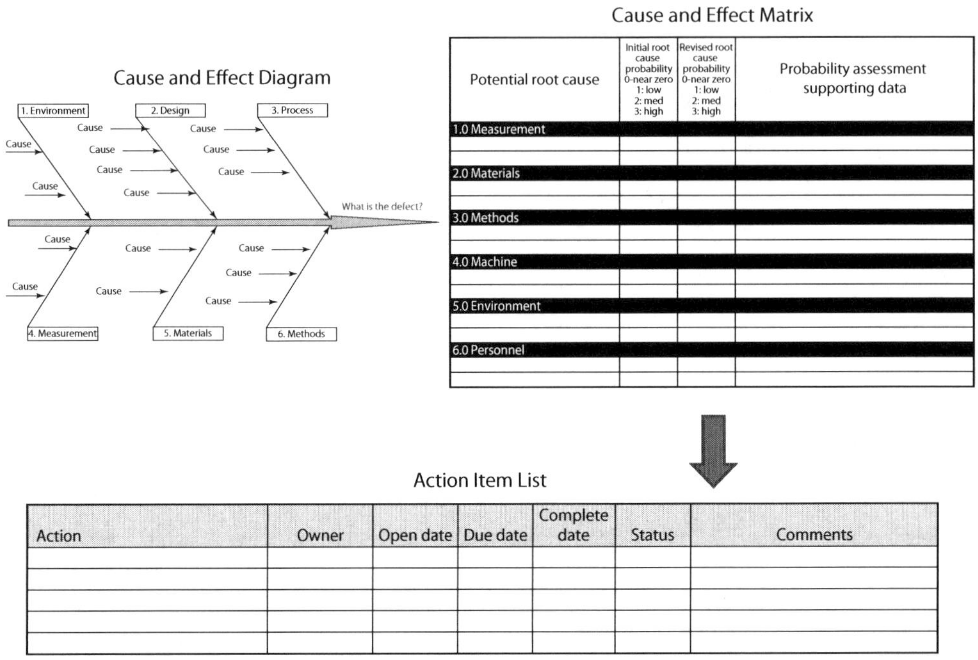

Figure 1.5 C&E (fishbone) example/matrix.

taken to reduce or eliminate each major SOV identified to improve process capability or measurement system precision and accuracy. A C&E diagram template is displayed in Figure 1.5 with a corresponding matrix and action item list to help drive variation reduction improvements.

Control Charts

A control chart can visually display undesirable process variation when process outputs exceed expected 3 sigma control limits, indicating the presence of special cause variation. The data range can also be used to gage acceptable process variation. The range is the difference between the highest and lowest values within the data set collected. The greater the data range, the more significant the variation. Unfortunately, range may not be the best parameter to measure variation in a data set since it only considers the difference between two data points, the data's maximum and minimum values. Standard deviation is typically a more appropriate parameter as it considers all data points when evaluating data variation relative to the data's central tendency. In short, control charts are a good starting point for identifying key sources of variation because outliers are classified as process defects that contribute to process waste and instability. More information on the topic of

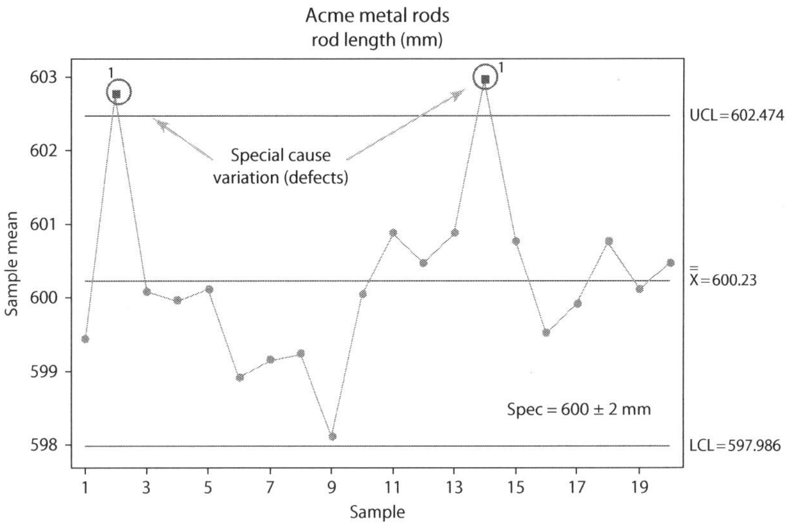

Figure 1.6 Control chart example (using Minitab® Statistical Software).

control charts will be provided later in Chapter 3 of this text. An example of a control chart is shown in Figure 1.6.

Controlling and Reducing Process Variation

Controlling variation is necessary to maintain process performance. The key is to control process variation within an expected range of optimized parameters so that the resulting output will be consistent and predictable over time. In order to do this, we must consider internal and external variation acting on our processes causing disruptive behavior. Internal and external contributors to process variation include:

- Raw material differences
- Operator experience levels
- Equipment wear and tear
- Available information
- Interpretation of procedures
- Environmental fluctuations

Variation in process and measurement system output can be decreased by reducing one or more input factors that significantly influences output performance. For example, controlling or reducing the factors that contribute to a car's fuel consumption (e.g. aerodynamics, weight, engine size and tire pressure) can have a direct impact on a car's fuel efficiency. Thus, consider the influence of process inputs such as materials, equipment, methods, operators and environment when looking to reduce process variation.

As an example, changes in raw material size, composition, color and other properties can have a considerable impact on process output. A latte from your favorite café will taste different if it is made from fresh versus boxed milk. If properly prepared requirements are in place for suppliers to control and continuously reduce material fluctuation, this is likely to translate directly to a reduction in process variation, especially in manufacturing operations.

Finally, it's important to understand how variation can impact process flow. Defects, rework, scrap and material shortages often cause overproduction to increase inventory as a way to compensate for these production shortfalls. These issues cascade into increased production cycle times and additional material transport to support bigger production volumes and excess material movement resulting from increased demands on the production system. All these factors work to disrupt product flow. Thus, process control, while working to minimize variation, should be an ongoing focus of any organization that is interested in continuously improving efficiency through waste and flow management.

Proactively Minimizing Variation

One of the most effective ways to reduce variation is to manage it through product, service and process design. Uncontrolled variation is difficult to deal with once a product or process design is frozen and accepted into production. However, there are methods, such as Design for Six Sigma (DFSS), which can be used during product and process development to understand and reduce the sensitivity of a product and process to the negative effects of uncontrolled variation while following established practices intended to minimize the impact of controlled variation inherent in all processes. A robust process is one that is insensitive to uncontrolled variation, also called "noise factors", intrinsic to the interactions, inputs and transformational activities occurring within a working environment.

SIDEBAR: MACRO VERSUS MICRO VARIATION

A Strategy for Continuous Improvement

The key to continuous process improvement is the reduction of variation. One can look at variation from a macro and micro perspective. Take manufacturing line performance for example, stability is the first step in process improvement followed by capability and efficiency. To achieve stability, we must first eliminate the "macro variation" contributing to instability. This is essentially the special cause variation that is evident when key process indicators deviate from targets such as line productivity (output), scrap, first pass yield and overall equipment effectiveness. By monitoring, identifying and eliminating these macro events (e.g. data spikes, trends and patterns), stability can be achieved and problems can be prevented from reoccurring.

Once stability is confirmed, we can work to improve process capability by removing the *macro* variation associated with significant deviations from customer specifications and engineering tolerances. When stability and capability are achieved and process control is established, we turn our attention to improving process efficiency by eliminating *micro* variations observed as process anomalies and fluctuations. Process anomalies are deviations from standard work routines while process fluctuations are deviations within standard work.

Looking for contributors to variation from standard work (anomalies) should reveal micro variations that can be removed, further improving process performance. Once process anomalies are addressed, the final step is the incremental removal of process fluctuations *within* the boundaries of standard work. These are typically minor process aberrations that frequently occur throughout a shift, contributing to process inefficiency when considering their additive impact on process cycle time. These fluctuations can be captured by an operator using a pen and check sheet listed with commonly occurring events. Every time an event occurs during a shift, the operator records the frequency of the occurrence on the check sheet. At the end of a week, these events can be prioritized using a Pareto chart to visualize their occurrence over time. Top events can then be methodically eliminated from the work environment in pursuit of perfection.

Summary

Understanding variation plays a key role in achieving process stability and pursuing continuous process improvements. Identifying and quantifying the sources of variation impacting processes must occur before we can determine actions required to significantly reduce major sources of variation on output performance. Process improvement involves reducing the variation of key process parameters. To do so, we must identify sources of variation in materials, machines, methods, people and the environment that negatively impact process output and take appropriate steps to manage them. We can start this activity by identifying major sources of variation influencing processes of interest using tools such as run charts, statistical process control charts, C&E analysis and MVA to highlight key sources of variation for reduction or elimination.

Key Points

- Variation is inherent in all processes and is characterized by differences in repeated process output measurements.
- Variation creates uncertainty in products and services output parameters.
- Variation within controllable (predictable) limits is acceptable; however, too much variation often leads to scrap and rework, which can significantly impact process efficiency and flow.
- The fundamental goal of continuous process improvement is to reduce variation in materials, machines, methods, operators and the surrounding environmental conditions.
- Variation reduction contributes to a "leaner" operation since a sustainable reduction in process variation can decrease production lead time and lower material buffers needed to regulate process flow.
- By reducing variation, we can increase the frequency (consistency) at which we produce products and provide services that meet or exceed customer requirements.
- The elimination of special cause variation will result in a stable process, leaving only common cause variation.
- Common cause variation is inherent in a stable process. A process is in control when only common cause variation affects process output.

- Variation must be understood and controlled to achieve process stability and capability.
- Variation reduction is universally recognized as key to reliability and productivity improvement.

Bibliography

Measurement Systems Analysis Reference Manual, Fourth Edition. Automotive Industry Action Group; Chrysler LLC, Ford Motor Company and General Motors Corporation, 2010.

Minitab Help Menu, Version 17. Minitab, Inc., Quality Plaza, 1829 Pine Hall Road, State College, PA 16801, USA.

Statistical Process Control (SPC) Reference Manual, Second Edition. Automotive Industry Action Group; Chrysler LLC, Ford Motor Company and General Motors Corporation, 2010.

Chapter 2

Process Standardization

> While stability is a necessary precondition for creating flow and improvement, standardization builds control into the process itself. Standardization is the supporting principle behind maintaining improvement, rather than springing back to preceding practices and results.
>
> **The Shingo Model for Operational Excellence**

Standards

The International Organization for Standardization (ISO.org) indicates that standards are *documents that provide requirements, specifications, guidelines or characteristics that can be used consistently to ensure that materials, products, processes and services are fit for their purpose.* Standards are documents that establish specifications and procedures intended to ensure the stability and reliability of materials, products, methods and/or services for which they are written. Standards are important because they form the fundamental building blocks for product development, process control and continuous improvement. They provide a common understanding, approach and discipline within an organization, influencing and transforming the way we work, interact and communicate. Standards, based on findings of science, technology and experience, bring credibility and value to processes in which they are employed. Meaningful standards are typically established by consensus and are approved by a recognized group or individual. The ISO goes on to say that standards reflect *common and repeated use, rules, guidelines or characteristics for activities or their results, aimed at the achievement of the optimum degree of order in a given context.* In short, standards are intended to establish a common set of activities that are expected to enhance process execution with the objective of stabilizing and optimizing process output.

SIDEBAR: GUIDELINES, PROCEDURES AND STANDARD WORK

Standard work instructions are ideal for highly repetitive work and should be continuously revised based on best practices and lessons learned. As we move up the hierarchy, tasks that are less repetitive may be better served by procedures and, in certain cases, guidelines. Guidelines should reflect the best-known or most practical way to perform certain activities or tasks with clear justification when deviations from the guidelines are warranted. A guideline may become the starting point for a new procedure that may eventually evolve into a standard work instruction. The benefit of a guideline is that it provides flexibility within boundaries when sufficient data or information is not available to define a more detailed set of instructions.

Process Standards

Process standards bring structure and discipline to the workplace. Without standards, the way people perform their daily tasks may vary significantly, leading to inconsistent results and, in the worst-case scenario, chaos. Process standards, reflected in work instructions, specifications, flow charts, procedures and the like, help to reduce variation, stabilize the process and provide clarity on how work should be performed.

Process standards set the baseline for controlling a process and can be used as a reference for detecting deviations that can destabilize a process and generate undesirable outcomes. Standards can also be changed (e.g. improved) to achieve a higher level of performance as measured by positive trends in output metrics. In short, standards are the backbone of a process and establish a reference for process control and continuous improvements. Figure 2.1 provides some tips on the do's and don'ts when preparing and using standards.

Do ...

- ✓ Keep it simple!
- ✓ Make it accessible.
- ✓ Use pictures, graphs, charts and drawings to support and complement text.
- ✓ Highlight and explain the "why" for critical steps.
- ✓ Prepare one standard document per work element.
- ✓ Use it to provide training and qualify new employees for their activities.

Don't ...

- x Make standards difficult to find!
- x Write standards without the input from those who use them!
- x Change the process without changing the procedure.
- x Make it difficult to change the document.
- x Use a lot of words when a simple picture or visual will do!

Figure 2.1 Work standards do's and don'ts.

Standard Work

Standard work defines the interaction between processes and their external factors including people, machines, materials and the environment under stable conditions. The objective of standard work is to provide clear and concise work instructions that, if executed properly, should minimize output variation and waste, helping maintain process stability and support efficiency improvements. In his book, *Creating a Lean Culture*, David Mann states it nicely [1], "The process is most likely to run as designed when operators ... are following their standardized work. If they are, things should run predictably".

Sometimes, the term "standardized" work is used in lieu of "standard" work to reflect a process whose standard work activities include changes to drive continuous process improvements. Standardized work is standard work that is continually updated as better material, equipment and methods are identified. These two terms will be used throughout the text with the understanding that work activities defined as standard work should be continuously updated (standardized work) as new and improved approaches to doing work are identified and demonstrated effective (Figure 2.2). With this in mind, there should be a clear expectation that any deviation in work activity or opportunity for improvement is highlighted, understood and acted upon, to maintain process control and continuously improve the way work is performed. Standard work should be periodically confirmed as a mechanism for rapid identification of process problems or deviations requiring corrective action in order to prevent undesirable events from occurring or reoccurring. If, at any point, an opportunity for improving the current

Standard Work

- Best current way to perform work
- Rigid, inflexible
- Activities / Sequence / Timing
- Predictable outcomes
- Includes cyclical and periodic work
- A reference for process control
- A way of working!

Standardized Work

- Act of comparing actual work to a standard way of working
- Used to maintain conformity with a standard
- Is continuously improved (never permanent)
- A starting point for Kaizen!
- Reflects current method of work
- Owned by manufacturing. Groups and team leaders own the Standard
- Available line side for managers to use (Workers already know it)
- A process expected to change, improve
- A way of life!

Figure 2.2 Standard work versus standardized work.

standard is identified and proposed, an evaluation or experiment should be conducted to determine if a change is warranted. This type of engagement promotes process stability, organizational learning and incremental efficiency improvement.

In a 1999 *Harvard Business Review* article, "Decoding the DNA of the Toyota Production System", the author highlighted four rules, one of which is *All work shall be highly specified as to content, sequence, timing, and outcome.* This is important because variation contributes to poor quality, lower productivity and higher costs, and significant deviations from specification can cause errors that lead to product and service defects. By following a clearly defined set of instructions, deviations from expected outcomes become easier to detect and quicker to correct. Correction may require operator retraining or a change in process to prevent reoccurrence.

The article continues: *Toyota's managers don't tell workers and supervisors specifically how to do their work. Rather, they use a teaching and learning approach that allows their workers to discover the rules as a consequence of solving problems.* In other words, the workers, with the support of their supervisors, are expected to define and refine their own work continuously over time. When preparing standard work, consider the following questions [2]:

- How do you do the work?
- How do you know you are doing it correctly?
- How do you know the outcome is defect free?
- What do you do if you have a problem or deviation?

Organizations should focus on standardizing highly repetitive processes where inconsistencies can lead to undesirable outcomes. When a clear, well-defined set of work instructions is established and followed, the resulting output is more consistent and predictable. In addition, deviations can be quickly identified and appropriate steps taken to address significant variances from process before they become bigger issues with the potential to escape and negatively impact customers.

It's important to reinforce the point that standard work can also be used as a way for supervisors and managers to check if the process is performed properly or for operators to know when a deviation from standard has occurred. Unfortunately, managers using standard work to check process conformance are engaging in an assessment that is a form of waste. However, if workers start using standard work as a reference for identifying deviations requiring corrective action, then standard work becomes a tool for them to influence and control process stability with value-added management support. Figure 2.3 provides the characteristics of good work standards.

Standard Work: A Basis for Control and Improvement

The objective of standard work is to clarify work roles, responsibilities and activities so that work can be performed consistently and safely with minimal physical impact on the person performing work activities. When properly deployed, standard work will reduce process variation and operator fatigue while making it easier to identify process deviations. In fact, standard work is a relevant tool for stability and continuous process improvement since it establishes the baseline from which improvements can be measured

Work standards should...

- Be clear, understandable and communicate expected results
- Be sufficient to allow process realization with minimal training
- Outline specific job responsibilities, expectations and ownership
- Detail how to minimize product / service variation
- Highlight critical activities
- Be prepared with the input of individuals performing the work
- Reflect lessons learned and best practices
- Be evaluated and modified before full-scale implementation
- Include job aids such as diagrams, photos, flow charts and examples
- Include directions on how to update the documents
- Be readily available for review
- Allow for operator discretion, flexibility and good judgment within clear boundaries
- Be easy to update when justified
- Encourage recommendations for alternative approaches

Figure 2.3 Characteristics of good work standards.

for the significance of their impact. It does this by reducing variation often associated with inconsistent, vague and ambiguous work activities workers struggle to understand and complete. Sometimes, it's the simple act of "drawing a line in the sand" as a way of establishing consistency in process output even if initial results may not be desirable. In essence, standard work sets the baseline for process monitoring, where the current state can be compared to a "fixed" reference and becomes the point from which process control can be maintained and improvements can be measured. Once a baseline is set and the target known, direction for improvement becomes clear along with obstacles blocking the path to a more desirable state of performance.

Facility/Work Area Standards: 5S

The 5S methodology is a systematic approach to organizing and standardizing a work area for more efficient and effective completion of work activities. It involves sort, straighten, shine, standardize and sustain. If done correctly, it leads to improved quality, less waste and safer work areas. 5S can help establish and reinforce the behaviors necessary for implementing and sustaining standard work and serves as a reference for identifying deviations for elimination, improving productivity.

As a matter of fact, 5S is a good practice for any well-run and disciplined operation. Who can argue with good housekeeping! A clean, uncluttered, orderly and well-maintained operation reflects an organization's ability to maintain control over its processes and operations. However, 5S is as much about safety and ergonomics as it is about housekeeping. Less time spent reaching, searching or walking around objects will reduce cycle time, fatigue and the potential for injury or accidents. In short, 5S is all about improvement and, like any tool, if it does not make work cheaper, easier, faster or safer, its value becomes questionable.

The first three phases of 5S (sort, straighten and shine) can be a starting point for establishing operational standards through the elimination of clutter by sorting through work area items, keeping what's needed and disposing of what's not. An objective of "sort" is to have everything that is required to perform the work accessible, within quick and easy reach, especially when repetitive work is involved. Sort is followed by "straighten" where order is created through the act of establishing a place for commonly used work items while labeling their designated location for efficient task execution. As straightening occurs, time should be taken to clean (e.g. "shine") all essential work areas, items and equipment that remain and ensure that they are in good working order by inspecting for abnormalities and fixing known problems. By engaging in sort, straighten and shine, you create a measurable baseline from which deviations can be detected for correction or improvement action. In short, you create a level of standardization from which safety, quality, productivity and cost can be monitored and controlled. It's a standard that is measurable.

It's best if 5S is not looked at as a tool or method. 5S should to be seamlessly integrated into work routines as a way to maintain a suitable working environment while creating a basis for sustainable process control. Regular 5S audits should become part of everyone's work routines and be periodically performed by cross-functional departments while allowing good practice sharing within the organization. An audit schedule can be prepared without identifying specific locations for conducting the review so that all areas remain vigilant in maintaining their area's 5S standard. Clearly, any deviation from standards identified during audits should be addressed using the deviation management process and reporting of 5S compliance visualized for all stakeholders to see. An overview of the 5S methodology is provided in Figure 2.4.

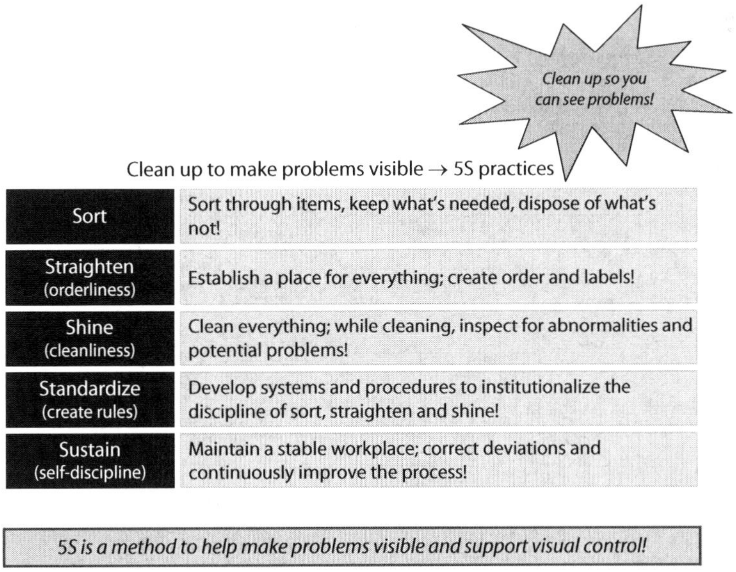

Clean up so you can see problems!
Clean up to make problems visible → 5S practices
Sort
Sort through items, keep what's needed, dispose of what's not!
Straighten (orderliness)
Establish a place for everything; create order and labels!
Shine (cleanliness)
Clean everything; while cleaning, inspect for abnormalities and potential problems!
Standardize (create rules)
Develop systems and procedures to institutionalize the discipline of sort, straighten and shine!
Sustain (self-discipline)
Maintain a stable workplace; correct deviations and continuously improve the process!
5S is a method to help make problems visible and support visual control!

Figure 2.4 5S overview.

5S is a fundamental practice that can serve as a barometer for assessing an organization's ability to follow standard work while gaging its impact on changing behavior. At a basic level, it can be used to establish organizational and personal structure, discipline and accountability. From a broader perspective, 5S can be used to assess the responsiveness of an organization to challenges such as lean, since lean, like 5S, becomes an integral part of an organization's core practices. Thus, if an organization can't implement a 5S methodology and sustain this discipline over time, efforts to implement lean may become questionable.

As an exercise, digitally record work being performed over several hours within a particular area of operations from a bird's-eye view (e.g. shipping and receiving) and start reviewing the video footage for waste improvement opportunities by asking "Are there any observed standards from which a performance baseline (measurement) can be established?". You may be surprised by the lack of standards that exist when observing an operation in motion and improvement opportunities that reveal themselves when engaging in this type of exercise.

Standard Work Instructions

One way to establish standards is through standard work instructions (SWI) developed from time studies and work breakdown diagrams. SWI are a way to document standards in the workplace by identifying who, what, when, where and how a process is to be performed. Standard work is an essential component in helping to minimize variation associated with the human factor. It defines a consistent approach for conducting work by capturing the most efficient and effective way to perform the routines required to deliver products and provide services that meet customer needs. More specifically, standard work is about specifying the content, sequence, timing and expected outcome of repetitive and periodic work routines to ensure that consistent and predictable work is accomplished with minimal variation.

The fundamental way to deploy standard work is through SWI, which answers three key questions:

- *What to do*: SWI capture distinct actions that are required to move the process from one task to the next. These actions describe "what to do". The objective is to identify the individual actions and logical sequence

of steps necessary for a worker to complete the expected work consistently and accurately.
- *How to do it*: SWI should document key steps, broken down into their fundamental elements, so that they are clear and understood. These instructions should describe "how" the work tasks are to be performed, including details of critical activities required to guarantee quality products and services are produced and provided safely and efficiently.
- *Why do it*: All critical steps should have a clear reason or explanation as to why the step is important and why it must be completed in a specific way. Potential consequences or the impact of not performing the step as described, should also be specified, when appropriate. This element answers the "why" of performing key steps and starts with terminology such as "to prevent" or "to ensure" as a way to reinforce the importance of vital actions.

A good work instruction should include pictures, drawings or photographs (e.g. one per major step) to visualize key points and highlight potential mistakes. Lessons learned from lean (gemba) walks, process audits and trouble reports (e.g. A3 or 8D) can also be used to identify and reinforce certain important activities.

In essence, SWI should explain the best way to produce a part or provide a service considering safety, quality and efficiency requirements. They can be written for many different types of tasks and, if done well, should lead to a reduction in waste associated with controllable variation and more consistent process output. At a minimum, consider preparing SWI for the following activities:

- Repetitive work routines
- Handling of supplied material to production lines and finished goods to shipping
- Handling of workplace tools, equipment and fixtures
- Handling of non-conforming materials and parts
- Preventive maintenance routines

SWI can also be used to train operators in performing standard work and as a tool to confirm standard work is being followed. When a supervisor or line leader is confirming standard work, a line operator can be asked to call out their key steps and highlight critical points within each step while performing their work routines. The assessor can use the SWI as a "checklist" to confirm all steps are understood and performed in the sequence required to verify that safe, quality and efficient work is being completed. Standard work routines should be reviewed periodically to confirm correct process execution and timing. If deviations in routines are noted, action must be taken to understand the nature of each deviation and appropriate steps followed to reinforce the standard work routine or initiate changes to continuously improve it. Ignoring deviations can lead to increased cycle times and waste resulting from defects. Standard work should be defined by shop floor management together with individuals expected to do the work.

Preparing for Standard Work

In preparation for implementing standard work, a process must be repeatable, reliable and capable. A repeat (stable) process is able to produce the same way every time. A reliable process is consistently available to produce and a capable process delivers consistent customer product quality.

Standard work requires a go and see approach for preparation. Expect to review the actual product, process, workplace, people and completion times at the work area, the place where value is created, utilizing the team's experience and observation skills to document (sketch) the following:

- Line layout
- Process flow
- Work in process
- Material handling
- Operator workflow
- Ergonomic issues

It's helpful to prepare worksheets to capture the characteristics upon which standard work is based including:

- *Standard operation sheet (SOS)*: Used to visualize the operator workplaces, workplace buffers and travel distances.
- *Standard work instruction (SWI)*: Used to detail operator work activities and the most effective sequence for performing those activities.

- *Standard work combination table (SWCT)*: Used to assess the interface of an operator with their machines and other operators and how these interactions align with planned cycle time.

  The SWCT may not be required for simple work activities; for example, an operator who is not using a machine or is only performing simple work steps.
- *Cycle time diagram (CTD)*: Used to show process stability and communicate actual cycle times.

Table 2.1 provides a brief overview of each document.

To assess various process characteristics, production capacity planning should be completed, process bottlenecks understood, setup and

Table 2.1 Standard Work Documentation

Document	*Abbreviation*	*Used by*	*Description*	
Standard operating sheet	SOS	Operators at line information board	The SOS displays production line layout and indicates the sequence of steps to be performed by the operator (position and motion). It may also include material entry points and storage areas within the work area.	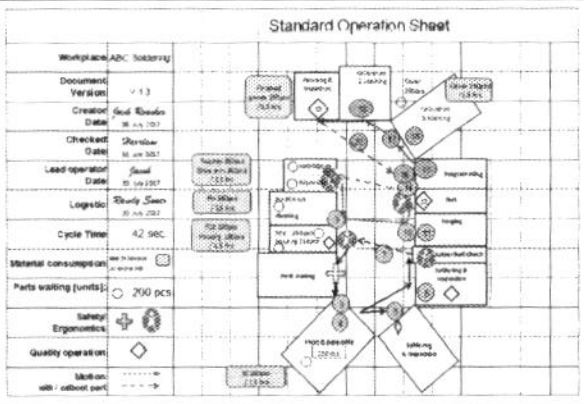
Standard work instruction	SWI	Operators at workplace	Work instructions explains how to perform work correctly. It describes the best way to produce a part for each process step in light of safety, quality and efficiency. The Work instruction specifies the part assembly sequence, handling of non-conformities, material supply requirements and tool management, if required.	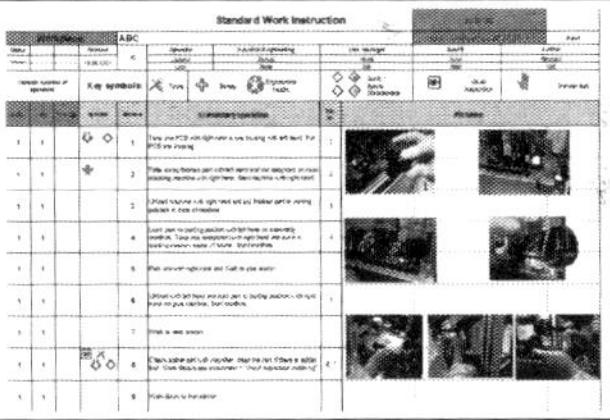
Work combination table	SWCT	Engineering to setup and verify SOS and SWI	SWCT describes a work sequence with a timetable combining manual work, walking, waiting and automatic machine time. It includes all fundamental operations necessary to produce parts that meet safety, quality and efficiency criteria. For multiple work systems, it shows the optimized sequence of work steps between operators and machines.	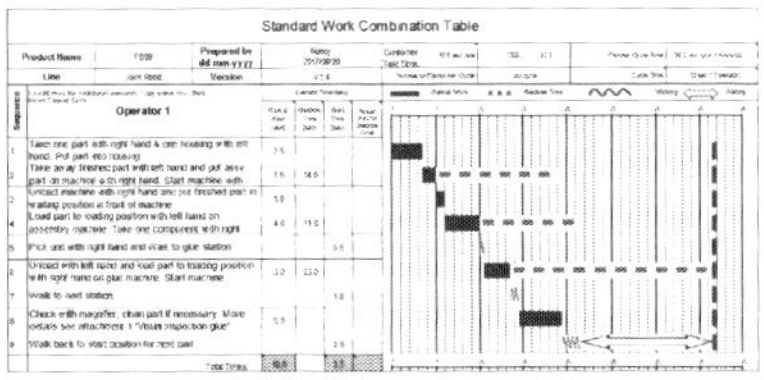
Cycle time diagram	CTD	Engineering to setup and verify SOS and SWI	CTD captures the required time for an average skilled worker, moving at a normal pace, to perform a defined operation following the SWI.	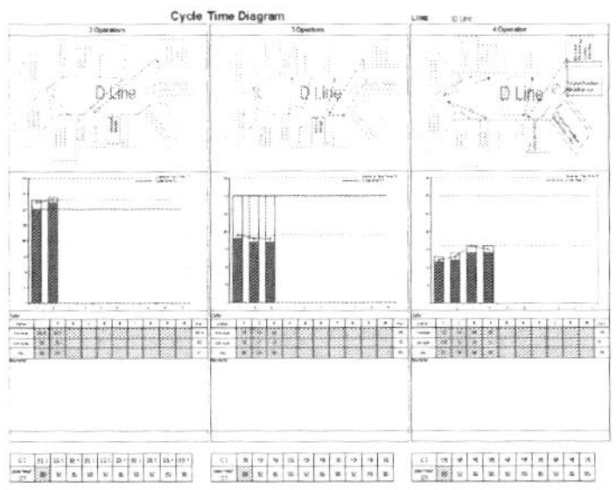

changeover time intervals determined and stable cycle times demonstrated. A clear breakdown (e.g. mapping) of process activities over time will help visualize gaps between planned cycle time and customer take rate, in addition to illustrating the interaction of people and machines to reveal excessive wait times. Periodic mapping of processes will highlight process improvement opportunities by comparing process performance before versus after process changes are made. A process workflow can be created to visualize the work sequence of operator movements within a work area while defining the quantity and location of standards stock in process (SSIP) needed to maintain line stability. A workflow can also serve to display manual versus automatic operations, operator walking times, cycle times, safety topics and quality checkpoints.

To identify which activities should be targeted for standard work, consider work that must be repeated to ensure the delivery of consistent and reliable products or services. One reason McDonald's is a successful restaurant chain is because its products and services are the result of consistent materials and highly detailed process activities performed in a very deliberate, controlled and consistent manner. You know what you are getting when walking into a McDonald's restaurant anywhere in the country, due to their structured, disciplined and standardized approach to process execution. In the case of standard work, McDonald's sweats the details to maintain consistency. Steps for creating standard work can be found in Figure 2.5.

Steps for Creating Standard Work:

- Video record workplace routine
- Collect cycle times (5–10 cycles)
- Identify key work activities and sequence
- Determine work element breakpoints
- Complete SW recording chart (Appendix VI)
- Identify the lowest repeatable cycle time
- Complete the Standard Work Combination Table (SWCT)
- Complete the Standard Work Chart (SWC)
- Complete the Yamazumi chart
- Balance workload, if necessary
- Prepare the Standard Work Instruction (SWI) and Standard Operating Sheet (SOS)

Achieve lowest repeatable cycle time

Kaizen events:

- Remove abnormalities
- Reduce fluctuations
- Eliminate waste

There is no improvement where there is no standard!

Figure 2.5 Creating standard work at the lowest repeatable cycle time.

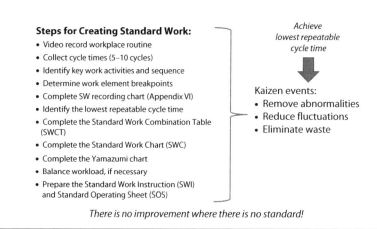

Implementing Standard Work

Before implementing standard work, make sure that there is a clear process, procedure or guideline for doing so. When training employees on a new process, it's recommended that a step-by-step method be prepared to facilitate learning new activities. This process should provide guidance, direction and a visual demonstration of how to perform specific work in order to deliver the knowledge, skills and practice needed to make execution of the required tasks habitual. The training and development of employees should communicate expected behaviors and reinforce task ownership. Consider the following steps when training an employee to perform standard work: preparation, demonstration, application and practice. Let's look at each in more detail.

Preparation

When preparing to train an individual to perform standard work, schedule training so that sufficient time is available to review the SWI documented for the work assignment. The content of the SWI should clearly address the who, what, when, where, how and why associated with the work to be accomplished. Training objectives should be discussed with the trainee before starting the session, along with the necessary documents and visuals to help facilitate hands-on instruction. Providing an employee with time to review work documents prior to instructor-led training allows them to identify concerns and ask questions that may arise during the initial face-to-face training session.

Demonstration

It's important to show the trainee what to do and how to do the work required at the workstation. Demonstrate the routine and explain the purpose of each task and significance of performing tasks in the specified sequence. If beneficial, highlight what may happen if the work is not performed as documented. Remember to take small learning steps with each person and frequently repeat what is being presented. Use simple examples. Easy-to-remember slogans such as "turn right to make tight" are sometimes helpful for the learner. Allow the learner to observe and ask questions.

Application

Watch as the trainee applies what they have learned. Initially, speed is not the objective, it's about understanding and demonstration. Answer questions to ensure understanding and encourage them to verbalize what they are doing and why, as they do it. Have the trainee explain key points and critical steps to reinforce their importance. If necessary, repeat routines, correct mistakes and give positive feedback to reinforce proper execution.

Practice

Have the worker try the routine on their own, without assistance. In the beginning, only stop and correct them when a crucial deviation from the work instruction occurs. Have them practice on their own and periodically check on their progress. Continue to provide positive feedback and correct deviations from expectation. As the trainee becomes more comfortable with prescribed tasks, work to improve cycle time and overall fluency of work-flow. To enhance the learning experience, consider video recording the work routine for review and improvement. Clearly explain output metrics expected as evidence of work properly performed. At the end of training, trainees should be aware of the following key points:

- ✓ What standard work is and why it's important
- ✓ Work activities, sequence, timing and expected outcomes
- ✓ Critical steps to ensuring quality and safety
- ✓ Importance of doing the work, as documented
- ✓ Who to notify when help is needed
- ✓ What to do in case of deviations
- ✓ Process metrics and targets affected by the work
- ✓ Where to find work-related documents
- ✓ Location of work to be performed

The following are some tips for training people to perform standard work:

- Use simple, precise words
- Explain unusual terms
- Refer to individual parts by their specific names

- Explain critical tasks and key relationships between work activities
- Speak slowly while facing the trainee
- Observe trainee performing the work task; correct them when appropriate
- Allow the trainee to practice and ask questions
- Hold multiple sessions to confirm the trainee's competence in performing the routines
- Follow up by observing application of the work standard in real time

Control of Standard Work

Once implemented, standard work must be maintained. One way to support the continuous and proper deployment of standard work is through periodic audits. The organization should establish an audit schedule with clear responsibility for conducting periodic assessments as a way to reinforce the importance of performing work to documented standards. All team members performing standard work should be part of a review. A standard work audit sheet or "checklist" may be helpful in performing structured assessments.

If deviations from standards are observed, take immediate steps to address the issue by showing the individual what's expected, conduct a retraining session and assess their understanding and capability to perform the required work. Confirm their ability to complete standard work correctly and consistently over time. Group leaders are responsible for ensuring compliance to standard work within their scope of responsibility. In short, there should be a system in place to verify continuous compliance with standard work routines while making it easy to manage deviations and pursue opportunities for improvement. Eventually, when a certain level of operational maturity has been reached, individuals should audit their own work in compliance with their SWI. If, at any point, they can't complete the work as documented, they should immediately contact their supervisor or designated support for assistance.

Why Standardized Work?

Standardized work involves documenting what you currently do (standard work) and continuously make changes to improve it. It's a way to establish clear methods for performing predictable and repeatable work tasks with a special focus on human movements. Standardized work is used by operators to ensure quality work is produced safely and efficiently; by engineering to allocate a balanced workload within a production line; and by management to confirm standards are followed. Standard work, as defined by SWI, drives repeatable work routines, resulting in a more stable process. Processes lacking standard work are typically less efficient, exhibit notable cycle time fluctuations due to changing work patterns and produce more waste due to poorly executed and missed operations. Safety may also be compromised if work is not performed correctly.

In addition to helping minimize waste through efficient application of work routines, standard work can also aid in regulating process flow. This can be achieved by setting the pace of production to customer demand (takt time) through balanced workload allocation, establishing a logical work sequence and defining a minimum number of in-process parts at each workstation (e.g. standard in-process stock [SIPS]) to regulate operator waiting time and process flow.

Standardized work is currently considered the best-known method for maintaining efficient production. It sets the foundation for process stability by establishing predictable and repeatable work tasks to drive consistent output performance. This is done through specifying work elements, sequence, location, timing and output requirements of cyclic work. In addition to facilitating process stability, standardized work provides a reference for seeing problems when obstacles to completing work exist. Standardization is also a force for maintaining improvements since enhancements in efficiency can be institutionalized by continually updating SWI. Standardized work, by its very nature, builds control and improvement into the process. Objectives of standardized work include:

- Clarifying roles and responsibilities
- Standardizing cyclic work activities
- Controlling process variation
- Establishing a baseline for detecting process deviations
- Providing a reference for continuous improvement
- Regulating quality, safety, time and cost

Operational excellence starts with standard work. As the organization matures, standard work can evolve to support changing needs of an enterprise in pursuit of perfection. Figure 2.6 displays the evolution of standard work in helping to create a sustainable culture of process control and continuous improvement.

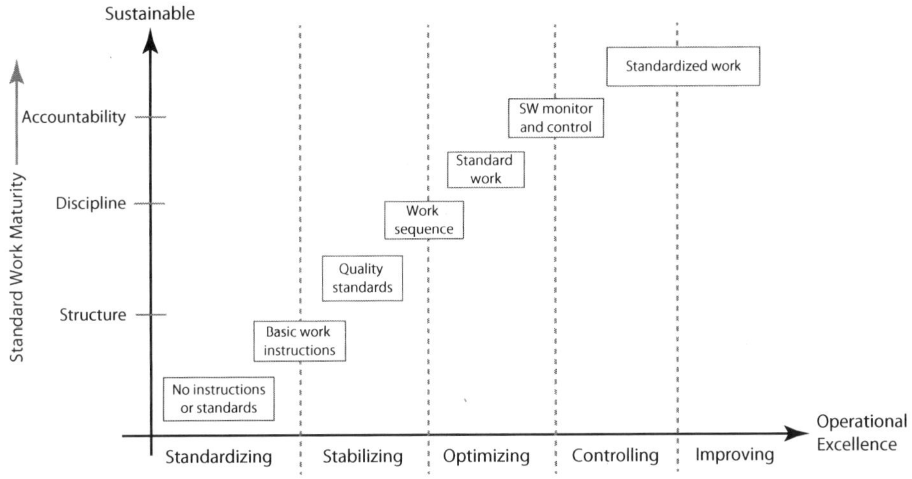

Figure 2.6 Standard work maturity: A foundation for sustainable operational excellence.

In summary, a common way to implement standardized work is through SWI and workflow diagrams. The SWI should contain a clear description of work tasks, work sequence and process cycle times. It may also contain the SIPS needed to ensure a smooth and continuous work rhythm. Once workers are trained in the SWI and deployment is confirmed effective, periodic assessments will likely be required to maintain expected performance. Figure 2.7 provides a method for assessing conformance to SWI.

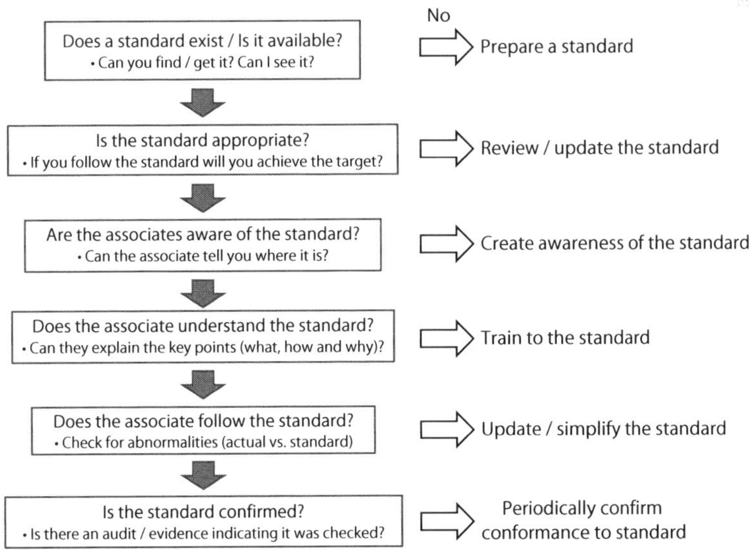

Figure 2.7 Questions to Assess Implementation of a Standard (Source: Toyota Production System.)

Key Points

- Standards avoid waste; not following standards allows waste to occur.
- Standards need to be continuously improved to remain relevant, otherwise people will become complacent and improvement opportunities will be lost.
- Standards make deviations easier to see.
- Standards reinforce the importance of performing critical work activities in a specific sequence to achieve a consistent, repeatable and efficient output.
- Standards should clearly explain "why" critical work activities are to be performed in the sequence specified.
- Standards set the baseline for process control, continuous improvement and sustainable results.
- Standard work instructions are expected to be prepared for the entire value stream, including material handling outside the line.
- Standards must be measurable.
- Standards provide a foundation for training.
- All work should be highly specified as to content, sequence, timing and outcome to achieve more consistent and predictable results.
- Standardization involves the continuous improvement of standards. One should constantly question how standards can be enhanced.
- Consistent process inputs and activities produce consistent outputs.
- Managing deviations to standards facilitates process control.
- Standard work should be periodically confirmed to ensure continued compliance.
- Update standard work when opportunities for improvement are evident.
- Involve employees in the development of their standards. People want a sense of involvement and control over what they are expected to do.
- Employees must demonstrate the discipline to follow standard work and be encouraged to share their ideas for improving work standards based on best practices and lessons learned.
- Leaders who follow their own standard work routines send a clear message to the organization they are serious about process control and continuous improvement.
- Consider standard work for material movers (e.g. water spider, milk run).

- Standard work is an extension of the roles and responsibilities commonly used to describe a job function.
- Standardized work is not about mandating compliance to specified procedures, it's about mutual agreement on how best to perform work and reveal problems.
- Standardization helps control variation while promoting production efficiency and timely process execution.
- Always communicate the "why" and the benefits of standards.
- Standards should be easy, clear, meaningful and safe to apply.
- Always question existing standards.
- Standard work provides a framework for control within which flexibility and creativity can occur.
- Standards are especially critical during times of high employee turnover because established routines, reflecting the best and most efficient way to perform work, remain firmly embedded in a company's documentation, instead of walking out the door in the heads of employees leaving the company.
- Standards create a predictable pace of work, creating less stress for operators.
- When preparing a standard workflow with multiple operators, avoid overlapping operator paths, if possible.
- Standardization is not done *to* people, it's done *with* people!
- Micro-manage the process, not the people.
- "I hear and forget, I see and I remember, I do and I understand" (Confucius).

References

1. David Mann. 2010. *Creating a Lean Culture*. New York: CRC Press/Taylor & Francis.
2. Steven Spear and Kent Bowen. 1999. Decoding the DNA of the Toyota Production System. *Harvard Business Review*. https://hbr.org/1999/09/decoding-the-dna-of-the-toyota-production-system.

Chapter 3

Process Stability

Stability in processes is the bedrock foundation of any improvement system, creating consistency and repeatability. Stability is a prerequisite for improvement providing a basis for problem identification and continuous improvement. Almost all of the continuous improvement principles rely on stability.

The Shingo Model for Operational Excellence

Process Stability Overview

Process stability is a requirement for process capability and a prerequisite for process efficiency. After standardizing a process, we must ensure stability before assessing process capability. A standardized, stabilized and capable process builds a foundation for sustainable lean improvements, which creates a thriving environment for operational excellence.

A stable process is one that is predictable. A process can be considered stable if the output parameters of interest are relatively consistent over time. For example, if a process produces steel rods whose average length and standard deviation are consistent and predictable with time, the process from which they are produced is considered stable. Characteristics of a stable process include:

- Randomly appearing data
- A consistent mean over time

- All points within process control limits
- Data points drift about the mean
- Uniform variation over time
- No observed trends, shifts or spikes in plotted data

A stable process is visualized in Figure 3.1.

If a process is not stable (Figure 3.2), we must understand the causes of its instability and take action to eliminate them. This will be our next topic of discussion.

Assessing Process Stability

Graphically plotting process output performance with time will provide a visual indication of stability. Observing a process in action will often reveal problems with material handling, procedural inconsistencies, equipment reliability, information flow and capacity constraints, all of which are symptoms of process instability. Observing the movements of line operators working the process will also provide clues as to its consistency. In short, signs of process instability abound when taking time to stop and look for them. Sometimes, we simply need to slow down, observe and visualize what's happening in a production line or work area to understand if a process is stable and if not, why not.

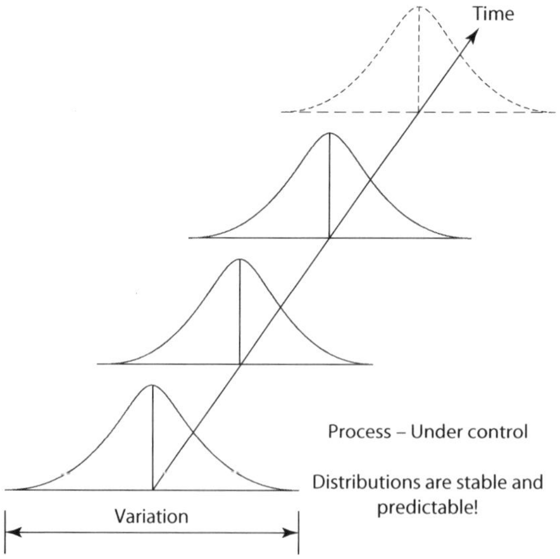

Figure 3.1 A stable process; mean and standard deviation are consistent over time. (Recreated from AIAG SPC Reference Manual.)

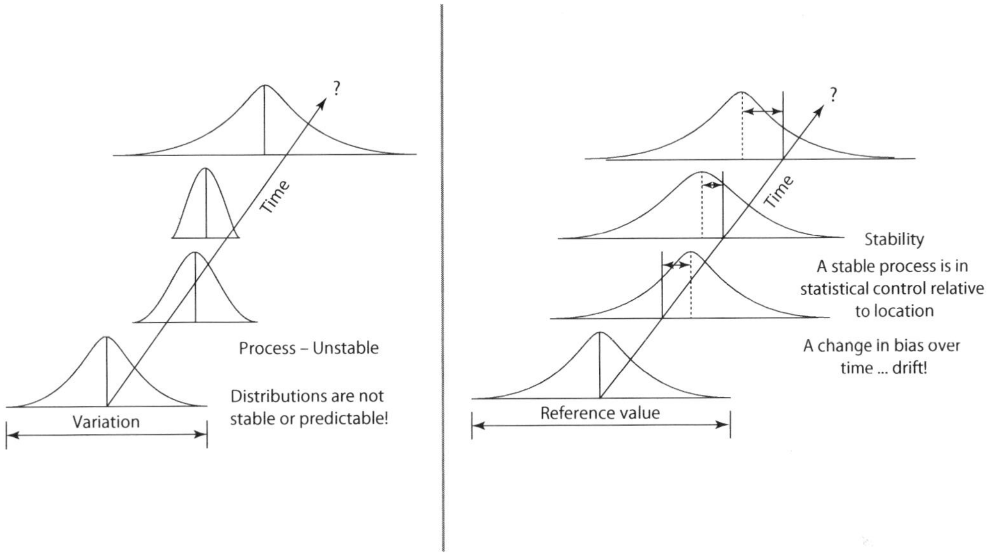

Figure 3.2 An unstable process; mean and standard deviation are not consistent over time. (Recreated from AIAG SPC Reference Manual.)

One of the more common ways to evaluate a process is by plotting work cycles, from start to finish. Using a stopwatch, observe and record around 20–30 work cycles while noting any unusual or abnormal work activities outside the scope of the standard work instruction. Plot the data in sequential order (run chart) and review it for potential trends, patterns and spikes. A run chart is a great tool to visualize the tempo of activities in a process and assess its stability.

Run Charts

Run charts can be used to expose instability in a process. Defects create instability revealed as special cause variation. Special cause variation often affects process outputs in intermittent and irregular ways. It's this unpredictable behavior that causes recognizable patterns, shifts, spikes and trends in data plotted over time, indicating the presence of defects. The causes of unusual process behavior must be identified, investigated for root cause and eliminated through root cause problem-solving to achieve a stable process.

Run charts can be used to study unusual (non-random) behavior exhibited by special cause variation over time to understand process stability and corresponding variation. They can help distinguish between common (natural) and special (assignable) cause variation and aid in the identification and elimination of uncontrolled variation through structured problem-solving. Run charts can exhibit a process's current state and serve as a baseline for output performance from which process improvements can be visualized, measured and evaluated. Statistical software, such as Minitab®, or tools like Excel® can be used to create run charts. Data can be collected at regular intervals (hourly, each shift, daily, etc.) and plotted in time series order. Statistical software can also be employed to analyze data, highlighting unusual values, trends and patterns in the data for further investigation.

A run chart can be prepared with sufficient data to reflect actual process fluctuation. This usually requires 20–30 data points. Upon analysis, a disproportionate number of "runs" on either side of the median is an indicator of special cause variation. Other trends or patterns to look for include:

- Too many or too few runs about the median relative to the number of data points plotted.
- A trend of six or more increasing or decreasing consecutive points.
- A pattern of eight or more consecutive points on the same side of the median.
- A pattern of 14 or more consecutive points alternating up and down.

These trends or patterns are contrary to random behavior expected of a stable process and can easily be identified with statistical software and classified in a way that helps with defect identification and root cause investigation. For example, a Minitab Run chart performs two tests for randomness that provide information on non-random variation due to data *trends, oscillations, mixtures and clusters!* Patterns in data suggest observed variation is due to special causes coming from outside the system and are targets for elimination. Common issues that cause certain patterns include:

- *Clustering*: may indicate sampling, measurement or process problems
- *Mixtures*: may indicate mixed data from two populations
- *Oscillations:* may indicate operator error
- *Trends:* may indicate changes in process, procedures or operators

These common issues provide a good starting point for root cause analysis needed to identify and eliminate defects contributing to undesirable variation and process instability. See Figure 3.3 for an example of a run chart and corresponding analysis results.

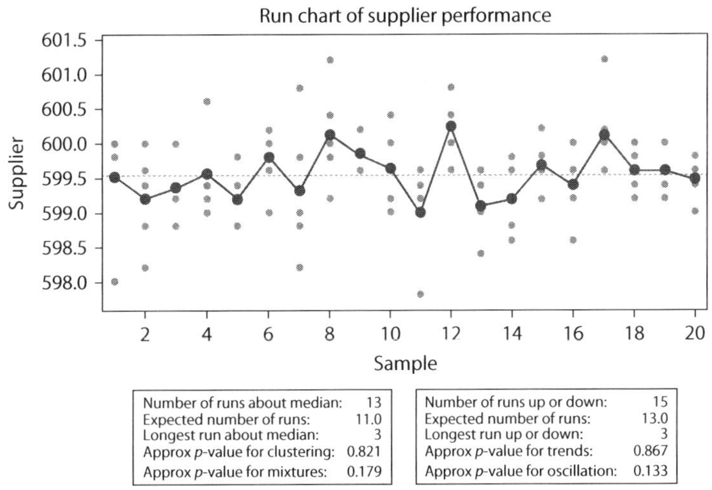

Figure 3.3 Run chart example (using Minitab).

Process Fluctuation

The last "in-cycle" workstation in a manufacturing cell is the *exit cycle*, which can be used to evaluate overall process fluctuation. The exit cycle time is how often an operator's work cycle occurs and can be determined by taking the time between completed units coming off or "packed out" of an operator's work area into a transport or shipping container (Figure 3.4).

To determine process fluctuation, select a reference point in the final operator's work pattern. Start your stopwatch when the operator gets to the reference point and time the operator until they return to that point, regardless of what happens. Record the cycle times and any notable observations (abnormalities) during the timing process, such as disruptions in the operator's expected work rhythm. Make sure the recorded cycle time includes operator wait times, out of cycle work, deviations from routine and other unusual activities or events. This could include a conversation with another person, moving a part to an unexpected location or obtaining a box for packing the next group of parts.

Plot the data collected as well as the takt time and planned cycle time (PCT). If you don't have a takt time or a planned cycle time, draw a line for the desired target exit cycle time.

Lowest Repeatable Time

Once the exit cycle time has been plotted on a run chart (see Figure 3.5), this information can be used to determine the lowest repeatable time (LRT) for the process. The LRT serves as an estimate of the cycle time, if

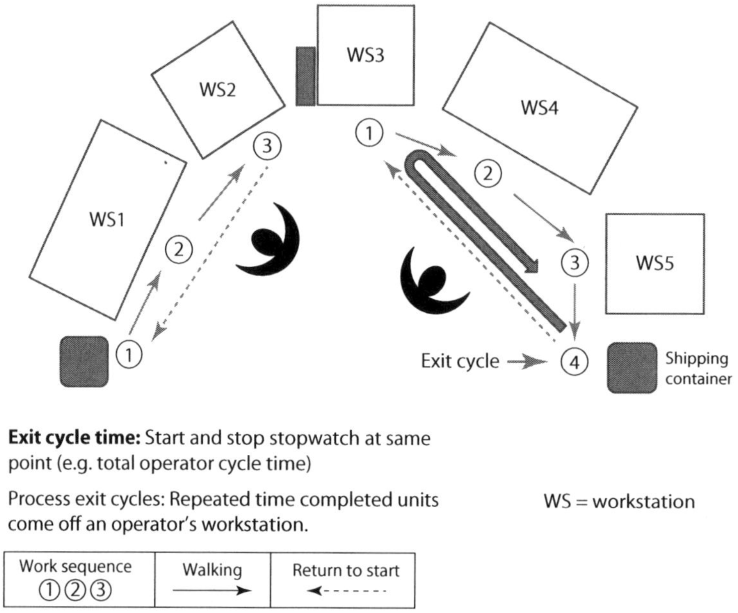

Figure 3.4 Process exit cycle.

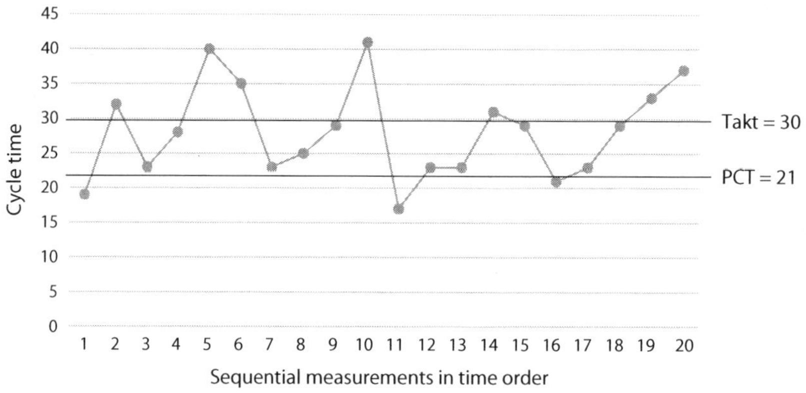

Figure 3.5 Run chart.

everything goes as planned. This is considered a sustainable cycle time for the operation under stable conditions. The LRT can be determined by moving a straight line (e.g. ruler) up from the bottom of the plot until data points start repeating (e.g. 3–4 points at the same value) (Figure 3.6).

Draw the "fat" bar to show the LRT and a thinner bar to show the data range (e.g. lowest and highest points). The data is now available to determine exit cycle fluctuation, or the percent variation, as indicated in Figure 3.7.

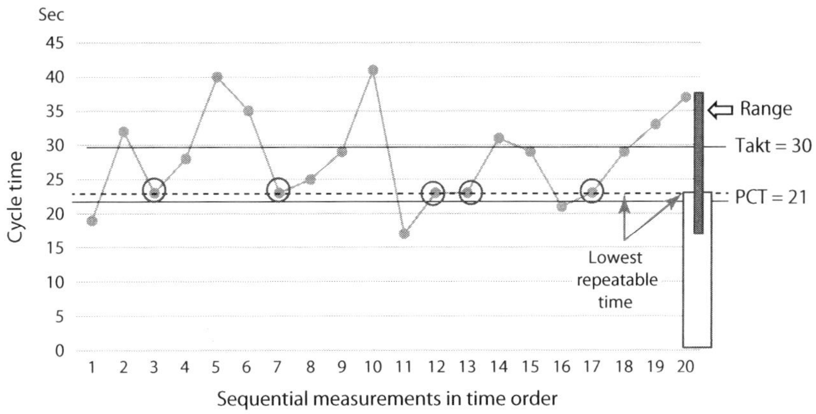

Figure 3.6 Exit cycle run chart: Lowest repeatable time.

Calculate current ± % variation:

- % + variation: (Highest point – PCT) ÷ PCT
- % – variation: (Lowest point – PCT) ÷ PCT

Example: Operator #2

- Highest point: 125
- Lowest point: 23
- PCT: 34

- % + variation: (125 – 34) / 34 x 100 = + 268%
- % – variation: (23 – 34) / 34 x 100 = –32%

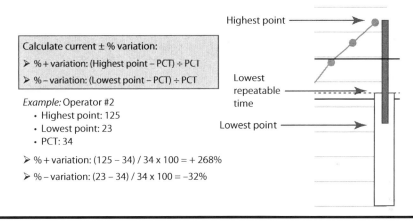

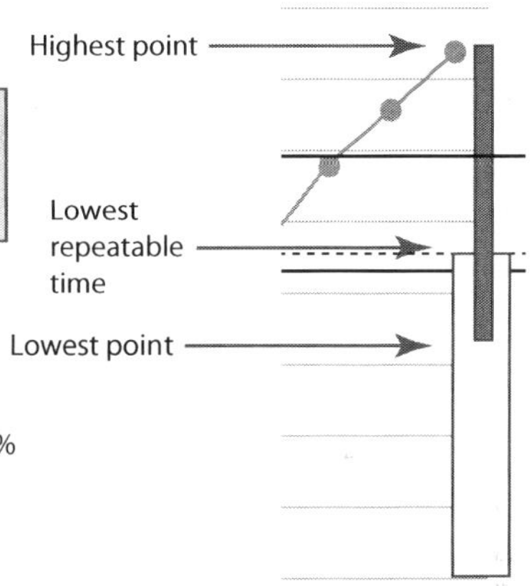

Figure 3.7 Exit cycle fluctuation calculation.

The goal should be to maintain process fluctuation between the takt and planned cycle times. This will facilitate meeting customer demand. To continuously improve the process, close the gap between takt and planned cycle times, further reducing variation while maintaining process stability (e.g. no patterns, trends or spikes in output data).

Statistical Process Control Charts

Statistical process control (SPC) is also an effective tool for assessing process stability. Similar to run charts, SPC charts are trend charts, with data-based control limits, used to assess if a process is in statistical control (e.g. stable) and can aid in maintaining statistical control (stability over time). Control limits provide an additional dimension for assessing process stability and, as in run charts, help distinguish between common and special cause variation while highlighting uncontrolled process variation. SPC is not only a good way to assess and establish stability, it's also a great tool to help monitor and maintain stability over time.

To clarify, control limits are lines on a control chart used as a basis for judging the stability of a process. They are calculated from process data and should not be confused with engineering or customer specification limits. Variation beyond a control limit is evidence that special causes are affecting the process and need to be investigated for their cause. A process is "in control" when all points fall within the boundaries of the control limits, and data does not display any distinguishing patterns. In essence, a statistical control chart is a tool used to analyze a process and trigger action to maintain process stability whenever process output exceeds calculated control limits.

An SPC chart differs from a run or trend chart in that a control chart has statistically based control limits and a center line. Ideally, control limits are calculated from process data taken under stable conditions. The center line is an estimate of process mean and is determined from process data taken over time.

Control charts are one of the best tools for reducing process variation and maintaining stability. There are up to eight conditions that can be incrementally applied to process data, and once one or more conditions have been realized, they can be continuously applied to reduce variation as a way to maintain tight control over stability. The eight conditions for SPC can be reviewed in the sidebar.

SIDEBAR: EIGHT RULES FOR STATISTICAL PROCESS CONTROL CHARTS

The eight tests for special causes are each intended to detect a specific pattern in process data displayed in a statistical process control chart. The existence of one or more patterns suggests special cause variation for investigation. The following are eight rules for SPC:

1. One or more points fall outside the 3 sigma control limits.
2. Two out of three consecutive points are on the same side of the mean beyond the 2 sigma limits.
3. Four out of five consecutive points are on the same side of the mean beyond the 1 sigma limits.
4. Nine consecutive points are on one side of the mean.
5. Six consecutive points are increasing or decreasing.

6. Fourteen consecutive points alternate up and down.
7. Fifteen consecutive points are all above or all below the mean.
8. Eight consecutive points on either or both sides of the mean without any within the +1 or −1 sigma range.

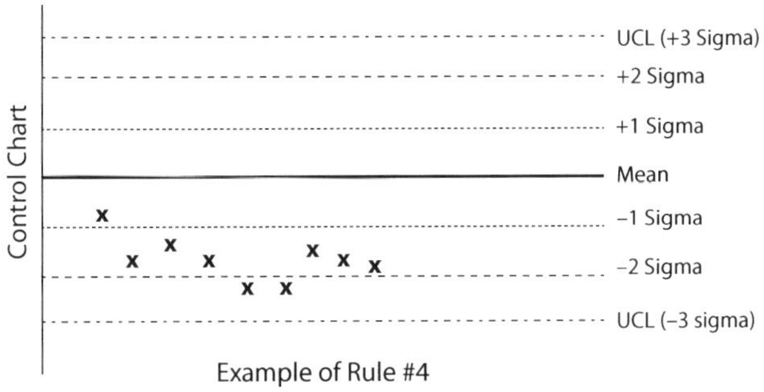

Control charts are used extensively in controlling manufacturing operations but are also practical for use in service and transactional disciplines whenever data is available. For example, one can use controls charts to monitor and control bank teller transactions, call center problem resolution times, a patient's blood pressure, personal spending habits and vehicle miles per gallon performance, to name a few. See Figure 3.8 for an example of an SPC chart.

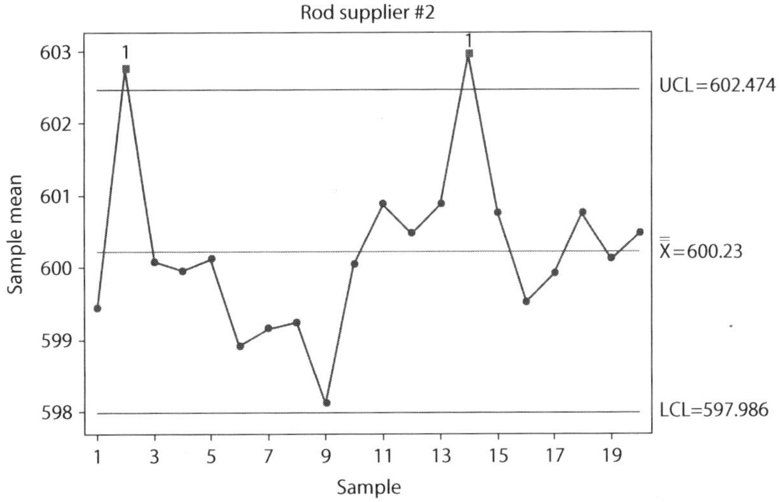

Figure 3.8 SPC chart example (using Minitab Software).

Achieving Process Stability

As discussed, process stability can be evaluated by plotting data on run or SPC charts and then reviewing the results for special cause variation characterized by unexplained patterns, trends or spikes in the data. Once these anomalies have been identified, action must be taken to understand their cause and determine appropriate countermeasures to eliminate unpredictable behavior. To do this, let's turn our attention to key inputs that influence a process's behavior and output stability.

Every process has inputs and outputs. Inputs are expected to facilitate a value-added transformation in form, fit and/or function of a product or create value in a resulting service. Process stability is greatly influenced by inputs and corresponding process activities. Five significant factors (or inputs) that play a key role in process stability include people working in the process, machines employed by the process, materials used in the process, methods followed during the process and the environment in which the process is performed.

The reliability, consistency and stability of these input factors directly impact the resulting process outputs. Understanding, monitoring and controlling these factors are important to ensure that a process remains in control over time. By controlling process inputs, you can significantly influence outputs and long-term process stability (Figure 3.9).

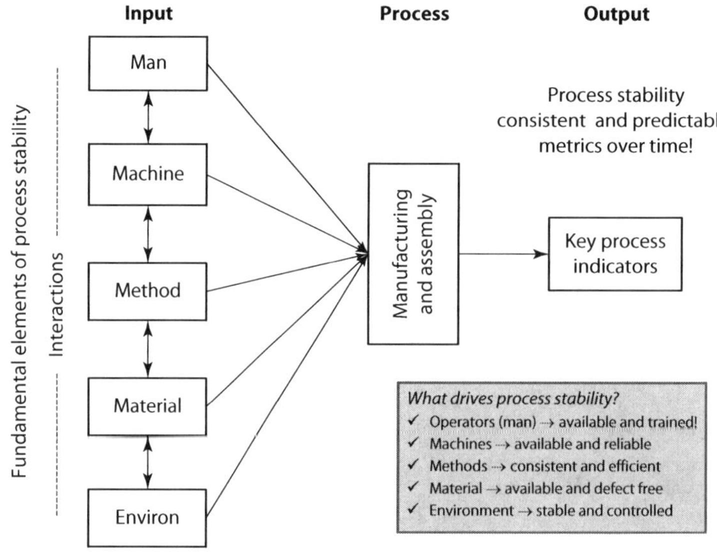

Figure 3.9 Inputs impacting process stability.

As indicated, five significant factors (or inputs) play a key role in influencing the stability of a process. These factors include:

- Man
- Machine
- Materials
- Methods (e.g. procedures and work instructions)
- Environment

Let's consider each factor in more detail.

Man

We will start with people or operators who work in executing the process. Individuals need to understand the best way to interact with their equipment, materials and their surrounding environment in order to minimize process output variation. This is typically communicated through training and work instructions and is reinforced through visual controls. For processes that require people to interface with machines and equipment, individuals must be available, knowledgeable and follow standard work to ensure defined process steps are performed in sequence and within the allotted time expected for each work routine. Standard work is a method to efficiently execute processes, ensuring a stable and consistent product or service is delivered to the customer.

Standard work is a good way to communicate how an individual should interface with a process in an effort to minimize input variation while establishing clear and unambiguous operating instructions. A reduction in input variation usually translates directly to a reduction in output variation.

Machines

If machines, fixtures, gages or other equipment are required in a process, their availability and reliability are critical factors in process stability. As with operators, equipment must run when expected to avoid unplanned downtime. Machines and relevant equipment must run within their control parameters and be maintained within their design specifications to support a smooth, steady and predictable output. Control parameters are to machines as standard work instructions are to operators. In either case, deviations from standards will compromise the integrity of results. Paying attention and making appropriate adjustments to machine settings and equipment parameters at start up and during process execution will significantly contribute to maintaining process stability. In addition, periodic equipment calibration and gage repeatability and reproducibility studies will ensure equipment continues to perform within their intended design parameters. Overall equipment effectiveness (OEE) is a quantitative measure of machine performance and consists of three factors: machine availability rate, performance rate and quality rejects rate. See the following sidebar for more information.

SIDEBAR: OVERALL EQUIPMENT EFFECTIVENESS (OEE)

Overall Equipment Effectiveness (OEE) is a quantitative measure of machine performance and consists of three values:

Machine Availability Rate

- Percentage of time a machine is supporting production
- Total hours of normal scheduled operation divided by the total hours, less downtime (e.g. total scheduled operating hours – downtime hours)

Performance Rate

- Percentage of available time a machine produces at a predetermined speed for individual units
- Measures the loss of speed due to inefficient batching, machine problems and other factors resulting from downtime

Quality Reject Rate

- The number of good parts divided by the number of all produced parts

$$\text{OEE} = \text{Machine Availability} \times \text{Performance Rate} \times \text{Quality Reject Rate}$$

Materials (and Information)

Defect-free, conforming material, available when and where needed in sufficient quantities to seamlessly support production demands is another essential component of stability. A disruption in material quantity, quality or availability often slows down or stops production, further affecting consistent and predictable process flow. Critical materials should be periodically, if not continuously, monitored for conformance to specifications before consumption since detection of problems after material usage can lead to significant scrap and rework.

The same is true of information. Factual information and reliable data must be available when and where needed to maintain continuous flow to prevent the unexpected interruptions that contribute to process volatility.

Method

Methods we use to interact with our processes, equipment and each other have a significant impact on process stability. The methods employed by an organization are often defined by its culture, documented in procedures, implemented by trained individuals and controlled by periodic work routines. The overall effectiveness of these methods in maintaining a stable process is commonly reflected in how well they are written, deployed, monitored and controlled by everyone in the organization. Periodic verification that standard work methods are being followed should be conducted while ensuring regular updates to these methods occur, reflecting a continuous learning and improving organization.

Process activities, including their sequence and timing, also drive consistent output. As indicated previously, the purpose of standard work is to clearly define the interaction between the process and its external influences (e.g. people, machines, material and environment) in order reduce the impact of external factors on output results. Clearly defined and efficient work instructions go a long way to minimizing process variation and maintaining stability.

Environment

The last factor to be discussed is environment. The environment can interact with many aspects of the process including people, equipment and materials, causing variation that may be difficult to control. Many organizations are taking a proactive approach to product and process design by using Design for Six Sigma (DFSS) as a method to reduce product sensitivity to controllable and uncontrollable factors. Although DFSS is outside the scope of this text, it can be an effective tool in minimizing the impact of input variation on process output.

Process stability is the result of good product and process design, effective process execution and disciplined process monitoring and control. Proper attention to key process inputs and control parameters will translate into stable and predictable process outputs. The application of tools and techniques such as control plans, control charts, standard work, leader standard work (LSW), total predictive maintenance (TPM), problem-solving and DFSS are essential in the effort to achieve and maintain process stability. Once process stability has been established, a process can be evaluated for work balance.

Workload Balance

Operator workload balancing is another way to improve stability and create a smoother workflow. In preparation for workload balancing, operator cycle time fluctuations (variation) should be assessed and maintained within ±5% of the planned cycle time. Reducing waste in work routines and the impact of bottlenecks on process disruptions will help to reduce operational cycle time. A Yamazumi chart is a good tool to visualize work area waste and facilitate workload balancing between process operators. It can highlight discrepancies in operator cycle times, display work cycle fluctuation and reveal wait times and obvious differences in incidental work time (work package changes).

Once operator cycles are stable, workload can be reviewed and rebalanced between processes by targeting non-value added activities for reduction and elimination before reallocating remaining labor tasks.

To prepare an operator balance chart for a work cell, generate a run chart for each operator. The LRT and range is then determined and visualized on individual run charts. Place the "fat" and "thin" bars from the individual operator charts together on one "operator balance chart" to create an operator cycle time view of the process. See Figure 3.10 for an example of an operator balance chart.

The appropriate number of operators can now be calculated for a production line if a stable process is maintained under controlled conditions. The number of operators needed for a process can be determined by summing up all the LRTs and dividing by the planned cycle time, as shown in Figure 3.11. According to the calculation, if the process were stable, it would require 4.2 people to operate.

Once the current situation is understood and visualized graphically, it's time to reallocate the workload to create a more balanced distribution of work activities. If the workload can't be evenly spread among all operators, put the "waste" burden on one operator so that it can be easily identified and eliminated from the operation over time (Figure 3.12). If job rotation is part of the operating procedure, all operators will share in the workload, regardless of where the waste exists.

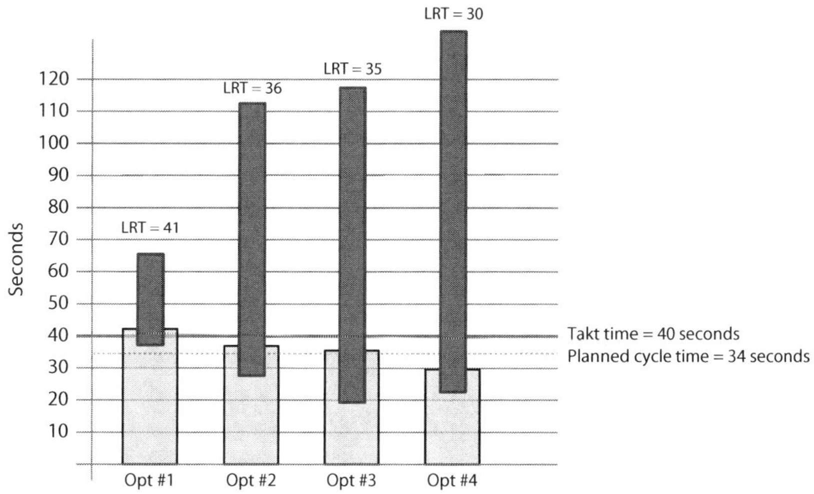

Figure 3.10 Operator balance chart.

Number of operators needed

Determine the number of operators need for this process by summing up all the LRTs and dividing it by the PCT as follows:

$$\text{No of people required} = \frac{\text{Sum of lowest repeatable time } (\Sigma \text{LRT})}{\text{Planned cycle time (PCT)}}$$

$$\frac{\Sigma\ \text{LRT}}{\text{PCT}} = \frac{30 + 35 + 36 + 41}{34} = 4.2 \text{ people}$$

Figure 3.11 Calculating the number of line operators required.

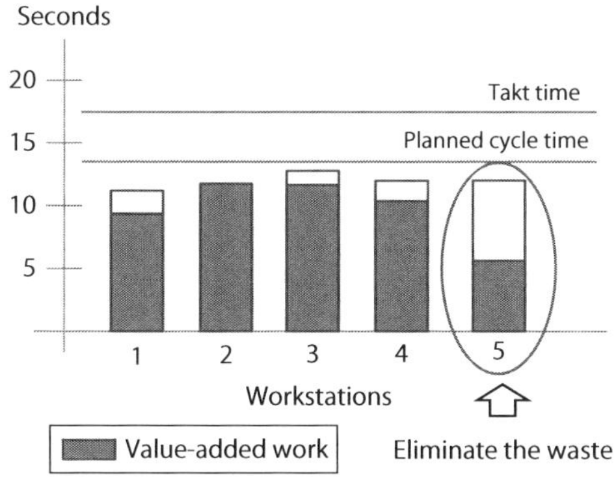

Figure 3.12 Shifting waste to one operator.

To move from an unbalanced to a more balanced workflow, consider the following rules:

- Rule #1: No operator should leave the cell for work-related activities!
- Rule #2: No one should enter the cell for work-related activities.
- Rule #3: Machines should not run any slower than 90% of the planned cycle time.

These rules set a expectation for every manufacturing operation. Continuous improvement activities can be focused on realizing these 3 rules as part of a strategy for achieving operational excellence.

The goal of workload balancing is to evenly distribute the workload among all operators in the production line in an effort to minimize waste while achieving the lowest possible cost, on-time delivery and defect-free production.

Maintaining Process Stability

Rapid problem-solving is required to prevent significant line disruptions when a production line operator encounters an issue requiring immediate attention. The availability of a qualified individual to assist with production problems is essential to ensuring a timely response and resolution within the expected cycle time defined by standard work instructions. This approach is counterintuitive to those who traditionally encourage workers to try and solve their own problems before calling for help. Line operators should not be spending time problem-solving as they are primarily employed to assemble product within a specified cycle time. However, they should be encouraged to make suggestions for continuously improving standard work since they have the knowledge, insight and expertise to do so.

When calling for assistance is not normal operating procedure, problems may take longer to solve or simply continue unsolved, forcing employees to create workarounds as a means to keep the line running, while process cycle times begin to increase. Organizations must adapt to the nature and frequency of problems they encounter to remain efficient and effective. The nature of a problem should dictate who is responsible for it and the urgency of an issue should determine the degree and level of support required to address it.

In summary, process stability can be evaluated by plotting output data on a run or control chart. These charts can help visualize trends, patterns or spikes in process data as a window into process performance. Non-random behavior in output data often indicates the presence of defects, causing instability. Once undesirable behavior has been identified, steps must be taken to determine the root cause and countermeasures initiated to eliminate defects. This can be done efficiently using a structured and disciplined approach to problem-solving. More importantly, this activity must become part of an organization's DNA since process stability is continuously challenged by the dynamic environment and the increasing complexity of manufacturing.

Key Points

- Defects contribute to special cause variation that leads to process instability.
- A stable process can be achieved by identifying and eliminating defects.
- A properly designed and stable process will produce expected results.
- Run and SPC charts are excellent visual tools for helping identify and eliminate defects.
- SPC is an effective tool for monitoring and maintaining process stability.
- Run charts reveal data trends while control charts reveal data anomalies using statistically based rules.
- Defects are eliminated through problem-solving.
- A stable process is one in which special cause variation has been eliminated; only common cause variation exists.
- Process stability is a prerequisite for sustainable process flow improvements.
- Once process stability has been established, a process is ready to be evaluated for capability.
- The LRT is not a standard but a reference point for continuous improvement. It helps focus attention on what's possible with a stable process.

Bibliography

Improvement Kata Handbook by Mike Rother, Version 22.0.

Statistical Process Control (SPC) Reference Manual, Second Edition. Automotive Industry Action Group; Chrysler LLC, Ford Motor Company and General Motors Corporation, 2010.

Chapter 4

Process Capability

An unstable process is unpredictable. If a process is not stable, you can't predict future performance and improve process capability or efficiency. Thus, a process must be stable before it can be determined capable and capable before improving efficiency.

Process Capability Overview

Process capability is the ability of a process to produce products and provide services that consistently meet engineering tolerances and customer requirements. It's important to note that a process must be stable before it can be determined capable. If a process is found to be *unstable*, the team must first identify reasons for its instability and engage in problem-solving to eliminate the offending causes.

Capability is assessed by comparing process output performance to corresponding customer requirements or engineering tolerances. To understand how to control and improve this process characteristic, it's important to consider factors that influence its behavior. Let's start by reviewing the relationship between inputs and process activities that work together to define process capability.

Process Inputs, Activities and Outputs

Every process has inputs, transformational activities and one or more corresponding outputs. Output parameters, sometimes called process metrics or indicators, are a measure of output performance commonly represented by the letter "y". Inputs that influence outputs are typically designated by the letter "x" and can consist of one or more controllable or uncontrollable variables. As an example, tire pressure and vehicle weight (x's) will affect a vehicle's overall miles per gallon performance (y). A transforming activity of vehicle acceleration, in combination with these two inputs (among others), will influence fuel efficiency.

A process can be defined mathematically by the relationship between y and x and can be represented by $y=f(x)$, where y is a function of one or more x's. Stated more specifically, $y=f(x_1+x_2+x_3+x_n...)$. This mathematical relationship, defined by "y" as a function of x, is considered a transfer function (e.g. a transfer of inputs to outputs). The term "y" can be viewed as a product output or metric that is influenced by one or more corresponding process input factors "x's". The objective is to control output (y) by understanding and managing significant input factors ($x_1+x_2+x_3+x_n...$).

The capability of a product output (y) is dependent upon its corresponding process inputs (x's). Understanding product and process capabilities is impacted by our ability to effectively measure these values precisely and accurately. First, confirm the equipment used to measure these parameters is capable of capturing data at a level of discretion required to distinguish between differences in measurements of interest with minimal contribution from measurement system variation. To understand process capability, we must understand the degree to which part and measurement system variation influences it. As a general rule, measurement systems should not contribute more than 15% to total process variation. Product capability should not be a major concern if proper steps are taken to design-in product reliability and verify process capability prior to production release. Let's review measurement system capability before process and product capability.

Measurement System Capability

Measurement systems analysis (MSA) is used to assess the quality of measurement data. It ensures data collection procedures and systems provide adequate resolution by understanding measurement bias and the influence of variation on specified tolerances. Bias is the difference between an average output measurement compared to a standard or reference value. It's an assessment of gage accuracy where the smaller the difference between the actual versus reference value, the better (Figure 4.1).

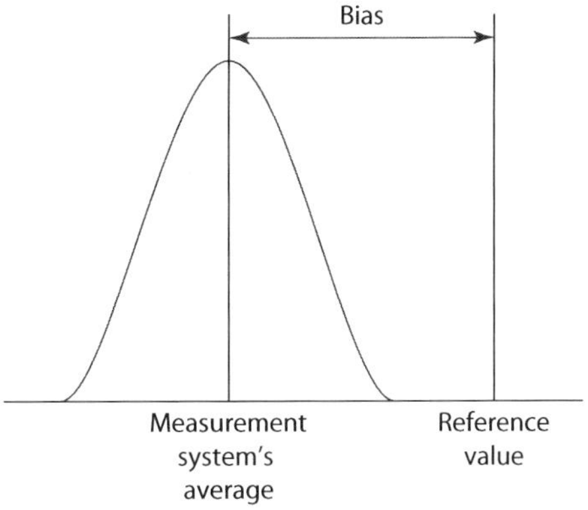

Figure 4.1 Visual display of measurement bias. Note: Bias considers the difference between the observed average measurement and a known reference value.

Measurement system variation encompasses variation associated with measurement tools, methods, setup procedures and system interactions. It's important that measurement equipment is calibrated before steps are taken to determine its reliability in providing quality data for assessing product and process capability.

A Type 1 gage study is used to evaluate the capability of a measurement process. This study evaluates the effects of bias and repeatability using multiple measurements from a single part. It should be performed prior to conducting a more comprehensive gage repeatability and reproducibility (GR&R) study, which is used to determine how much of your observed process variation is due to measurement system variation [1]. GR&R studies can be performed to ensure the integrity of measurement systems for a specific application. For more details on this topic, see Sidebar: Measurement System Error.

Once you are confident that the measurement system is stable and capable of providing accurate and precise data, it's time to determine if the process is capable of producing consistently good products defined by customer requirements.

SIDEBAR: MEASUREMENT SYSTEM ERROR

Source: Minitab Inc. V17

Measurement system errors can be classified into two categories: accuracy and precision. Accuracy describes the difference between the measurement taken and the part's actual value. Precision describes the variation you see when you measure the same part repeatedly with the same device. Within any measurement system, you can have one or both of these problems. For example, you can have a device that measures parts precisely (little variation in the measurements) but not accurately. You can also have a device that is accurate (the average of the measurements is very close to the accurate value), but not precise, that is, the measurements have large variance. You can also have a device that is neither accurate nor precise.

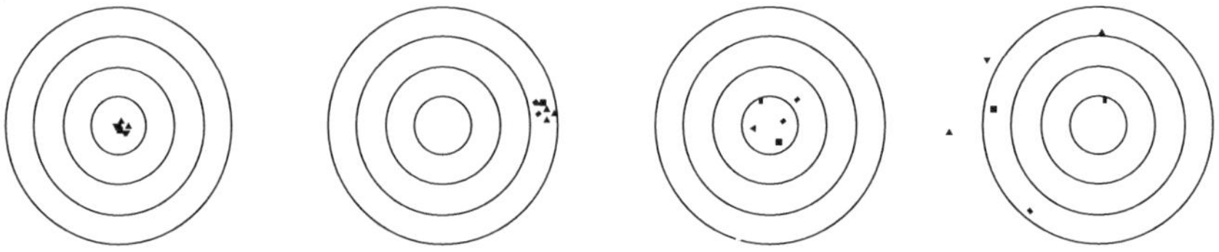

Accurate and precise | Precise but not accurate | Accurate but not precise | Not accurate or precise

Accuracy

The accuracy of a measurement system is usually broken down into three components: linearity, bias and stability.

- Linearity is a measure of how the size of the part affects the accuracy of the measurement system. It is the difference in the observed accuracy values through the expected range of measurements.
- Bias is a measure of the bias in the measurement system. It is the difference between the observed average measurement and a master value.
- Stability is a measure of how accurately the system performs over time. It is the total variation obtained with a particular device, on the same part, when measuring a single characteristic over time.

Precision

Precision, or measurement variation, can be broken down into two components: repeatability and reproducibility.

- Repeatability is the variation due to the measuring device. It is the variation observed when the same operator measures the same part repeatedly with the same device.
- Reproducibility is the variation due to the measurement system. It is the variation observed when different operators measure the same parts using the same device.

Process Capability

Once stability has been achieved and the measurement system is determined capable, we must understand and assess process capability as we move closer to creating an environment for sustainable lean improvements. Common ways to assess process capability include capability analysis, which compares actual process variation to specification limits (customer or engineering), or visually superimposing specification limits over a distribution of output data to see if the process is consistently producing products within the upper and lower boundaries. This must be done over several time periods to assess repeated conformance to requirements (Figure 4.2).

Figure 4.2 provides a snapshot in time comparing process variation to customer-defined limits. In this example, the process is not capable since actual process capability exceeds allowable customer tolerances for the upper (USL) and lower (LSL) specifications. A similar approach would be to collect data, prepare a histogram and overlay specification limits on the chart to determine capability as demonstrated in Figure 4.3. A histogram will provide insight into the data mean, standard deviation, shape and common values collected within a sample.

The following steps can be used to assess process capability. Although calculating capability is a relatively simple process, there are plenty of software options to assist with this activity.

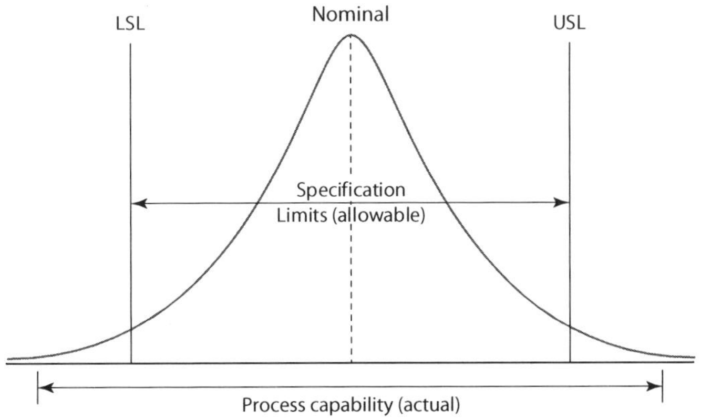

Figure 4.2 Comparing process variation to specification limits.

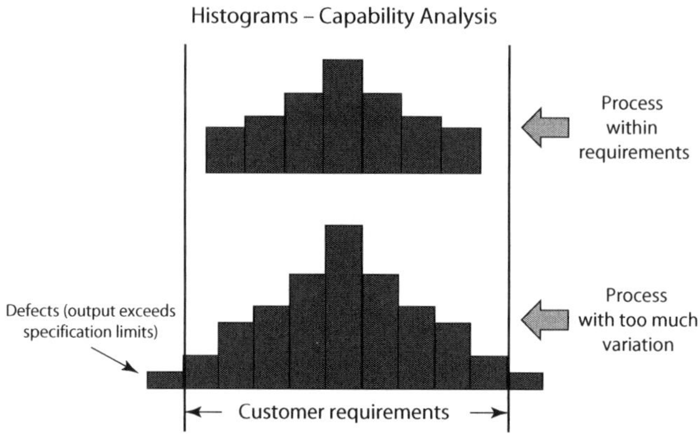

Figure 4.3 Histogram with customer requirements.

Step #1: Ensure Process Stability

Process stability must be confirmed before starting a process capability study of this type. If the process is found to be unstable, identify and eliminate defects causing instability and confirm output consistency before moving forward. Chapter 3 on process stability will provide more information on how to evaluate, achieve and maintain consistent output results.

Step #2: Confirm Data Normality

The proper interpretation of a capable process, using capability analysis, requires that the data approximates a normal distribution, which is characteristic of many industrial processes. Data collection may require a minimum sample size of 30 data points before sample means can be evaluated for normality. The Anderson–Darling normality test is often used to determine data normality with an understanding of its limitations. Data that is normally distributed will be exhibited as a straight line when using a normal probability plot and have a p-value >0.05. If the data is not normal ($p < 0.05$), consider options for transforming the data set into a normal distribution or an alternate method for assessing process capability. Sometimes, a simple visual display of distributed data will justify a normality assessment.

Note: A p-value is used to determine the degree to which data exhibits random behavior. For example, if a p-value is less than 0.05, there is a low probability (5% or less) the data is behaving randomly and thus suspect for non-random behavior due to special cause. Special cause in this case is a non-normal data distribution.

Step #3: Capability Analysis

The next step is to determine capability. The capability index (Cpk), also called Potential capability or short-term capability is a measure used to define the capability of a process and reflects the distribution of a process about a target value and percentage of measurements within specified limits. It can be used to estimate the defect percentage and determine the need for process improvement. It's also a metric to baseline process performance and assess the effectiveness of process improvements over time. Cpk is a good indicator for comparing multiple process capabilities with different units of measure and specification limits since it's based on a ratio. It's often used to gage a product's readiness for release to manufacturing or acceptance of a supplied product for production. Remember, Cpk analysis is only valid if data is normally distributed. If data is not normally distributed, there is no value in using Cpk to assess process capability. Capability assessments are generally divided into two groups, Potential capability and Overall capability. Potential capability considers variation within subgroups, not between subgroups. It's considered short-term capability since it does not account for process variation between subgroups but, is reflective of what the process is capable of doing. Overall capability is more representative of what customers experience since they receive multiple groups of product reflective of true process variation to specification requirements over time. The gap between Potential and Overall capability closes as the process approaches a statistically stable state of control. See Figure 4.4, a comparison between Potential and Overall process capability.

Step #4: Calculating Capability

Cpk compares the sample data mean to corresponding specification limits. It considers process centering relative to the upper and lower specification limits independently and the capability value is based on the worst case of the two resulting calculations. See the formulas for calculating Cpk in Figure 4.5 and an example of a Cpk calculation in Figure 4.6.

Strive for a minimum Cpk of 1.0. This reflects a process output producing to specification requirements. If there is no variation in process performance, all outputs produced will meet expected tolerances. However,

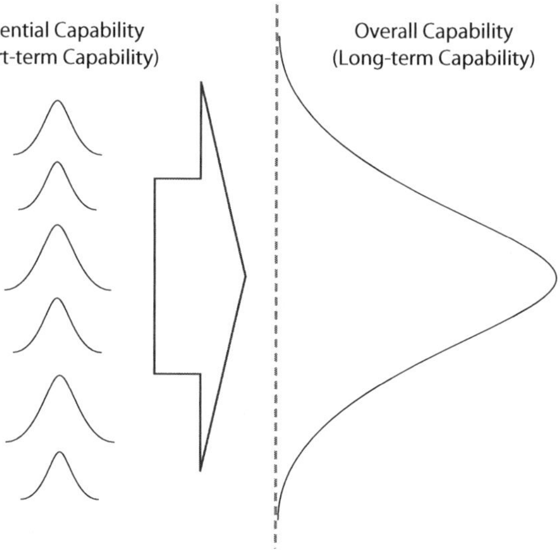

Figure 4.4 A comparison between Potential and Overall process capability.

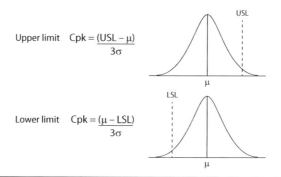

Upper limit $\text{Cpk} = \dfrac{(\text{USL} - \mu)}{3\sigma}$

Lower limit $\text{Cpk} = \dfrac{(\mu - \text{LSL})}{3\sigma}$

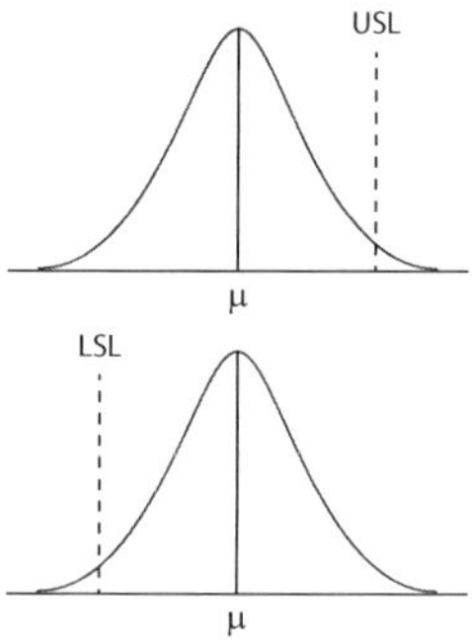

Figure 4.5 Process capability formulas.

- ➢ Lower specification limit = 130
- ➢ Upper specification limit = 140
- ➢ Target = 135
- ➢ Standard Deviation (SD) = 2.7
- ➢ Mean = 131

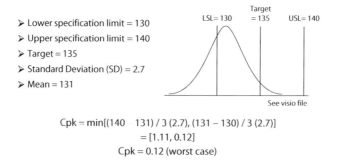

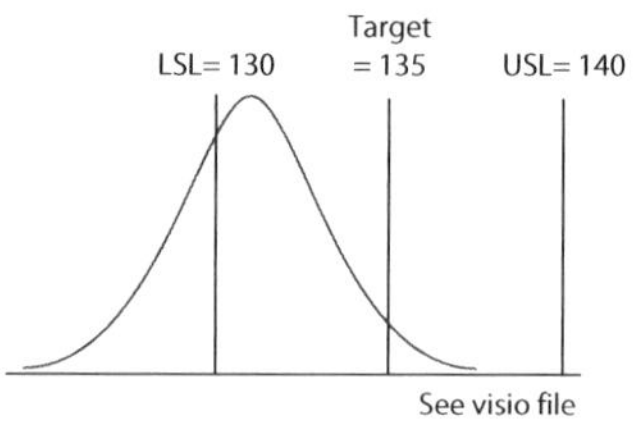

Cpk = min[(140 – 131) / 3 (2.7), (131 – 130) / 3 (2.7)]
= [1.11, 0.12]
Cpk = 0.12 (worst case)

Figure 4.6 Calculating process capability.

a Cpk of 1.0 will not allow for any additional variation in process before a non-conforming product is observed. A performance target for Cpk of 1.33 is generally accepted by most industries and will permit minor deviations in process variation without compromising output quality. A Cpk of 1.0 reflects a 3 sigma quality level or a process yield of 99.73%. A process capability of 1.33 is equivalent to 4 sigma quality or the equivalent of 99.99% of output produced within specification. A Cpk of 2.0 is considered "Six Sigma" quality. See Figure 4.7 for further details on Cpk and quality performance. Minitab® software has options for calculating capability, an example of which can be found in Figure 4.8.

Step #5: Determine Next Steps

Once you have achieved acceptable capability on all key processes within your control, turn your focus to material suppliers since they typically have the next biggest impact on capability. If you are unable to achieve a Cpk of 1.0 or greater, you must work to reduce common cause variation within your process. To do so, identify major sources of process variation and

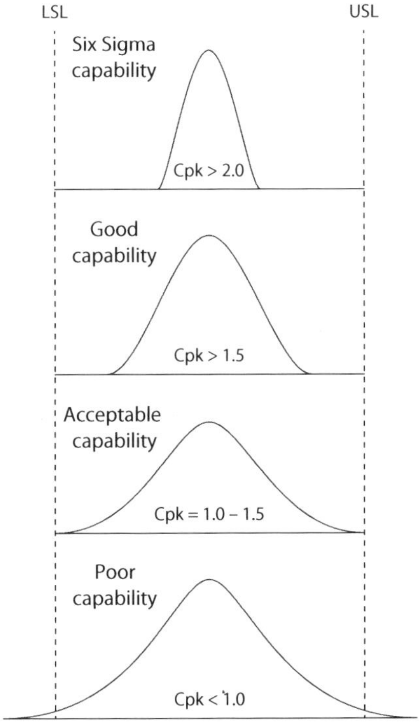

Cpk	Sigma level	Process yield	Process loss (per 1,000,000)
0.33	1	68.27%	3,17,311
0.67	2	95.45%	45,500
1.00	3	99.73%	2,700
1.33	4	99.99%	63
1.67	5	99.9999%	1
2.00	6	99.9999998%	0.002

Figure 4.7 Level of Cpk performance.

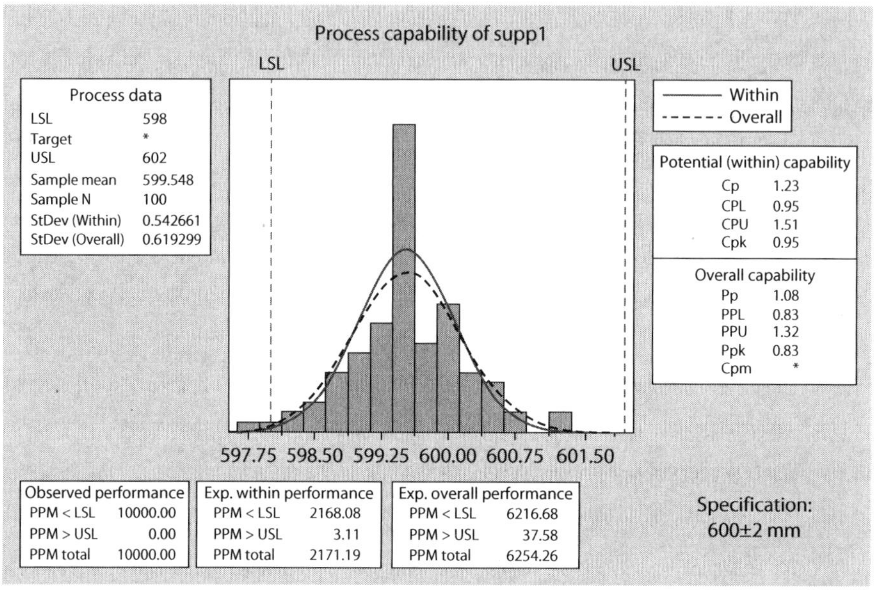

Figure 4.8 Capability analysis (using Minitab).

take action to reduce, if not eliminate, one or more contributors to output variation. Sensitivity analysis can be used to determine which input factors have the most significant impact on output parameters of interest. Consider evaluating the five primary sources of variation:

- Part to part
- Change over time
- Customer use
- Environment
- System interaction

Once a major contributor to variation has been identified, work to reduce the sensitivity of this input on output variation by considering one of three methods:

- *Method 1*: Tighten input variation. Reduce output variation (y) by reducing variation in process inputs (x's). In this method, variation in output is reduced proportionally to input variation. Figure 4.9 shows this relationship between input versus output.
- *Method 2*: Shift target values. Shift input values (x's) to a region in which the output (y) has less sensitivity to variation. This method is only useful if there is a reduction in the rate of change from inputs

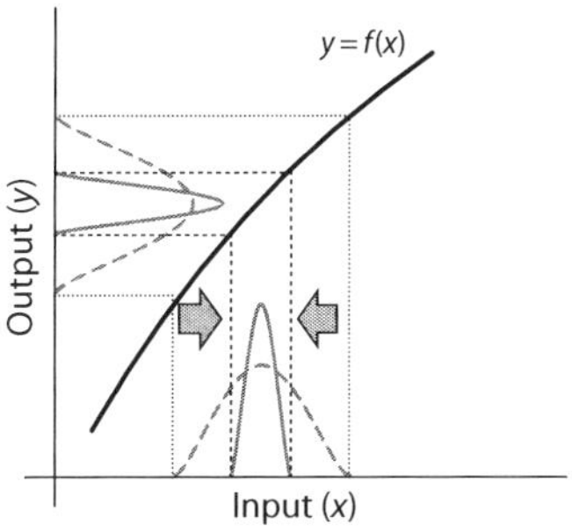

Figure 4.9 Reducing input proportional to output variation.

to outputs while still meeting specifications. As indicated previously, the input (*x*) and output (*y*) relationship defined by the curved line in Figure 4.8 is considered a transfer function. The objective of Method 2 is to shift the design means to a different region along the transfer function where the slope is reduced and output (*y*) becomes less sensitive to input variation (*x*). This approach is graphically displayed in Figure 4.10.

- *Method 3*: Modify the relationship. Although frequently difficult to do, an option may exist to change the relationship (e.g. transfer function) between inputs (*x*'s) and output (*y*) through product design or redesign. This is not recommended due to the complexity of doing so and is often considered a last resort when too much variation in *y* exists to create a robust design. As usual, shifts in inputs and output must still satisfy product requirements and process specifications (Figure 4.11).

Maintaining Process Capability

Once established, both stability and capability must be maintained. Process capability should be continuously monitored for conformance to requirements. This can be done by periodically observing product output for

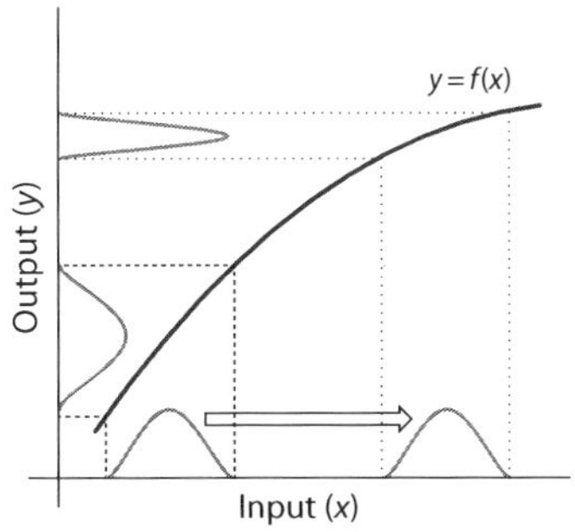

Figure 4.10 Shift input target value.

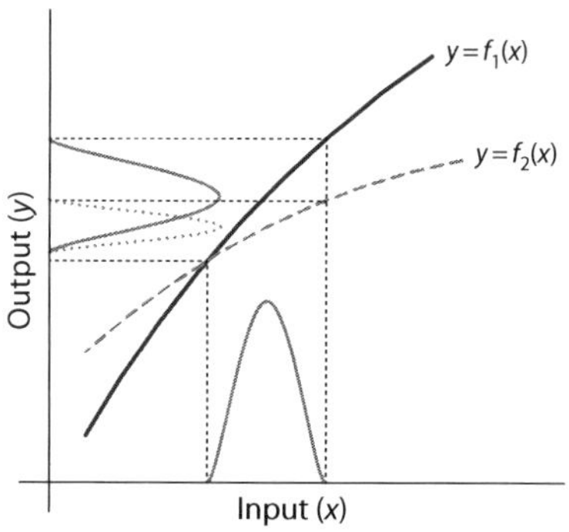

Figure 4.11 Transfer function modification.

deviations from specification and can often be automated using tools such as control charts. Control charts are useful for monitoring both stability and capability in addition to providing a good visual for revealing significant process outliers. Statistical process control limits are commonly used to assess process stability while customer specification limits are used to determine process capability. Both measures can help baseline a process's current state as well as highlight deviations. Of course, significant deviations must be identified, investigated and eliminated to maintain both stability and capability. Figure 4.12 visually displays an unstable, stable and capable process.

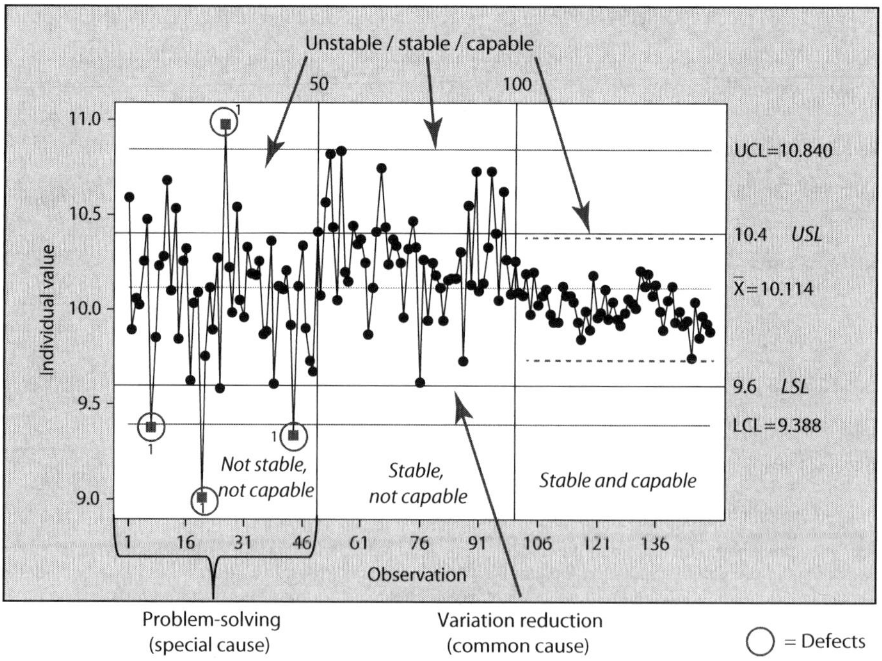

Figure 4.12 Stability and capability demonstrated.

An unstable process is evident when one or more outputs exceed the upper or lower *control limits* (UCL, LCL), highlighted in Figure 4.12 as defects. Stability is achieved when all outputs fall within those limits. However, a stable state does not imply capability since output results may still exceed upper and lower *specification* limits (USL, LSL). Stability and capability are achieved when process outputs are within both upper and lower *control* and *specification* limits.

Improving Process Capability

Capability is increased (improved) as process outputs are more aligned with their target values and process variation is reduced relative to process tolerances (Figure 4.13). Variation reduction starts with understanding the type and sources of variation acting on a process and systematically working to reduce significant variation. To understand sources of variation negatively impacting a process's capability, consider variation due to factors such as equipment wear, material differences, system interactions and environmental influences. Sometime, a small shift in mean output toward the target is all that's needed to improve process capability.

By comparing the voice of the process (control limits) to the voice of the customer (specification limits), you can determine the difference between your current and desired capability and work to close the gap. Investigate obstacles preventing you from closing the gap and taking actions to reduce, if not eliminate, obstacles through creative problem-solving. Also consider reviewing and validating existing specifications for adequacy. Widening

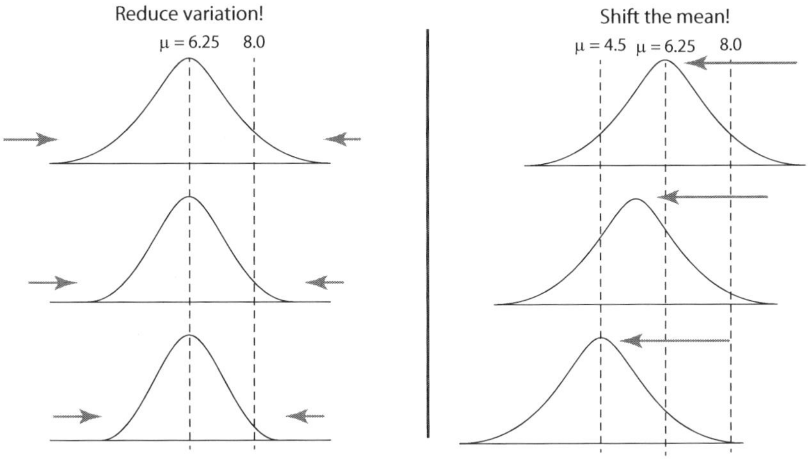

Figure 4.13 Improving process capability.

specification limits may be justified if data-based evaluations support no significant impact on product quality. An unrealistic or incorrect specification tolerance can challenge a process's ability to achieve capability, sometimes at great sacrifice to time and resources.

Product Capability

Product capability takes a slightly different focus since it's ultimately determined during the design phase. When we talk about product capability, we often discuss it in the context of design optimization by choosing product and process parameters and parameter settings that are less sensitive to variation. This is commonly discussed as design robustness where a robust design is one that consistently meets customer requirements and demonstrates a capability (or Cpk) of 2.0 or greater. A capability of 2.0 or greater allows variation to occur without significantly compromising product quality. To ensure robust designs are achieved, prototypes, computer simulations, mathematical equations and historical data are employed early in the design process to evaluate product capability and make adjustments during the concept phase when it's easier and cheaper to do so. Once a design is frozen, more time and money are required to realize product changes.

Design for Six Sigma has become a proven method for evaluating and improving design robustness in the development process. It's intended to improve design predictability and capability early in the process, avoiding market delays and production defects due to design shortcomings detected late in the development life cycle. This approach minimizes the influence of variation at the point of design, ensuring products will meet customer requirements prior to production launch. Upon releasing a product for manufacturing, it becomes the responsibility of operations to maintain product and process control, which will be discussed in the next chapter.

Capability analysis will help determine if a process is able to meet customer requirements, once stability has been demonstrated. It can also assess the risk of producing product outside of specification limits, providing insight into process reliability. Capability often serves as a barometer for how well improvements are implemented and sustained over time, but it must be constantly measured and analyzed to do so. Our next topic highlights the importance of process control in maintaining process stability and capability as we reinforce a foundation for lean efficiency improvements.

Key Points

- Control charts can be used to monitor both stability and capability.
- Capability is increased (improved) as process outputs are more aligned with their target values and process variation is reduced.
- Once achieved, process capability should be continuously monitored for conformance to requirements.
- Increasing specification tolerances will improve capability but this must be done without compromising quality.
- Process capability is a measure of how able a process is to produce the desired outcome to specifications. It's used to determine the percentage of defects a stable process will produce within defined specification limits.
- Since process information is reduced to a single index value, you can use capability statistics to compare different types of processes.
- Capability analysis reveals how well a process can produce a product that meets customer specifications, and provides insight into how to improve processes.

Bibliography

1. Minitab Help Menu, Version 17. Minitab, Inc., Quality Plaza, 1829 Pine Hall Road, State College, PA 16801, USA.
2. *Statistical Process Control (SPC) Reference Manual*, Second Edition. Automotive Industry Action Group; Chrysler LLC, Ford Motor Company and General Motors Corporation, 2010.

Chapter 5

Process Control

Standard daily management creates a reference point from which continuous improvement can be based. Standard daily management can lead to greater process control, reduction in variability, improved quality and flexibility, stability (i.e. predictable outcomes), visibility of abnormalities, clear expectations and a platform for individual and organizational learning.

The Shingo Model for Operational Excellence

Process Control

Process control is one of the most important but often neglected activities in manufacturing today. It's sometimes tedious, boring and time-consuming, but it's vital to the long-term health and integrity of a process. It's a way to ensure work accomplished and improvements implemented are sustained and don't revert to a less desirable state of performance. Process control is important for several reasons. It's a way to confirm process outputs are meeting desired performance expectations and identifies if a process has significantly deviated from its preferred state. Process control also includes establishing and maintaining standard work so organizations can sustain an efficient level of consistent performance. A process is considered in control when

- Critical process input parameters (x's) that affect the output (y) are known.
- Significant uncontrolled variation affecting process output is known and controlled (through robust product and process design).
- Measurement system variation is known, within acceptable limits, and controlled.
- Process capability is known and acceptable (Cpk $\geq$ 1.33).
- Process is stable (consistent, predictable).
- Process control practices are defined, implemented and effective.

Process stability and capability are fundamental to a reliable process. These process characteristics create the foundation upon which continuous improvements are rooted. As with any foundation, if it's not sound, it will not sustain whatever is built upon it. You can't improve a process whose behavior is unpredictable and you can't produce consistent output from a process that is not stable. Without stability and capability, any effort to improve process efficiency will likely fail.

When a process is first developed and launched into production, it's expected to be in control. The objective of process control is to ensure the process remains stable and capable of consistently delivering acceptable products and services to customers. Unfortunately, over time, if little attention is given to maintaining a process, the law of entropy comes into play and the process slowly deteriorates to a point where stability is compromised and its ability to consistently satisfy customers with conforming product is lost. Issues such as a lack of clear ownership, limited process knowledge and constant demands from other work priorities can cause us to overlook the importance of maintaining regular daily routines conducted to keep the process within its expected tolerances.

Controlling a process requires a structured approach and a set of disciplined routines to ensure continued compliance with working parameters. These routines should facilitate the identification, disposition and deployment of actions to manage periodic departures from standard practice as part of every individual's work responsibilities. Through daily process monitoring and control, we can ensure continuous stability and capability. Disrupting, shortchanging or ignoring these daily routines sets the stage for slow process deterioration leading to underperformance and significant inefficiencies over time. An inefficient process is likely to end up delivering substandard quality products and services that cause customer dissatisfaction and impact business profitability. Control requires an optimum operating range for each critical input parameter be defined and maintained through the discipline of deviation management.

Deviation Management Process

As stated previously, we are hired to support the process in two primary ways: to maintain process control and drive continuous improvements. Process control is achieved, in part, by deviation management. Deviation management is a relatively simple concept that is not always easy to implement since it takes a structured and disciplined approach to deploy and maintain it properly.

A deviation is any change of direction or position; a significant departure from a standard or norm. When a deviation occurs, we need to detect its existence and take action to understand its cause so we can engage in a swift and decisive response to counteract its potentially negative effect on the process. Visual controls are put in place to help us recognize deviations or gaps between what's expected and reality.

Deviation management involves the activity of continuously monitoring process performance to standards, looking for deviations from process inputs and expected outputs. If significant deviations are detected, an approach is to classify them into one of three categories: performance, process or system.

The *performance* category involves mistakes that people make when interacting with the process. If a person deviates from procedure or causes a defect, this is considered a performance issue normally addressed directly and immediately with the offending individual. This type of issue can result from a number of different sources or error precursors [1], leading to a divergence from standard. Failures in performance can stem from time pressures, excessive workload, misinterpretation of information, lack of knowledge or work distractions, to name a few. In cases where there is a lapse in worker judgment leading to a process mistake or defect, the error precursor should be identified and lessons learned should be shared with all who are actively engaged in the process to prevent reoccurrence. There is no need to create a follow-up action if the issue can be addressed in real time. However, a record of the event and how it was handled may serve as valuable information for future reference.

If the issue turns out to be *process* in nature, such as a misinterpretation of standard or unexpected equipment failure, steps should be taken to prevent further understandings such as making changes to work instructions or preventive maintenance procedures to avoid reoccurrence. Process issues generally require documented actions for follow-up since support functions are usually responsible for making changes and often require time to complete necessary actions to prevent reoccurrence. Process issues are mainly line or area specific and can be managed by the team in the location or function of the organization where they occurred.

If the issue is *systemic*, where it impacts multiple lines, areas or functions within a facility, it should be escalated to the appropriate department and owner within the hierarchy for attention, review and timely correction. A higher level priority should be assigned to eliminating systemic issues since they have a broader impact on an enterprise (Figure 5.1).

Time and resource limitations are evident when working to identify and eliminate deviations. Due to the substantial number of potential findings, it's vital that deviations are categorized, prioritized and managed at a level in the organization best suited to address them. It's also good practice to visually communicate the number of deviations identified, acted on and dismissed. This builds integrity into the deviation management process. It's recommended that any decision to dismiss recorded actions be justified and communicated as to why. This will to maintain transparency and promote trust within the organization.

Deviation management consists of four essential activities: identification, investigation, correction and follow-up (see Figure 5.2). Let's explore each in more detail.

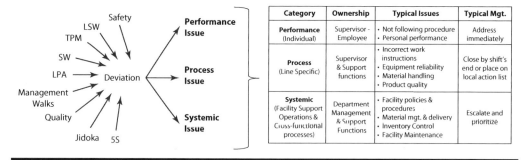

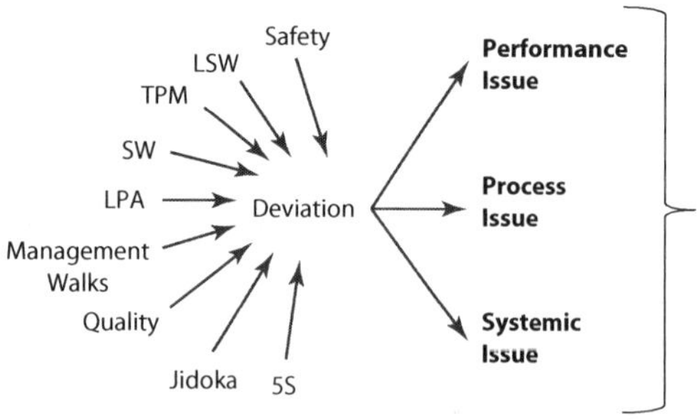

Category	Ownership	Typical Issues	Typical Mgt.
Performance (Individual)	Supervisor - Employee	• Not following procedure • Personal performance	Address immediately
Process (Line Specific)	Supervisor & Support functions	• Incorrect work instructions • Equipment reliability • Material handling • Product quality	Close by shift's end or place on local action list
Systemic (Facility Support Operations & Cross-functional processes)	Department Management & Support Functions	• Facility policies & procedures • Material mgt. & delivery • Inventory Control • Facility Maintenance	Escalate and prioritize

Figure 5.1 Classification of deviations.

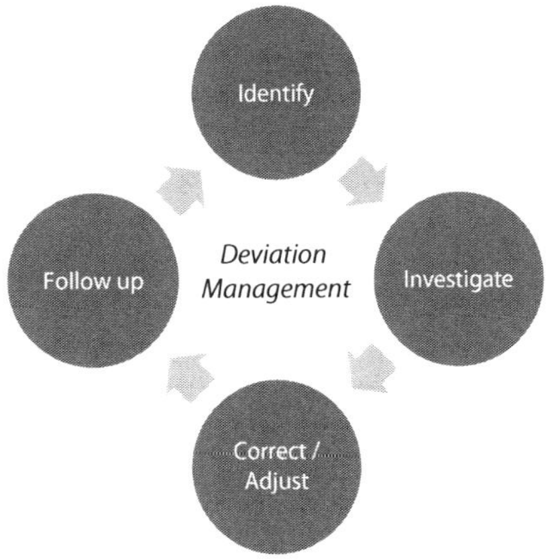

Figure 5.2 Deviation management activities.

Identification

Deviations can reveal themselves in many different ways: during shop floor walks, process audits, standard work and performance reviews, to name a few. They can pop-up instantly or emerge over time. It's important we constantly look for deviations from standard and, if possible, address them before they adversely impact process outcomes. Identification usually occurs while conducting daily work routines as we monitor process execution for unusual characteristics or behaviors and key output metrics for unexpected trends or results. Typical metrics that deserve monitoring are the number of units produced per hour, process stops per shift, equipment downtime and standard work cycle times. Deviations can also arise when those performing standard work encounter obstacles that need assistance from their support network to address. As indicated, performance issues should be addressed immediately, while process and systemic issues are documented as follow-up actions, allowing appropriate time and attention for resolution.

Investigation

Once a deviation has been detected, the next step is to evaluate its impact on process performance. An immediate action or temporary containment may be required to prevent additional defects from occurring or to avoid further process disruptions, allowing the process to continue while a more permanent fix is being pursued. This is where a triage is performed to determine the most appropriate action for the current situation. An effort should be made to understand the reason behind why a deviation occurred so its root cause can be determined and targeted for elimination.

Good root cause investigation starts with a simple, clear and concise problem statement followed by a problem description capturing the what, when, where and how big of an issue exists based on data and information collected. One question often asked upon detection of a deviation is, what changed? Has there been a change in people, materials, methods, machines or the environment? Confirm machine settings are correct, verify material is within specification and standard work is being followed. Employees are familiar with the work they perform and would be a good source for understanding the current state of process performance. Inquire into their current level of comfort with the way operations are running. Ask if they have any information or have observed anything unusual recently. Are there any unresolved issues that may be contributing to existing deviations? Do they feel the process is performing as expected? People working closest to the process are often best suited to assist with understanding its behavior.

If good structure and process discipline are in place, start your investigation quickly by considering what changed or what's different from when the issue first occurred. Clues to solving a problem are often easier to detect around the time a problem was first observed. A classic cause and effect diagram can assist with the investigation. Other structured problem-solving methods can also help a team get to root cause quickly, facilitated by different tools such as Brainstorming; Cause and Effect matrix; 5 Whys analysis; SIPOC (suppliers, inputs, process, outputs and customers); Pareto chart; DMAIC methodology (define, measure, analyze, improve and control) and Plan-Do-Check-Act (PDCA) cycle.

In short, always look for what might have changed first, since changes in process are a likely cause of deviations we identify and seek to understand.

Correction

Once the investigation phase is complete, there is generally one of two outcomes: no action required or a corresponding corrective action is needed. It's important to determine, understand and verify root cause before implementing a countermeasure. There are many sources of inspiration for generating solution ideas, including co-workers, subject-matter experts, mind mapping, lessons learned and best practice databases. When selecting a solution for corrective action, consider giving more "weight" to factors of importance to key stakeholders such as cost, time, resources and quality. For example, what's the financial impact of each solution, how many people may be required to implement a particular action, how long will a solution take to implement and what's a solution's effect on process reliability and performance. Often, a decision matrix can be used to identify, weigh and quantify solution attributes for comparison. See Sidebar: Decision Matrix for more details.

Don't evaluate a solution by implementing it and waiting to see if the problem goes away. Verify corrective action effectiveness prior to deployment, especially if the corrective action is expensive to implement or difficult to reverse. Consider performing a trial evaluation before full-scale implementation to assess possible issues and risks with the selected solution. Try to turn the problem on and off willingly, to confirm you have found the true root cause and can control the outcome. Remember, a corrective action (solution) should be verified effective at the point where the problem or defect first occurred and where it may have escaped the system before reaching the customer.

SIDEBAR: DECISION MATRIX – *CASE STUDY*

A *decision matrix* is a structured process for selecting the best and most appropriate solutions or corrective action. It's used to identify, weigh and quantify solution attributes for comparison. The following case study involves a decision to determine the best way to protect a production line against a newly installed air-condition (AC) unit above it which was found to cause scrap when recently turned on for the first time. Air flow from the AC was disrupting the cooling profile of parts exiting the molding machine causing surface flaws. In this example, several options were identified and assessed, with and without a weighted score. Note, when the weight of the various factors are not considered, all value in the weighted row = 1.

Factors ▶	Cost	Time	Quality	Resources	TOTAL	
Weight ▶	5	2	4	3	w/o weight	w/weight
Options						
Turn off AC	5	5	3	5	18	62
Move AC	2	3	3	2	10	0
Insulate machine 2	4	4	4	4	16	72
Move machine 2	1	2	3	1	7	19
Make on night shift	5	5	2	5	17	68
▶ Score each option by how well it satisfies each factor						
▶ Factors: 5-Important; 1-Not important						
▶ Options: 5-Best; 1-Worst						
▶ Quality = Stakeholders satisfacton / Effort						

Solution: 5x5 + 5x2 + 3x4 + 5x3 = 62

Follow-Up

Follow-up activities should verify actions taken have been properly implemented and confirmed effective. The corresponding metrics affected by the action should be periodically monitored for problem reoccurrence. It's best to close out actions after a specific time period in which solution tracking does not detect any further problems with the concern. Monitoring for problem reoccurrence is a good way to assess effectiveness of an organization's problem-solving acumen. Checking for reoccurrence of recently corrected problems can be a line item on a daily team meeting agenda. A checklist is a good tool to verify process improvements remain in place and are effective.

Follow-up is an essential activity for ensuring process control. It not only confirms the effectiveness of deviation management, but also holds people accountable beyond implementation by upholding problem ownership until solution integrity has been verified. Deviation management plays a key role in process control by integrating the tools and techniques of 5S, visual control, work routines, problem-solving and daily accountability meetings into a system intended to quickly and effectively respond to process abnormalities harboring the potential to disrupt a stable state of operation.

A deviation management system (Figure 5.3) creates the bedrock for a robust operation when made part of daily work activities. Putting deviation management into context, Figure 5.4 highlights the role of this system within the scope of process improvement where it is intended to maintain standards. As standards change, deviation management activities remain the same.

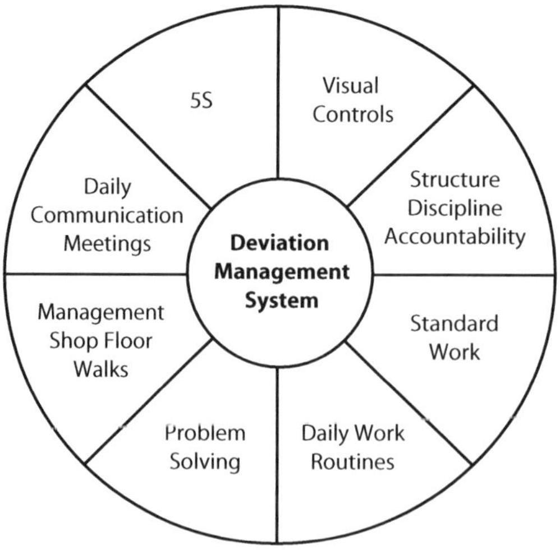

Figure 5.3 Deviation management system.

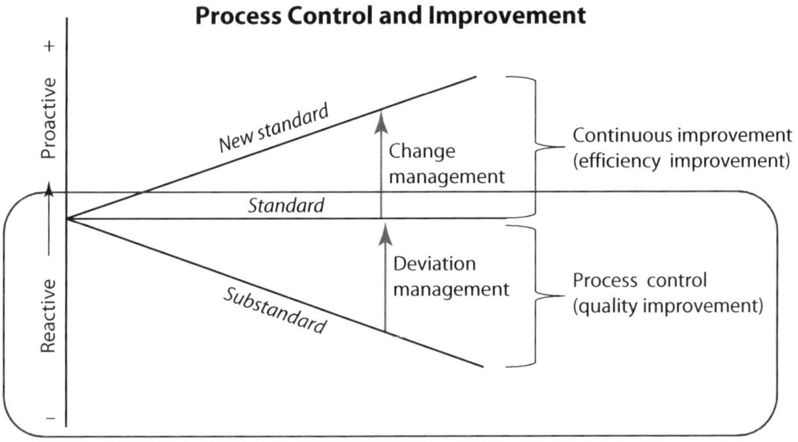

Figure 5.4 Deviation management as a subsystem of process improvement.

Process Control Routines

Process control requires a set of disciplined routines to ensure compliance to product and process performance parameters. These routines should be part of a support team's daily work and include activities such as verifying standard work, reviewing visual controls, conducting process audits and performing scheduled equipment maintenance, while completing actions to address known issues. All these activities, and other work-related routines, have been described as leader standard work (LSW), process management and daily shop floor management, among others. Regardless of what you call them, routines need to be documented and allocated to appropriate functions and individuals throughout the organization. These routines further clarify existing roles and responsibilities as a way to ensure essential work required for maintaining a stable state of control is defined, understood and executed.

Work routines should be formalized and institutionalized at all levels of the enterprise with an emphasis on continuous improvement routines at the upper levels of the hierarchy, process monitoring and control performed by mid-level management and process execution of work standards at the lowest level, where the greatest value creation is occurring (Figure 5.5).

Routines for process control are expected to include activities intended to prevent current process performance from reverting to its previous, less desirable state. These routines should maintain a stable, capable and efficient process; document and communicate process improvements; capture reasons and benefits for changes; train, evaluate and reward employees for desirable behavior; identify key metrics to monitor and manage the process

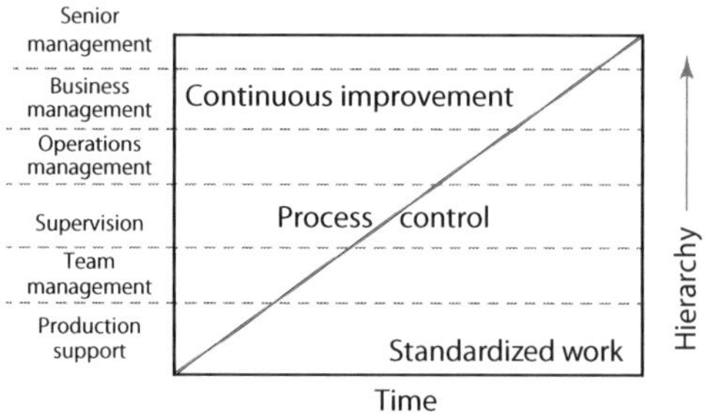

Figure 5.5 Focus of hierarchical work routines.

over time; measure process outcomes for conformance to requirements; and track as well as assess process improvements for effectiveness.

The activities or daily routines that we are referring to as process control are often considered an integral part of daily shop floor management and are crucial for maintaining a healthy and productive work environment. Every organization should know the critical product and process parameters that must be controlled to remain a viable operation. It's paramount that these routines are quick and easy to execute as a way to reinforce their continued deployment. Routines should be supported by whatever visual controls will facilitate their timely and effective execution.

In many instances, the simple act of periodically monitoring key process indicators (KPIs) for patterns, trends and spikes is sufficient to maintain control as long as action is taken when deviations from normal operations occur unexpectedly. This is not very different from a car dashboard that displays KPIs for monitoring and controlling a vehicle's performance. If the dashboard indicates a problem, immediate action is required to prevent a potentially bigger issue. For example, would you ignore a gas gauge indicating the tank is nearly empty?

Leadership sets the example for how the organization should behave. Thus, they must be the role models for performing daily work routines and reinforce the importance of completing scheduled routines by continuously holding themselves and others accountable for their proper and timely execution in order to achieve and maintain an environment of operational excellence.

Process Control: Tools and Techniques

The activities and periodic routines needed for process control will vary with the product, process, organization and industry. They must be defined by the individuals who have responsibility for operations since they are the most knowledgeable about what's needed for consistent and lasting process reliability.

Before we can apply the methods, tools and techniques of lean, we must first verify the prerequisite tools and techniques for process control exist, are practiced, and a structure is in place to ensure their long-term sustainability. What well-established and proven activities are associated with good process control practices? As mentioned previously, the following tools and techniques must work in concert to facilitate a system approach to long-term process stability and capability by helping to reveal and manage significant process destabilizers.

Visual Controls

Visual controls are a way to quickly communicate data and information in a working environment. They help facilitate the monitoring, control and improvement of key process parameters to maintain process stability and capability in addition to helping drive continuous improvement. Three key objectives of visual controls include communicating current process status, highlighting performance trends and revealing reoccurrence of problems.

Effective visual controls help workers see how well they are doing, indicate when work is deviating from standards and facilitate rapid response to problems. Visual controls should answer the question: *How do I know if this process is working as intended?* To add value, visualization must clearly communicate what is important to people using them. Visuals must

- Be simple and timely
- Be easy to update
- Quickly indicate if there is a problem requiring action
- Allow comparison of actual versus expected results
- Have a designated owner responsible for updates
- Specify update frequency to be effective

The frequency at which visual controls are updated will determine their usefulness in helping to monitor and manage process deviations. Implementing warning signals such as audio or visual devices can help employees respond immediately to problems, avoiding waste. Data visibility is important because it enables workers to make information actionable. Visual controls are only as good as they are useful. Visual controls can take many forms, some of which include:

- Color-coding parts
- Floor markings

- Accountability and information boards
- Indicator lights
- Andon lights/boards
- Colored bins and designation cones
- Max/min levels

Typical visual controls for manufacturing line operations include hourly output, first pass yield (FPY), overall equipment effectiveness (OEE), scrap trends and action lists. A broader list of frequently available visual controls and other key manufacturing documents can be found in Figure 5.6.

Line Information Boards

Line boards are a form of visual control. In a manufacturing facility, line boards display key information and data necessary to efficiently and effectively manage the line. They serve individuals who work and support the line. Teams should decide on the data and information they need to manage their operations and define the frequency at which data is updated to effectively monitor and control line dynamics. The board is a tool of the people, by the people, for the people and should be positioned close to those who use it to make decisions, manage deviations and drive continuous improvements. A line board is simply waste if it does not serve the people whom it's intended to support. A good line board will provide what's needed, when it's needed, in an easy-to-understand format that is visual, meaningful and actionable. It should be easy to update, regardless if it's a manual or electronic display. Additional information can be found in the following sidebar.

Safety	Quality	Delivery
• Number of accidents • Number of near misses • Consecutive days without an accident	• Scrap • FPY • Rework / Repairs • Capability • Manuf. caused returns	• Schedule status • Quantity delivered • Delivery date • On-time delivery status • Backlog
Productivity	**Costs**	**People**
• Units produced per hour • Lead time • Machine downtime • Number of line stops	• Material costs • Labor costs • Cost per unit • Expenses	• Attendance rate • Meeting participation • Number of suggestions • Injury / Illness rate • Open and escalated actions

Figure 5.6 Typical visual control indicators.

SIDEBAR: LINE INFORMATION BOARD

The line board is a tool for frontline teams to manage their work activities and a starting point for management to engage with employees. This is where targets are displayed, progress is reported and issues of concern are highlighted. It's a way to display the current activities that teams are working on to control and improve their processes as well as displaying risks and managing trends in output performance.

Line information boards should only contain information and data teams need to perform their work routines. The data and information posted should be useful, easy to update, display the required information and facilitate effective process control through corrective and preventive action. The availability of trend charts will reveal the impact of recent actions and indicate the sustainability and direction of current process performance. It's a tool for process control and continuous improvement, not a platform for criticism or a showcase for customers. A typical production (line) information board layout is presented in Figure 5.7.

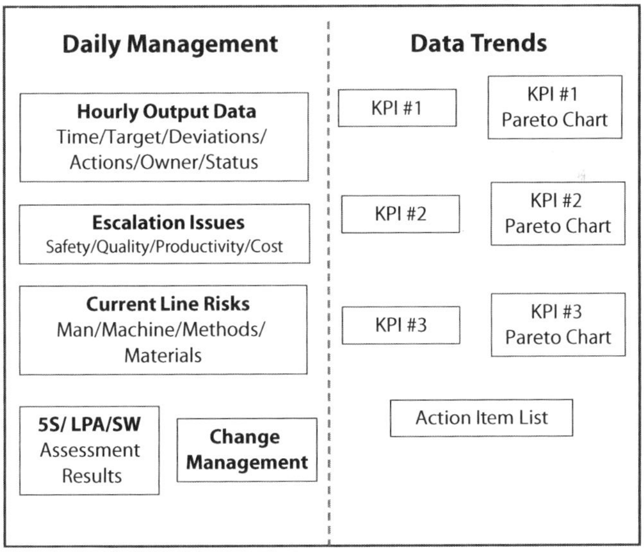

Figure 5.7 Example of a Production (Line) Information Board.

Key Process Indicators

KPIs are high impact metrics used to measure or assess the performance of an activity or process in order to know when appropriate action is necessary in response to flat or negative trends. KPIs are used to monitor and control processes and can include leading indicators, process parameters and output performance metrics. The selection of a good leading indicator depends on a number of factors including its usefulness in determining actual compliance to requirements. The grid in Figure 5.8 can be used to assess the improvement potential and impact of KPIs when deciding which ones are best suited for predicting output performance. KPIs with high "business-relevant impact" and high "improvement potential" (upper right quadrant) are the best leading indicators for driving desired outcomes as long as in-process activities remain within their defined specification limits. In addition to their impact and potential for influencing output results, criteria for selecting these indicators should include their degree of influence, their sensitivity to variation and effort required for their periodic monitoring and control.

Standard Work

Standard work contributes to process control by reducing variation in how processes are executed and establishing a baseline from which control is maintained and continuous improvement is measured. Process control needs a reference point from which actual performance can be compared, without which neither control nor improvement can occur. Standard work composes the roots upon which stability, capability, control and improvement are supported. Chapter 2 on process standardization covers this topic in detail.

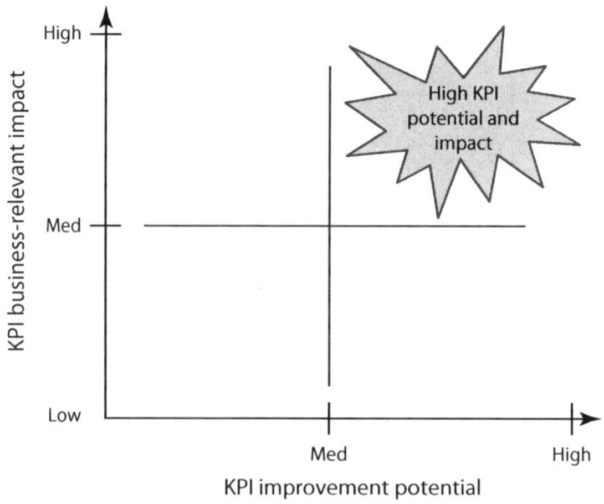

Figure 5.8 KPI performance potential and impact grid.

Control Plans

Control plans provide a summary description of activities, highlighting the key inputs, process parameters and equipment settings that minimize variation and keep outputs within desired tolerances. These plans include key actions required at each step in the process to ensure all process outputs are in a "state of control".

A control plan typically starts with a review of the process flow diagram and documents the number and name of process activities being addressed. Inputs (x's) are critical product or process characteristics being controlled within defined specifications or tolerances to ensure output stability. The measurement technique highlights the measurement system being used to confirm process parameters are in compliance with expectations and can include gauges, fixtures, tools and test equipment. Sample size and frequency are documented when required.

The control method contains a brief description of how the operation is to be controlled by techniques such as SPC, inspection, attribute data and error-proofing. An owner is the contact person for answering relevant questions and the reaction plan defines actions to help avoid product nonconformances and out-of-control operating conditions. The control plan is an effective tool for process standardization and control when properly documented, followed and updated using lessons learned. See Figure 5.9 for an example of a control plan template.

Leader Standard Work (Work Routines)

LSW or "work routines" is about defining and executing the activities and routines for maintaining and continuously improving processes. It involves the continual monitoring of key performance indicators and parameters

Control plan									
Product		Owner:		Date: Rev #:		Core team:			
Process number	Process name	Input (x)	Specification / tolerance	Measurement technique	Sample size	Sample frequency	Control method	Owner	Reaction plan

Figure 5.9 Control plan template.

(including process inputs, activities and outputs) by organizational management, support functions and leaders. It's intended to maintain the integrity of a lean management system. At a minimum, work routines for process control should ensure standard work instructions are followed, layered process audits (LPA) are performed, performance reviews are held and deviations from expectation are identified, investigated and corrected using structured problem-solving when appropriate. When opportunities for improvement present themselves, actions are taken to evaluate a change's impact on process performance and updates to work standards are initiated upon justification.

Work routines are not new, they simply document the "value-added" actions that should be periodically performed to ensure the right activities are getting done to control and continuously improve processes. A well-prepared system for deploying enterprise work routines will contain clearly documented responsibilities for each functional role, and visual controls displaying the status of completed routines. A public display of individual status is a way to create transparency and maintain accountability while holding key individuals accountable for completing their routines in a timely manner. Figure 5.10 is an example of a typical work routine template. The "*activity*" column generally contains key activities performed as part of the organization's daily shop floor management including performance reviews, layered process audits and management shop floor walks. *Topics* may include 5S, SPC, problem-solving, safety or error-proofing. *Routines* should be documented in sufficient detail to avoid any misunderstand of expected actions and outcomes. The "*Why*" should provide justification for performing the work routine based on its contribution to process control and continuous improvement. The "*time*" column is optional for those who want to specify a particular time of day or week to perform a routine while the last 6 columns

Work routines: Function / Role										
Activity	Topic	Routines	Why	Time	Shift	Daily	Weekly	Monthly	Quarterly	Annually

Figure 5.10 Work routine template.

define the frequency of performing each routine. The frequency at which routines are performed can change based on information and data gathered. If a work routine to check an operators' cycle time every shift produces a consistent result over several weeks, consider reducing the frequency of observation. However, the reverse is also true. If a work routine continuously reveals deviations from standard, increasing the work routine frequency may be justified until the situation is stabilized. Actual work routines are best defined by the individuals responsible for the work while being assisted by subject-matter experts. Remember, work routines reinforce the desired behaviors and practices expected of a lean thinking and acting organization. Operational excellence is reflected in the work routines of an organization.

Layered Process Audits

LPAs are process audits performed by various levels of management to look for deviations from work standards, product specifications, process tolerances and process controls. LPAs ensure standards are being adhered to and process outcomes serve customer needs. If significant deviations are noted, a root cause analysis should be performed and action taken to bring the process back under control. LPAs are expected to monitor process inputs and corresponding outputs in real time to highlight deviations and facilitate a rapid response to non-conformances.

During these audits, in addition to checking for deviations, opportunities for improvement are likely to present themselves. It may be of interest to document these findings and escalate them to the appropriate process owners for evaluation and prioritization. At the same time, there is often an occasion for real-time, face-to-face coaching of the workforce personnel during these audits; seize the opportunity to do so when presented. By engaging in this type of conduct, an audit becomes a forum for learning and adding value, instead of a "hunt" for the guilty, leading to fear and mistrust. Typical topics covered in an LPA include:

- 5S compliance
- Standard work compliance
- Work routines completion
- Visual controls: Available and up to date
- Performance trends
- Scrap/FPY (Jidoka) events and trends
- Total productive maintenance (TPM)

- Employee engagement
- Environment, health, safety

An example of an LPA audit can be found in Appendix V. It's not unusual for organizations to combine an LPA and LSW into one set of activities since their objective serves a similar purpose. In fact, a well-developed and deployed LPA system may become the basis for LSW.

Control Charts

Control charts are utilized to monitor process stability over time and quickly identify instabilities by highlighting abnormal or unexpected data trends, patterns or spikes. For many, control charts are essential tools in the struggle to reduce process variation and maintain control. Variable and attribute control charts exist with statistically based control limits to help visualize data variation and a center line to establish the data mean. The application of control charts requires that control limits are revisited when significant process changes impact performance output. At times, it may be necessary to stop the process in order to understand and eliminate problems before too much waste is generated in the form of process outliers (e.g. defects). Rapid problem-solving is a critical skill set for all employees who use control charts for process monitoring and control. See an example of a stable and unstable control chart in Figure 5.11.

Problem-Solving

I once visited a company in Appleton, Wisconsin, which separated their problems into three categories: boulders, rocks and pebbles. This characterization provided a clear delineation as to the magnitude of a problem in terms of time, priority, resources and approach. This classification also helped set expectations for management in allocating time and resources required to solve specific problems. Figure 5.12 outlines these three classifications in more detail and the methods to consider when deciding on the best problem-solving approach.

Problem-solving is critical to establishing and maintaining process stability and capability. If actions are not taken to correct significant process or product deviations, control is quickly lost and problems mount. As you become "leaner", the urgency to solve problems quickly becomes more prevalent since reductions in material buffers and finished goods inventory decrease available time and material before disruptions in process rhythms impact customers.

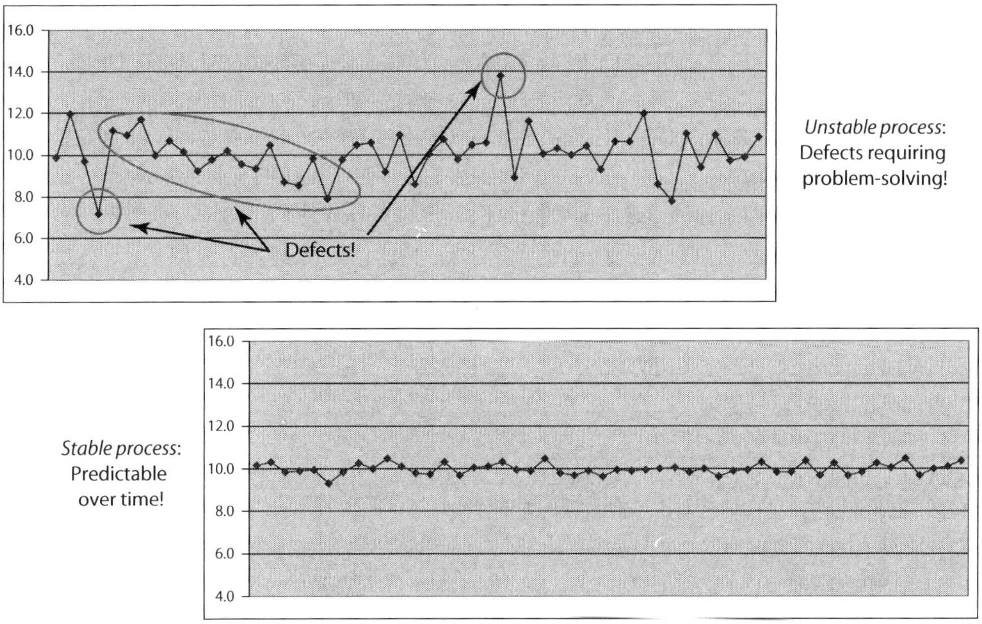

Figure 5.11 Example of a stable and unstable process displayed in a control chart.

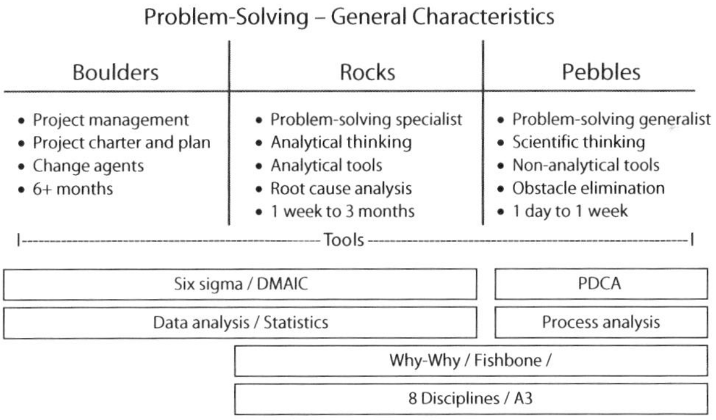

Figure 5.12 Problem-solving classifications.

Preventive Maintenance

Preventive maintenance is a key contributor to process control since it serves to proactively maintain machines and equipment in good working order to avoid unexpected breakdowns leading to disruptions in process flow. Preventive maintenance should focus on maximizing machine availability while continuously improving equipment reliability. One efficient way to engage in preventive maintenance is to involve operators in low-level maintenance of their equipment (e.g. replacement and lubrication) to reinforce process ownership while promoting employee development.

The tools and techniques previously discussed are only a few of the many methods used to maintain process control. The key is to apply them in a structured and disciplined manner, continuously refining them and holding process owners accountable for their proper execution and timely completion. A summary and a brief description of these and other common tools and techniques can be found in the following sidebar.

SIDEBAR: PROCESS CONTROL TOOLS AND TECHNIQUES

- *Standards and procedures*: Drive a consistent, predictable process output.
- *5S/Visual controls*: Making problems visible.
- *Lean (gemba) walks*: Looking for and exposing problems.
- *Deviation management*: Managing process deviations.
- *Problem-solving*: Structured, disciplined approach to eliminating defects.
- *Error proofing*: Detecting and preventing defect reoccurrence.
- *Control plans*: Implementing key process controls and response plans.
- *Control charts*: Monitoring process stability and capability over time.
- *Audits/checklists*: Looking for anomalies and deviations; maintaining process controls and highlighting improvement opportunities.
- *Inspections and testing*: Verifying conformance to specifications and other defined requirements.
- *Process metrics*: Continuously monitoring key process input, activities and output parameters for conformance; a focus on process and results.
- *Performance reviews*: Identifying and assessing deviations from KPI trends and ensuring appropriate countermeasures are taken when required.
- *Total preventive maintenance*: Maintaining equipment availability and improving reliability.
- *Daily work routines*: Maintaining process control and driving opportunities for improvement.

Proactive Process Control

Once a stable and capable process has been demonstrated, a lean-thinking organization can focus its attention on establishing a more proactive approach to process control by understanding and controlling the primary inputs that drive desired outputs. Since process inputs and activities affect process outputs, by identifying, monitoring and controlling key inputs, organizations can influence output' results instead of reacting to them. Consider the following key input parameters and contributing attributes when looking to proactively engage in process control to achieve more predictable outcomes:

- *Operators (man)*: Available, trained, experienced and disciplined
- *Machines*: Maintained (TPM), available and reliable
- *Methods*: Standardized, simple, clear, unambiguous and efficient
- *Material*: Available, consistent, conforming and defect free
- *Environment*: Defined, consistent and controlled

SIDEBAR: TIPS FOR GOOD PROCESS CONTROL

- Define meaningful daily work routines.
- Focus on daily execution of work routines; identify and manage deviations by following up on prioritized actions.
- Understand *what* you are doing and *why* you are doing it; avoid mindless activities and execution.
- Focus on controlling process inputs and activities, not just reacting to results.
- Seek to understand the root causes of deviations and react accordingly.
- Implement simple, easy, cheap and sustainable countermeasures.
- Allow employees to develop an expertise in their discipline.
- Mistake proof whenever possible.
- Continuous incremental improvement; everyone, every day.

Summary

Process control is often an overlooked activity within an enterprise. It's a fundamental practice to maintaining existing process performance as well as sustaining process improvements through disciplined monitoring and control. The data and information needed for process management should be visualized to provide a quick and clear assessment of current performance so accountability can be reinforced throughout the organization. The ultimate objective of process control is process stability and capability in an effort to continuously deliver consistent products and services that satisfy customers. Defining and following work standards can go a long way in helping to achieve this objective while work routines including LPA, management walks and performance reviews can also aid in this regard.

When significant deviations are detected, it's important for process owners to understand what to do, how to do it, when to do it and why it's important to do it. It's also critical to exercise the disciplines required to ensure key process control parameters are respected, as a way to avoid waste associated with no action or over-reaction. For example, would you ignore a vehicle's gas gage as it nears the empty symbol? The action to avoid this problem from occurring will likely be a lot less painful than the mandatory action taken to address it, once it occurs.

Process control requires a conscious effort to execute daily, weekly, monthly and quarterly activities (e.g. routines) necessary to maintain consistent and predictable outcomes. Good practices and organizational discipline are part of the formula for creating a well-run operation. This is the starting point for lean. Once process control is established and a consistent output is demonstrated, an increased focus on process efficiency can begin. This is where lean principles and practices are applied for continuous process improvement and value stream optimization. A consolidated and simplified version of process control is presented in the following sidebar.

SIDEBAR: PROCESS CONTROL SIMPLIFIED

Process control strives to institutionalize process activities necessary to maintain the current state of performance. It involves maintaining a stable, capable and efficient process through organizational structure, discipline and accountability. It requires documenting and qualifying process improvements; communicating the reasons for and benefits of changes, training, evaluating and rewarding employees for desired behavior; and identifying key measures to monitor and maintain actual process performance over time. Process control requires organizations to measure process outcomes for conformance to requirements, manage deviations, track process improvements and evaluate implemented improvements for effectiveness.

Key Points

- All outcomes are the result of a (controlled or uncontrolled) process.
- Process control is a way to ensure work accomplished and improvements made are sustained and don't revert back to a less desirable level of performance.
- Process control is concerned with maintaining the output of a specific process within specified parameters.
- Process workarounds occur because people don't feel they have a mandate to stop and diagnose the problem, especially when process ownership is unclear.
- Control charts are an effective tool for monitoring and maintaining process stability and capability over time.

- Keep the process in control; when a refrigerator cools down, do you unplug it?
- Trust is good, verification is better. *Trust but verify!*
- Data and facts eliminate conflicts.
- If a process is capable and in control, it will produce what it was designed to produce, not necessarily what we want it to produce.
- Process control is an essential activity for achieving sustainable lean improvements.
- Deviation management is about finding gaps between actual and expected performance and eliminating them to maintain current process performance.
- Process control eliminates the gap between actual and expected performance.
- The job of process owners and workers is to ensure production runs as designed and is continuously improved.
- LSW is a collection of periodic work routines (activities) performed to ensure the process remains in control and continuous improvements are identified, implemented and sustained.
- Routines establish a desired behavior that produce predictable results.
- An expected outcome favors control over luck.
- Visual controls make problems easier and quicker to detect.
- Deviation management is used to maintain what was improved.
- Visualizing deviations from procedures and specifications facilitates a quick response to minimize potential defects.
- Problem-solving is used to bring underperforming processes back to standard or within target and is best approached systematically to achieve an efficient and effective solution for defect elimination.
- Results are final. If you want to control output, focus on process inputs and activities that influence the results.
- Work routines should place the focus on process, not people.
- Solutions don't come from high technology, they come from people.

Reference

1. Shane Bush – Battelle, Idaho National Laboratory, 03-May-2005. LANL Mirror. int.lanl.gov/safety/online.

EFFICIENCY IMPROVEMENT

II

Improving Process Efficiency

Many organizations have tried and failed to implement lean practices or they have implemented them only to achieve marginal or short-term benefits at best. This is not necessarily due to their lack of knowledge or understanding of lean; it's more likely they did not have a solid foundation upon which to support these practices or sufficient discipline to sustain them. Lean is evolutionary. It must be built upon a process that has demonstrated stability and capability over time to be sustainable. If you think about it, without a reliable and predictable process, little additional value can be gained from the application of lean principles and corresponding practices that can't be sustained long term. Once a solid foundation for process stability and capability has been demonstrated, it's time to focus on efficiency improvements. This is when the concepts of "lean" improvement can be applied with confidence.

Many practices such as 5S, total productive maintenance (TPM) and gemba (management) walks associated with lean are not specific to lean. In fact, these practices have been around for a long time; they may be recognizable under different terms. Arguably, 5S can be viewed as good housekeeping, TPM is regular maintenance intended to prevent unexpected equipment breakdowns (e.g. car maintenance) and a gemba (management) walk is similar to what we used to call "management by walking around" in the early to late 1980s. The fundamental premise of a gemba (management) walk and management by walking around is the same; management spending time where it matters, learning firsthand what's happening from observation and people in their organizations. In fact, much of what we are "re-learning" are "old" practices, embraced by Toyota, and made an integral part of their culture based on demonstrated value.

The idea of efficiency improvement uses these proven practices while building upon them by providing additional context in which they can be more effectively applied. At www.lean.org/lexicon/kaizen, Rother and Shook [1] discuss two levels of Kaizen: process Kaizen focused on improvement of individual processes primarily driven by work teams and systems as well as flow Kaizen intended to optimize material and information flow through the entire value stream. The approach to engaging in process Kaizen versus flow Kaizen can be viewed from the perspective of the tools and techniques used to pursue improvements. Value analysis, using process mapping and Pareto analysis, has been demonstrated to be a valuable approach for process Kaizen, while value stream mapping and design is an effective technique for visualizing the value stream in support of both process and flow (Kaizen) improvements.

Process efficiency improvements are often referred to in the context of waste elimination (process Kaizen) and process flow improvement (flow Kaizen). Although both activities overlap and complement each other, waste elimination is sometimes considered a "lighter" version of lean with its focus on individual processes, while process flow improvement can be considered the "real deal", involving optimization of the value stream as we strive for a smoother, more continuous and reliable flow.

Achieving process efficiency is illusive since efficiency can be subjective. The "ultimate" goal of any efficiency improvement effort is to change the mindset of an organization to one of incremental process improvement with a continuous focus on waste elimination and flow improvement as part of a relentless pursuit of operational excellence.

Change Management

Process improvement occurs in many ways; there may be a change in material or procedure, perhaps a new piece of equipment is installed or a highly skilled operator is added to the production line. Regardless of how it happens, a change to documented methods or standards usually occurs to establish and help sustain a new standard or level of performance. A new standard resets the baseline for process control. Any deviations from this new reference point will require deviation management as a daily shop floor management tool (see Figure P2.1).

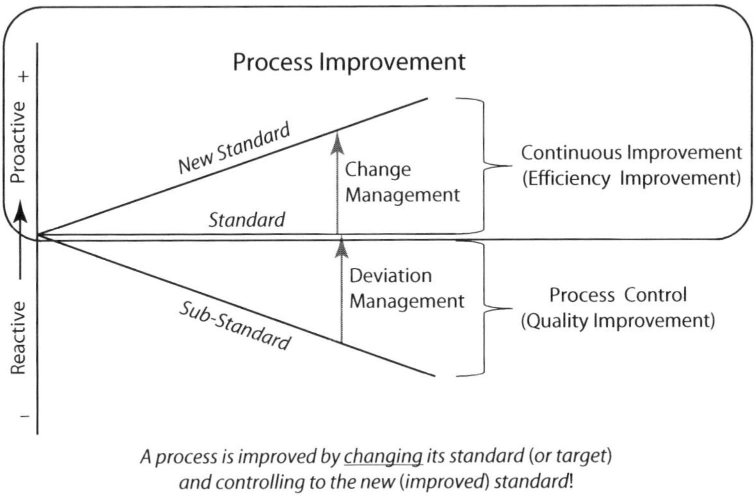

Figure P2.1 Change management's role in process improvement.

Change management itself is a process. It requires an opportunity be identified before an evaluation is conducted to assess feasibility. Once a change has been proven effective, it should be implemented and verified as sustainable. Let's take a moment to review the basic steps of change management.

Opportunity Identification

As indicated, changes are identified in many ways. A change can be proposed by a line operator based on their work experience, it can result from an analysis of a problem or stem from an idea captured during a shop floor management walk. Regardless of its origin, there should be a system in place to document the proposed change, evaluate its potential impact, prioritize its importance, track its implementation progress and, if approved, communicate its status until completed or cancelled. Improvement ideas are the backbone of any good continuous improvement program. How you manage idea generation, disposition and implementation will be a defining factor in the success of a process improvement initiative.

Impact Evaluation

Once a change proposal has been acknowledged, it's often necessary to evaluate its validity and effectiveness. A process should be defined to assess a change's impact, ensuring it will not adversely affect other aspects of work being performed or the work environment where it's likely to be implemented. A checklist of activities or a "prove-out" plan can be employed for this purpose.

Complex changes should be reviewed by a change review board (CRB) of knowledgeable individuals (e.g. subject-matter experts), familiar with the change under consideration and likely to be impacted by the change. It's best that supporting functions, with a stake in the proposed change, be part of the review process for maximum effectiveness. Only proven changes should be implemented to minimize the risk of needless process disruptions and potential customer dissatisfaction.

Often, a small trial or pilot run can be performed to assess the effect of a change prior to acceptance and full-scale implementation. A pilot provides an opportunity to quantify the cause-and-effect relationship between a change's input and output results. A pilot should be considered when a solution will significantly impact the organization or reversing a change will be difficult, costly or time-consuming. Pilot evaluations are considered beneficial investments when a team can obtain significant information and data that can minimize the risk associated with a managed change.

Implementation/Training

Once a change has been thoroughly vetted, it's time to implement it. A deployment or change management plan is recommended and should consider the following elements:

- A training plan
- A communication plan
- Resource requirements
- A detailed work plan (of activities)
- A schedule and budget
- Monitor and control metrics (sustainability)

For many, implementation is about updating documents and training people to follow a new work standard or procedure. However, it's as much, if not more, about getting people's buy-in and commitment to the new change. It's human nature for people not to like change, so if you don't take the time to explain the importance of change, why change is necessary and how change will impact them, they are less likely to support it, making it unsustainable. People need to understand why change and what's in it for them as a key step in driving meaningful and long-lasting change. A change can be the best, most significant improvement in years, but if you have not obtained the buy-in and commitment of those responsible for making the change, it's unlikely to take permanent hold.

Verification/Audit

In verification, it's important to evaluate the effectiveness of the implemented solution by tracking expected performance to targeted results. If effectiveness is confirmed, the implemented solution should be communicated to key stakeholders, standardized and replicated across the organization while documenting lessons learned for future reference as part of a learning organization.

If significant shortcomings are identified, consider if the change was documented, evaluated and implemented correctly. Question if additional actions are necessary to address unexpected problems or close unanticipated gaps in change deployment. A checklist can be helpful for ensuring all relevant documents affected by the change are updated and appropriate people trained.

Personal Commitment to Change

One interesting thing about change management is that high-quality changes are not guaranteed to be implemented. In fact, poorly managed change is one of the most significant causes of failure in realizing and sustaining improvements over the long haul.

People's emotional response to change often facilitates resistance to change due to a lack of understanding about the who, what, when, where, why and how of change. Not being honest and forthcoming about change can undermine people's commitment to making a change. Alternatively, resistance to change can provide a wealth of information and insight into what's needed to obtain commitment. Take time to listen, understand and work to remove barriers creating resistance to change. Develop a change management plan to help think through points of resistance and prepare to address them, one issue and one individual at a time. Doing so will improve the likelihood of success and increase its effective institutionalization.

Part II of the continuous improvement journey to operational excellence will focus on efficiency improvement now that we are confident in what's required to establish and maintain process control.

SIDEBAR: MORE ON EFFICIENCY IMPROVEMENT

Production efficiency has been used as a standard for evaluating productivity in equipment and/or labor. It can be viewed as efficiency achieved through an increase in production output relative to a given time period, with or without considering sales. A more realistic reflection of efficiency considers a saleable quantity of units produced within the shortest possible labor hours, taking into account costs resulting from inefficiencies due to material transport, excess inventory, over-processing and rework, among other factors. In addition, forecast-based production schedules are inherently inaccurate, often leading to under or overproduction, which significantly contributes to production costs that can often be avoided with pull-based systems. In essence, efficiency should be determined by the holistic cost of manufacturing saleable goods based on the fewest labor hours required for realization. Any non-value activities in production flow negatively impacts efficiency.

Efficiency improvement can be driven at a workstation, within a production line and throughout plant support operations. It's best to work on efficiency systematically, starting with individual processes, followed by production lines and then at a plant level, always considering how improvements at each level may impact the value stream. If there is a need to increase production capacity, determine how to do it within existing labor hours. Conversely, if production quantities are maintained or start to decrease, focus on reducing labor hours as a way to improve efficiency.

Key Points

- Efficiency improvements are focused on reducing cycle time through waste elimination and process flow improvement.
- Continuous improvement should strive to make things easier, better, faster, cheaper, safer and more flexible!
- Efficiency improvement is not about implementing lean tools, it's about understanding process flow and eliminating the obstacles that disrupt

flow such as equipment downtime, material shortages and operator distractions.

- Changes resulting in measurable improvements should be institutionalized to ensure they can be sustained indefinitely.

Reference

1. Rother and Shook. 1999. Lean Lexicon. KAIZEN: p. 8. http://www.lean.org/lexicon/kaizen.

Chapter 6

A Lean Mindset

> Dr. Shingo taught that understanding the principles behind the tools leads to higher-order thinking and answers the question, "why?" When people understand more deeply the why behind the how and the what, they become empowered to innovate and take individual initiative. As more and more people within a single organization begin to act independently based on their understanding and commitment to the principles, culture begins to shift.
>
> **The Shingo Model for Operational Excellence**

What Is Lean?

There are many ways to describe lean. Terms used to describe lean include "lean manufacturing", "lean production" or simply "lean". The fundamental concept of lean focuses on the creation of value for the end customer through the systematic elimination of waste. Waste can be described as any non-value-added activity resulting from poorly designed or executed processes, overburdening of people and equipment as well as unevenness of workloads.

The Lean Enterprise Institute [1] describes lean in several different ways:

- Maximizing customer value while minimizing waste.
- Creating more value for customers with fewer resources.

- Optimizing the flow of products and services through the entire value stream.
- A way of thinking and acting for an entire organization.

Regardless of how lean is defined, lean means different things to different industries, organizations and people. The concepts behind lean are fundamental and have been around for years. Toyota did not "invent" lean more than they practiced and "perfected" how methods, tools and techniques now associated with lean can be used and continuously improved to optimize processes, proving that, if done with a purpose and a goal in mind, a significant competitive advantage can be achieved. Toyota built their culture on fundamental principles and practices important to the development and growth of their business. These principles and practices evolved over time, contributing to Toyota's increasing success and eventually became synonymous with the Toyota culture. These principles will be discussed in Part III of the book.

According to the Lean Enterprise Institute, the term "lean" was coined by a research team headed by Jim Womack, PhD, at MIT's International Motor Vehicle Program to describe Toyota's business practices during the late 1980s. The characteristics of a lean organization and supply chain are described in *Lean Thinking* by Womack and Dan Jones [2], founders of the Lean Enterprise Institute and the Lean Enterprise Academy (UK), respectively.

Lean is a management philosophy derived from the Toyota Production System (TPS). It involves a set of tools deployed in a structured way to identify and eliminate waste and improve process flow. It can be viewed as part of a continuous improvement philosophy that strives to enhance the quality and efficiency of operations, leading to more reliable and cost-competitive products, processes and services that satisfy customer needs. Conceptually, lean focuses on process efficiency improvements with a goal of continuous, one-piece flow. It presents a way of thinking and acting for an entire organization, by promoting an attitude and behavior consistent with a continuous improvement mindset and culture.

Traditionally, people focus their improvement efforts at the process or task level, within their own area of influence or control. This is where Six Sigma projects tend to concentrate. Lean, on the other hand, takes a broader view of the organization by minimizing waste and maximizing process flow across business processes to create a more efficient value stream. To optimize operational efficiency, we have to move from a process-centric focus to a value stream focus where cooperation between functions leads to a more cohesive and efficient flow of materials and information to support a receiving to shipping movement of raw material and product through a facility. Traditional operational leaders focus on results; modern-day lean operations take a more proactive focus on process inputs and activities that influence and ultimately drive desired outputs. As companies improve their process efficiency, productive resources are often freed-up and reallocated elsewhere in support of new value-creating work.

Over the years, many of us have forged successful careers on our ability to recognize, react and solve problems. As most of us have observed, if not experienced, praise and reward were often given to "firefighters" of the organization, those who could extinguish problems quickly. Unfortunately, this recognition tended to overlook those who actively prevented fires from occurring, reinforcing the "wrong" or, shall we say, less than ideal behavior.

If a culture rewards firefighters, we all become firefighters preparing ourselves to extinguish fires. We sit in wait for that next big opportunity to prove our worth to the company. Historically, looking for problems has not been a wise career move; it's best if we arrive "just-in-time" to douse the fire in order to maximize our visibility and reinforce our commitment to those who value such behavior. Sound familiar?

Exposing problems, although important, has not been a popular way to create favor with management. In fact, finding too many problems could lead to an undesirable reputation, similar to the boy who cried wolf a few too many times. We have learned to accept the old adage: if it's not broken, don't fix it. My intent is not to be critical of this approach but simply to point out that it differs from a lean approach, which encourages people to look for problems and rewards individuals for finding, highlighting and solving them expediently before they negatively impact the process.

Waiting for problems to occur creates a stagnant environment, one in which the status quo rules the culture. By contrast, if we actively engage ourselves to look for the next likely concern, identify it and implement a countermeasure quickly, we move incrementally closer to an ideal state of behavior. It's a state that we never expect to reach, but one that creates an attitude or mindset of continuous efficiency improvement. In short, lean thinking is about taking a proactive approach to continuous improvement by actively looking for and exposing problems versus waiting for them to disrupt our world before reacting.

Learning to See

If you have been around as long as I have and observed the process world from its many perspectives, then you have most likely concluded that very little about lean is new! This is not to say that more can't be learned from lean principles and practices. Most of what we are learning from lean comes from incremental improvements toward achieving the perfect state since every opportunity to apply lean further enhances our unique insight into its possibilities.

As stated before, Toyota recognized and applied fundamental principles and practices, learning from their experiences and those of others to grow and advance their operations. They settled on a set of core principles and practices that served as a basis for their continuous improvement work style. In particular, they realized the untapped potential of employees contributing to their journey of operational excellence and made it a strategic initiative to engage everyone, every day and everywhere in incremental improvements.

Early on, there was a misconception that lean was only for manufacturing. Time has since debunked this belief with a renewed understanding that lean applies to any business where processes exist. However, there remains a prevailing misconception today about lean; one that could limit organizational potential for those who can't shake it. It's the misconception that lean is about identifying and eliminating waste. Clearly, there is truth to this statement but it's a partial truth. More importantly, lean is about finding waste. It involves looking beyond one's normal "frame of reference"; it's about learning to see what has always been there but not inherently obvious to the untrained eye or preoccupied mind. Sometimes, learning to see is as simple as taking time to look and contextualize what you are observing. At other times, it may require a bit more effort to see what lies just below the surface of a seemingly normal process or operation.

In general, identifying defects (waste) involves a mostly passive approach since the prevailing tendency is to monitor our environment for deviations and react to significant variations to maintain process control. Finding waste takes on a more proactive role in our quest for continuous improvement by actively seeking out waste through stressing systems (processes) to expose the next problem in line for elimination as we work toward a more efficient operation. This is what continuous improvement is about – a slow, structured and disciplined approach to finding and eliminating waste, not waiting for waste (e.g. problems) to occur and then doing something about it.

Lean Thinking and Culture

As discussed, process control is the starting point for lean improvements. A stable and capable process creates the foundation upon which continuous improvements are rooted. As with any foundation, if it's not sound, it will not sustain whatever is built upon it. As is the case with lean efficiency improvements. Without a stable and capable process, any effort to improve the efficiency of an existing process will eventually fail.

Lean thinking changes our mindset by focusing attention on looking for problems to solve versus waiting for the next one to occur before solving it. Continuous efficiency improvement requires that we actively stress systems to reveal the next problem or obstacle on the path to the "ideal" state. This may include reducing material inventory or batch size as a way to reveal the next improvement opportunity. Lean thinking also takes a systematic approach to finding and eliminating waste while improving process flow through employee engagement. It leverages employee capabilities throughout the organizational hierarchy to highlight waste for elimination while applying tools and techniques that move a process closer to a smooth, steady and continuous rate of flow, consistent with customer demand.

Lean thinking can't be defined in one simple statement. It's a multidimensional concept that can be expressed in many different ways and from many different perspectives, some of which include:

- Changing an organization's focus from optimizing the efficient use of people and equipment to optimizing the flow of goods, services and information through the entire value stream.
- Continuous and incremental highlighting of problems for permanent elimination. Problems can take many forms including defects, deviations, obstacles and non-value-added activities, among others. As we solve problems and eliminate waste, process quality and efficiency improves.
- An organization that understands customer value and focuses its efforts to maintain and continuously increase it.
- Changing a service-driven organizational focus from an internal business perspective to include an external customer value perspective through the elimination of waste in the value stream.
- Switching from a traditional focus of enhancing *value-added* opportunities to one of eliminating *non-value-added* activities within and among processes.
- Eliminating unnecessary complexity through process simplification.

Lean thinking requires a shift in mindset from a results-orientated focus to one that includes process inputs and activities that drive output results. Common sense dictates that a well-designed, developed and maintained process will produce desired outputs. Proper attention to the right inputs and key process activities will go a long way to delivering desirable, predictable and consistent results over time. The benefit of being process focused is that you can proactively influence the outcome versus passively accepting results and reacting to their consequences.

A lean mindset *is not* about waiting for problems to occur and eliminating them (reactive), it's about looking for problems by stressing the system little by little over time to see where the next problem is hiding (proactive). How do you "stress" a process to expose the next biggest problem?

- Stop to fix problems
- Reduce inventories/buffers
- Reduce batch size
- Speed-up the process

The pursuit of perfection means never being satisfied with the status quo. A true mindset of operational excellence requires that we continuously look for problems. As stated by Taiichi Ohno of Toyota fame, no problem is a big problem!

SIDEBAR: WHAT IS OLD IS NEW AGAIN

All too often, I have observed a new initiative being rolled out by management knowing it did not have long to live. During a typical "kick-off" phase, a lot of fanfare and excitement masks the time and effort required to achieve success. However, one often hidden reality is that most initiatives are not new at all. Over time, an industry takes a renewed interest in a topic or tool because someone wrote a book or published an article that put a new twist on an old concept or demonstrated the successful application of a proven technique when executed properly. Some examples include 5S, formally housekeeping; Toyota kata, formally continuous incremental improvement; gemba walks, formally management by walking around; and my favorite, leader standard work (LSW), formally daily shop floor management.

Although these comparisons may not be completely fair, they are based on a sound premise; what is old is new again. In my years of experience, what appears to be "new" is often old and is reintroduced when someone rediscovers its intrinsic value. However, before deciding to make a big deal about launching some "new" initiative that will "change the course of the company's future", consider what is already in place and build upon what currently exists. People become less resistant to change when change is incremental and builds upon existing infrastructure. Build upon what already exists and consider the best way to introduce something "new" with minimal disruption and resistance from those individuals being targeted. Re-energize existing activities by making enhancements to existing processes, procedures and work routines, and sell it as continuous improvement to existing systems. In this way, it's nothing new to them and you can reinforce the "why" you are doing it and "how" to do it in a more meaningful way. Remember, in business, it's rare that something is truly new or "revolutionary" and it is likely to exist in some aspect of what you are already doing.

The Lean Toolbox

All too often we hear stories about implementing tools such as 5S, Jidoka, kanban and load-leveling (heijunka) boxes in manufacturing simply because Toyota uses them and therefore they must be lean. In addition to adding to the workload of operators, concerns with these new tools and techniques start to appear when people begin asking questions as to why they are doing something for which management can't provide valid justification. We implement a tool when it helps us solve a problem. If a tool does not make a job easier, better, faster, cheaper or safer, ask yourself, why are we doing it? It's important to understand the relationship between the guiding principles or concepts of an organization, its systems and supporting tools. If there is no clear reason for using something new or doing something different, other than "it's lean", the mindset is misguided and it's time to change it. Tools should enable a system to accomplish its purpose, not complicate it.

Continuous improvement can't be sustained on a tool-based approach. The application of a tool should be the consequence of problem-solving or process improvement, not blind deployment. Part of lean thinking is knowing "why" a tool is being used and understanding "how" to use it properly to obtain the benefits for which it was intended. Lean tools should be implemented with purpose, without which they become meaningless. As presented in the opening quote of this chapter:

Dr. Shingo taught that understanding the principles behind the tools leads to higher-order thinking and answers the question, "why?" When people understand more deeply the why behind the how and the what, they become empowered to innovate and take individual initiative.

The Lean Mindset

Changing the mindset of an individual is not easy; never mind that of an entire organization. So how does one change a mindset? Where do you start? Before anything else, you need to articulate what type of working atmosphere you want to create and what individual characteristics reflect that expectation. A workplace environment is defined by the attitudes and behaviors of the people working in it and reflects their values and beliefs. Although values and beliefs are difficult to recognize, behavior is one of the tangible characteristics we can observe in others. It's an indication of how people think and are likely to act. If we want people to think and act a certain way, we need to observe their behavior and influence the factors that align their behaviors with organizational expectations. Changing a mindset is about controlling the factors that influence individual behavior. If we accept the Shingo Institute model that systems drive behaviors, by observing current behaviors and corresponding results, we can adjust existing systems so that consequential behaviors produce the results we aspire to achieve.

One of the most powerful systems for driving behaviors and results is that of incentives. When incentives are focused on results and not the behaviors expected to produce those results, "creative" steps are often taken to achieve outcomes with little regard for the behaviors required to get there. Therefore, when looking to change or adjust an organizational mindset to better align with the desired principles and practices, consider specifying the behaviors you want organizational personnel to demonstrate in obtaining those results instead of simply stating the desired results and allowing employees to decide what behaviors they will exercise to achieve them. The following points will help facilitate changing behaviors in an organization:

- Obtain management's commitment to change.
- Manage change as a project.

- Communicate the why and how of change.
- Develop systems that drive desired behaviors.
- Encourage management to continually display the behaviors expected of all employees; lead by example.
- Expect organizational leadership to coach and mentor others on work expectations, behaviors and desired results.
- Correct undesirable behaviors.
- Recognize and reward desired behaviors and corresponding results.

A 1999 *Harvard Business Review* article titled "Decoding the DNA of the Toyota Production System" [3], sums up the lean mindset nicely by stating that Toyota has a clear and common vision of what they want to achieve. This vision defines the path forward for all employees: an ideal state of products and services that are

- Produced on demand
- Produced without waste
- Defect free (form, fit and function meet customer expectations)
- Delivered one request at a time (e.g. batch size of one)
- Delivered immediately
- Produced in a safe working environment for all employees

The achievement of this vision translates into some of the following behaviors:

- Stop, think, plan, execute, learn
- Fast and efficient reaction to problems
- Visual controls available for rapid problem identification
- Following standardized work and reacting to deviations
- Performing daily work routines focused on process control and improvement
- Frequent monitoring of productivity for deviations from target
- Managing deviations quickly and effectively (Jidoka)
- Understanding line capacity with a plan to continuously improve it
- Operators who communicate problems when they can't follow standardized work
- Equipment maintenance to ensure reliability (TPM)
- Key process indicator (KPI) analysis for trends; actions taken to ensure control

- Continuous improvement of the value stream
- Proactively looking for the next biggest problem to solve
- Timely sharing of accurate information

The mindset of an organization is established and demonstrated by leadership. If the mindset needs to change, leadership must formulate a vision of what it should be; identify, create and drive systems and behaviors that support it; hire people that align with it; and be the first in their organization to demonstrate it. People do what their managers and leaders do, not necessarily what they are told to do.

SIDEBAR: THE BOTTOM LINE

On occasion, I have the privilege of working with a particular American manufacturing plant that is continuously competing for business in the global automotive market. What's interesting about this particular facility is that everyone working there has a clear and focused mindset about continuous improvement. If an improvement opportunity is being considered, the same question is always asked: "How will this change help keep us competitive?" As an American manufacturing facility, they are continuously competing against lower-cost companies in Mexico, Eastern Europe and Asia for business. To survive, every improvement must contribute to the bottom line. It must improve safety, quality, delivery or productivity in a meaningful way. Waste is not an option when competing on a global scale. Therefore, every decision they make is done within the context of short- and long-term survival. There is true clarity to continuous improvement in this facility; if a change or improvement supports keeping the plant doors open, it's value added. If not, it's waste. Simple!

Continuous Process Flow [4]

Flow is the smooth, steady, uninterrupted movement of materials and information through a value stream. The value stream is defined by the workflow required to satisfy a customer order from the moment received (e.g. order entry) to the point of delivery. A characteristic of a lean process is one in which nothing is produced until a customer order is received or a request is made by the next person, operation or step in the process.

Continuous manufacturing flow is supported by just-in-time material delivery and a kanban pull system, driven by an integrated production system and continuous improvement mentality. It requires the continual removal of waste while consciously working to minimize costs and maintain on-time delivery of quality products. The "goal" is to realize a batch size of one or "one-piece" flow from one process step to the next. This is often facilitated by a work cell configuration where equipment and workstations are arranged in close proximity. If a line is responsible for producing multiple models, special attention must be paid to product changeover time since resource capacity is consumed by changeover. It's wise to note that reducing batch sizes can increase handling time as well as the complexity in planning and controlling production. Regardless of potential difficulties in achieving a more favorable flow, many believe that continuous flow is the most efficient way to produce.

If incremental improvement suits your work style and organizational strategy, continuous flow, facilitated by a pull-based production system, can help move operations closer to a one-piece flow. However, reductions in changeover time and improvements in equipment reliability will likely be required.

Batch versus One-Piece Flow

Batch flow is considered a traditional approach to manufacturing. The movement of batched material is reflective of mass production systems that harbor *overproduction* caused by making large lots of goods that contribute to excess and idle inventory. In a batch process, multiple parts are processed together as a group at one time. Often, these batches or lots contain large volumes of product that wait in line for subsequent processing. In contrast, single-piece flow involves the pulling of one part at a time through the process.

As discussed, a traditional batch process contains large volumes of material. For example, when making a "smile" button, Department #1 makes the button with the pin on the back, Department #2 prints the button light gray while the third department (Department #3) prints the smile face. In Figure 6.1, a batch size of 10 is used. At 1 minute per unit, it takes the batch 10 minutes in each department for a total of 30 minutes per batch to complete. The first button would be completed in 21 minutes (10 + 10 + 1) with only 3 minutes (1 + 1 + 1) of value-added work to complete.

One-piece flow involves physically lining up processes in a sequence that will produce the customer's order in the shortest possible time. In lean, the

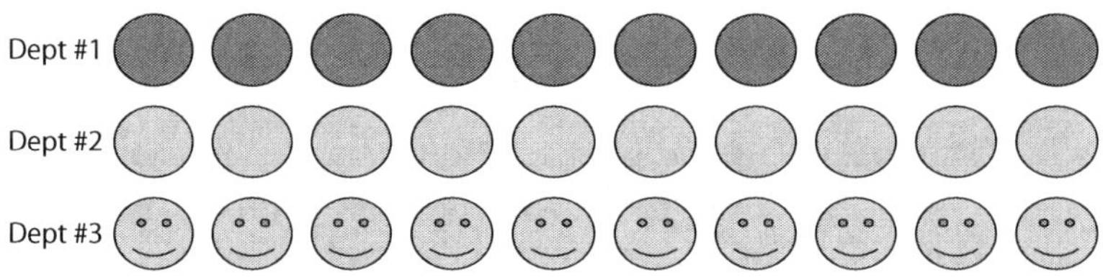

Figure 6.1 Batch processing of smile buttons.

ideal batch size is always the same, one. The focus is on material optimization, not people or equipment optimization. A reduction in batch size and optimization of material flow allow for quick movement of product through the process. Use of work cells, grouped by product versus process, often reduces the process time further while helping to decrease overproduction and inventory. Figure 6.2 demonstrates a one-piece flow for the button fabrication process where a button can be produced every 3 minutes to a specific order quantity without overproduction.

Figure 6.3 shows the difference between batch and continuous flow using a work cell configuration. In many instances, there are clear benefits to moving toward a more continuous flow. However, there are situations where continuous flow is not practical and batch processing will remain the preferred method.

The clear advantage of a cell configuration producing one piece at a time is the making of parts to a specific order quantity. If a special order is received for 5 parts, a batch process of 10 units must produce 10 units at a time to satisfy an order size of 5. The five remaining parts may end up being sold (at a lower cost), stored, reworked or scrapped. A work cell supporting one-piece flow will only make the quantity ordered, no more, no less, no waste. If there is a special order for three light gray and three dark gray buttons, a batch process will need to make 10 light gray and 10 dark gray buttons to satisfy the order, overproducing by 14 units, 7 of which are dark gray. Will they be able to sell seven dark gray buttons? In a work cell configuration, three light gray buttons are made and a changeover occurs to make three dark gray buttons. Order satisfied; no overproduction. As indicated, work cells are not practical for all applications, but can provide a significant operational advantage when

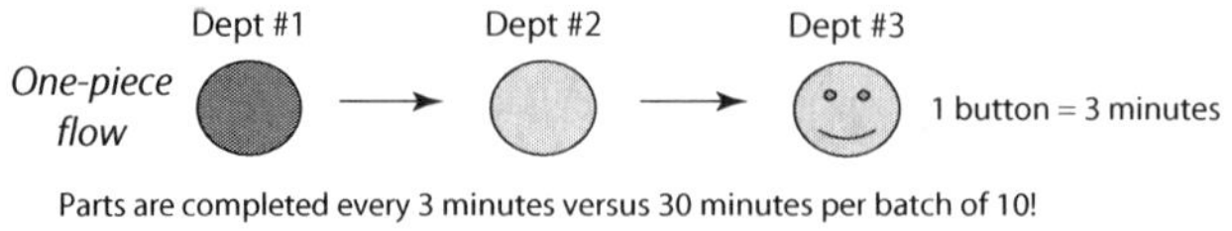

Figure 6.2 One-piece flow button fabrication process.

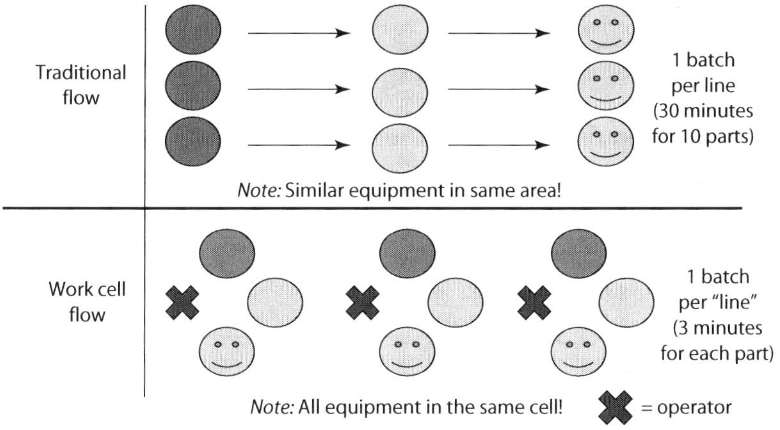

Figure 6.3 Batch (traditional) versus continuous flow (e.g. work cell) process.

overproduction is a concern and flexibility is paramount. If one-piece flow is a realistic option for an existing process, there are clear benefits including:

- *Quality improvement*: Operators can inspect their work output for problems or issues that can be corrected before the product moves to the next operation or the next part is made.
- *Flexibility*: Work cells are more agile since they are more easily adjusted to suit changing customer needs versus dedicated batch process equipment.
- *Productivity*: Non-value-added activities (waste) are minimized, improving process efficiency.
- *Floor space*: Work cells require a "tight" configuration, reducing the need for excess space commonly used for storing work in process (WIP).
- *Safety*: Small batches reduce the need for transport, decreasing opportunities for accidents (e.g. forklifts are a major cause of accidents).
- *Morale*: As value-added work increases, morale increases as people see their results and recognize their value to the company.
- *Inventory*: Less inventory frees up capital for investment and reduces the occurrence of obsolescence.

Pull (vs. Push) System [4]

Pull systems are used to avoid overproduction by providing "downstream" customers with what they want, when they want it and in the amount they want. This helps minimize WIP and inventory that contribute to excess costs. An effective pull system will facilitate a more controlled response to day-to-day shifts in customer demands. Pull systems rely on a just-in-time support system to be effective.

In a traditional push system, a forecast-based schedule drives the production of goods whereas a "pull" system uses a customer request (a purchase order) to initiate the "pull". An office example is provided in Figure 6.4, where coffee is produced in batch or on demand. In the case of a batch process, it's not unusual to produce too much or too little coffee. A pull system (coffee on demand) avoids this problem. In preparation, lean operations must be simple, reactive and flexible in response to changing customer requirements.

As indicated, the purest form of "pull" is one-piece flow, 100% on demand; zero inventory. However, some inventory or "buffer" will be required to compensate for the natural disruptions (variations) in flow when transforming raw material into finished goods. The ultimate goal of a pull system is to eliminate the "storing of parts" and strive for an "on-demand" one-piece flow of parts, making only what's required, when requested. If production flows perfectly, there is no inventory.

Forecasts are based on customer projections several weeks or months in advance of their actual need; therefore, forecast-based schedules are not very accurate and often lead to *underproduction* causing overtime or *overproduction* resulting in inventory. Not all systems can be converted to a pull system. Schedules, reflective of a push system, work best when lead times are very short. Finally, a successful "pull" system requires a just-in-time inventory management system, stopping to fix problems, a kanban signaling system and in-process buffers.

Well-run supermarkets use pull systems by maintaining sufficient inventory (buffers) to keep shelves stocked. Customers create demand by taking (or pulling) items from shelves while supermarket clerks review and replenish them from a small store of inventory before they run out. Overproduction is minimized to a small "store" of goods based on trends in

Figure 6.4 Push versus pull system.

customer take rate. Clearly, even pull systems require inventory "buffers" to compensate for uncontrollable variation to maintain a smooth, steady flow.

As indicated, pull systems require replenishing. Kanbans are used to alert internal (and external) suppliers of the need to replenish material. A kanban can be a sign, card or empty bin used to trigger action. In the case of a supermarket, a periodic review of shelves for low stock is a signal for the store clerk to replenish them. An effective kanban system is simple, highly visual and minimizes inventory while increasing the availability of correct materials and parts for production.

SIDEBAR: AN OFFICE "PULL" SYSTEM

Most well-run offices use a pull-replenishment system to control office supplies (pens, paper, tape, etc.) to save money and avoid a supply shortage. An office that maintains a standing order (e.g. a schedule of supply deliveries) will experience variation in available supplies over time, including a lack of critical items. An office that maintains a pull system, which triggers material orders based on availability, is less likely to run out of critical supply items, creating a more stable inventory.

Leveling the Work Schedule (Workload Leveling) [4]

Building exactly what the customer wants when they want it is a nice idea; however, it is not very practical when considering the unpredictable nature in which orders are received on a daily, weekly or even monthly basis. Building to schedule often leads to over or underproduction, stressed employees and underutilized equipment when schedules change due to significant variation in customer demand and interruptions to accommodate "expedited" orders. This type of dynamic contributes to increasing lead times, often resulting in disorder and chaos while preventing a steady flow of material through production. Recognizing the difficulty of building to order, Toyota pioneered the approach of leveling out the production schedule to maintain customer quality while improving manufacturing efficiency.

To achieve a steady flow, one must first ensure the workload is balanced within a production line. If not, any improvements in process flow efficiency will be quickly overshadowed by spikes in customer demand causing production "stops and starts" that will stress equipment and people while disrupting the very flow an organization is working hard to maintain. This is the idea behind the Japanese term "heijunka", leveling of production schedules by regulating both product volume and mix.

A good example of this concept in action is traffic management. Figure 6.5a displays traffic congestion while Figure 6.5b shows the area that a vehicle occupies on the road as a "service" unit. The service is to provide a drivable surface for cars to travel. Cars move along the road in "service units". The goal is to maximize the number of cars reaching their destination per hour.

The objective is to optimize the flow of work products (service units), not the capacity utilization of workers (cars). One hundred percent capacity utilization leads to congestion due to a lack of "buffer" to compensate for variations in traffic flow (see Figure 6.6).

Adding more capacity (an additional lane) is an expensive solution with limited effect!

- 3 lanes = 50 cars/minute
- 4 lanes = 66 cars/minute ($$$)

Changing traffic management focus from *capacity utilization* to *vehicle flow* yields a much bigger return on investment (Figure 6.7).

A typical approach in manufacturing is to reduce capacity utilization to 80%, by adding 20% more people. A different approach is to change workflow to achieve more output with less input. This is why you may have noticed activated traffic signals at entrances to major highways during rush hour. These lights are intended to change or regulate vehicle flow by controlling capacity as a way to increase system throughput.

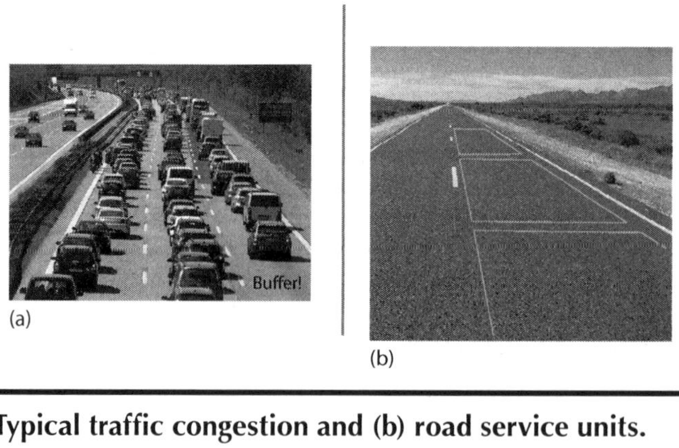

Figure 6.5 (a) Typical traffic congestion and (b) road service units.

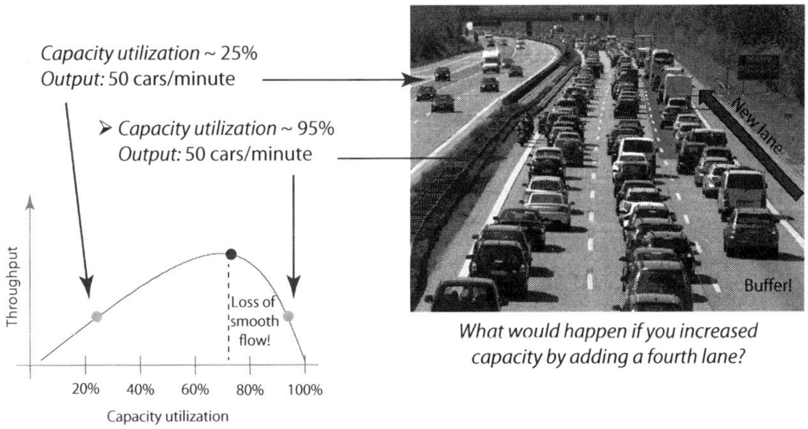

Figure 6.6 Capacity utilization.

Want to improve workflow? Reduce the number of tasks in process, which allows WIP to be completed on schedule. In addition, exceeding 80% capacity (reducing your buffer) will start reducing your system throughput and increase the time to complete in-process tasks due to "stops and starts" as observed in heavy traffic conditions.

Stop to Fix Problems [4]

Stopping to fix problems is fundamental to lean. Problems ignored during production commonly results in rework or scrap (waste) later in the process and have the potential of escaping to the customer. Fixing problems at the source is usually faster and more efficient since evidence may still exist for root cause identification. As time passes, critical information can be lost, making it more difficult to determine the cause of a problem for decisive corrective action.

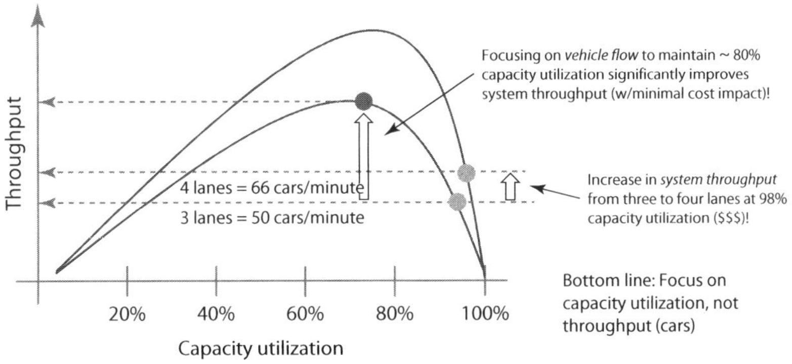

Figure 6.7 System throughput versus capacity utilization.

Use simple visual controls to help highlight problems. Once an issue is discovered, using proven quality tools and techniques is an effective way to address concerns. Slowing down or stopping the process may be required to eliminate a problem from reoccurring. Go and see the problem firsthand, analyze the situation (why-why analysis), identify the root cause, implement a permanent corrective action and follow up with error-proofing, if feasible. It's important to get quality right the first time to prevent waste due to problem reoccurrence.

SIDEBAR: STOP AND FIX PROBLEMS

Process control must happen in all areas of a business, including research and development. I once attended a plant review between the central function staff, business unit personnel and plant management. This plant was struggling to launch over 15 new projects into the facility of which 87% of them were shown to be yellow or red over the past 15 months. Although the business units responsible for product launches were represented in the meeting, the discussion barely touched on this chronic issue. It was a failure of central and business management not to address a crisis that was continuously plaguing the manufacturing facility, not to mention the significant cost and launch delays that were impacting multiple customers. Even more disappointing, the head of the central function, leading the operational excellence initiative, failed to take decisive action with the business unit representatives on this red flag issue, missing a significant opportunity to address a clear weakness in the organization and to demonstrate the behavior expected of a continuously improving enterprise in which he plays a key role. If we don't stop and fix problems, we continue to generate waste.

In Jeffrey Liker's book, *The Toyota Way*, the chapter titled "Principle 5: Building a Culture of Stopping to Fix Problems, to Get Quality Right the First Time" has an interesting comment about the Toyota mindset written as follows: *Toyota learned long ago that solving quality problems at the source saves time and money downstream. By continuously surfacing problems and fixing them as they occur, you eliminate waste, your productivity soars, and competitors who are running assembly lines flat-out and letting problems accumulate get left in the dust.* This is a mindset we can embrace but with caution, as we manage through the complexities of doing so. A good practice is to have a reaction plan in place for dealing with different types of situations and process anomalies employees are likely to encounter during production. At a minimum, deviations should be documented, prioritized and followed up based on available time and resources.

Standardized Work [4]

Standardized work creates the foundation for process control and continuous improvement. It establishes a repeatable process that helps reduce process variation, improve stability and drive a more predictable output. Standardized work should capture three key elements:

- Takt time or rate at which products must be produced to meet customer demand.
- Precise work sequence in which an operator performs tasks within the expected cycle time.
- Standard inventory (buffer), including units in machines, required to keep the process operating smoothly.

Work standards support processes in many ways including elevating safety awareness, providing stakeholders with expected outcomes, onboarding new employees and eliminating waste. Standards must be specific enough to be useful but general enough to allow some flexibility. Work standards need to be simple and practical for those doing the work, incorporate best practices and lessons learned for continuous improvement and allow individuals creative expression to augment existing practices within clearly established boundaries. As said many times before: *Quality is ensured by doing it the right way and the same way every time!*

Standardized work is not meant to be punitive; if implemented with the right intent, it can lead to worker empowerment and innovation. Consider professional athletes initially developing their skills; they learn the basics by following the directions of their instructors and continuously practice until their technique is stable and consistent. What eventually makes a professional athlete great is their ability to build on what they learn, experimenting and refining their technique within the fundamental boundaries of their sport, while continuously optimizing their performance. This takes innovation, creativity and commitment. It's been said that the only difference between good and great performers is the consistency of their optimal performance.

Proven and Reliable Technology [4]

Technology is a tool that is only as good as its ability to make achieving a specific purpose easier, faster, cheaper or safer. Before a change in technology is introduced, it's best to work out the "bugs" and iterate changes manually before going digital. Manual changes tend to be easier, faster and cheaper to implement than digital; once mature, a digital solution can be considered. Harness technology to propel your continuous improvement efforts forward. Pursue technology only if it's relevant and adds value to the situation for which it's being considered.

Technology should support people and processes, not replace them. It should be introduced once proven effective, value-adding and reliable. Consider available technologies when evaluating new approaches or new applications.

A3 Thinking/Reporting

A3 thinking provides a structured problem-solving approach to improvement using coaching and scientific thinking to experiment at one's threshold of knowledge. Scientific thinking involves developing a hypothesis and testing it to see what can be learned through experimentation. The A3 also serves as a reporting tool for documenting and communicating problem-solving progress and continuous improvement status reporting.

An A3 approach often involves plan-do-check-act (PDCA) cycles and encourages employees to obtain a deep understanding of a problem or opportunity in order to identify permanent and sustainable solutions and improvements for implementation. Expectations of A3 thinking involve going to the workplace to see what's happening, talk with employees, elevate awareness and seek data and facts for decision-making.

There are other methods that serve a similar purpose such as 8 Disciplines (8D), Lean Six Sigma (DMAIC) and Kepner-Tregoe Decision Analysis all of which serve to provide a structured and disciplined approach to critical thinking in order to solve problems efficiently and effectively. In the end, it's not about the methodology as much as the ability of skilled employees to apply a methodology in a way that achieves sustainable results.

A3 Reporting: Preparation

A3 reporting is intended to provide a coherent, logical story of a project's progress in reaching a workable solution. The term "A3" obtained its name from the paper size it's printed on. The intent of using A3 paper is to present the current or final status of a problem or improvement opportunity on one page as visually and quantitatively as possible. A3 is not about the document but use of a structured (PDCA), disciplined approach (scientific thinking) to learning and developing one's capability to manage knowledge work.

When preparing an A3 report, the preparer should know their audience. Consider what the audience expects from the report and the time allotted for presentation. Anticipate their questions. Make sure data and facts are presented. Avoid misunderstandings by providing sufficient detail; use the 5W 1H method (Who will do What by When? Where? Why? How or how much?) to communicate a comprehensive picture of the current state. Clarify when data and information are preliminary or have not been substantiated and require further analysis.

The A3 template has been prepared in a logical sequence. If followed, it helps facilitate the telling of your story. The audience may be familiar with the template and anticipate your next topic. If possible, before the presentation, go and see the room. What equipment is available? What's missing that you will need during the presentation (e.g. projector, flip chart and markers)? Practice your talk; be prepared. A lack of preparation can be interpreted as not respecting the audience's time and attention.

A3 Reporting: Presentation

Periodic meetings should be held to review the status and quality of A3 activities. These create organizational awareness and opportunities to mentor individuals in the A3 thinking and reporting process. A3 presentations should focus on what's important, providing clear and concise reporting. Initial A3 reviews tend to focus on defining and understanding the problem while later reviews concentrate more on confirming results and effectiveness of implementation. The presenter should tell the whole story within the time allotted and use audience questions to determine where to spend extra time on a specific topic, if time permits.

At various points throughout the presentation, check for audience comprehension. Observe body language. Ask if they understand or need clarification on any points covered. Confirm audience agreement with your logic and thinking. If necessary, stop and answer questions and address concerns. A3 reporting often brings experts and executives into a room to review organizational activities. Take this opportunity to ask questions of them. Consider preparing several questions to ask participants such as how to perform an analysis or about alternative approaches to validating results.

At the end of your presentation, be sure to outline the next steps and follow-up actions. If additional activities are required prior to the next update, confirm understanding and the best way to proceed. Be prepared to answer final questions and ask for feedback upon completing your talk. Listen to what is being said.

An A3 template with a brief description of each topic is provided in Appendix xv. Tips for A3 reporting are as follows:

- Scope the A3 with the team's skill set in mind.
- Background information should "set the stage" for the A3 review.
- A problem statement should clarify what is wrong with what; the improvement opportunity should define the current condition.
- An A3 should have a goal or target condition that is quantifiable and includes a "due by" date.
- A3's should be visual, quantitative and follow a methodology (e.g. PDCA; define, measure, analyze, improve and control [DMAIC]; 8 Disciplines), typically defined by the template.
- State the facts and include supporting details.
- Information reported should focus on understanding the problem/opportunity, validating the solution or confirming improvement effectiveness.
- A3 should contain a logical flow that tells a story; avoid unexplainable gaps.
- Actions taken should eliminate the root cause or redefine the performance baseline.

Scientific Thinking

Scientific thinking involves gathering and interpreting new information to enhance our understanding and increase our knowledge. It's systemic and analytic in nature; systemic in terms of taking a structured, logical approach to understanding issues and solving problems; analytic in one's desire to pursue a deep knowledge of how things work in order to effectively address new challenges and unique situations. The Shingo Institute considers scientific thinking "a natural method for learning and the most effective approach to improvement". Systemic thinking is about understanding the interrelationships and connections of components in systems. It is

- Fact based and data driven
- Structured problem-solving
- Exploration of new ideas without fear of failure

- Cycles of experimental learning to augment understanding
- Reconciliation of the difference between predicted and actual results

Scientific thinking is something people do, not something they have or earn. It's a reflection of personal observations and statements supported by clear, relevant and reliable data, factual information and undisputed evidence. Meaningful scientific thinking often leads individuals in unexpected directions and to surprising places, enhancing their knowledge and perspective of the world in which they live and work.

SIDEBAR: THE SCIENTIFIC THINKER ...

An experienced scientific thinker:

✓ Raises vital questions and problems
✓ Gathers and assesses relevant data
✓ Evaluates assumptions, implications and realistic consequences
✓ Has well-reasoned conclusions and solutions
✓ Communicates effectively with others

*Excellence in thought must be systematically developed!***

**Source: The thinker's guide to scientific thinking by Dr. R. Paul and Dr. L. Elder

Want to develop your scientific thinking?

➢ Question what you observe → How does this gel cure? What caused this material to melt? When does this crack first occur?

➢ Investigate further → Determine what's already known about your observations.

➢ Be skeptical → Should you believe what you hear or verify it yourself?

➢ Try to disprove your own ideas → Consider different sides of your own argument.

➢ Seek out more evidence → If insufficient evidence exists to support your position.

➢ Be open-minded → Change your mind, if logic and evidence supports it.

➢ Think creatively → Consider multiple possibilities to explain what you observe.

Source: http://undsci.berkeley.edu/article/think_science

Simplicity

By definition, simplicity is the quality or condition of being easy to understand or do. It's an attitude, a way of thinking, behaving and communicating. In essence, simplicity means different things to different people. It involves staying focused on what matters, reducing the complex into its fundamental components, making things clear to see and easy to understand. If applied insightfully, it can provide better, cheaper, more reliable outcomes. Leonardo Da Vinci stated it very well when he said "Simplicity is the ultimate sophistication". Simplifying a complex process, procedure, idea or concept brings clarity and focus to one's work. An example of this concept would be avoiding the application of electronic controls when simple mechanical devices are sufficient. This will likely reduce downtime while allowing for easier and quicker equipment maintenance. Focus on automation where it adds value since automation increases complexity and capital costs. As Albert Einstein once said, *Everything should be made as simple as possible but not simpler.*

SIDEBAR: WASTE REDUCTION – BANK ONE
SOURCE: WHAT IS LEAN SIX SIGMA?

A good example of simplicity comes from a story I encountered concerning a Bank One multi-million dollar bank transaction improvement project. They set out to improve customer satisfaction by significantly reducing the processing time of their high-dollar-value transactions. Their objective was to achieve a 4 hour processing time for financial deposits with the expectation that deposits received by 8 a.m. would be credited to customer accounts by noon.

A "wholesale lock-box" process was being used to handle business-to-business financial transactions. An analysis of this "current state" process revealed 1.5 miles of floor-to-floor and office-to-office transport of these transactions. One-and-a-half miles of travel inside the Bank One office.

They analyzed the process by preparing a process flow and performing a value analysis. Upon identifying and completing improvement actions, offices and workspaces were moved to create a new flow that required only 386 walking steps to complete the process. This resulted in an 80% reduction in cycle time (travel) while increasing the ability to consistently meet a 4 hour processing commitment.

Respect for People

Respect for people starts with ensuring a safe workplace. This can be achieved by striving to reduce potential work hazards, maintaining adherence to standard work and enforcing a 5S discipline within the facility. A positive and creative workplace can also enhance worker morale, demonstrating respect for all.

Leadership should enhance the knowledge, experience and creativity of every employee as a way to show respect for people. Individual dignity and self-worth creates an environment of trust and cooperation essential to exploit the best of people. Organizations should work to develop, mentor and coach individuals as a way to augment organizational skills while building trust among cohorts. Respect for people can also be demonstrated by involving everyone in problem-solving, not just experts. For example, machine operators can be taught to perform various levels of preventive maintenance on their equipment, providing them an opportunity for personal growth and development while freeing up other technicians to work on more urgent and technically complex issues.

When growing and developing people, it's important to keep responsibility for problem-solving and improvement with those doing the work as a way to engage and empower the workforce to take ownership of their activities and results. However, the workforce must understand and honor their threshold of knowledge by knowing when and how to escalate an issue for extra-ordinary attention. This must be complemented with ongoing recognition and reward as to demonstrate leadership's commitment to the workforce for whom they are responsible. As has often been said: *Treat people the way you want to be treated. Talk to people the way you want to be talked to. Respect is earned, not given.*

Go and See

Go and see is a mindset. It's about visiting the source of an issue or problem with an open mind to seek reliable data and factual information for understanding and decision-making. It may involve observing the process, talking with operators, taking measurements or documenting facts. Observation may involve simply standing and watching operators continuously perform their routines or reviewing the cyclical flow of material through a workstation for 30, 45 or 60 minutes in order to capture valuable insights unlikely to be recognized during brief visits, reviews or discussions at the workplace. When you "go and see" people, don't just see people as they are, see their potential; talk to them, ask questions, understand their perspective and show your respect for their contribution to the enterprise. Go and see is about comprehending a situation, establishing relationships and building trust.

Before leaving this chapter, I would like to share some thoughts on how lean thinking may reflect differently from a more traditional view of efficiency improvement. Keep in mind, this list is not exhaustive but is intended to start or evolve your thinking about a lean mindset and how an individual or organization's focus may gradually shift over time.

SIDEBAR: TRADITIONAL THINKING/LEAN THINKING

- Push system/Pull system
- Focus on results/Focus on process and results
- Address many issues/Address strategic issues
- Firefighting to solve problems/Process controls to prevent problems
- Specialists work on problems/Everyone works on improvements
- Resources fixing problems/Resources prevent problems
- Complex processes/Simple and visual processes
- Manage by meetings/Manage by go and see
- Batch production/Continuous flow production (small batches)
- Long lead times/Shorter lead times
- Process optimization/Value stream optimization
- Technical expert/Technical resource
- Low cost units/Low cost system production
- Full capacity production/Demand capacity production
- Restricted production/Flexible production
- High inventories/Low inventories
- Dedicated operators/Flexible, cross-trained operators

Key Points

- Go and find problems, don't wait for them to disrupt the process.
- Good companies solve problems; great companies fix the processes that created the problems.
- Tools help address the how, not the why.
- If you want the facts, go and see!
- Go and see; do not trust systems.
- Eliminating obstacles will improve the flow of ideas, information, decisions, materials and products.
- Improvement is the result of experimentation, observation, continuous learning and application.
- Leaders must ensure continuous improvement is part of everyone's standard work.
- Every leader should dedicate time to demonstrating and reinforcing the importance of continuous improvement.
- Question assumptions to achieve a deep understanding. Assumptions guide and constrain the way people solve problems.

- Challenges people to fully explore all improvement opportunities.
- All organizational levels should engage in coaching; coaching is important to develop the desired behavior/culture for operational excellence.
- Do not reward firefighting, reward problem prevention and continuous improvement.
- Use lean tools in meaningful ways to eliminate problems, waste and obstacles preventing a smooth, steady process flow.
- Tools are not a concept for achieving operational excellence.
- The mindset of continuous improvement is never being satisfied; always striving to make things better. There is always a better way.
- Lean is learned by doing.
- Motivate members by providing value and meaning to their jobs.
- Toyota believes work = problem-solving. Every production line should have skilled problem-solvers.

References

1. Lean Enterprise Institute. https://www.lean.org/.
2. James P. Womack and Daniel T. Jones. 1996. *Lean Thinking*. New York: Simon & Schuster.
3. Steven Spear and Kent Bowen. 1999. Decoding the DNA of the Toyota Production System. *Harvard Business Review*. https://hbr.org/1999/09/decoding-the-dna-of-the-toyota-production-system.
4. J.K. Liker. 2004. *The Toyota Way: 14 Management Principles from the World's Greatest Manufacturer*. New York: McGraw-Hill.

Chapter 7

Lean Preparation

> The rules, not the tools, drive the decisions and direction of the organization. A rule used by Toyota (The Toyota Way) include the notion that all work shall be highly specified as to content, sequence, timing and outcome (e.g. standardized work) and taking a scientific approach to problem-solving.
>
> **The Shingo Institute**

Introduction

The lean initiative takes a considerable degree of thought and engagement in order to change the mindset and behaviors of those who are willing to make the journey. Toyota's journey over the past several decades focused on two primary concepts, Just-In-Time (JIT) and Jidoka, both of which required a cultural shift in thinking about how inventory is managed and problems are solved in order to deliver the right products, at the right time, in the required quantities and with minimal resources. In essence, they needed to reduce production output variation relative to customer demand while decreasing inventory in support of a JIT material delivery system.

Lean Process Design and Development

A lean mindset actually starts at the point of product and process design, which has many dimensions and characteristics for consideration including manufacturing line layout and equipment flexibility as well as scalability.

Traditional companies design manufacturing equipment based on peak capacity and a buffer relative to forecast. This typically results in increased equipment cost and complexity driven by more functionality and automation. Unfortunately, complexity often has a negative impact on equipment flexibility and reliability, making it difficult to modify equipment to compensate for dynamic market conditions. A more progressive or "leaner" approach would be incremental investment in equipment to obtain an early payback by focusing on purchasing simple, modular equipment designs with basic functions that can be customized internally, as needed. This helps increase organizational flexibility and capability in response to changing customer requirements. See examples of modular equipment design concepts (basic and variable) in Figure 7.1.

Line design must be optimized based on available funds, costs, needed flexibility and physical workplace constraints. Strive to create an integrated process (U-Cell) where continuous flow between all equipment stations is possible (Figure 7.2). Avoid isolated process steps since they require buffers at input and output points, increasing throughput time. Factors that will influence the level of cell equipment integration include pieces of equipment, number of process steps, number of operators, machines capability and production volume. Designs should work to optimize each factor relative to overall system performance.

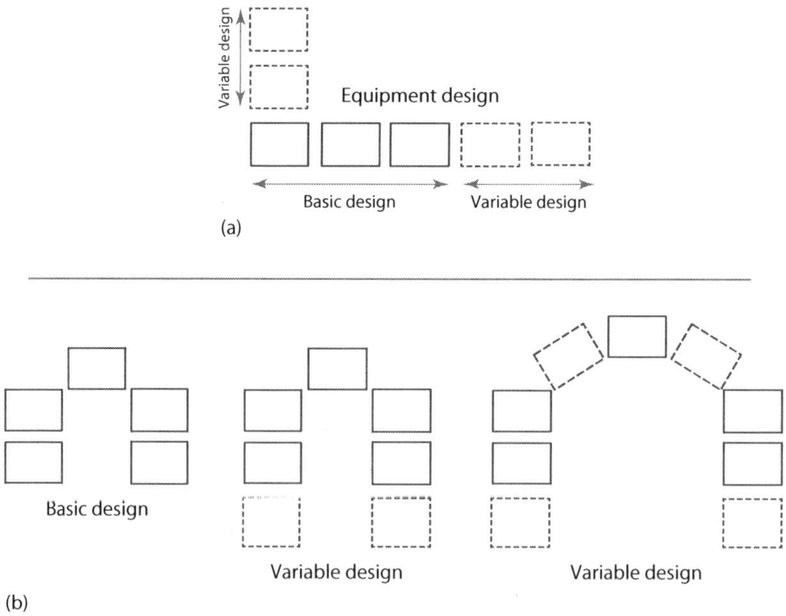

Figure 7.1 (a) Equipment design. (b) Line design.

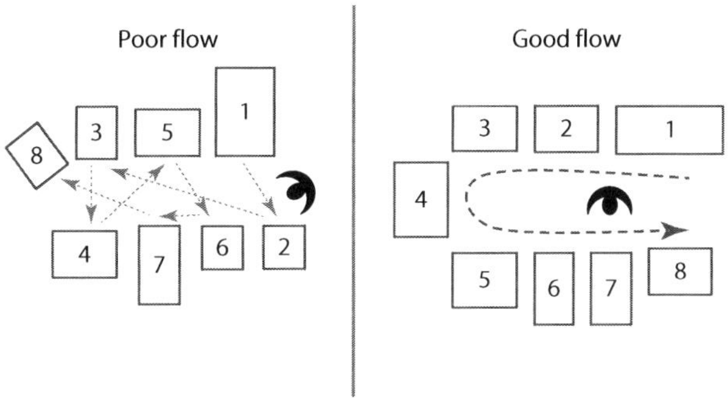

Figure 7.2 Examples of line flows.

Production lines should be flexible in response to variations in customer takt time. This can be achieved through operator balancing (relative to volume) and scalable line configurations (e.g. ease of adding and removing equipment). Avoid conveyors since they often negatively impact scalability. An example of excessive and good use of conveyors can be found in Figure 7.3a and b.

If possible, manual workplaces should be consolidated in one area to reduce the waste of walking and transport. This may help facilitate operator balancing. See Figure 7.4 for examples of line space layout.

If different size equipment, machines and storage racks are to be integrated into a U-Cell design, consider placing the longest objects at the front to minimize wasted space. See Figure 7.5 for an example.

In addition, minimize space between machines to avoid the placement of inappropriate objects for storage and to prevent the accumulation of dust and debris for cleaning (Figure 7.6).

Maintain consistent work height and depth; avoid part rotation. This will minimize motion, reduce the risk of handling damage and improve ergonomics (Figure 7.7).

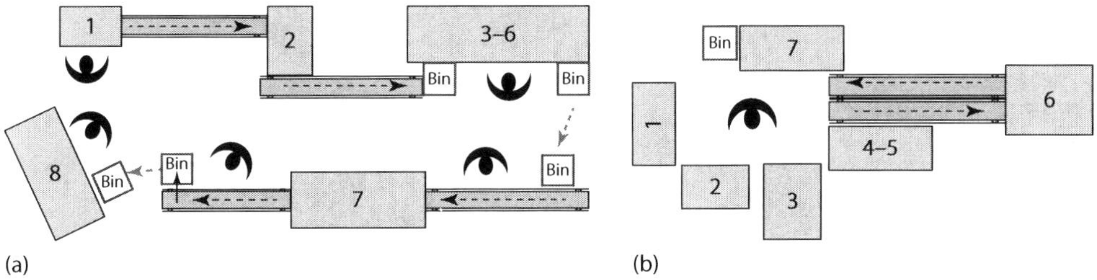

Figure 7.3 Examples of conveyor practices. (a) Excessive use of conveyors. (b) Good use of conveyors.

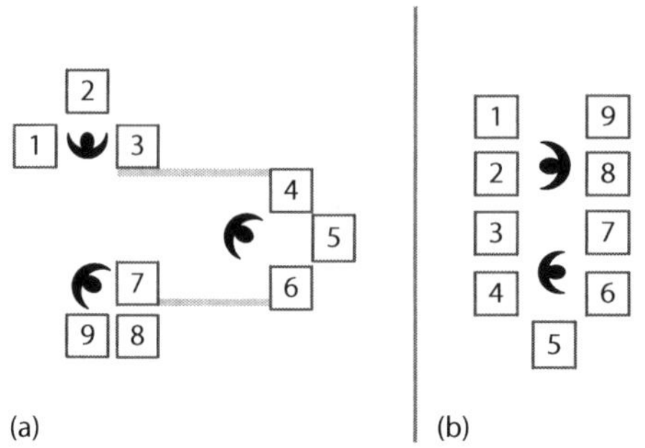

Figure 7.4 Examples of space layout. (a) Poor space layout. (b) Good space layout.

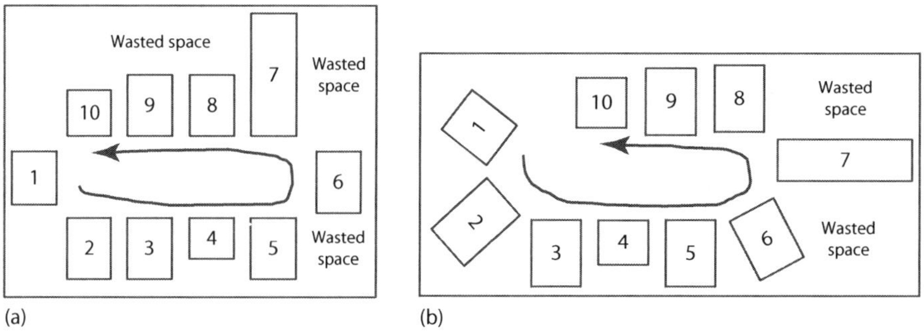

Figure 7.5 Examples of space utilization. (a) Poor utilization of space. (b) Better utilization of space.

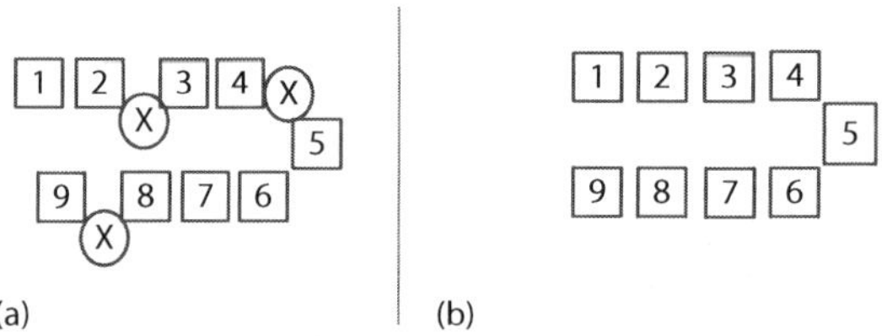

Figure 7.6 Examples of machine spacing. (a) Space between machines (poor practice). (b) No significant space between machines (good practice).

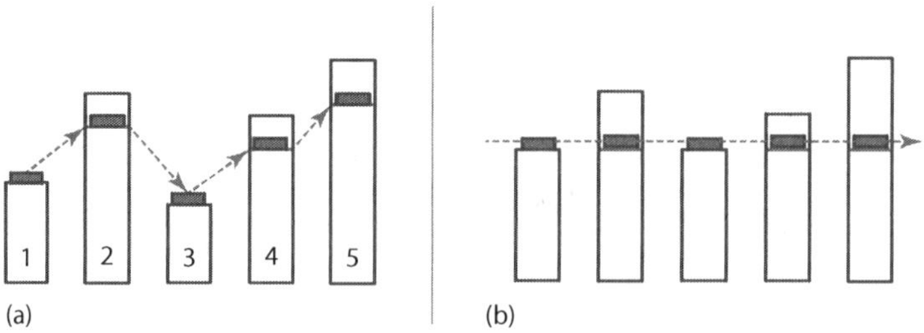

Figure 7.7 Work height considerations. (a) Inconsistent work heights (poor practice). (b) Consistent work heights (good practice).

Install flexible units to supply compressed air, vacuum and electricity for easy layout adjustments. Workstation characteristics reflective of the lean process design include:

- U-shaped workstations
- Workstations on wheels
- Easy part loading and unloading
- Automatic start after production loading
- Automatic part ejection after processing
- Bad parts automatically blocked from further processing
- Mistake proofing at the point of design
- Access to production line equipment from the front or back (vs. sides)
- Use of simple mechanisms for machine construction including gears, cranks, cams and levers or gravity principles

Just-In-Time

A JIT system will produce and ship parts upon customer request. This means that upstream processes will deliver the appropriate quantity of material when required by downstream operations. This type of response necessitates the right balance of man, machine, methods and materials to produce the right product, at the right time, in the amount needed with minimal resources and waste. This also means production systems will require people, equipment and material to be available, on demand, while upstream supply is prepared to compensate for downstream fluctuations in product volume and mix. Ideally, a production system capable of supporting this type of situation will retain only a minimal amount of inventory to regulate for expected variation.

A significant reduction in raw material, work in process (WIP) and finished goods is not an unrealistic task. However, to do so, one must take intentional steps to incrementally reduce inventory while rapidly responding to hidden problems as they are revealed. This is the essence of a JIT mentality, by continually decreasing the quantity of raw material, in-process and finished goods supply, you expose problems otherwise hidden by overproduction, requiring the organization to take action in order to eliminate waste that litters the road to improved efficiency.

A quick response to emerging problems and exposed abnormalities will require early warning systems (visual controls) that must be continuously monitored (via work routines) and responded to (through deviation management) when trigged. To prepare an organization for this type of scenario, a handful of experts will not be sufficient to prioritize and address the multitude of concerns that will present themselves, requiring immediate attention. The engagement of an entire organization in the monitoring and control of process anomalies and deviations will require everyone to become problem-solvers working to eliminate waste, without which the weight of unresolved issues and roadblocks to flow will quickly erode the enthusiasm of people and stifle the momentum of a lean journey.

The Achilles' heel of a JIT operation is the inability of many organizations to initiate a timely response to significant process deviations preventing disruptions in flow. Supporting practices such as Jidoka, pull systems and production leveling helps realize a stable and predictable output with an increase in inventory turnover. JIT must become a core competence of an organization interested in maintaining a lean management system, leading to the production of smaller part quantities, shorter lead times and increased operational flexibility.

Manufacturing often involves a complex system of interactions among individuals, functions and departments to create a workable flow of information and material door-to-door through a facility. For JIT to work, it will not only be important to understand these interactions, but also to manage them in an intentional and meaningful way to avoid confusion, frustration and failure. A pull system, a key component of JIT, will be the next topic of discussion.

Pull (vs. Push) Systems

Pull systems are part of a JIT mentality, preventing excessive under or overproduction by regulating the flow of parts to those required by subsequent processes. Pull systems help minimize inventory levels, controlling the cost to produce and store excess material. Unfortunately, pull systems also face the challenge of responding to day-to-day shifts in customer demand. As stated by the Shingo Institute [1]: *Pull is the concept of matching the rate of production to the level of demand, the goal in any environment. Yet pull is not feasible or cost-effective without the flexibility and short lead times that result from flow.*

Pull systems are driven by customer requests while more traditional push systems are driven by a forecast (schedule). Forecasts tend to be inherently variable and often require high levels of inventory to compensate for their changing dynamics. More competitive companies use pull systems as a way to minimize inventory costs while rapidly responding to customer orders. This improves operational efficiency but it demands reliable equipment, a rapid response to problems and an ability to quickly change from one product type to another during the manufacturing process.

Pull systems are a practical method for controlling production between processes that cannot be connected via continuous flow. However, they have limitations when trying to manage custom parts with excessive part variations, parts with short shelf lives or costly yet infrequently used parts. In these situations, batch processing may be a more realistic option. In addition, pull is not feasible or cost-effective without the flexibility and shorter lead times that result from incremental improvements in flow over time.

There are two primary pull systems – replenishment and sequential pull – with a third one a hybrid of the two. A replenishment pull is a supermarket-based concept that involves the transfer of parts from a supplier or supermarket to the point of consumption. Parts are triggered for replenishment when they are taken "off the supermarket shelf" for use. The supermarket comes with the disadvantage that every part used in the downstream process must be available in the market.

A sequential pull is the transfer of a predetermined type and quantity of material, typically one unit. It can be used to compensate for the inability to keep all needed parts in the market, essentially serving as a make-to-order system of supply.

A hybrid pull system combines the supermarket and the sequence approach and tends to be practical when a small percentage of part numbers constitutes a majority of the daily production volume. A sequence pull can be established for low volume of infrequently requested parts such as special orders or service parts while the remainder is managed through a supermarket. A supermarket usually contains multiple units of the same part. An effective pull system is paced to takt time. It pulls product in small batches in an effort to level product mix and quantities in response to changing customer demands and is supported by a replenishment system driven by a signal kanban.

Takt Time

Takt time is the average time it takes to produce one unit over a given time period. It's based on the customer order, demand or take rate. For example, in one month, a production line must produce 2000 units of product X and 16,000 units of product Y. The normal operating schedule is two 8-hour shifts with a 10-minute break in the morning and afternoon and 20 minutes for lunch.

Let's assume a typical working period as one 8-hour shift. If the factory works 2 shifts per day, 5 days per week and 20 days per month, we can calculate takt time for a single shift as follows: 18,000 units per month/20 days/2 shifts = 450 units per shift.

The next step is to determine the available manufacturing time per shift (typically in seconds) to produce one unit. Since we defined a shift as 8 hours minus 40 minutes for breaks and lunch, the available time will be 480 minutes − 40 minutes = 440 minutes or 26,400 seconds (440 × 60 seconds). Thus, the customer demand rate or takt time for one shift is

$$\text{Time Available/Customer Requirement} = 26,400 \text{ seconds}/450 \text{ units} = 58.7 \text{ seconds}$$

This means that a unit must be produced every 58.7 seconds with the current manufacturing conditions to meet customer demand.

Takt time helps clarify the production quantities needed to drive more effective operations by allowing for more efficient scheduling of production equipment and labor, especially when load leveling is required to manage multiple models.

SIDEBAR: ORIGINS OF TAKT TIME

Source: *Mark Graban, Colin Ducharme and Todd Ruddick* "Takt Time" (pdf)

Takt time originated from the German word *Taktzeit,* meaning clock interval or beat of music. It was borrowed by the Japanese (most likely in the 1930s) and captured by the Japanese word *takutotaimu* (タクトタイム) meaning cycle time. It's now used extensively to describe the rate at which customers request parts, setting the pace for continuous production flow.

Kanban

Kanbans are visual signs or signals, such as a card or empty bins, used to trigger the withdrawal of parts from a market or storage area or to alert suppliers of the need to make more product. Pull systems require replenishing. Kanban is used to create a "pull" concept in production that allows the rate of production to align with the level of customer demand.

Kanban is like a gas gage in a car, when the gage indicates low fuel, it triggers the driver to get more gas. Kanban takes on a similar role in manufacturing processes by signaling a previous process or step that more parts are needed. This creates a "pulling" of parts through the system at a rate defined by the next step in the process.

Kanban helps to drive controlled inventories while regulating the availability of correct parts for production. It controls the flow of material (right parts, right amount, right time), minimizing inventory and overproduction in the workplace. However, a poorly established or managed kanban system can generate excessive WIP, causing a disruption in flow. An effective kanban is simple, highly visual and follows a standardized practice.

In knowledge work, where problems are more difficult to see, kanban boards are often used to visualize the flow of work or projects through a system. Visualizing workflows helps to reveal problems and understand capacity limits.

There are several types of kanban:

- *Production kanban*: A card or device that instructs a process to produce a specific quantity of product for consumption or replenishment.
- *Withdrawal kanban*: A card or device that instructs the material handler to acquire and transfer parts, typically from a supermarket to a consumption point.
- *Signal kanban*: A supplier notification to produce another batch of material when a trigger, lower limit or threshold is reached. Batch production is usually required to compensate for changeovers.

A signal kanban can be defined or represented by a production pattern, a batch board or a triangle. In the case of a production pattern, order quantity and part type are made in a fixed sequence over a given time period (e.g. shift or 24 hours). As an example, quantities of each part type, A, B and C, are specified by their kanban card and are made in the following sequence (pattern) every 24 hours: A BB CC, A BB CC, A BB CC and so on.

A batch board will contain a space for each kanban card in the system. As a supermarket runs out of a specific part, the kanban from the empty container is returned to the batch board as a trigger to produce the part and replenish the supermarket (Figure 7.8). This style of production establishes a fixed part quantity but varies the type of parts made next. A production sequence may look like BCAAC, CACBB, AACBB and so on. The batch board method provides a clear visual of material consumption and potential issues emerging at the central market.

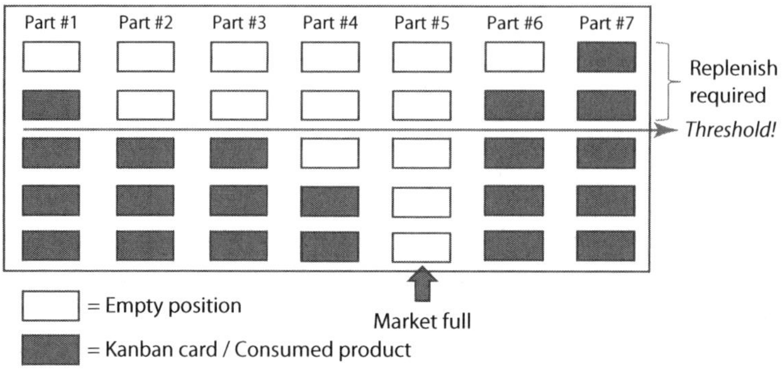

Figure 7.8 Batch (lot-making) board.

A triangle kanban (▼) is a request for a batch of material from an upstream supplier, which can vary in batch size and part type. The supplier must produce in batches due to significant variation in product demand, equipment constraints or to compensate for a required changeover.

The Lean Enterprise [2] highlights six rules for using kanban effectively:

- A production process requests material in the exact amount specified by the kanban.
- The supplier process produces material in the exact amount and sequence specified by the kanban.
- All parts and materials must have a kanban.
- No items are made or moved without a kanban.
- Defective parts and incorrect amounts are never delivered to the next process.
- Kanban quantities are slowly reduced to lower inventories while revealing problems for resolution.

Quick Changeover (Setup)

Creating flow allows an organization to produce and deliver products that consistently meet changing customer requirements. To achieve a high degree of flexibility without building excessive inventory, organizations need to respond quickly to dynamic requirements by managing the volume and mix of products produced in a specified time period. To do this, we must first consider factors influencing the time to change from one part type to another on the same production line. This is why rapid changeover is important.

Manufacturing changeover involves the process of converting a manufacturing line from producing one product to another, typically within a part family. Rapid changeover aids in reducing production lot size because it allows a manufacturing operation to quickly change from one product type to another to meet customer requests without keeping extra inventory on hand to compensate for long changeover delays. It can also allow a manufacturing operation to support a higher product mix when the facility must manage a diverse portfolio of low volume products.

To reduce changeover time, a creative approach may be required. Creativity and innovation often start by asking questions that challenge prevailing assumptions. People should articulate basic assumptions and their understanding of what can and cannot be changed. For example, can two bolts do the same job as four? Are all changeover steps needed? How much work can be done off-line?

When working to reduce line changeover time, consider some of the following points:

✓ *Hand tools*: Ensure required tools are available prior to setup.
✓ *Fasteners*: Ensure the availability of every fastener needed during setup.
✓ *Changeover parts*: Move all change parts to the machine while it's running. All parts should be cleaned when not in use, while the machine is producing. None of the items used for setup should require any maintenance during setup. Establish a procedure ensuring items needing maintenance are attended to before setup begins. Consider preparing parts in pre-assembled kits or carts to minimize setup time.
✓ *Lubricants, chemicals and solvents*: Ensure these items are easily accessible during setup.
✓ *Guard removal*: Guards requiring time-consuming removal of fasteners should be replaced with "one-quarter turn" fasteners.
✓ *Scrap and rework*: Ensure causes of scrap and rework are identified and eliminated during changeover.
✓ *Setup procedures*: Develop written setup procedures to standardize and streamline the process. Follow the standards; improve them over time.
✓ *Tooling*: Use standard tooling, wherever possible.

Production Leveling

Production facilities are often expected to manufacture multiple product model types with minimal fluctuation in the production schedule. Unfortunately, customer demands can create significant schedule disruptions.

By leveling production, resources can be managed to maintain an even production flow. Level production involves leveling or "averaging" of product model mix and volume over a specified time period. This is best facilitated by moving small lots of material through the value stream with an "ideal" batch size of one part produced at a time.

Leveling production by normalizing volumes and model mix will improve process stability, predictability, resource utilization and flow. However, model mix and volume leveling in production often require improvements in equipment reliability, reductions in changeover time and incremental reductions in batch size. If done correctly, these activities should lead to a decrease in process buffers needed to regulate flow.

As an example, a customer demand for 100 units per day can be produced as a lot size of 500 units per week or 100 units per day. When executing a lot size of 500 units per week, there will be more WIP (or inventory) to manage at the beginning of the week, gradually decreasing as inventory is consumed throughout the week. In contrast, if the facility can manage a lot size of 100 units per day, there will be a smaller, consistent number of units to manage each day. Clearly, it's easier to manage and maintain a consistent flow when a smaller more consistent lot size is possible. Figure 7.9 shows the difference between a 500 unit per week and a 100 unit per day lot size distribution.

Smaller lot sizes will reduce the investment required to maintain inventory, reduce the space required to store extra material, decrease handling and handling damage as well as reduce large batches of material hiding defective parts. When a single product type is required (no model variants), only product volume needs to be regulated. When variants are added to the product mix, leveling helps minimize the waste due to changeover inefficiencies.

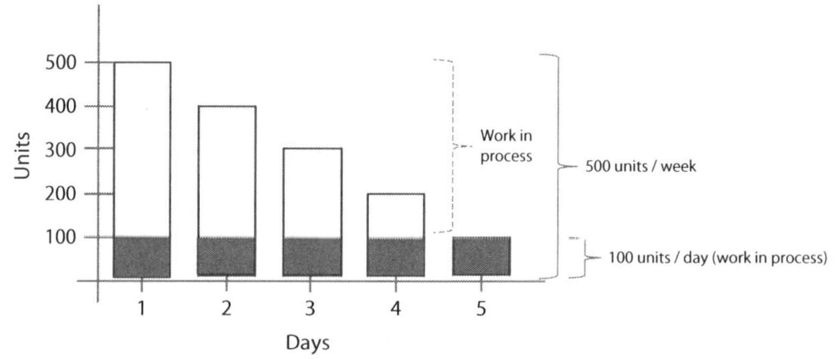

Figure 7.9 Lot size inventory management.

Note that production leveling will take time since many input factors influencing leveling such as equipment reliability, changeover time and batch size need to be improved independently. Through these collective enhancements, increasing flexibility in production leveling can be realized.

Workload Leveling

To achieve a more continuous flow, work processes need to be performed at a relatively even pace. Factors contributing to workload imbalance are uneven work tasks, overburdening people and running equipment beyond its design capability. Unevenness is the result of areas where work products do not flow well, where activities within systems are not in sync or systems are not aligned with each other. Unevenness is often due to irregular production schedules, fluctuating production volumes (due to internal problems or missing parts), incomplete work orders and defects, among many other process destabilizers.

Systems become overburdened when machines are pushed beyond their design capability causing excessive wear, unexpected breakdowns and defects. Likewise, when people are pushed to perform beyond expectation, they may become stressed, increasing the potential for errors and safety concerns. One way to reduce excessive burdening of people and machines is to identify and eliminate process constraints or bottlenecks. Bottleneck management is the basis for the theory of constraints made popular by Eliyahu M. Goldratt in his 1984 book titled *The Goal* [3]. Other ways to reduce unevenness and overburdening is through cross-training individuals, enhancing operational flexibility and increasing responsiveness to changing dynamics within the production environment.

Equipment Reliability

Unpredictable equipment availability forces many operations to increase inventories to buffer against unexpected downtime or to invest in additional equipment to compensate for the shortfalls of existing equipment. A key to improving equipment reliability is total productive maintenance (TPM). TPM is a production discipline intended to optimize equipment and machine performance throughout their expected life span using known maintenance techniques and total workforce engagement. If executed properly, TPM could increase operational efficiency with minimal investment in maintenance. A good TPM program leverages lessons learned, best practice and standard work procedures to improve maintenance efficiency and effectiveness.

Maintenance includes technical, administrative and process activities performed during an equipment or machine life cycle to generate output that is consistent with expected design quality and availability. TPM is intended to increase overall equipment effectiveness (OEE) by preventing equipment deterioration while facilitating an environment of ownership between operators and their machines.

OEE is composed of three components multiplied together to establish a value. They include performance, availability and quality or

$$\text{Performance} \times \text{Availability} \times \text{Quality} = \text{OEE}$$

Availability is the amount of time equipment is operational during the period of planned usage (e.g. uptime). Performance is the amount of production realized divided by planned production relative to established standards and available time. Quality is the percentage of product that meets specifications (e.g. no defects). Sometimes, this is referred to as "first run yield", "first pass yield" or simply "yield".

OEE can also be decomposed into six elements (or losses) as follows:

- **Performance** = Reduced equipment speed / Idling and minor stops
- **Availability** = Breakdowns / Product conversions or changeover
- **Quality** = Startup losses / Running defects and rework

Continuous improvement of OEE can be forged with self-directed teams using their problem-solving acumen to prioritize and eliminate the causes contributing to these six types of losses.

Equipment reliability can be improved at the point of design by implementing robust improvements based on historic failure modes. The availability of equipment can be increased by maintaining an inventory of spare parts that are difficult to obtain or are likely to be needed during unplanned breakdowns. In addition, TPM-certified operators in combination with fault tree analyses can serve as a first line of defense in reacting to problems before they become bigger issues. Finally, preventive maintenance activities should be standardized and scheduled to ensure work gets done in a timely manner, according to equipment manufacturer recommendations.

SIDEBAR: AUTONOMOUS MAINTENANCE

In the world of manufacturing, operators typically produce parts and rely on trained technicians to repair and maintain the equipment they use. Unfortunately, with increasing levels of automation and complexity, more maintenance personnel are required to support equipment needs. Thus, a logical approach is to have machine operators accept more responsibility for their work area by performing routine machine maintenance and learning to address minor equipment issues. This approach releases trained technicians to focus on critical issues aligned with their skill set. This concept of *autonomous maintenance* improves enterprise efficiency through increased utilization of both operators and technicians. It also allows more time for the maintenance group to perform equipment modifications suited to their expertise, improving equipment reliability while minimizing the life cycle cost of production equipment.

SIDEBAR: OPTIMIZING LINE DOWNTIME

Although unplanned downtime of a production line is not a desirable event, its impact on the organization can be minimized by preparing pre-established activities for manufacturing teams to engage in while waiting for the line to resume production. To optimize the unexpected availability of time, activities "packaged" in various time periods can be prepared for deployment when the opportunity arises. For example, basic TPM routines, operator training modules, 5S and Kaizen events can be carried out during down time, occupying people's time in a meaningful way while reducing the waste associated with waiting.

Supplier Impact

Before leaving the topic of JIT, it's important to remember that a chain is only as strong as its weakest link. This means that lean thinking and application must eventually make its way to key suppliers the enterprise depends on to provide quality components and materials on time and in the right quantity. Disturbances in flow can easily occur at the front end of operations when poor-quality material or short shipments arrive at the receiving dock. In the interest of productivity and improvement, take time to identify critical suppliers and develop a plan to bring them into the lean fold of activities, treating them as partners when preparing to move the value stream beyond the boundaries of your door-to-door lean efforts. Include key suppliers in lean training, invite them to view recent improvements in operational efficiency, offer to conduct a Jishuken workshop at their facility, invite them to participate in a Kaizen event and offer to perform a capacity analysis on one of their production lines feeding your value stream. At some point, you will reach your "span of control" limits, beyond which you will require the cooperation of certain suppliers to maintain continuity in flow while pursuing improvements. Proactively embrace the future by including critical suppliers in your strategic thinking and make supplier development a conscious part of your roadmap to operational excellence.

Jidoka

Jidoka, translates from Japanese into English as "automation with a human touch" or sometimes simply "autonomation". It involves a machine automatically stopping whenever an abnormality such as a quality issue or equipment problems is detected. It prevents defective products from being produced and promotes rapid problem-solving at the source by immediately stopping a workstation when an issue of concern first occurs. This leads to improvements in process quality and efficiency by facilitating quick root cause identification for defect elimination. Jidoka is a tool that is used to ensure a system is working properly and is a critical activity in the pursuit of continuous flow.

The concept of Jidoka, as developed by Toyota, involves separating man and machine by designing machines capable of detecting anomalies and automatically shutting down to prevent further defect generation. This idea of stopping a process upon immediate detection of a non-conformance helps to minimize waste while avoiding the potential escape of defects to downstream customers. In turn, this may help limit machine damage and reduce potential operator injury.

"Smart" machines that detect and notify the existence of abnormalities increase operational efficiency by eliminating the need for an operator to continually monitor the process, thereby freeing them up to work multiple machines or assist with other value-added activities. This also allows for operational flexibility in responding to changing customer demands. Jidoka helps build quality into the product.

The only way to immediately detect and prevent additional defects from occurring or moving to the next process operation is by building quality into each process step. This requires that areas where defects occur are held accountable for eliminating defects through root causes analysis to prevent reoccurrence. To work most effectively, associates must inspect the quality of work they produce as part of their standard work to ensure "built-in quality" is achieved and maintained. This may require the application of test equipment or visual inspection at key process points. The Jidoka concept aligns with eliminating off-line quality inspectors, removing a layer of process waste.

Operators are expected to ensure quality of their work at each process step to prevent passing defects to the next customer, downstream of their workstation. Implementing defect detection, such as Jidoka, should aid in maintaining quality at the source (Figure 7.10).

Jidoka is rooted in the idea that problems are solved where they occur by stopping and fixing problems when they occur. If an issue can't be resolved within the takt time of the line, a containment must be put in place for the line to continue operating and the problem escalated to the appropriate level and owner for timely resolution.

Andon

Andon is a system to notify the workforce of a quality or process problem. It uses signal lights to indicate which work area or station has a problem. The alert can be activated manually by a worker using a cord

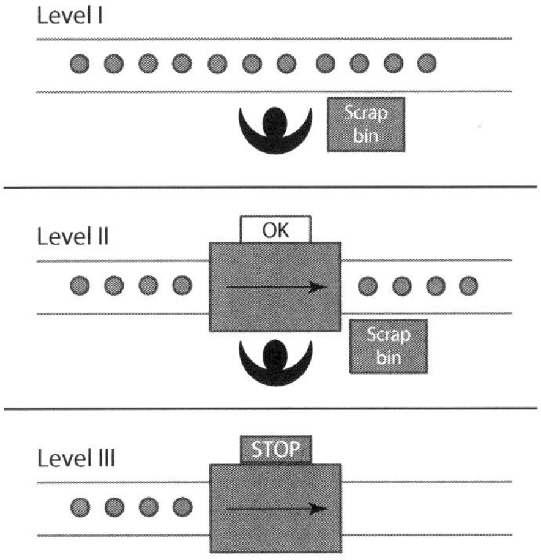

Figure 7.10 Jidoka evolution.

or button, or automatically by the affected equipment. The system sometimes stops production so issues can be corrected. Andon empowers workers to stop the line when a defect is detected to call for assistance. Defects can result from material shortages, operator error, equipment issues or safety concerns. Work is resumed when a solution is identified and implemented.

Andon can also be realized by a series of lights used to communicate equipment status. Lights can be integrated into machine design or retrofitted to existing equipment. Colored lights are typically in a top-down sequence of red, yellow and green. It's recommend light-emitting diode (LED) lighting be used for energy efficiency and installed directly onto the equipment to optimize flexibility.

A red light can indicate a stopped process resulting from an out-of-tolerance condition or detection of a defect by the equipment, signaling a need for action. A yellow light can indicate special attention is needed due to an anticipated problem such as material shortage or equipment breakdown. Green indicates a normal state of operation, where all is running well (see Figure 7.11).

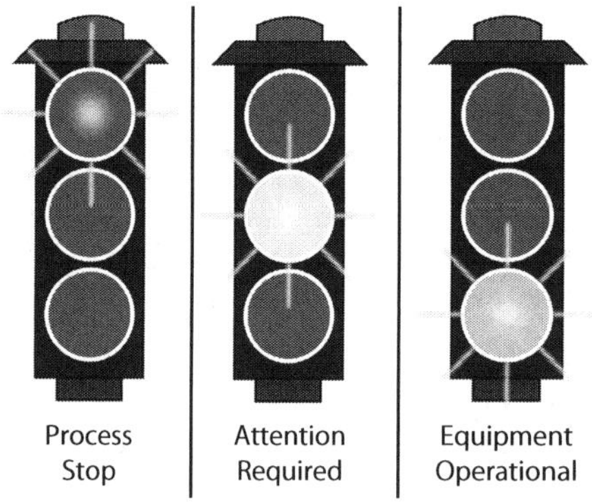

Figure 7.11 Andon Lighting System.

Error Proofing

To err is human, thus people will make mistakes. Sometimes, those mistakes end up as defects that escape a workstation or facility and reach the customer without detection. Many organizations initiate inspections or audits to minimize or prevent mistakes from escaping. However, it has been found that human inspections are only about 80% effective. At a 1% error rate, it would take five inspectors to maintain 6 sigma quality; therefore, mistake proofing is a logical approach to preventing errors!

Error proofing is a tool that can be implemented at the point of design or manufacture to prevent mistakes and consequently defects from occurring. The Japanese use the term "poka-yoke", which translates as "prevent inadvertent mistakes". Error proofing is applicable in all processes and should be kept simple and cheap since complicated mistake proofing tends to be less cost-effective. Consider integrating error proofing into a process to increase its likelihood of successful deployment. Use simple objects like fixtures, sensors and warning devices to prevent human error. When designing processes, consider incorporating features to prevent incorrect setup and part assembly. The optimization of facility attributes such as lighting, ventilation, temperature and seating will increase people's comfort while decreasing the likelihood of human error.

In an article on the topic of preventing human error released by Shane Bush from Battelle, Idaho National Laboratory [4], Bush indicated that 80% of occurrences are caused by human error; 70% of those occurrences are organizational-based errors while 30% are individual errors. The average human error rate is five errors per hour, indicating that errors can't be eliminated but can be reduced by mitigating or eliminating error precursors. Error precursors are existing conditions that increase the error rate. Typical error precursors cited by the article can be found in Figure 7.12.

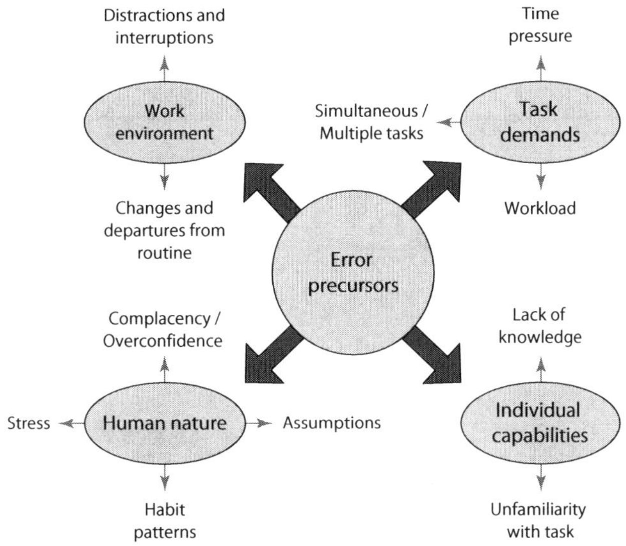

Figure 7.12 Error precursors.

Human error is a result, not a cause. To prevent mistakes, precursors that lead to errors must be understood and addressed. Errors can be classified and dealt with as follows:

- *Skill-based errors*: Are the result of a "slip, trip or lapse", an unintentional error. The best mitigation approach is to share lessons learned and address the error precursors that lead to the occurrence.
- *Rule-based errors*: A misinterpretation of rules or standards. Best mitigation approach is to understand why there was a misinterpretation of the rule and take action to prevent future misinterpretation.
- *Knowledge-based error*: Unfamiliarity with the task or a lack of knowledge. Best mitigation approach is training.

Rapid Problem-Solving

The objective of rapid problem-solving is to identify and implement a fast solution within an operator's cycle time, preventing additional defects from being produced and escaping to downstream customers. It may require a slow down or stopping of the production line until the issue is resolved or contained, allowing the process to continue without generating additional waste.

Rapid response requires availability of information, material and a support network to maintain a continuous workflow within planned cycle time parameters. Workers encountering a problem must have the knowledge and skills to address certain issues and know when to escalate concerns to the next level of operations or ownership. People are preconditioned to solve problems, thus management's job is to ensure deviations are easily observed and responded to in a timely manner.

Existing knowledge, information and experience can be used to facilitate rapid problem-solving, especially in highly repetitive process environments. In this situation, a decision tree can be used to exploit existing data and information to create an effective problem-solving tool for troubleshooting. This tool uses a series of questions leading an individual to a likely root cause and corrective action when a known, repetitive issue reoccurs. A decision tree is usually presented graphically to facilitate quick assessment and is updated whenever a new problem and corresponding root cause are identified. This allows the decision tree to remain relevant and effective. It's important to use data and information from known problem solutions to build and maintain the decision tree. Consider some of the following questions to shape the environment, culture and behavior required for rapid problem-solving:

- Is problem-solving a core competency of all employees?
- Is there a standard or procedure in place to support rapid problem-solving?
- Does the standard or procedure provide an adequate structure for efficient and permanent solutions to problems?
- Does the team understand the importance of using reliable data and factual information as part of their problem-solving activities?
- Do organizational discipline and accountability exist to execute and follow the problem-solving process as intended?
- Do training and coaching exist to develop and enhance employee skills needed to solve problems quickly and efficiently?
- Are tools and techniques available to make problem-solving easier?
- Do coaches or mentors exist to provide support when needed for problem-solving?

Buffer Management

A manufacturing buffer is a defined amount of material such as raw material, in-process or finished goods that enables a line or value stream to maintain a smooth, steady flow through the process. It's commonly used in manufacturing to compensate for product line fluctuations due to periodic work such as material replenishment, end-of-line packing activities, handling of scrap units and other intermittent events. Buffer management is the act of maintaining sufficient amounts of material at critical operations to stabilize material flow against known and unknown fluctuations in process. Buffering minimizes the impact of process variation on flow.

Three types of "buffers" are typically used in manufacturing to manage process variation, including inventory, capability and time. Although the ideal state is zero inventory, we use inventory in different ways to manage process dynamics. For example, it can be used to counteract the impact of unexpected equipment downtime, buffer against excessive scrap, compensate for time-consuming setups and hedge against excessive volatility in product mix and volume.

In-process material buffers can be used as a tool in response to process fluctuations by providing material, when needed, to keep the process flowing smoothly. Proper inventory levels can stabilize a process, allowing time to identify and address process disruptors like machine changeovers, uneven distribution of work and unexpectedly high defect rates. For example, faster changeovers require less inventory to "buffer" the time equipment sits idle while being converted from one product variant to another. Once a process is stable, one can slowly lower the inventory (buffer) level as a way to stress the system and reveal the next biggest problem or obstacle for elimination as you move closer to an ideal state of continuous flow where no inventory is required.

In situations where customer demand is volatile and the ability to respond is unmanageable, buffer stock can help handle swings in demand. When working to minimize inventory, it's good practice to separate inventory used as safety stock (process instability) from inventory used to buffer fluctuations in customer demand since the causes driving these two conditions typically vary as does the ownership for improvement. A planned buffer to combat common cause variation is ok and is typically part of an initial line design. However, buffers must have clear objectives so that they can be monitored, controlled and reduced over time.

Safety stock is a form of material buffer used to hedge against special cause variation and can buy a team response time to material shortages negatively impacting process stability and customer deliveries. As defect trends decrease concurrently with root cause problem-solving, safety stock can be reduced correspondingly.

A capacity buffer can take the form of overtime or employment of extra lines to meet capacity demands, both of which typically lead to increased cost. If inventory or capacity buffers are not options, time can be used as a buffer. When demand exceeds capacity, expedited freight may provide a "buffer of time" needed to make and deliver product according to customer schedules. On the other hand, if inherently unreliable suppliers deliver materials late, delaying shipments to customers will avoid the expense of building extra inventory or increasing internal capacity but at the likely expense of considerable customer dissatisfaction. In the end, it's best to determine how and where you would like to manage your buffers and work to eliminate buffers by reducing or eliminating the variation for which buffers were put in place to regulate.

Key Points

- It's not about the tools you use but the rules you follow that drive your continuous improvement progress. Tools help facilitate the next level of achievement.
- Jidoka is a technique for highlighting and addressing deviations from expectation.
- Jidoka may provide the ability to detect abnormalities in, machines and methods, preventing defects from reaching the customer.
- Lean tools can highlight production problems; however, it takes ownership, ability and empowerment to respond in a meaningful and productive way.
- Buffers regulate the impact of process variation. Planned buffers are an acceptable part of initial line design with the expectation that variation will be reduced over time.
- Production capacity is consumed by changeovers whenever a setup is required to switch from one part model to another.
- If you can't stop the line, contain the defect!
- Mindless application of tools is simply waste.
- Gravity feed, auto-reject and mistake proofing (poka-yoke) are recommended practices for making work easier and cheaper to perform.

References

1. Shingo Institute, Utah State University. 2016. *The Shingo Model for Operational Excellence.* Logan, UT: Jon M. Huntsman, School of Business.
2. The Lean Enterprise: Kanban. https://www.lean.org/lexicon/kanban.
3. Eliyahu M. Goldratt and Jeff Cox.1984. *The Goal: A Process of Ongoing Improvement.* Great Barrington, MA: North River Press.
4. Shane Bush – Battelle, Idaho National Laboratory, 03-May-2005. LANL Mirror. int.lanl.gov/safety/online.

Chapter 8

Waste Elimination

> Dr. Shingo's advice: "Improvement means the elimination of waste, and the most essential precondition for improvement is the proper pursuit of goals. We must not be mistaken, first of all, about what improvement means. The four goals of improvement must be to make things easier, better, faster and cheaper".
>
> **The Shingo Model for Operational Excellence**

What Is Waste?

Waste can be defined in many ways. It can be considered anything that does not add value to products or services destined for the customer. The Shingo Institute™ [1] defines waste as *anything that slows or interrupts the continuous flow of value to customers.* The former president of Toyota, Fujio Cho, defined waste as *Anything other than the minimum amount of equipment, space and worker's time, which are absolutely essential to add value to the product.* What does this mean? It means waste is in everything we do, from product design and development, to assembly, delivery and servicing. We need to recognize it and take meaningful, intentional actions to eliminate it from the products and services we provide to our customers to create more value for all stakeholders.

Waste exists in many forms including inventory, procedures, equipment, material flow and product design. The causes of waste are equally as diverse as waste itself and can be observed in systems we define, actions we take, ways we manage and how we communicate with others. Waste can impact organizations from many different aspects as reflected in a stressed-out workforce, unpredictable equipment failures or an inability to deliver products on time.

Toyota has identified seven major types of non-value-added (NVA) waste in manufacturing processes. These wastes are not unique to manufacturing and can be found in most industries. Figure 8.1 highlights and provides a brief description of each waste category as defined by Toyota.

In addition to the seven types of process waste defined by Toyota, waste has also been highlighted in other areas including information, human resources and the physical environment in which work is performed. Information waste primarily deals with incorrect, missing or collection of unused data. Human resource waste comprises the underutilization of human potential or talent, and physical environment waste encompasses the safety and movement of people or objects. Figure 8.2 displays examples of waste in other operational areas.

Value versus Non-Value Added

Waste is considered NVA work. If waste is considered NVA work, what constitutes value or value-added work? Changes to a product, service or process for which the customer is willing to pay as well as any task or activity

Defects	Production or correction of defective parts or service mistakes (e.g. scrap, repair, rework, replacements, repeats, etc.)
Excess motion	Wasted motion of employees while performing work (e.g. looking for, reaching for, or stacking ... parts, papers, tools, etc.)
Waiting	Workers waiting for the next process step, tool, components, equipment, order ... (e.g. processing delays, equipment downtime, bottlenecks, slow communication, etc.).
Unnecessary transport	Moving work in process (WIP) long distances; creating inefficient transport; moving materials, parts or finished goods into or out of storage ...
Excess inventory	Excess material, WIP or finished goods; causing longer lead times, obsolescence, damaged /spoiled goods, transportation / storage costs, delays, etc.
Overproduction	Producing goods / services for which no orders exist (e.g. production ahead of demand, services without request)
Overprocessing	Performing unneeded steps to process parts / provide services (e.g. inefficient processing due to poor planning or scheduling)

Figure 8.1 Seven wastes identified by Toyota. (From Jeffrey Liker, *The Toyota Way*, 2004).

Information Waste

- Redundancy (data inputs and outputs)
- Incompatible information
- Manual accuracy verification
- Unused data
- Re-entering data
- Converting formats
- Unavailable or missing data
- Unclear or incorrect data

Physical Environment Waste

- Safety-related waste
- Waste in the movement of people or objects

Employees who are not sufficiently protected from harm ...

- Poor ventilation
- Insufficient lighting
- Excessive noise
- Unstable office furniture
- Trip hazards
- Ergonomic issues

Underutilized Human Potential

- Unclear roles
- Lack of training
- Work interruptions
- Multi-tasking
- Underutilization of talent
- Hierarchy and structure
- Recruitment errors
- Lack of strategic focus

Figure 8.2 Waste other than process.

deemed "valuable" by the customer is considered value. An *activity* is "value added" when it meets the following criteria:

- The customer is willing to pay for it!
- It positively changes (transforms) the form, fit or function of a product or service.
- It's done right the first time.

What constitutes NVA work? Internal activities of no value to the external customer or work not completed correctly the first time (e.g. rework) is considered non-value added. Inspections, reviews, approvals and scrap are often categorized as NVA work. Essentially, value is based on who you define as the customer and how the customer perceives value.

Waste Categories

Waste, according to Toyota, can be viewed from three different perspectives: unnecessary activities (*muda*), overburdened resources (*muri*) and variation or unevenness (*mura*). The challenge becomes identifying and eliminating these groups of waste from the process as part of an organization's continuous improvement efforts.

There is a clear cause-and-effect relationship between all three types of waste. For example, variation in production scheduling can lead to overproduction whereas an uneven workload can result in under or overutilization of people and equipment at various times during process execution. Consequently, these events can result in equipment downtime, process errors and increased inventories among other forms of waste. When put into perspective, variation and unbalanced workloads can cause any of the seven process wastes. Process waste results in loss of money, time and resources spent with little or no increase in customer value.

Waste impacts just-in-time (JIT) material management by creating "obstacles" or bumps, disrupting the efficient flow of material and information through a value stream on its way to the customer; the consequence of which is loss of valuable material, energy and time. Thus, variation reduction and balancing workloads can go a long way to help reduce waste while facilitating a smooth and continuous flow of material and information to internal and external customers. Let's explore the different types of process waste in more detail, starting with defects.

Defects

Defects are the result of non-conformance to requirements or a deviation from procedures (standards). They can result in product rework, scrap or repeat service to correct an unresolved problem. Defects often increase costs due to extra time, material and handling required to manage rework and scrap. Increased production and inventory often reflect defect levels to buffer against late and missed shipments caused by material shortages. Defects also threaten customer satisfaction since poor internal quality decreases efficiency while increasing the risk of delayed shipments or defective product escaping the facility and impacting customers.

Overproduction

Overproduction is typically from producing more or faster (sooner) than customer demand resulting in excess inventory that requires handling and storage. Unfortunately, overproduction ties up capital in raw materials, work in process (WIP) and finished goods stock, while reducing available cash for other more immediate and fluid expenses. Overproduction is a common response to unreliable material suppliers, unstable processes, inaccurate schedules, large batch sizes and unbalanced workstations. It is used to hedge against unexpected issues such as equipment breakdowns, spikes in defect levels and operator absenteeism as well as to compensate for unpredictable customer orders. Overproduction is one of the major contributors to waste since it's the cause of waste in other process areas.

Waiting

Workers waiting for the next process step, tool, material, part or simply having no work because of equipment downtime, capacity bottlenecks, changeovers or material and information delays, are some of the issues contributing to waste found in NVA time. As we all know, time is money and a finite resource. Thus, preventive maintenance, accelerating changeover rates and ensuring reliable information and material flow are practical ways to reduce waiting and corresponding cycle time losses.

Conveyance/Transport

Excess or inefficient movement of information, materials and assemblies is commonly attributed to poor facility design and layout. The objective is to move these items quickly and efficiently from one work area or cell operation to another without interrupting flow. This can be facilitated by positioning workplaces closer to each other in addition to moving incoming and shipping areas closer to production lines. This will minimize conveyance of material, assemblies and information between process operations, increasing efficiency. A spaghetti diagram can reveal the movement of material, information and people throughout a work area and is a good tool for identifying waste in transport.

Over-Processing

In the realm of project management, over-processing is termed "gold plating". Doing more than what's necessary to meet customer requirements is considered waste since it does not add any additional value to the product or service. Teams must work closely with customers to identify and clearly define, in measurable terms, product and service requirements so workers understand what constitutes value-adding work in order to deliver to the expectations of customers without deviation or delay. Doing more than what's required often costs time and money while generating more waste.

Excess Inventory

A certain level of inventory will always be required to compensate for variation that inherently exists in all processes. However, the need for inventory should be minimized through a reduction in variation to complement a smoother, more continuous flow of work through the value stream. Balancing workflow between workstations which exhibit uneven task assignments will help minimize WIP needed to buffer against existing or unexpected process variation.

Excess inventory can be costly due to the need to purchase extra material and parts, handling and storage of more finished goods, conveyance of additional containers and increased urgency for storage space to house excess. It also hides problems such as production imbalances, late supplier deliveries, defects and equipment downtime. It is best to identify and address problems early to avoid being caught off guard when unexpected defects encountered during low inventory levels negatively impact customer deliveries.

Motion

Organizations should strive to remove unnecessary human motion from workplaces since it consumes valuable energy and time. The waste generated by people motion is often difficult to identify since it's frequently overlooked by those executing process routines every day. When items are placed close to each other, within an arm's reach or without having to take unnecessary steps to perform a task, wasted motion is minimized. In addition to reducing waste, the elimination of excess turning, lifting, bending and reaching will reduce the potential for absenteeism caused by repetitive motion injuries and fatigue.

Overburden (Muri)

Waste includes overloading people, equipment or systems beyond their expected or design capacity. Stressing people and equipment past peak performance can cause injury and unexpected breakdowns, respectively, leading to disappointing outcomes. Common practices that lead to overburdening process operations include changing employee expectations, urgent drop-in orders, poor schedule management, overtime, significant fluctuations in customer orders and lack of performing or skipping preventive maintenance routines.

Unevenness (Mura)

Variation in system performance and fluctuation in product mix and volume can significantly stress people and the systems within which they work, leading to process defects and delays. Unevenness can cause absenteeism due to fatigue or illness as well as equipment failure when demand exceeds design capability. The impact of unevenness on flow is evident when people and machines are prevented from operating at design capacity. Underutilization of people and equipment can also cause long periods of idle time, contributing to process waste.

Unevenness in production volumes is primarily the result of two situations: variation in production scheduling and uneven workloads (or work pace) in production. Batch processing is one cause for unevenness. Large batch production is intended to maximize the utilization of resources while minimizing production costs. Unfortunately, this can negatively impact an operation's flexibility in response to rapidly changing customer demands. A logical response to limited flexibility in meeting customer demands is to build buffers in order to compensate for an inability to quickly set up equipment in reaction to continuously changing production requirements. This response can actually exacerbate fluctuations in production volume due to the "bullwhip"* effect that results in waste from producing and storing inventory and potential losses driven by excess and obsolescence. Although often overlooked by management teams, significant variations in production can be a major contributor to unevenness and operational waste.

The ultimate goal of continuous improvement is to reduce costs through waste elimination. There are many ways to tackle waste reduction from the point of design through to customer product or service delivery. Waste exists from product inception, through design and development, in production and to the point of customer delivery. Waste can be found in methods we choose, systems we use, procedures we define and training we provide. Waste is everywhere. It needs to be understood and eliminated, one opportunity, one obstacle, one step at a time.

---

* The *bullwhip effect* refers to increasing swings in inventory in response to shifts in customer demand as you move further up the supply chain.

Waste Metrics

If there is a desire to actively manage a lean transformation and periodically assess overall lean maturity of an organization, quantifiable metrics can be identified and used to track waste elimination and process flow improvements. In a paper titled "Waste Measurement Techniques for Lean Companies", written by Maciej Pienkowski, the topic of quantified waste metrics is discussed [2]. In this publication, the idea of using waste metrics to manage a company's efforts to eliminate waste and implement a JIT system was explored. The author suggested dividing waste into two categories: passive and active waste. Passive waste refers to losses (inefficiencies) in performing work according to an organization's operational standards and procedures while active waste is the result of inefficiencies resulting from actual work accomplished.

Several other common metrics are used to assess a system's efficiency including lead time, cycle time and throughput. They are clearly linked and are briefly described as follows:

Lead Time and Cycle Time

Lead time and cycle time are two key metrics for assessing workflow through a process. They can help identify trends and serve as a baseline for measuring the effectiveness of process changes. Although similar, lead time measures the total process time for work completion (e.g. from order entry to delivery), whereas cycle time measures the total time to process a unit within a defined work sequence (cycle) including delay time. For example, cycle time can be the time it takes for one operator to complete their work routine within the total assembly or processing time of a part. Cycle time is commonly used to understand the current flow of work through a specific part of a system or workplace and is a good metric to assess the impact of changes over a given time period. Whether you are interested in workflow within a work area or throughout the value stream, cycle time and lead time (Figure 8.3) can be used as measures, respectively.

A quick assessment of lead time can be calculated using a variation on Little's law.

$$\text{Lead Time} = \text{Amount of Work in Process}\ (\text{WIP}) / \text{Average Completion Rate}$$

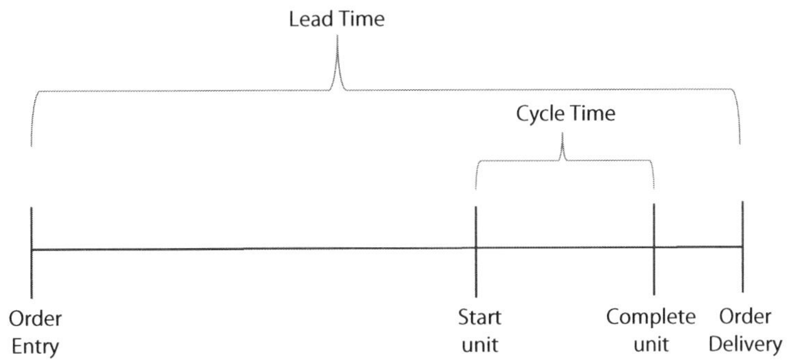

Lead time - measures total process time for work completion (e.g. from order entry to delivery),

Cycle time - measures total unit process time within a defined work sequence (cycle) including delay time.

Figure 8.3 Visual Comparing Lead Time to Cycle Time.

This reflects how changes in system input can influence output. The formula indicates an increase in WIP will lead to an increase in lead time, if throughput remains the same. Thus, reducing WIP will decrease lead time. Correspondingly, an increase in throughput (completion) rate can improve lead time. However, this is often a more challenging task. If interested, a lead time map can visualize the distribution of WIP throughout the production area by documenting units among and between process operations. The time needed between each process step can then be taken to determine current buffers to optimize flow.

Throughput

Throughput, sometimes called process output or yield, is the number of units produced per specified time period. Throughput is a good indicator of process stability since a consistent output (e.g. mean and standard deviation) over time is reflective of a stable process. Changes in throughput directly correlate to changes in process inputs and activities. If process improvements are made to reduce cycle time, changes in output quantity can be measured to assess the significance and degree of difference using statistical comparative analysis.

Inconsistent output can result from many factors including deviations from process standards, material shortages, excessive scrap or unexpected machine downtime. Negative trends or inconsistencies in throughput need to be investigated for root cause and addressed with appropriate countermeasures. Once a stable output is demonstrated, forecasting future results is expected to be more reliable and actionable.

Waste Identification and Visualization

Waste elimination is a process and, as with any good process, there is a logical series of steps to methodically identify, prioritize and eliminate waste. The prioritization of waste for elimination is often required due to limited time and resources. A clear set of criteria for waste prioritization and elimination will set the stage for an effective culture of incremental process improvement. The follow methods have been found helpful in identifying, visualizing and prioritizing waste for removal.

Process Mapping (Value Analysis)

One way to calibrate people on the amount of waste that exists in their work activities is to perform a value analysis using process mapping. This activity is likely to reveal significant waste within a process and helps visualize as well as prioritize waste for elimination.

Value analysis is a proven method for improving process efficiency and cycle time in manufacturing and transactional operations. Value analysis starts with a process map detailing the current process by visualizing its activities and corresponding sequence in a flow chart. When preparing an existing process flow, all activities must be considered, including wait time, operator movement, machine time and part handling. The process map should account for all activities and the time it takes to perform the entire process from beginning to end. The map must reflect the "as is" or "current state", revealing a process in all its glory and ills, including workarounds, periodic work and reoccurring abnormalities. This map becomes a baseline, reference or starting point for improvement. Swim lanes can be added as a visual element to reveal various departments or functions that perform tasks within a cross-functional workflow. See Figure 8.4 for an example of a loan approval process map. Figure 8.5 is an example of a basic process map with swim lanes.

When preparing a process map, don't hesitate to use Post-it™ notes when identifying activities within a process flow. They can easily be moved to

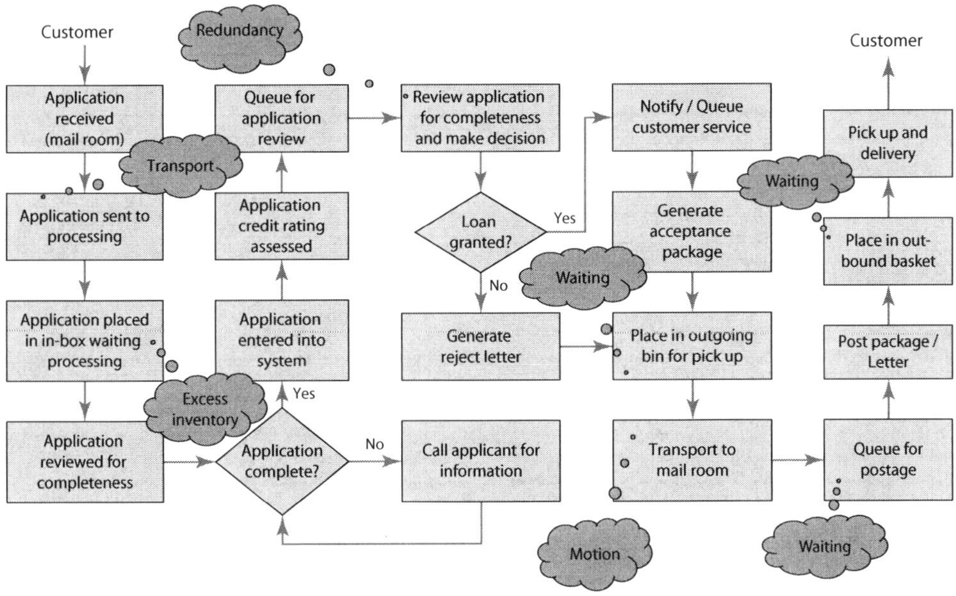

Figure 8.4 A loan approval process map.

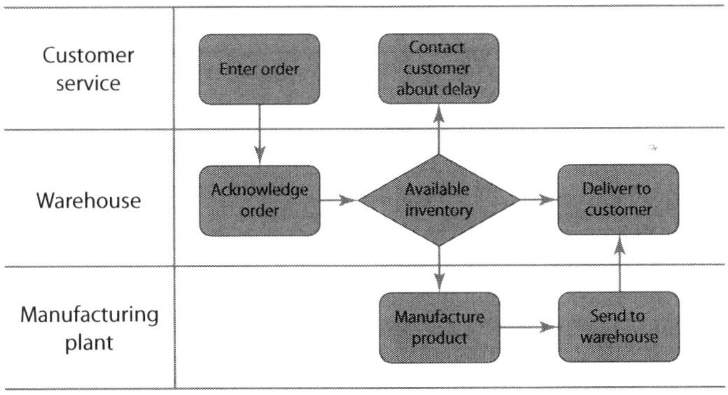

Figure 8.5 A basic process map with swim lanes.

establish the process sequence and placed in such a way as to represent an activity (square) or decision point (diamond). In addition, don't forget to record the time it takes for each activity since this information will be required to determine time spent on value and non-value activities. It's recommended several cycle times be taken to determine an average time for each activity. Multiple cycle data will provide a more representative view of process fluctuation and may reveal anomalies encountered during process execution.

At the point where your process flow has been visually mapped, sufficient detail should be captured to highlight obvious process problems or areas for improvement. The following process areas and characteristics may help identify waste reduction or elimination opportunities:

- *Disconnects*: Poorly managed handoff points or inadequate communication of requirements by suppliers and/or customers.
- *Bottlenecks*: Points in the process where volume exceeds capacity, slowing process flow. Could impact timeliness and adequacy of delivery quantities.
- *Redundancies*: Repeat of process activities or existence of parallel activities; duplication of activities (e.g. entering the same data in two different places).
- *Rework loops*: Process points where significant work volume is fixed, corrected or repaired.
- *Decisions/inspection points*: Process points where choices, evaluations, checks or appraisals could create potential delays.
- *Entry and exit points*: Points where significant manufacturing line/cell cycle time fluctuations occur due to material handling issues.

Once key steps have been identified in their actual sequence and an estimate or average time has been recorded for all process activities, including waste, a simple matrix can be used to classify these steps or activities identified into value-added, non-value-added and business requirements. Business requirements, sometime call "incidental" activities, are required to facilitate value-added activities or to ensure compliance with requirements, but don't add value themselves. Each group can be summed to reveal the total time spent within each classification with priority given to NVA activities. See Figure 8.6 for an example.

It's often said the majority of time performing a process is spent on NVA activities. It's clear from Figure 8.6 the majority of time in this process is spent on NVA activities. Value-added time is typically a small percentage of the total lead time. It's not unusual for a service process to run about 5% value-added time. A lean process is characterized by value-added time typically greater than 20% of its total cycle time.

Traditional cost-saving efforts focused on improving value-added activities; however, with this providing so little opportunity for improvement, attention turned toward reducing NVA activities where the most significant opportunities for cycle time reduction exist. We consider NVA activities within a process because the majority of process activities contain NVA work, which consumes unnecessary time and money.

Value analysis: Process mapping

Value analysis - Loan approval process				
Process activity	Time (min)	Value added	Non-Value added	Business reqs.
Application received (mail room)	5	x		
Application sent to processing	10		x	
Application placed in in-box waiting processing	90		x	
Application reviewed for completeness	30	x		
Call applicant for information	15			x
Application entered into system	20		x	
Application credit rating assessed	10			x
Queue for application review	60		x	
Review application for completeness and make decision	40		x	
Notify / Queue customer service	10		x	
Generate acceptance package	45	x		
Place in outgoing bin for pick up	120		x	
Transport to mail room	10		x	
Queue for postage	70		x	
Post package / Letter	5			x
Place in out-bound basket	90		x	
Pick up and delivery	10			x
Customer received package / Letter	5	x		
Total:	645	13%	81%	6%

Business requirement - work that keeps the process running but has no value to customer

Figure 8.6 Classification of process activities.

It's important to include a business as well as customer view of process value and non-value activities so as not to overlook key requirements to function as a business (e.g. filing tax returns, administering benefits and paying employees). Although these may not be value-added activities from a customer perspective, they are essential for maintaining a compliant and properly functioning business operation.

Once process activities have been broken down into their value components, it's time to focus on opportunities for waste elimination. This is where a Pareto chart is helpful. NVA activities are considered "waste" and are often presented in a Pareto chart as a way to visually identify and prioritize the greatest sources of process waste. Figure 8.7 provides an example of the visual impact a Pareto chart can offer when looking to identify the most significant source of waste for elimination.

The goal of waste elimination is to reduce process cycle time. In doing so, there are some clear avenues to pursue, including

- ✓ *Simplification*: Simplify confusing, ambiguous and complex procedures and processes.
- ✓ *Complexity*: Implement mistake proofing; make it easier to do something right than to do it wrong.
- ✓ *Parallel processing*: Perform tasks in parallel to reduce cycle time while being mindful of communication and coordination issues.

✓ *Alternative paths*: Identify process paths designed to optimize workflow based on key product or service characteristics.
✓ *Bottlenecks*: Analyze and rework process steps that limit workflow, causing slowdowns or backups.

Process Cycle Efficiency

Figure 8.8 is an example of a loan approval process presented as a time value map. A simple calculation of process cycle efficiency (PCE) reveals considerable waste, the bulk of which is waiting.

PCE is a key metric for establishing a baseline for waste in service processes. It's used to determine the percent of value-added activities versus waste relative to a process's total cycle time. PCE can be calculated for the foregoing example as follows:

$$\text{Process Cycle Efficiency} = \frac{\text{Value-added Time}}{\text{Total Lead Time}} = \frac{90}{1350} \times 100 = 7\%$$

A PCE of 7% indicates value-added time is small relative to the overall lead time and presents significant opportunity for improvement. Another way to more directly determine value added versus total lead time is to place a physical tag on an item and have people handling it record the time they spent processing it. For example, place a routing tag on a

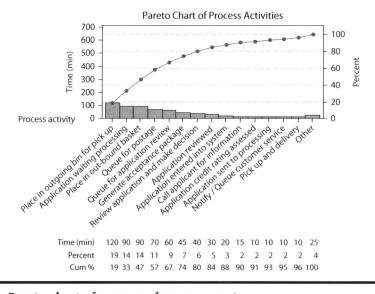

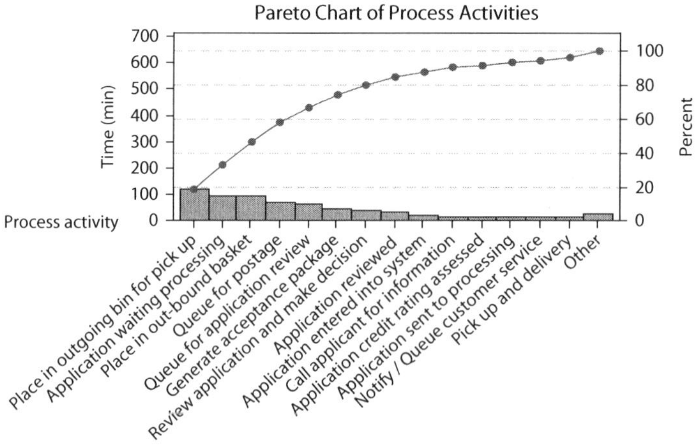

Time (min)	120	90	90	70	60	45	40	30	20	15	10	10	10	10	25
Percent	19	14	14	11	9	7	6	5	3	2	2	2	2	2	4
Cum %	19	33	47	57	67	74	80	84	88	90	91	93	95	96	100

Figure 8.7 Pareto chart of sources of process waste.

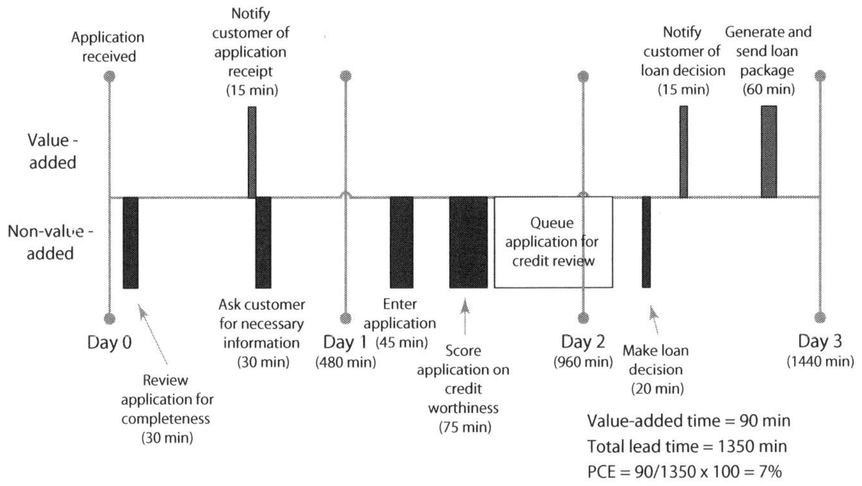

Figure 8.8 Time value map: Loan approval process.

personal computer purchase order and have each operator time stamp the tag during its assembly process. An alternative to this method is to physically time an item moving through the process with a stopwatch. In general, lead time is quick and easy to calculate and can uncover WIP problems.

PCE can also be displayed visually in the form of a time value map. In Figure 8.9, a relative display of value added and NVA time for each process step has been visualized over the manufacturing life cycle of a part, from raw material to completion. The shading of value-added activities can quickly reveal areas where waste elimination opportunities exist.

Yamazumi Chart

Yamazumi is a Japanese word that means to *stack up*. Yamazumi charts visually present the work tasks (content) of an operator and reveals this information to facilitate work balancing by isolating and targeting NVA work

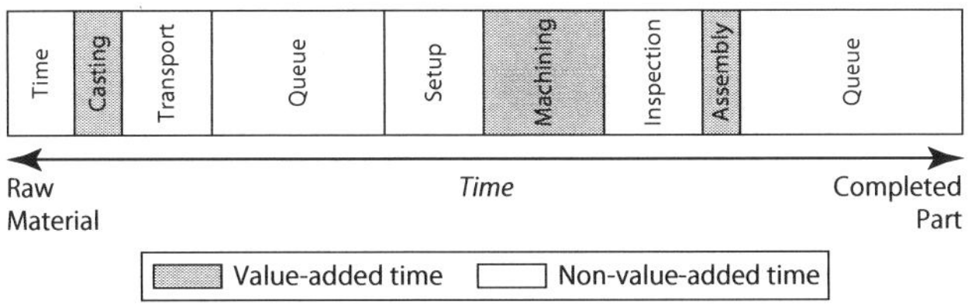

Figure 8.9 Example of a time value map.

for removal. Yamazumi charts can visually display the workload of multiple operators in a work area relative to takt time and planned cycle time. See Figure 8.10 for an example of a Yamazumi chart.

Yamazumi charts display all operator work activities within a repetitive work cycle as value added, NVA or incidental work (e.g. business requirement). Each category is displayed as a different color on the chart. NVA work is displayed in red so it can be quickly identified and targeted for reduction or elimination.

Operator activities can be captured by video recording 10–15 repetitive work cycles and performing a detailed analysis of the recording (using software). The recording is then separated into individual "work elements" from which the time to perform each work element is documented. Work element descriptions and corresponding times are then recorded in the standardized work recording chart. Figure 8.11 is a "snapshot" of a repetitive routine broken down into its job elements. The results of three cycles are displayed in Figure 8.11.

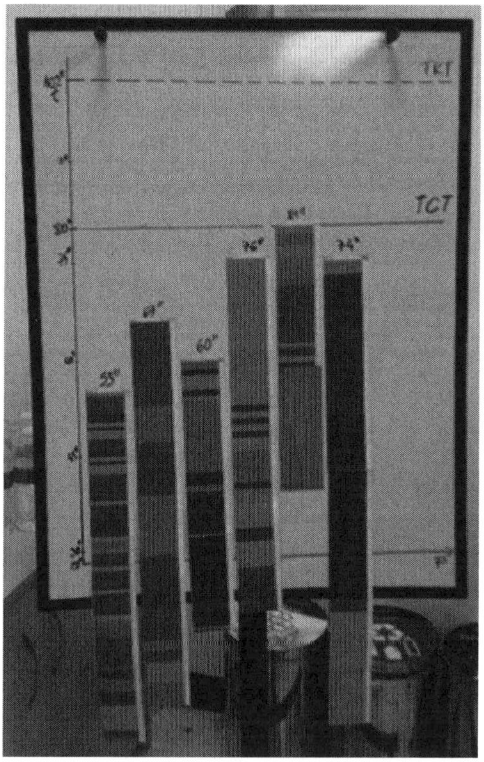

Figure 8.10 Yamazumi chart example.

Work elements Video time Cycles Observer

	Clear sheet:		1	2	3	4	5	6	7	8	9	10	Min	Max	Fluctuation
		Filename	00385.min		C2	C3									
		Start time	0:01:54		06:30.0	09:14.0									
A	Place housing on fixture		01:54.8		06:31.0	09:15.6									
			00:01.0		00:01.0	00:01.6									
B	Press housing to frame		01:55.1		06:32.0	09:15.9									
			00:00.3		00:01.0	00:00.3									
C	Move hand to dial plate		01:55.6		06:32.0	09:16.4									
			00:00.5		00:00.0	00:00.4									
D	Pick up dial plate		01:56.8		06:33.0	09:17.4									
			00:01.2		00:01.0	00:01.1									
E	Bring dial plate to light		01:57.3		06:34.0	09:17.9									
			00:00.5		00:01.0	00:00.5									
F	Inspect dial plate		01:58.9		06:35.3	09:19.6									
			00:01.6		00:01.3	00:01.6									
G	Bring dial plate down		02:00.2		06:36.0	09:20.1									
			00:01.3		00:00.7	00:00.6									

Figure 8.11 Standardized work job element breakdown template.

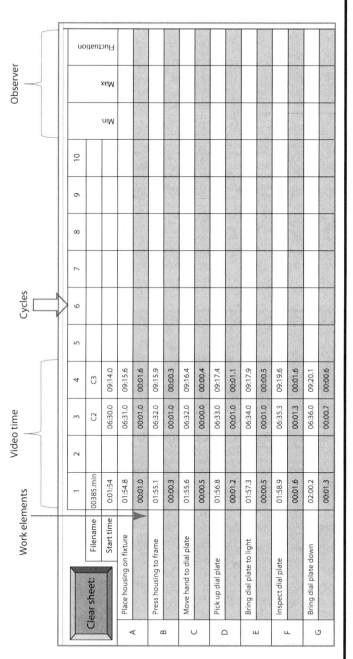

Work elements and their corresponding times can be transferred to an Excel macro that requires an individual to manually assign each work element a color based on its classification as value added (green), non-value added (red) and incidental. Incidental can be further divided into avoidable (orange) and necessary (yellow). Typical examples of each category can be found in Figure 8.12.

Upon executing an Excel macro, the work activities expand in size relative to their average completion times (e.g. 1 second=1 mm). At this point, the results of each operator's work elements are printed in color, cut to size and posted relative to takt time. The total average time to complete each operator's routine can be written above each column on the display along with the operator designation. You now have a relative visualization of the manual work content for each operator separated into value added, NVA and incidental work. This information can be used to balance the operator's work content by focusing on the most significant waste reduction opportunities to improve cycle time. Figure 8.13 is an example of work elements and timing.

	Incidental		
Non-value added	Avoidable	Necessary	Value added
Walking	Hand movement (with or w/o part)	Pick up part	Apply protective coating
Inspection	Press button to start inspection	Press button to start assembly machine	Connect cable
Move part	Reposition part	Place part in fixture	Manual assembly
Repair part	Air blow part	Pick up screw	Adhere label
Waiting for part	Press button to start inspection	Automatic scanning	Tighten screws
Manual scanning	Remove bag	Remove part from assembly machine	Package for shipment

Figure 8.12 Work element classification and examples.

Job elements	Time (sec)
Pick up part with right hand	0.8
Move part to fixture	1.7
Open fixture with left hand	1.2
Place part in fixture	0.9
Close fixture with left hand	1.1
Grab screwdriver	0.6
Tighten screw	1.7
Return screwdriver	0.8
Open fixture with left hand	1.3
Pick up module with right hand	0.7

Figure 8.13 Example of work elements and timing.

During video analysis, you may observe periodic work, fluctuations and anomalies occurring. This is not unusual since we live and work in a dynamic environment. Periodic work is interval work performed while executing work routines (e.g. material reloading, handling failed units, assembling packing boxes). Fluctuation is variation *within* standard work while anomalies are deviations *from* standard work. If interested, this additional information can be visualized with existing data by adding periodic work, fluctuation and abnormality times to the top of each operator's Yamazumi chart stack-up to get a complete picture of the total time spent within each category as demonstrated in Figure 8.14.

A Yamazumi chart is an excellent tool to visually display the current allocation of process time and activities within a work area while revealing opportunities for improvement. However, it's just a tool to expose opportunities to balance work and reduce NVA activities. It's up to the team to take action to realize these improvements.

SIDEBAR: STEPS TO BUILDING A YAMAZUMI CHART

1. Confirm standard work is being performed on the line; if not, do so.
2. Video record 10–15 cycles of each operator's work cycle.
3. Perform a workplace video analysis, separating each operator's actions and motions into *work elements* and their corresponding times using a data recording chart (see Appendix VI).
4. Cut and paste the information into an Excel spreadsheet, classify each work element as value added, NVA and incidental, using a color scheme and adjust each column width according to the time required to complete each work element (1 second = 1 mm). Create a stack-up column chart for each operator (a macro can be created to perform chart sizing relative to time).
5. If interested in visualizing the total process time, include times for periodic work, fluctuations and anomalies in the operator stack-up charts (see Figure 8.13).
6. Color print, cut, post and label each operator stack-up, placing one next to the other, referencing takt time.
7. Decide on the actions required to reduce waste and rebalance workload, if required.

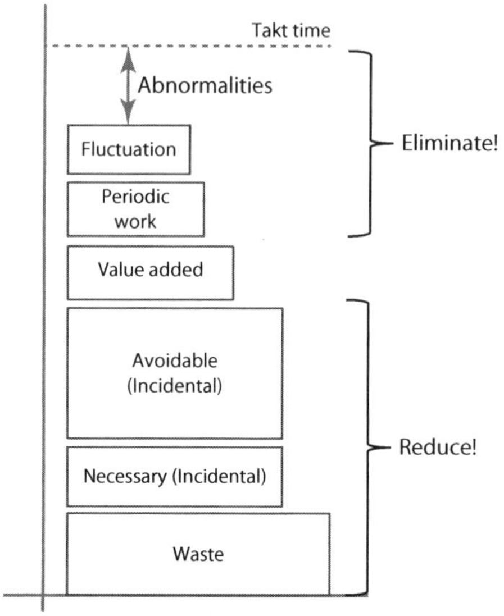

Figure 8.14 Work element descriptions and contributing variation.

Waste Elimination

There is no silver bullet for removing waste from a process. The best and most efficient way is to take a structured, disciplined approach, experimenting when necessary and evaluating results for lessons learned. The plan-do-check-act (PDCA) method can provide a systematic way to identify and methodically eliminate obstacles blocking the path to easier, faster, cheaper and safer process execution. Waste elimination starts with a "plan", establishing the objectives of what needs to be accomplished, understanding the current state and defining the activities necessary to improve performance. "Do" involves executing the plan while observing and collecting data for charting and analysis in the "check" phase where progress to plan is monitored and assessed. The final step of "act" requires knowledge acquired and lessons learned through observation and study be considered in planning the next PDCA cycle as a way to control and drive process enhancements.

Deming's PDCA cycle can be applied iteratively. The key is to understand the sources of waste, similar to defect root cause analysis. Once a source of waste is determined, various countermeasures can be considered and the best solution selected for permanent waste removal. It's not unusual for multiple PDCA cycles to be performed before an obstacle, blocking the path to improvement, is removed. The goal in eliminating obstacles is to continuously set new standards (baselines) for process performance while maintaining those standards through process control (Figure 8.15).

The PDCA cycle can help promote a more scientific thinking mindset to problem-solving and continuous improvement. Scientific thinking requires a hypothesis be formulated as to an expected outcome upon executing a "plan". During the "check" phase, the actual result is compared to the expected result, leading to one of two outcomes: confirmation of what you expected, or acquisition of new knowledge when the question "why was the result different from expectation" is answered.

Waste elimination differs from problem-solving in that it's a more proactive approach to process improvement. Whereas problem-solving is typically a reaction to process deviations such as a defect, the elimination of waste requires process analysis to highlight waste opportunities for preemptive removal. This is why Jishuken workshops can be an effective method for pinpointing sources of waste for eradication.

Jishuken Workshop

How often have you been in a situation where you were told to improve a system, process or perhaps even the performance of a production line with little or no direction other than a cost saving or performance improvement target? Unless you do this type of activity every day, it may be a difficult assignment as you start to ponder, where do I start? What should I focus on? What's my first step? A Jishuken workshop can be an effective method for

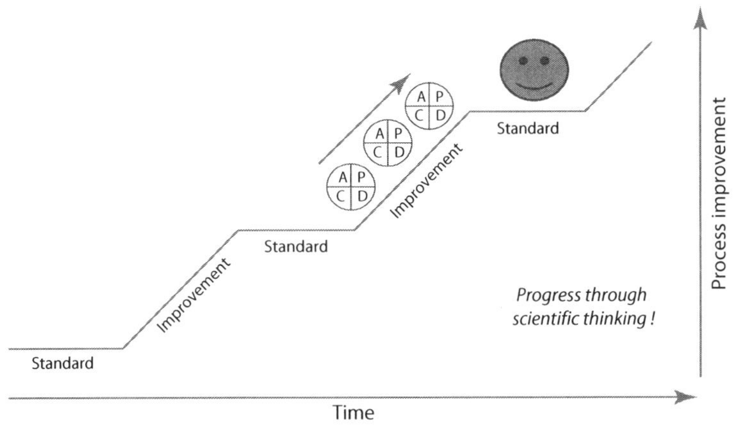

Figure 8.15 Iterative role of PDCA in process improvement.

understanding the current state of production performance and provide clear direction for action when tasked with driving efficiency improvements.

Jishuken workshops are management-driven, target-focused, process improvement initiatives designed to understand, identify and prioritize opportunities for improvement. When combined with Kaizen events, an effective cycle of activities can be set in motion, inching an organization closer to a state of operational excellence. One of the main tenets behind Jishuken is the practice of going to the shop floor to see, study and learn, often through trial and error. The objective is to act on information and data acquired through observation, once a proposed change has been evaluated (often real time, on-site) and confirmed effective.

A Jishuken workshop can be targeted to a specific production line to understand the interaction of man and machine in order to highlight NVA work for elimination. The improvement goals can be general or targeted. For example, there may be a specific need to reduce the number of line operators, increase line capacity, decrease changeover time or improve workload balance. These would justify a targeted approach for a Jishuken workshop. On the other hand, a team may be interested in conducting a workshop to look for new efficiency improvements as a way to promote a continuous improvement mindset. Unfortunately, many of these workshops are at the request of management to recover losses in production capability or capacity already impacting operations. The objectives of a Jishuken workshop can involve:

- Guiding people to find opportunities for improvement on a production line.
- Helping people determine what to do, when to do it, where to do it and why they are doing it.
- Coaching people to continuously ask "why" until they understand the fundamental elements behind a problem, issue or improvement opportunity before taking action.
- Ensuring every action taken has reasonable justification.
- Making improvement with no additional investment ($0 spend).
- Completing many of the improvements identified during the workshop, only leaving longer-term actions for team follow-up.

Jishuken workshops are considered self-study activities where all participants, at various levels of the organization, spend time observing the production line for improvement opportunities relative to safety, quality productivity and cost. Consideration is given to making work safer, faster, easier and cheaper to perform. Jishuken workshops may result in Kaizen events, led by individuals who are assigned ownership of an improvement opportunity not completed during the time period allotted for the workshop.

Jishuken workshops are a multifaceted series of activities required to comprehend the process under study. The following are typical steps taken to deepen one's understanding of the process being studied and prepare participants to determine the best course of action for achieving targeted workshop objectives. These steps are presented in a logical but not mandatory sequence of activities and may be tailored to the expected outcomes of the workshop.

- *Improvement area*: Select an area or production line for improvement.
- *Improvement opportunity*: Define your target objective. Typical focus for improvement includes capability, capacity, first pass yield (FPY), standard work, *overall equipment effectiveness* (OEE), operator reduction, workspace reduction, buffer management, material flow, etc.
- *Current performance*: Review historical data and production line key process indicators (KPIs; e.g. output, FPY, OEE, scrap) over the past several weeks. Review trends and determine your current state or level of performance.
- *Team selection*: Choose a team consisting of management and supporting operations based on the targeted improvement (e.g. engineering, quality, production, maintenance). Quality may need to review and approve changes during the event. Line leaders and supervisor should be included in the workshop since they will be the conduit for communicating and implementing changes with the local workforce and, in many cases, assigned ownership of improvements. Management must be aware of the time and effort required to analyze the line and identify targeted improvements for evaluation and implementation.
- *Production rate (takt time)*: Establish the expected flow rate of product through the line. This sets the tempo or pace upon which line output performance can be measured. It you want to deliver the right quantity of products on time to the customer, you will need to understand the required rate of production and continuously monitor your output performance to this expected value. The topic of calculating takt time is covered elsewhere in this text.
- *Planned cycle time*: Determine the planned cycle time; the intended rate of production. This rate of flow is typically faster than takt time to

compensate for losses due to issues such as scrap, equipment downtime and changeovers. If you are unable to determine potential losses, a rule of thumb is to multiply takt time by 0.85 as a basis for planned cycle time.

- *Standard work*: Confirm the existence of and verify operators are following their standard work by assigning team members to observe and assess compliance. Establishing and following standard work is essential for process stability and a reference point for process improvement. Any improvements made in the absence of standard work may not be sustainable.
- *Go, see and observe*: Once standard work has been confirmed, it's time to video record each operator's interaction with their work environment and determine the cycle times of each machine in the process. While recording operators performing their standard work, note any fluctuations (variations) with their standard work routines and anomalies (e.g. deviations) from standard work within each process cycle being recorded. Also note any periodic work occurring during multiple work cycles. As indicated previously, periodic work is work performed by line operators outside the cyclic routines performed on every part. They are typically process-related work activities supporting product handling and material flow. Examples of periodic work include product packaging, defective unit isolation and material replenishment. Strive for 10 "clean" or "abnormality free" repeatable cycles (e.g. no periodic work, machine breakdowns or other disturbances) in preparation for work element analysis. Software can be used to assist with data collection.
- *Block diagram/line layout* (optional): Go to the workplace again (if necessary) to take dimensional measurements of equipment and worker travel distances while operators are on their break. Draw a layout of the process equipment and operator movements. Use the video for detail. Highlight safety and quality topics of concern. This helps visualize and quantify the current layout of operations.
- *Process analysis*: Cycle times of each operator can be plotted on a graph relative to takt time and planned cycle time. In doing so, you will be able to visually assess the stability of a process and its current ability to produce to takt time and planned cycle time. In addition, you can look for several repeatable points at the low end of the cycle time chart and draw a straight line through them. This becomes your lowest repeatable value and an indication of your current process capability under stable conditions (Figure 8.16).

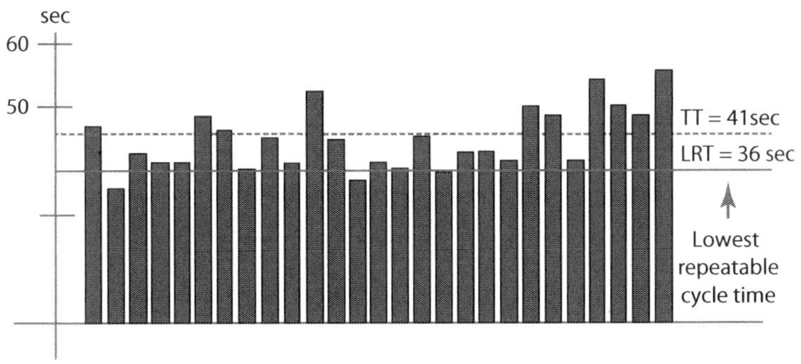

Figure 8.16 Example of operator cycle time chart.

- *Machine cycle time diagram*: A machine cycle time diagram captures the cycle time of machines and combines them into one document for review. It can be used to understand the impact of machine time on process cycle time performance and highlight potential bottlenecks in process flow (Figure 8.17).
- *Production (zone) capability chart*: A plot combining average operator cycle times, machine times, quality losses, periodic work and planned stops can provide an overall picture of production capability relative to planned cycle time and takt time. It shows the production capacity of each process, which can be divided into zones for further analysis. Separating the production line into "zones" allows a predetermined amount of WIP to act as a buffer between zones, minimizing the impact of planned stops on material flow.

  The production capability (zone) chart reveals process challenges to takt time and planned cycle time while visualizing bottlenecks. Focused attention can be paid to the interconnection of zones and how they interact to impact flow for the entire process (Figure 8.18).

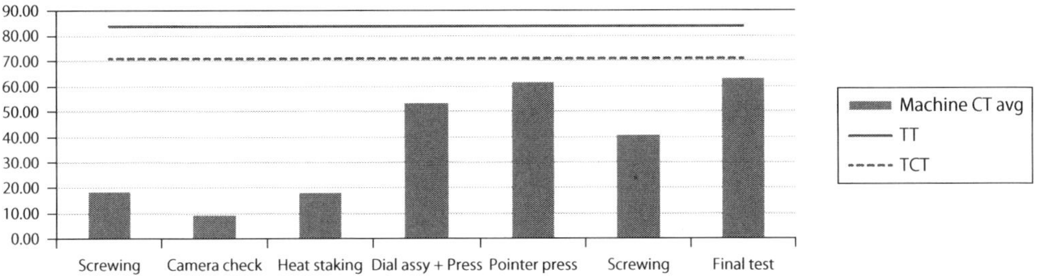

Figure 8.17 Machine cycle time diagram example.

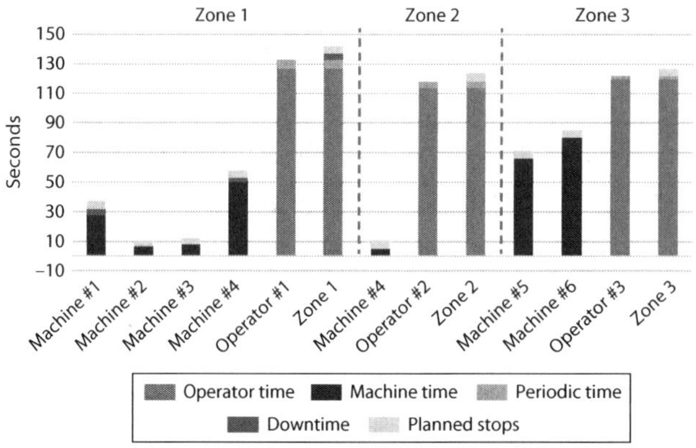

Figure 8.18 Example: Production (zone) capability chart.

Typical process metrics available from the Jishuken workshop activities should include:

- Takt time
- Planned cycle time
- Process lead time ($\sum$MT + $\sum$CT + $\sum$Travel T)
- Number of required operators = $\sum$CT / PCT
- Process fluctuation (% ± variation)
  - % + Variation: (Highest point − PCT)/PCT
  - % – Variation: (Lowest point – PCT)/PCT
- Variation factor (%) = V = [(Max. value − Min. repeatable value)/Min. repeatable value] × 100
  - $V \leq 10\%$: SW is in place; no significant anomalies
  - $V > 10\%$: SW not in place or process may not be capable
- Output min. and max. values
- Lowest repeatable time (LRT)
- **Terms:**
  - TT = Takt time
  - PCT = Planned cycle time
  - MT = Machine times
  - CT = Operator cycle times
  - Travel T = Travel time
  - Variation factor = V
  - SW = Standard work

■ *Process work table*: When manual work, machine time and walk time are combined into one chart, a visual display of process work performed over time is revealed. A standard work combination table (SWCT) is used to gather and display this data and information (Figure 8.19).

Product name	ACME	Prepared by dd-mm-yyyy	J. Preacher 09-04-2016	Operator cycle time:	76 sec / 2 piece(s)	Takt time (TT):	140 sec / 2 piece(s)
Line	Cell-6	Version	1	Number of pieces per cycle:	2 pc/cycle	Design cycle time (ATT):	76 sec / 2 piece(s)

Sequence	To add rows for additional elements: Copy entire row, then insert copied cells. Operation	Element time (sec) Manual work (sec)	Machine time (sec)	Walk time (sec)
1	Unload and load testing	20.0	20.0	
2	Walking to flash			2.0
3	Unload and load flash		104.0	
4	Put PCB into fixture and insert into oven			
5	Walking to tester			2.0
6	Unload and load for Test	14.0	122.0	
7	Take housing and PCB, assembly and checking	12.0		
8	Walking to press fit			4.0
9	Load for press fit	10.0	48.0	
10	Walking to air			4.0
11	Load and scan for air	16.0	58.0	
12	Walking to height measurement			4.0
13	Load for height measurement	8.0	36.0	
14	Walking to welding, load and place cover	24.0	30.0	
15	Walking back			13.0
	Total times:	104.0		29.0

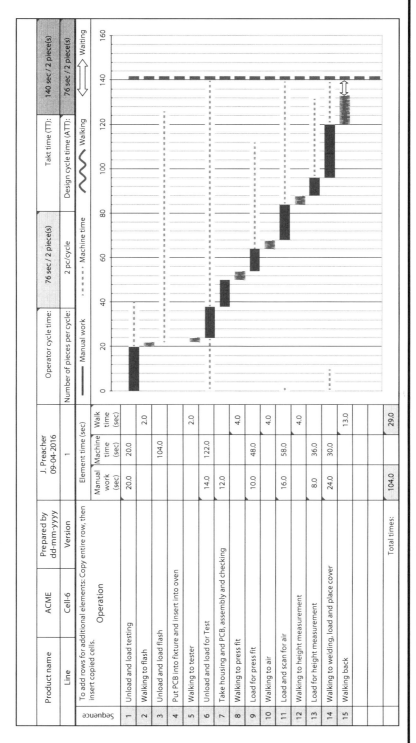

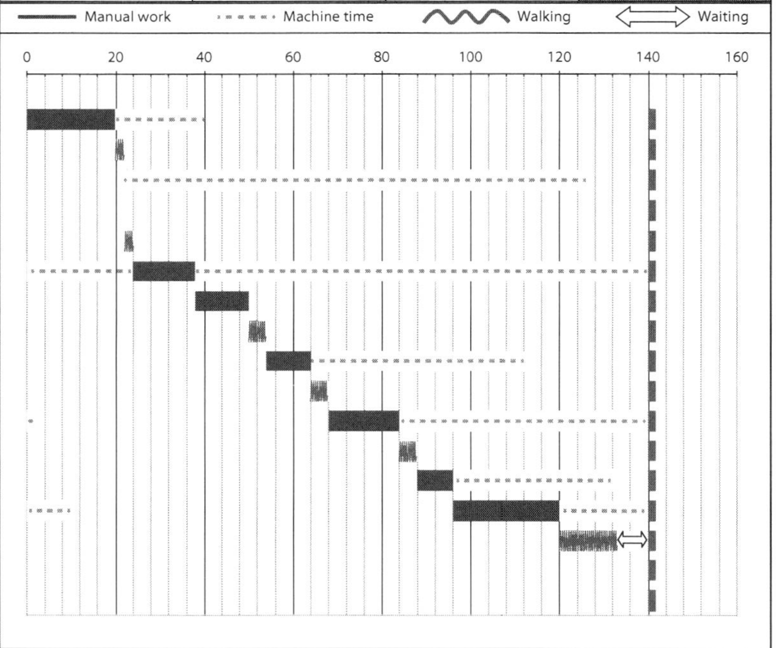

Figure 8.19 Standard work combination table.

- *Yamazumi chart*: There should be sufficient data to prepare a Yamazumi chart. Refer to the previous discussion on this topic for more details. As indicated, a Yamazumi chart is designed to visually display the workload of one or more operators in a work cell relative to takt time and planned cycle time. It can help visualize and balance operator workloads, address bottlenecks and reduce process cycle time by illuminating the job activities and operator motions that contribute to waste (Figure 8.10).
- *Opportunities for improvement*: At this point, various opportunities for improvement are likely to have revealed themselves. Consider reallocating operator work or decreasing waste due to waiting, excessive motion and other NVA activities. Review and discuss the findings with operators, line leaders, process owners and other key personnel. Get their input and feedback on what waste opportunities should be the initial focus of workshop improvements and follow-up Kaizen events. Determine potential countermeasures to be taken. Document any suggestions for improvement and determine which ones can be implemented within the remaining time frame of the workshop. Identify action owners and due dates. Plan for management follow-up as a way to maintain accountability.
- *Implement changes*: Obtain management's and quality's support to evaluate and implement changes. Confirm the validity and effectiveness of each change prior to approval and implementation. Where possible, conduct simulations and trial runs to collect data and assess results relative to expectations. Use a structured approach such as PDCA for proving out changes and change control for implementing changes upon approval.

  Monitor the status of changes and follow up as appropriate. Use a checklist, if helpful. Create a deployment schedule, perform an evaluation, redefine standards and update relevant documents. Schedule additional Kaizen events for improvements that can't be completed during the workshop.
- *Update standard work*: Whenever changes are made to the process, update standard work to reflect the current state of operations. Train operators on all shifts to the new standard using a proven method such as training within industry (TWI):
  - *Step 1*: Trainer demonstrates; trainee observes (1 cycle)
  - *Step 2*: Trainer demonstrates and explains key points; trainee observes (2 cycles)

- *Step 3*: Trainee demonstrates; trainer observes and corrects (2–3 cycles)
- *Step 4*: Trainee demonstrates and explains key points; trainer observes (1–2 cycles)

Jishuken is a "self-study" approach to process improvement where you learn by doing! It can be used to recover from capacity issues resulting from production problems or to enhance process performance by improving flow rate and operator workload balance. Through data collection, experimentation and process analysis, key visuals such as a production capability chart, process work table and Yamazumi chart can be created to reveal specific actions to take in order to achieve performance targets. Jishuken can also help to improve process flexibility by focusing on activities to reduce batch size and changeover times.

SIDEBAR: HIGH FREQUENCY, SHORT DURATION ERRORS

In pursuit of perfection, you will likely reach a point in your journey where all the "low-hanging fruit" improvement opportunities will be picked clean and you begin searching for new ways to continuously improve line performance. One approach is to start recording high frequency, short duration errors that contribute to line fluctuation. These errors, although short in duration, begin adding up when they occur frequently, resulting in potentially seconds of savings over a shift. Examples of these types of errors include chronic machine resets, multiple barcoding attempts and part repositioning.

These errors can be captured by creating a check sheet of typical events observed over a shift. Keep the sheet close at hand when the shift starts and begin recording these events with a single stroke of a pen whenever they occur throughout the shift. At the end of the day or week, Pareto the frequency of events and initiate actions to eliminate the highest frequency or longest time events, one by one. An example of a worksheet to prepare and document these error events can be found in the Appendix X.

Kaizen Events

Kaizen is known as the process of continuous improvement. The phrase "Kaizen event" goes against the grain of continuous improvement. Kaizen events take a "batch" approach to continuous improvements since events are short duration activities that tend to focus on very specific objectives rather than being part of a more holistic continuous improvement program. These events are typically led by a facilitator who works with area personnel and support team members over a one- to five-day time period making targeted process improvements. These activities have been called many different names including Kaizen Blitz, Kaizen Bursts and Continuous Improvement workshops. Sometimes they involve the application of lean tools and techniques such as standard work, Jidoka, 5S and total productive maintenance (TPM), while other times they may be more focused on a specific objective such as reducing work cell space, changeover times, buffer size or increasing capacity. Although each Kaizen event is unique, the following are typical high-level activities that occur as part of these events:

- Identify a change (pre-event)
- Evaluate the change
- Review results; verify effectiveness
- If acceptable, update standard
- Implement and train individuals (operators) to new standard
- Sustain results by updating work routines and other relevant documents

The following is a more detailed breakdown of a Kaizen event that can be customized to meet specific objectives.

Definition and Planning

Successful Kaizen events start with management commitment, followed by targeted objectives, detailed planning, disciplined execution, rigorous monitoring and attentive control while being led by a trained facilitator. A good facilitator will have appropriate management skills to keep the team on track and focused; lean skills to maintain efficient event execution; and people skills to exploit the energy and creativity of all participants. It's also important to define clear boundaries and metrics for each event so as not to derail the team from their stated objectives while establishing unambiguous achievement goals. A schedule of activities will also help people prepare and work within the time limits defined for each activity.

Common activities likely to occur during a Kaizen event include agenda review, data gathering and analysis, simulation and modeling, time studies, layout changes, standard work updates and management presentation of results (e.g. A3 reporting). Training should be provided before the event to those who may not have sufficient knowledge or experience in any of the lean tools or topics to be covered. This will ensure a basic level of understanding, allowing for more efficient execution of project tasks. Most of all, no surprises; clearly communicate the who, what, when, where, how and why of the event. This will minimize uncertainty and anxiety about the work to be accomplished. A pre-event checklist is often useful in planning ahead, highlighting the people, materials, equipment and documents needed to minimize waste of "excess motion" in looking for items needed during event execution.

Be open and transparent about the event. Keep stakeholders informed about activities and outcomes. Clearly communicate what's happening and reinforce how various activities align with strategic objectives of the enterprise.

Baseline Performance

Improvement activities start with defining your current state of performance. Once an output measure has been defined for the target performance you want to achieve, data should be collected to establish the current baseline in preparation for the event. This baseline becomes the reference point from which progress can be assessed. Pictures and video of the area layout and operator movements prior to the event may help save time during the event. Typical metrics that may be useful for the team to collect in preparation include:

- Line layout diagram
- Cycle time measurements
- Number of operators
- Operator and part travel distances
- Average changeover times
- Work in progress/buffer quantities
- Scrap rates/FPY

Flow charting the process helps to reveal NVA activities that can be targeted for removal.

Event Execution

As activities unfold, the facilitator should keep people focused and efficient. Be aware of additional resources that may be required to support task completion. For example, if changes in line layout are required, assistance in moving equipment and reworking electrical connections may necessitate the availability of maintenance personnel.

Facilitation will require as much pre-planning as possible and disciplined execution of planned activities once the line is available, since there will be limited time to deviate from scope. Expect to provide coaching and mentoring to newer members of the Kaizen team since there is often an abundance of problem-solving and decision-making occurring in concert. Special attention should be paid to deviations from the plan and expected results as this may be a symptom of an underlying, unidentified issue.

Solutions to problems come in many forms. Team members should not go into these events with preconceived notions of how things should look, feel or function. Teams need to observe and experiment through trial and error, acquiring the knowledge needed to exercise their creativity and good judgment based on data and factual information. The objective is to come up with easy, cheap, fast and workable options for consideration, selection and implementation. Keep things simple and concentrate on delivering practical solutions. Be open-minded. If a solution is simple but crude yet it works, implement it!

Conduct pilots and manual simulations; use technology and software to facilitate motion analysis and assess potential process changes, if possible. Most of all, be conscious of how team actions will impact production activities and schedules. Lest we forget, continuous improvement is about making work easier, faster, cheaper and, I might add, safer. Remember, countermeasures identified and implemented by individuals who work in the area are more likely to be sustainable.

Event Closure

A presentation to management and other key stakeholders is encouraged at the end of a Kaizen event to reinforce the benefits of these activities and provide an opportunity for team members to interact with management, promoting their value-add to the company. It's best to quantify and document improvements for presentation. A one-page A3 keeps the message simple and focused on significant issues. Provide facts, figures and visuals; an example of clearly visualized improvement results is provided in Figure 8.20. It's difficult to dispute reliable data and factual information, especially when presented in a clear and logical way. Also, if done right, a good A3 or equivalent report will leave a lasting impression with leadership.

Metric	Before	After	Improvement
Inventory (Qty)	19	6	70
Productivity (min/100 units)	111.3	78.2	30
Space (m^2)	25 m^2	25 m^2	0
Weekly output	11.3 K	14.3 K	20
Operators	2	2	0

Figure 8.20 Display of improvements metrics.

Once a new level of performance has been confirmed, the last step is to define a performance measure that can be periodically monitored to ensure gains achieved are sustained.

Each Kaizen event should end with some degree of recognition and reward. There are many ways to do this; see Figure 8.21 for several easy and inexpensive suggestions.

To approach recognition and reward properly, the following tips are recommended:

- *Match the reward or recognition to the person*: Strive to provide a reward of value suited to an individual. Consider public recognition, time off, lunch or a gift certificate as examples.
- *Match the reward or recognition to the achievement:* Customize recognition to reflect the level of achievement. For example, completing a task versus leading a successful project demands a different level of recognition. Focus on measures, performance and customer impact when recognizing individual achievement.
- *Be timely and specific*: Effective recognition should be delivered soon after the desired achievement is obtained or behavior has been demonstrated. Clearly and specifically state why the recognition or reward is being provided.

Recognition / Rewards

- ✓ Bonus / Merit raise
- ✓ Increased responsibility
- ✓ Public recognition
- ✓ Coffee/Lunch with the boss
- ✓ Training opportunity
- ✓ Time off
- ✓ Paid vacation
- ✓ Certificate or plaque
- ✓ Books
- ✓ Thank-you letter
- ✓ Gift card

Figure 8.21 Suggestions for recognition and reward.

Kaizen events should not be an avenue for solving critical business problems but a mechanism for incrementally enhancing organizational performance. They can be planned and executed in service areas as well as production. These events are intended to reduce costs and cycle time through elimination of NVA activities in production and transactional operations. Obviously, the work of the team is never finished since continuously looking for opportunities and implementing improvements should be the norm for all areas of operation.

Toyota Kata: Improvement through Planning and Coaching

In his book *Toyota Kata* [3], Mike Rother introduced Toyota kata to the world. In doing so, he revealed a very practical yet disciplined side to Toyota that few people understood. A disciplined culture of continuous improvement is a way of life for Toyota employees rooted in the simple but powerful PDCA methodology using scientific thinking to advance their knowledge and develop every employee to be a better problem-solver. Increasing the problem-solving skill level of every employee allows Toyota to exploit underutilized resources while accelerating their problem-solving acumen without the need to hire more "experts". Through creative thinking, Toyota can increase their capacity to manage the complexity of a changing world, keeping ahead of the crowd by offering a development path for their employees. Through greater ownership of their work, Toyota empowers employees to support and advance company objectives. The Toyota culture, which Mike Rother coined as "Toyota kata", was born of a need within Toyota to develop internal employees who could help accelerate continuous improvement with minimal cost impact on the organization. Let's explore the concepts behind Toyota kata a little more, if for no other reason than to better understand Toyota's mindset of continuous improvement every day and everywhere.

First of all, I will frequently refer to "Toyota kata" as just "kata". Simply stated, kata is developing people to be more efficient and effective problem-solvers. The word "kata" refers to movement sequences in martial arts used to train combatants so their actions become instinctive, essentially second nature. This word reflected what Rother observed Toyota doing when attempting to describe the culture in which Toyota develops its people. The display of continuous improvement being developed within Toyota included the application of a disciplined methodology (PDCA) combined with repetitive practice (kata) while maintaining an open-minded approach to scientific thinking when unknown solutions to problems were encountered.

Kata is based on a mentorship between a coach and learner (or improver) intended to develop an individual's process improvement skills through critical thinking, disciplined execution and continuous repetition to create and reinforce a desired behavior, pattern or habit. The idea of scientific thinking is about gathering and interpreting new information to refine our understanding and evolve our thinking. In short, Toyota kata is a standard, structured approach to continuous improvement involving systematic and scientific thinking reflective of Toyota's culture for developing people and driving operational improvements. It's intended to change people's way of thinking and solving problems by coaching and reinforcing desired behaviors through a deliberate, practiced routine that, upon extensive repetition, becomes an unconscious habit. It's a way to engage untapped or underutilized resources to create an organizational culture of continuous process improvements.

If done right, kata can bring structure, discipline and accountability to problem-solving using the PDCA routine. It can help stabilize a process by removing obstacles causing instability while establishing and reinforcing a *desired* pattern of behavior within an organization, slowly moving it toward a more sustainable culture of improvement. If you want to learn more about Toyota kata, visit Mike Rother's Internet page where you can download his *Improvement Kata Handbook.*

SIDEBAR: TOYOTA KATA

It's not uncommon for organizations to struggle with understanding how kata "fits" into their business systems simply because, kata is a reflection of Toyota's continuous improvement culture which has evolved, within Toyota, over several decades. Just because Toyota does it, does not mean it will work (as documented) for your organization. Different companies have different cultures.

I observed an organization trying to implement kata without a clear understanding of why they were doing it or how to best integrate it into their business system. They were not trying to solve a problem but, simply trying to implement an "improvement" tool. Like any tool kata can be effective, as long as it's being implemented for the right reason, with a clear purpose and plan in mind.

In summary, waste elimination will only allow you to improve operations so far; if you want to optimize the efficiency of your entire system, you must consider doing it from a system perspective. This perspective takes into account the interaction of activities necessary to support the successful production of parts destined for the customer, from receipt of raw material to the delivery of finished goods. A system approach looks to optimize interconnected processes along the value stream to deliver a quality product in the most efficient and cost-effective way possible.

When we talk about improving systems, it involves understanding, identifying and eliminating waste impacting product flow throughout the value stream. Improving process flow will be the next topic of discussion on the journey to operational excellence.

Key Points

- Continuous efficiency improvement requires the elimination of waste.
- Waste is anything that slows or interrupts the continuous flow of product through the value stream.
- Waste elimination can be used to rally employees around a unifying cause that benefits the organization and provides customer value.
- Unnecessary materials, information and activities are targets for elimination to improve quality and productivity.
- Constant changes in production schedules can reduce the efficiency of people and equipment.
- The ultimate objective is to eliminate waste with the goal of creating fast and flexible processes that supply customers with what they want, when they want it, at a competitive price.
- Overproduction can harbor defects, in large batches, that go undetected with time.
- Repair work requires additional handling, time to fix or replace bad materials or components and sometimes retesting to confirm quality. All these extra activities cost money, time and generate waste.
- Hiding problems through overproduction and inventory undermines a production system.
- Everything can be improved, and all improvements, regardless of how small, are valuable.
- Workers are a key source for improvement ideas.

- Lean implementation requires a learn-by-doing approach to improvement.
- Jishuken is a good method to improve production line efficiency in a disciplined and systematic way.
- Data that is collected but never used is waste. A lack of information, when needed, creates waste.
- Don't automate waste.

References

1. Shingo Institute, Utah State University. 2016. *The Shingo Model for Operational Excellence.* Logan, UT: Jon M. Huntsman, School of Business.
2. Maciej Pienkowski. 2014. Waste measurement techniques for lean companies. *International Journal of Lean Thinking*, Volume 5(1): 6–9.
3. Mike Rother. 2010. *Toyota Kata.* New York: McGraw-Hill Education.

Chapter 9

Process Flow Improvement

> Flow thinking is the focus on shortening lead-time from the beginning of the value stream to the end of the value stream and on removing all barriers (waste) that impede the creation of value and its delivery to the customer. Flow is the best driver to make processes faster, easier, cheaper and better.
>
> **The Shingo Institute: Principle – Flow and Pull Value**

Continuous Process Flow

In today's competitive world of manufacturing, rapid response to changing customer demands is essential to remaining profitable. Customer orders can vary from day to day, week to week or month to month. An uneven build-to-order production schedule can create large inventories needed to meet customer requirements, hiding defects not discovered until weeks later. Replacing defective product facilitates the need for overtime to cover the cost of building replacement parts while elevating employee stress and equipment availability required to satisfy unanticipated demand.

In a 1999 *Harvard Business Review* article, "Decoding the DNA of the Toyota Production System" [1], the author highlighted four rules of the Toyota Production System, one of which is "Every product and service should flow along a simple, specified (direct) path. Goods and services don't flow to the next available person or machine, but to a person or machine". This rule was implemented as a strategy to combat the daily struggle of managing dynamic swings in customer orders while minimizing process waste. Thus, the concept of continuous flow evolved as a strategy for minimizing waste with the goal of achieving continuous or "one-piece" flow to minimize overproduction.

Continuous process flow is the movement of information and material through an entire production system without interruption. It's built on fundamental concepts such as standardized work, rapid changeovers, pull systems and error proofing, and is facilitated by an optimized just-in-time (JIT) structure driven by a kanban system to regulate the rate of flow relative to customer takt time. Kanban facilitates production "pull", which allows the rate of production to align with the customer's rate of demand. Yet, "pull" is not feasible or cost-effective without production flexibility and shorter lead times that result from incremental improvements in flow over time.

As previously discussed, process stability and capability must be demonstrated before meaningful flow improvements can be pursued. Improving process flow is achieved by understanding and optimizing factors that influence information and material flow within the value stream. Any cause for a stop in flow is considered waste that becomes a target for removal.

The Value Stream

The value stream is considered the flow of a product from raw material to delivery, application and final disposition. It can include the design and development process, starting with a concept to release a product into production. It's the compilation of all steps required to deliver customer value. Understanding what constitutes customer value can be a difficult task. This chapter will focus on production flow from raw material to delivery, sometimes called "door to door", since this is where the majority of today's lean activities are concentrated.

The value stream perspective takes a holistic view of process efficiency by optimizing the value of interconnected processes within a specific product family versus focusing on individual processes that make up the whole. A proven approach for improving flow across multiple processes is value stream mapping (VSM), a method used to map material and information flow through the value chain, which is contextualized in the book *Learning to See* by Rother and Shook. This mapping tool helps document the current state of material and information flow through a product's value stream while facilitating the visualization of a future state (Value Stream Design) to aid in establishing a clear path for improvement.

Moving from the current to future state takes time, patience and creativity to identify and remove obstacles along the improvement path, once the gap is understood. It also takes structure, discipline and accountability to do it efficiently. In this chapter, we will seek to understand the factors that influence process flow, explore concepts behind flow and highlight some of the proven tools and techniques that will move us toward a more continuous, ideal one-piece flow.

Flow Disruptors

Aligning process flow to complement customer demand requires continuous evaluation, identification and elimination of obstacles along the value stream preventing the smooth, steady, uninterrupted flow of material, information and product destined for the customer. Disruptors to process flow include unexpected equipment downtime, changeovers, process defects, material shortages, inexperienced operators and deviations from standard work, to list a few. To combat these "negative" forces, there is an arsenal of ways to reduce or minimize the impact of flow disruptors along the value stream including:

- Straight line, forward-moving material flow through the production facility
- Line layouts optimized for space and minimal operator movements
- Accurate and timely information flow
- In-line buffers to compensate for process fluctuation
- Simple, flexible and reliable manufacturing equipment
- Operator ergonomics (to minimize fatigue and injury)
- Rapid changeovers (to increase flexibility and customization)
- Ease of maintenance (e.g. external line maintenance to decrease scheduled line downtime)
- Preventive maintenance (e.g. operator ownership)

We will consider these and other lean improvement opportunities as we work to enhance information and material flow. However, before doing so, we must ensure standard work is in place and functional work routines are defined and properly followed. Deviations from standards and opportunities for improvement should be captured, prioritized and acted upon in a timely and professional manner. At this point, we will consider material and information flow separately before combining them later when optimizing the value stream. Let's start with material flow since it's a major player in maintaining a steady process.

Material Flow

To fundamentally improve material flow to a manufacturing line, four areas must be considered. They include shop floor (or facility) layout, warehouse layout, material flow to production and work area (production line) layout. Let's start with shop floor layout. Figure 9.1 considers flow improvement from a plant as well as a product family perspective.

Facility Layout

Facility layout is a major factor in defining the limits of an organization's lean capabilities. The best scenario for an efficient production environment is starting with a new plant blueprint followed by changing an existing facility layout. Adding a new assembly line is more common, reflecting the ebb and flow of product life cycles within a dynamic manufacturing environment.

When laying out a new plant or changing an existing layout, the first step is to create a vision of the raw material and finished goods flow throughout the facility. Creating a vision for material flow takes a team effort (Figure 9.2). All support operations need to work together to define common objectives

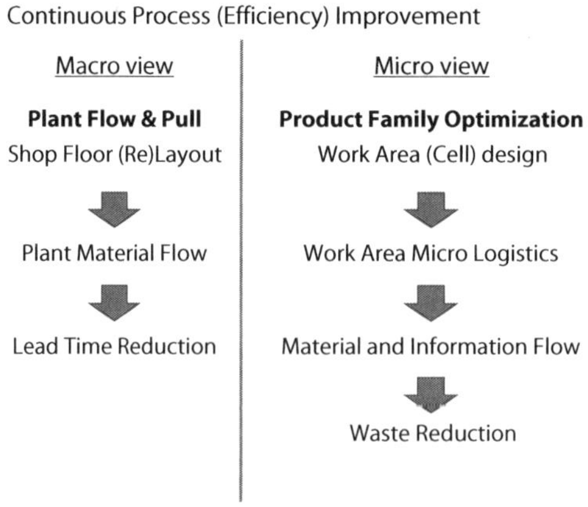

Figure 9.1 Flow improvement considerations.

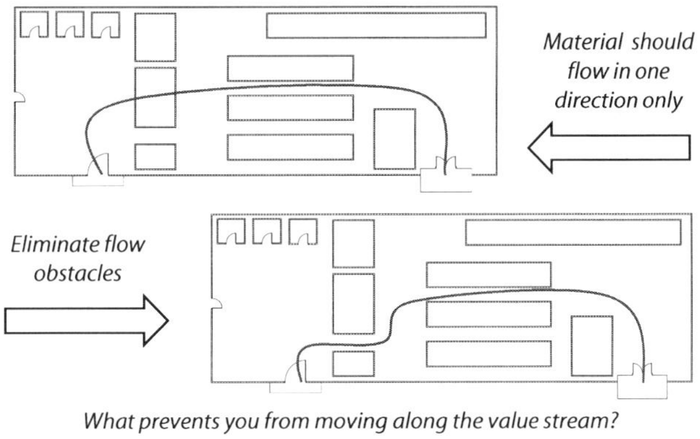
Material should
flow in one
direction only
Eliminate flow
obstacles
What prevents you from moving along the value stream?

Figure 9.2 Create a facility flow vision.

and cooperate toward realizing those objectives with clear actions in mind. Project planning must consider the requirements, resources, assumptions, constraints and risks associated with the significance of the undertaking. However, material flow must not be the only factor under consideration; design layout must also take into account the movement of information, people and equipment; storage of raw materials; work in process (WIP) and inventory; placement of work areas and machines; as well as accommodations for kanbans, storage racks and information boards. These are a few key considerations.

When optimizing a facility layout, the objective of most efforts would be to increase the size of value-adding areas (e.g. production areas) and reduce the size of non-value-adding areas, including shipping, receiving, warehouses, offices and social areas. Assembly lines can be organized into many sizes and shapes including linear and cellular configurations. No one line layout satisfies all needs. However, a good line layout is one that meets operational requirements and satisfies the needs for which it was intended while minimizing WIP and optimizing flow in the cheapest way possible.

The first step in changing a new or existing facility layout is location of the material receiving and shipping dock relative to high and low runner production lines. Material movement through the plant will be defined by where raw materials are received and finished goods are staged for shipping. The shortest path of material flow through a facility should be the most efficient. If possible, lay out or rearrange production lines according to their material flow requirements (high to low volume runners).

Physical site constraints, existing production lines and the location of utilities will influence the flow patterns within a facility. Visualize the work area layout and various constraints along a path to the work areas where materials need to flow. Software simulations can help define efficient ways to move raw materials and components through a facility to each work area and how best to stage finished goods for shipment. Once an optimal layout has been defined, review the current layout to determine what actions will be necessary to move from the existing state to a more efficient one. A clear plan, complemented with a series of projects and good project management, should help realize the vision.

A shop floor layout usually consists of many different value streams with multiple products, shared machines, capacity constraints and other factors. Designing for a single value stream is often too simplistic for a new facility layout. Consider existing product families, the likelihood of future value streams, management of capacity and investment issues.

Warehouse Layout

Since warehousing is considered non-value-added space in a production facility, look to minimize its footprint in the facility layout. Consider maximizing vertical as well as horizontal space for storage. Any warehousing "off-site" would likely be considered waste since transport of materials clearly fits into the category of non-value added. When incoming material storage is on-site, organize the storage locations according to product line demand.

Material Supply/Flow to Production

A lean facility layout requires understanding and optimizing material and information flow to production lines. Material flow needs to be carefully considered since it can have a significant impact on process waste due to excessive movement and storage on its journey to consumption. Good facility layout designs exhibit short, simple flow patterns across the facility, from material receipt to product shipment.

The flow of material from incoming to the production lines is a primary component of any manufacturing facility arrangement. It's best to lay out the facility from high to low running production lines so high runners are closest to incoming where the majority of incoming material can be consumed with minimal travel within the facility. Material feeding lower volume lines will need to be transported further from the receiving dock but in smaller quantities, minimizing transport waste. Metrics that can be used to measure the efficiency of material movement include transport effort and distance, the number of replenishment runs and the number of empty runs.

The flow of supplier material to the production line is sometimes called micro-logistics. Since production lines can be significantly impacted by the flow and feeding of material to the line, careful consideration must be given to factors impacting these activities including:

- Quantity and frequency of material delivery to the facility and production lines
- Facility storage of supplied material (inventory)
- Line storage of material
- Line storage space (assembly material and finished goods)
- Standardized feeding of parts into the cell/workstations
- Use of gravity feed (typically a preferred method)
- Use of supermarkets, first-in-first-out (FIFO)
- Application of a pull system
- Introduction of materials and removal of empty containers within the cell

Ways to reduce the complexity of line access for material feeding and maintenance include:

- Application of standardized components
- Use of common tools and fixtures
- Selective availability of spare parts
- Attention to ergonomic when designing line controls and fixtures
- Easy access to equipment for maintenance and repair (e.g. front or rear access)
- A good preventive maintenance plan

In addition to defining a material flow pattern to work areas or cells, it's important to consider the maximum and minimum material inventory levels for each production location and how those levels will be monitored and controlled to ensure material levels are maintained. For example, a line autonomy of 90 minutes may be defined as an acceptable running time before additional material supply is required to maintain seamless production. Before shifting topics, it's important to make one additional comment; material flow should always follow information flow.

Production Line Design for Material Feed

Material handler accessibility to the line and material feed are an essential part of line design. Exterior gravity feeding of a line typically minimizes operator disruptions. Lines should be designed with material buffers in mind. The quantity of in-process stock at each workstation should be calculated based on material consumption rates.

Material supply packaging should be designed according to production line needs. Avoid excess packaging, repackaging or a need to adjust the quantity/box type to suit line demand. Aim for 1–2 hours of material in the production line, when practical. The less material required at the line, the less space needed to store it, pending use. Use vertical storage to exploit available space.

Production Cell Design

There are a number of different production line layout configurations. Some of the more common ones include straight line, L-shaped and U-shaped production flows. They all have advantages and disadvantages and can be used in combination to optimize existing floor space and processing needs. Although the U-shaped flow is common to lean, other patterns can be just as efficient. Do not focus on "U" cells; create a production line configuration that works within constraints of the existing facility while satisfying the needs of the line. Production cells have the advantage of making it easier to minimize cycle time and travel distance for operators because of better space utilization and operator access to multiple workstations.

Straight production line layouts make it difficult to balance work tasks among operators because they are often unevenly distributed. A U-shaped configuration provides more flexibility in balancing workloads (Figure 9.3).

Changing to a cell configuration introduces the challenge of determining which equipment should be shared or allocated to various production lines. Unless capacity of a production line is dominated by one product, it's more feasible to establish a production line that supports a product family. Clearly, if workflows need to share common equipment and/or resources, easy access and proximity become a consideration. As layout complexity increases, feeder cells can be an effective way to supply modules or subassemblies to workstations.

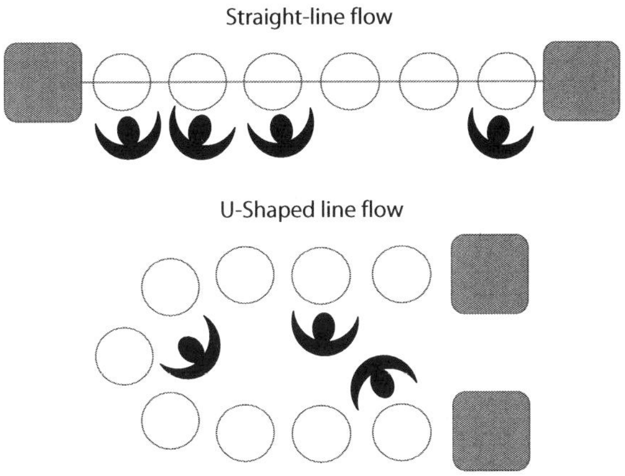

Figure 9.3 Straight versus U-shaped line.

Work cell design should start with an understanding of some fundamentals to create a framework within which to work. These include:

- *Takt time*: Material consumption rate.
- *Block diagram*: Use to visualize workstations and sequence of steps required to produce a part.
- *Machine balance chart*: Use to compare machine cycle time to takt time.
- *System layout*: Use to arrange equipment to optimize material flow and operator motion.
- *Operator balance chart*: Use to display the value and non-value-added work content for each operator with the objective of minimizing waste and number of operators required to produce at takt time.
- *Buffer and batch size*: Use to maintain continuous flow once an optimized layout has been established.
- *Lead time*: Use to determine production line efficiency.
- *Containers and packaging*: Prepare necessary containers and/or packaging to support material flow requirements.
- *Error proofing*: Evaluate opportunities for error proofing the line with systems and devices to prevent defects.

Good cell design is difficult to achieve. Typical characteristics of good design include:

- Running according to standard work
- Simple machines; no conveyors

- No buffers between stations
- One-piece flow (make one, move one)
- No waiting on processes (e.g. balanced workload)
- Minimal setup and changeover times
- No machine runs slower than 90% of planned cycle time
- Material storage outside cell
- Exterior material loading of cell
- Operator start and finish points close to each other
- Minimal material handling (by operator) after entering the cell
- No operator waiting on a machine to finish
- All non-cyclic work done outside of cell by the support team
- Use of auto-unload to improve balance and workflow

In a well-run, efficient manufacturing cell, an operator's only task would be to perform cyclic work according to their standard work instructions, nothing more. Operators do not leave the cell and no one enters the cell. Consumed materials are supplied to the cell externally, via a material handler. Clear transfer points are established to move product from the cell to the next process step. No temporary storage of product should exist in the cell.

To optimize material flow, a material handler transports material from the warehouse to the line material buffer and picks up finished goods, empty containers and waste. Scrap needs to be removed from the cell via the material handler or other means (Figure 9.4).

Material Availability and Handling

Material shortage is one of the main disruptors to flow. Simply stated, if there are no materials or components to build, there will be no parts to ship. Material deliveries should be scheduled in small, frequent batches to minimize storage and excess handling at the line. Raw materials should be stored where used to minimize transport. Line storage is recommended (in small batches) for all WIP and raw materials to support line flow. Material, upon entering a facility, should flow in one direction only, always moving forward, never backward, while being introduced at the specified rate.

Less handling minimizes damage and waste from excess transport and motion. To minimize material handling, standard work instructions should be available and layered process audits performed to ensure proper procedure is exercised and opportunities for improvement are identified, evaluated and implemented, if proven favorable. If excess handling is observed or damage

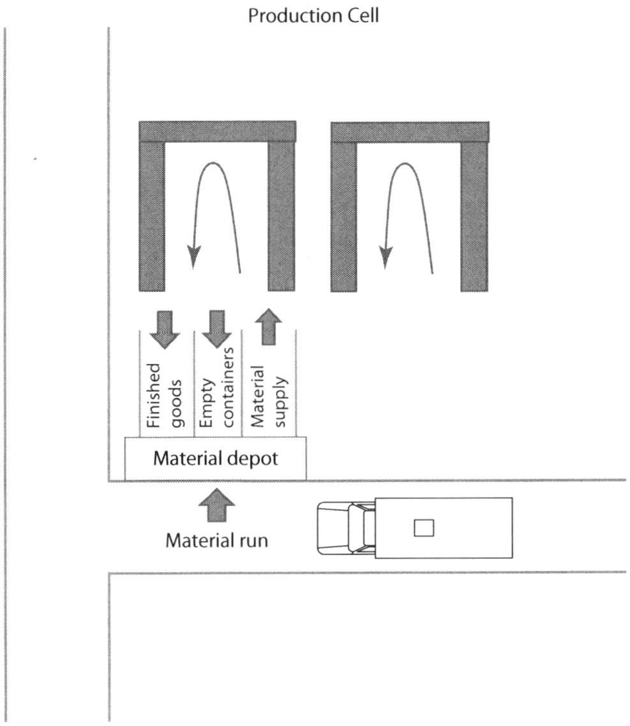

Figure 9.4 External material supply to and from the production cell.

occurs due to improper handling practices, action must be taken to eliminate the source of waste or improve the material handling procedure, respectively.

Another aspect to consider is the equipment used in the handling process. One should evaluate and choose the best equipment for safe and efficient movement of material within the facility. This would include transport vehicles, conveyors and containers.

One of the best approaches to improving material handling is the reduction of "touch points", specifically manual ones. Manual intervention increases the potential to damage parts, can lead to improper placement or storage and can induce contamination.

To ensure a fast response to issues, a process should be tailored to quickly identify, eliminate or escalate problems or obstacles impacting material flow to work areas. Clear work routines should include periodic verification that the material delivery process is working as expected.

When looking to improve material availability, ask yourself, "What's preventing reliable movement of material along the value stream?" The answer to this question should provide clear direction for waste elimination as you inch closer to seamless flow and operational excellence.

Assessing Process Flow

True process flow is never really known until a study is performed to document the actual flow pattern. In doing so, it's not unusual to find the expected flow to be different from the originally approved version since time has a way of changing flow patterns not actively controlled. Subtle changes to line layouts occur for many reasons including line consolidations, introduction of new equipment, equipment sharing and changes to standard work routines. One of the best ways to assess line flow is through preparation of a spaghetti diagram, which visually captures product flow through a work area. Once product line flow has been documented and confirmed, a team of subject-matter experts can convene to review the existing state and propose an optimized version for consideration. A before and after version of a facility layout change is presented as a spaghetti diagram in Figure 9.5a and b. As a result, considerable reduction in cycle time was achieved.

Information Flow

Information flow is observed in many different facets of production including forecasting, ordering, scheduling and shipping, when information is exchanged between suppliers and customers. Production flow involves the movement of material and information through the value stream. It's important to note the source, reliability and flow of critical information to key points within the operating environment.

Walk along the information flow path to visualize the flow pattern and map it so you can see how information interacts with various process activities. Ask people how they know how much to produce and what to produce next. Understand how information influences material inventory, line buffer quantities and replenishment activities. When mapping the flow of information, draw forecasts and daily orders as separate lines since they denote different information paths.

Generally speaking, information flow provides notification of what to make and when to make it. Information as well as material must be available to operators to facilitate continuous workflow within planned cycle times. To be useful, information must be accurate, accessible, easy to understand and timely.

Information flow is simplified when companies identify a single point for communicating schedule requirements (e.g. a pacemaker process) from which upstream material flow will be controlled. This will reduce the number of communication paths observed within traditional

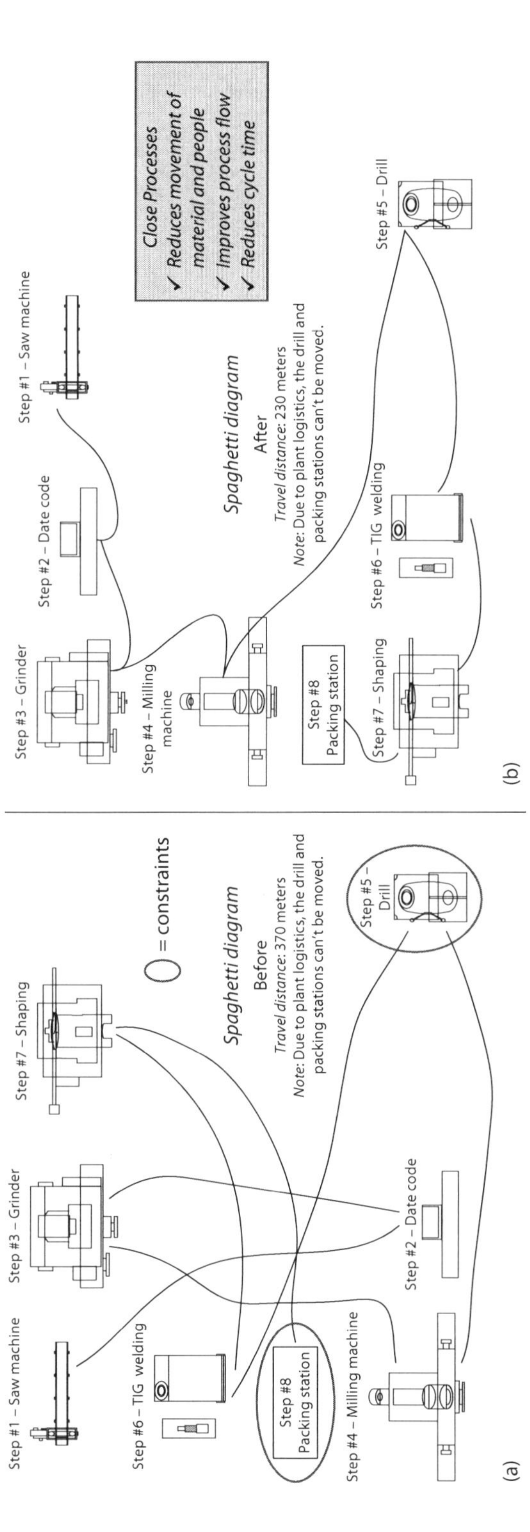

Figure 9.5 Spaghetti diagram: (a) before and (b) after a facility layout change to reduce cycle time.

operations. However, this does not eliminate forecasting since suppliers, several layers removed from customers, still need advanced information to plan their capacity, workforce and other needs, to satisfy longer-term expectations.

Product Flow

To rapidly respond to changing customer demand without the need for storing excessive inventory, production must manage fluctuations in product volume and mix, creating a predictable flow of material through the manufacturing process. This can be accomplished by taking the total volume of orders in a specified time period and leveling them so the same amount and mix of parts are being made each day. To achieve this objective, first and foremost, a product line should be designed with simplicity and practicality in mind. This is not a trivial task and requires some foresight and planning to minimize manufacturing disruptions. Let's explore some of these key influences to product flow.

Manufacturing Line Layout

As indicated previously, a production line designed to enable flow and apply the principles of pull must consider the following characteristics:

- Straight line, forward-moving material flow
- Accurate and timely information flow
- Minimal in-line buffers
- Simple, flexible, reliable equipment
- Operator ergonomics
- Rapid changeover
- Ease of maintenance
- Flexible production expansion/reduction
- Preventive maintenance

Many mistakenly believe a work cell represents lean production. This is only true when a cell configuration is selected with a specific lean objective in mind. It's important to remember that every action taken should intentionally move the organization closer to a desired state, consistent with its vision and strategic plan. When striving to achieve a more efficient line design, focus on fluid product flow. Some of the following concepts will help achieve this aim:

- JIT part availability and material buffers to regulate flow
- U-shaped cell design to optimize operator availability and minimize movements
- Connected sub-processes to avoid waste and excess transport
- Gravity feed of parts to minimize operator movement
- Machines placed in logical sequence
- Counterclockwise workflow (see Sidebar: Why a Counterclockwise Work Cell Flow?)
- Small lot/batch sizes
- Rapid changeovers to facilitate adjustable/flexible line flow rates

Activities that support the work area should be performed by a support team outside the work area or cell so operators don't have to leave their work areas during scheduled work hours. As a rule, operators should not leave the work area and support teams should not enter the work cell during scheduled work times.

During the concept phase, work areas or cells should be designed so machines and other equipment can easily be moved within the work environment. Consider flexible utility lines such as ceiling dropdowns to make layout changes simpler. Maintaining flexibility in workstations will allow easy adjustments to changing requirements.

Creating a flow-orientated line design and managing the value stream can move an organization closer to producing and delivering products that meet real-time customer needs versus building a costly bank of inventory that can become damaged or obsolete.

SIDEBAR: WHY A COUNTERCLOCKWISE WORK CELL FLOW?

It's often recommended to design a U-shaped cell with a counterclockwise workflow because most people are right-handed. Our natural tendency is to use our dominant hand when we need to "aim" and reach for something while our less dominant hand can be used for placing an object down with less precision. Since over 70% of people are right-handed, a counterclockwise direction would support using the right hand more often to pick things up and the left hand to place things down when less "aim" is required. Since the majority of people are right-handed, it makes sense to flow counterclockwise or "left-hand inside".

Manufacturing Line Equipment

Manufacturing line equipment must be designed for ease of operator use and maintenance to ensure its availability in sustaining a smooth work flow. Fixtures must be easy and quick to change or replace (e.g. fast changeovers). These include test fixtures and gages.

The application of mistake proofing (e.g. poka-yokes) will help minimize defects. Equipment access from the rear of a machine will allow equipment maintenance from outside the production area, reducing work cell disturbance and equipment downtime. When designing equipment, consider speed and ease of changeover, ease of maintainability, repair as well as a modular design approach for future reuse.

Simple equipment will require less money to make and is typically easier to maintain. Consider the benefits of installing manual backup tools at automated stations, with low reliability, as a way to hedge against significant disruptions to process flow due to unplanned events.

When designing equipment to interface with operators, think about separating the loading and unloading position, especially when working with large parts requiring manipulation by two hands. As indicated previously, consider gravity feeding of materials, simple fixtures and jigs, basic automation, auto-eject, mistake-proofing equipment designs and application of smaller dedicated equipment versus large shared equipment which tends to reduce flexibility.

Use the knowledge of experienced technicians to develop low-cost customized solutions. Keep it simple and cheap. A modular approach will increase flexibility in adding and removing equipment as a way to regulate changes in product demand. Equipment design should also consider the interaction of equipment, operators and materials with the objective of maximizing an operator's skills and flexibility while facilitating the flow of materials through the process. Equipment design guidelines include:

- *Equipment size*: Keep equipment small and dedicated to one task. Maintaining a balanced flow may require development of slower, simpler, less-automated equipment. Minimize machine surfaces; machine widths should only be slightly larger than the smallest part dimension width. This will help to reduce walking distances and material movement. Keep gages simple and flexible.
- *Equipment features*: Design should consider equipment use within arm's reach of an operator (e.g. ergonomics), one-touch automation for

ease of execution, auto-eject whenever operators are required to use both hands for manipulating parts, safety features to prevent accidents and continuous feedback to assess system status (e.g. sensors to signal abnormalities). Consider automatic stops (Jidoka) when abnormalities occur. One other thing, a lean machine is a quiet machine!

- *Machine placement*: Machines should be located as close to each other as possible, taking into account connects and future access needs. Optimizing placement distance helps to minimize operator motion and work area footprint.
- *Machine loading*: Manual loading provides increased process flexibility, especially when part orientation is required to move material from an existing location to the machine. Chamfer nests can ease the burden of placement and reduce wear. Auto-eject may be of benefit when performing multiple processes.
- *Make equipment portable and flexible*: Equipment should be able to adjust to changes in product volume and mix with the goal to run every part, every day. Portability makes equipment relocation easier and facilitates continuous improvement. Portability can be achieved, in part, by designing self-contained equipment, flat floor mounting (e.g. no pits, foundations or catch basins) and avoiding floor fastening, unless necessary. Consider lockable wheels as a way to keep equipment in place until relocation is necessary.
- *Visual and audit controls*: Keeping operators informed of equipment and work status helps leverage their skills while maximizing their work engagement. Consider what information will provide operator value and equipment features necessary to deliver it.
- *Workplace organization*: What tools, gages and fixtures will be required for operator access? Ensure these items have a designated place within the guidelines of good ergonomic practices.

Designing to requirements is lean, anything more is over-engineering or waste from a lean perspective. Minimize or eliminate the use of conveyance as this only adds to non-value movement of parts. Avoid customizing machines, unless necessary, since this can lead to significant cost and time commitments. A lean equipment checklist may help facilitate application of lean principles and practices during the design process.

Part presentation to the line also plays a role in line equipment design efficiency. The positioning of a rack or storage device supports material delivery to point of use (preferably FIFO), followed by the retrieval of containers (empty or full). These should also be designed with flexibility, reuse and reconfiguration in mind.

Line Personnel

One of the primary factors contributing to a smooth line flow is the balancing of operator cycle times. It's a lot easier to maintain a smooth and steady line flow when operator tasks take approximately the same time to complete. Small in-line buffers can be used to compensate for variations that periodically challenge a smooth line flow.

An operator balance chart can be prepared to visualize the cycle time of multiple operators working as a team within a cell. If there are significant differences between operator workloads, a Yamazumi chart can be created to show work activities with the largest degree of waste and Kaizen events can be scheduled to eliminate some of the more significant waste contributors before updating standardized work instructions to reallocate work routines.

During work area layout, ergonomics can play a significant role in maximizing operator performance by preventing unnecessary injury due to excessive movement and repetition. Waste reduction opportunities include positioning materials at workers' optimum height and instructing operators in the proper lifting of heavy loads. Lighting should be sufficient to avoid eyestrain (leading to errors) and tools should have dedicated storage locations within a worker's field of reach. Also consider flexible tool mounts to accommodate workers with different heights and reaches.

Provide a location for standard work instructions and other key information; avoid flipping work pieces when moving from one workstation to the next. A unit from the previous operation should be in the same orientation as it was unloaded. These are examples of ways you can ease the stress and strain on operators performing repetitive tasks and minimize the disruption of workflow due to human error and absence.

Improving Process Flow

The book, *Learning to See*, by Rother and Shook [2] discusses the topic of the "lean value stream", which presents a logical and disciplined approach to improving flow within a product family's value stream. One objective of lean manufacturing is to reduce lead time from raw material to finished goods.

This requires more than searching for and eliminating waste, it requires attacking root causes of waste in the value stream and implementing solutions that prevent reoccurrence. According to Toyota, the most significant source of waste is overproduction, which contributes to several different types of waste including excess handling, inventory and rework.

Overproduction is producing more, sooner or faster than required, causing a shortage of parts currently needed to fill orders because processes are busy satisfying the "wrong" order. In-process parts not in demand at the present time consume operator time and equipment capacity to make and handle them. These "extra" parts cost money to produce and don't generate any revenue while being transported to storage (waste) only to occupy valuable space (waste) in the hope someone will request them before they are damaged, become obsolete or scrapped (waste). Overproduction also lengthens lead time, since valuable time making the "wrong" parts delays fabrication of the "right" parts customers are waiting to receive. In turn, this impacts an operation's ability to respond to current customer requirements in a timely manner.

Unfortunately, a traditional "push" or batch process facilitates overproduction due to inherently inaccurate forecast-based schedules leading to excess production, material handling, counting and storage. To move from a "push" system of manufacturing, based on a forecasted schedule, to a "pull" system, driven by a rate of flow consistent with customer demand, process improvements must focus on identifying and removing barriers to flow.

An ideal flow rate is based on the notion that a work area only makes what the next process needs, when it needs it. Parts flow seamlessly from raw material to finished goods, one step at a time, without hesitation or deviation at a rate of flow consistent with customer orders. Thus, if the goal is one-piece flow, in the spirit of continuous improvement, how do we achieve it?

Let's focus on a set of guidelines, outlined by Rother and Shook, which can help organizations move closer to creating a flow-orientated process consistent with customer takt time (Figure 9.6).

The first step to achieving a more continuous flow is to establish an appropriate rate of flow. If we want to produce what the customer wants, when the customer wants it, it only makes sense to determine the rate at which customers order parts. This rate is what the industry calls the "takt" time. Once determined, we need to work toward creating a process flow rate consistent with takt time. If you have not already tried it, you will quickly learn this is not necessarily an easy task.

Creating a smooth flow, with the shortest lead time, highest quality and lowest cost involves the following guidelines:

#1 – Produce to your takt time.

#2 – Develop continuous flow wherever possible.

#3 – Use supermarkets to control production where *continuous flow* does not extend upstream.

#4 – Try to send the customer schedule to only one production process ... *the pacemaker process!*

#5 – Distribute the production of different products evenly over time at the pacemaker process → Level the production mix!

#6 – Create an "initial pull" by releasing and withdrawing small, consistent increments of work at the pacemaker process → Level the production volume!

#7 – Develop the ability to make "every part, every day" ... *then every shift, then every hour or pallet or pitch* in the fabrication processes upstream of the pacemaker process.

Figure 9.6 A lean guideline for improving flow. (From *Learning to See* by Rother & Shook, 1999. Cambridge, MA: Lean Enterprise Institute.)

Establishing Takt Time

The first order of business is to create a reference or target condition. What is the appropriate rate of production for your manufacturing line? The objective is to cycle your pacemaker process as close to the customer demand rate or "takt" time as possible. Takt time is calculated by dividing the rate of customer demand (in units per day) into the available working time (in seconds per day). See Chapter 7: "Lean Preparation", for an example of a takt time calculation.

Often, an operation will focus on producing to a planned cycle time lower than the customer takt time to compensate for variation in process. A realistic approach is to control the rate of production between the planned cycle time and takt time with the goal of closing the gap between the two. A significant gap between takt time and planned cycle time indicates the existence of production problems causing line disruptions. To maintain flow within the customer takt time, support operations must respond to problems quickly, improve equipment reliability and work to reduce, if not eliminate, changeover times.

Continuous Flow

Process flow is the continuous movement of items through a production system *without interference*. When flow is being restricted, items will begin to back up at certain points; this is called a "constraint" or "bottleneck". Too many *constraints* will cause production to slow down, increasing lead times and time to deliver finished goods to customers.

SIDEBAR: BOTTLENECK MANAGEMENT

Bottlenecks are points in a process where volume exceeds capacity, causing a slowdown in production and affecting the rate of flow through the production line. Continuous process flow is the movement of items through an entire production system without interference. Restricting process flow often results in backups at certain operations along the supply chain, creating a constraint or "bottleneck". These constraints will slow down production, increasing lead time and delaying delivery of finished goods to the customer. One way to improve flow is through bottleneck or constraint management. Process flow can be improved by identifying a process constraint, determining its root cause, eliminating the cause and verifying the effectiveness of the implemented solution. This process is repeated with each subsequent constraint encountered.

A lean operation requires a focus on achieving a more continuous, uninterrupted flow. Simple as this may seem, it's not a trivial task since time, patience and a lot of creativity is often required to achieve this objective. Continuous flow is commonly viewed as an ideal state of "one-piece flow" where one unit passes from one process step to another in a defined sequence without interruption. It's more realistically characterized by small batch sizes, minimal inventory and standardized processes. When implemented correctly, continuous flow processing:

- Reduces waste
- Saves money by reducing inventory and transportation costs
- Increases productivity; more units completed in the same or less time
- Improves quality by making it easier to spot and correct defects
- Cuts down on overhead due to increased stability and reduced lead times

Aligning process flow with customer demand often requires continuous evaluation, identification and elimination of obstacles preventing the smooth, steady, uninterrupted movement of material, information and product destined for the customer. It reflects a process without queues, unscheduled work stoppages or rework.

Supermarkets/FIFO

Since it's not always possible or practical to achieve continuous flow due to unusually long or short cycle times, changeovers, large distances between sequential processes, unrealistically long lead times or unreliable processes, the option of supermarkets exists to control production quantities in a "pull" environment where continuous flow is not practical.

As discussed, a schedule is only an estimate of what the next process will actually need. It's better to control production by linking processes to their downstream customers, most often via a supermarket-based pull system. According to Rother and Shook [2], a pull system is typically installed where continuous flow is interrupted and the upstream process must operate in a batch mode.

When establishing a supermarket, a "production" kanban is used to trigger the making of parts, while a "withdrawal" kanban notifies the material handler of the part type and quantity to transfer to the customer process downstream of the supermarket. See Figure 9.7 for an example of a *production* and *withdrawal* kanban.

A supermarket contains a small, controlled inventory of parts based on customer take rate. In production, the customer is the downstream user who "orders" parts from the upstream supplier by taking parts from a designated location for consumption. The removal of parts from the "supermarket" serves as a trigger to the upstream process (supplier) to make more parts, typically by movement of kanban cards from the supermarket to the supplier process. This mode of operation establishes product demand at the supplier process, without the need for a schedule. Product is controlled by the flow of parts between customer and supplier processes with the downstream process (customer) being the only source for determining when

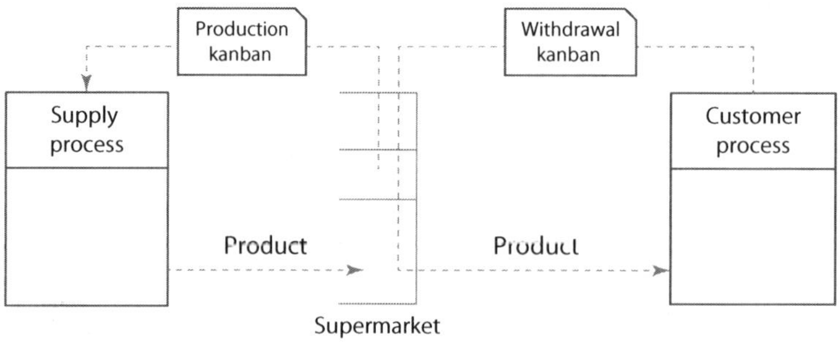

Figure 9.7 Example of a production and withdrawal kanban. (From *Learning to See* by Rother & Shook, 1999. Cambridge, MA: Lean Enterprise Institute.)

and how much to produce (e.g. pull process). On the factory floor, supermarkets are typically located near the supplying process to maintain a visual link with customer requirements. However, one disadvantage of a supermarket is that it must hold a stock of all parts that downstream operations need to produce.

FIFO lanes between decoupled processes can *substitute* for a supermarket and maintain a controlled flow between them. In this case, a supermarket is not practical due to excessive part variations, short shelf life parts or infrequently used components. FIFO lanes should only hold a specified amount of inventory. If the FIFO lane is full, the supplying process must stop producing until the customer has used some of the inventory. The FIFO lane is a tool to prevent the supplier process from overproducing.

In order to bridge the flow gap between disconnected processes and maintain flow, FIFO lanes can be used to compensate for various flow disruptors including:

- Equipment downtime
- Equipment setup time
- Rework (first pass yield [FPY])
- Batch/lot size
- Information flow
- Transport time

For example, a FIFO lane can be used when there is a large difference in cycle time between two adjacent workstations and the supplying workstation is able to produce other products. An example of a FIFO lane is presented in Figure 9.8. More on FIFO can be found in the following sidebar.

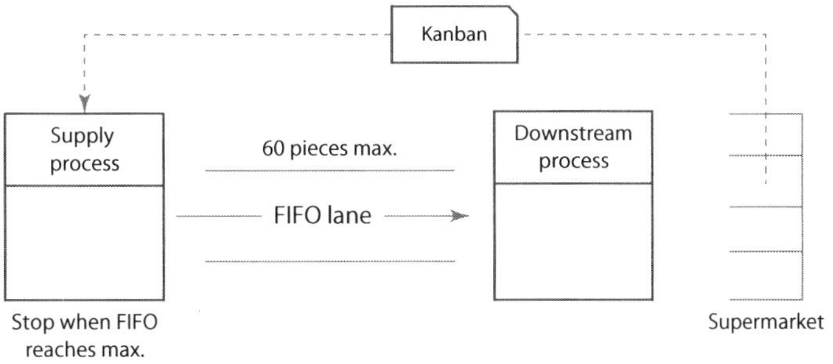

Figure 9.8 Application of FIFO lane between two processes. (From *Learning to See* by Rother & Shook, 1999. Cambridge, MA: Lean Enterprise Institute.)

SIDEBAR: FIFO'S CONTRIBUTION TO PROBLEM-SOLVING

FIFO facilitates problem-solving. When a defective unit occurs, it's easier to isolate a problem to a time period or serial number when the sequence of production is maintained. The absence of FIFO can hide flow problems. When the output of two machines performing the same work is expected to occur at the same rate, a degradation of one may go unnoticed as operators favor the other. Simply stated, if you have no problems, there is no benefit to FIFO.

Establish a Pacemaker Process

The pacemaker process is the point in production where you "set the pace" for the rate of production. The idea behind the pacemaker process is to designate only one point in production for controlling customer orders. If production orders can be pulled at the rate of customer demand at one location (e.g. pacemaker process), this sets the rate of pull for all upstream processes while eliminating the need for a schedule. On the other hand, any variation in production volume at the pacemaker process will impact upstream capacity requirements.

No supermarket or pull should occur downstream of the pacemaker process since material transfer from the pacemaker process to finished goods needs to occur as a flow. There will be a tendency for the pacemaker process to move upstream as the work product becomes more customized. See Figure 9.9 for examples of pacemaker processes.

Look for an opportunity to schedule production from only one production process; this becomes the pacemaker process where you will eventually work to release production orders evenly, with the objective of pulling consistent increments of work through this control point. Once you have established the pacemaker process, it's time to consider leveling the volume and mix of production through the line.

Production Leveling

To achieve a high degree of customer responsiveness without building significant piles of inventory, organizations need to respond quickly to changes in customer demand by managing the volume and mix of products produced in a week, a day, a shift or even an hour. The initial goal of leveling production is to minimize supply chain inventory by smoothing out the volume and mix of parts produced each day. This will require more control

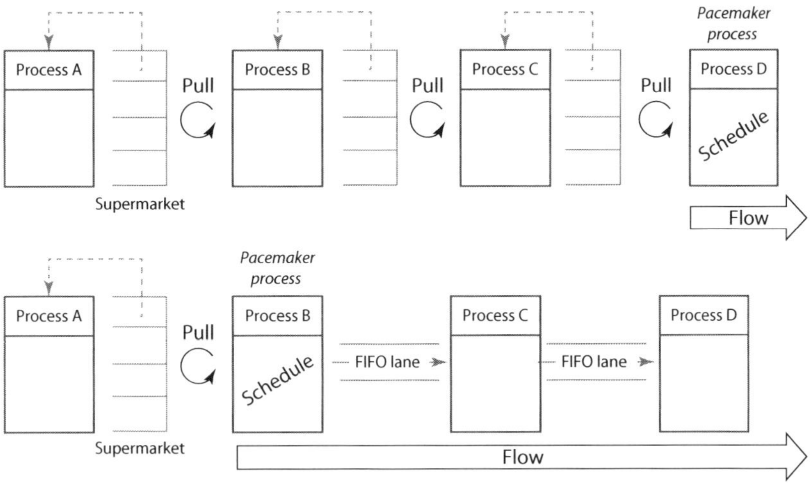

Figure 9.9 Identification of the pacemaker process. (From *Learning to See* by Rother & Shook, 1999. Cambridge, MA: Lean Enterprise Institute.)

over incoming materials, helping to regulate production variation and enhancing flexibility in response to dynamic customer requests.

Level Production Mix

To further improve process flow, work to distribute the production of different product variants evenly at the pacemaker process over a specific time period; the shorter the time period, the better. This requires a level of flexibility that comes from reducing changeover times to near zero.

Scheduling long runs of one product type without corresponding demand and avoiding changeovers means fabricated components will be consumed in batches, increasing process inventories needed for upstream supermarkets. Batching products and producing them all at once requires more finished goods inventory to meet changing customer requirements. The more you level product mix at the pacemaker process, the more responsive you will be in meeting customer demands through shorter lead times while minimizing finished goods inventory.

Leveling Production Volume

Releasing large batches of work into production often causes shuffling of work orders to meet inaccurate forecasted schedules. This eventually puts an undue burden on machines, people and supermarkets struggling to respond, leading to increased lead times and expedited shipments. The purpose of leveling production volume is to create a "pull" of small, consistent work batches at the pacemaker process. If done in a controlled and consistent manner, you should be able to simultaneously take away an equal amount of finished goods currently being produced, maintaining a consistent flow.

Leveling production volumes will require scheduling small batch sizes upstream of the pacemaker process, requiring less inventory in the supermarkets. If you only produce one product, this may be relatively easy to do. However, more likely than not, multiple variants are produced on the same line, highlighting the need to reduce changeover times to the shortest possible duration in order to facilitate a reduction in batch size. An example of production leveling is shown in Figure 9.10.

Batch Size Reduction

A lean approach seeks to improve process flow by reducing batch size. Smaller batch sizes facilitate customization of goods and services. It increases an operation's ability to respond more quickly to changing customer demands, reducing cycle time and inventory generated by overproduction. Unfortunately, it also makes a process more vulnerable to process hiccups such as unplanned downtime or unexpected spikes in defect levels since a decrease in inventory reduces the number of available parts needed to "buy" time to correct an issue before it negatively impacts the customer. Thus, operations need to respond quickly to problems, within the available

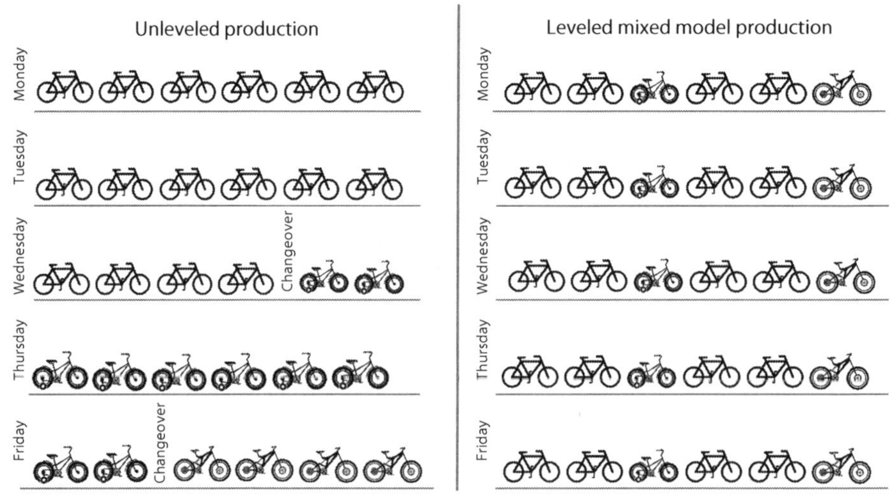

Figure 9.10 Production leveling of product volume and mix.

time frame of existing inventory levels, to avoid impacting customer deliveries.

Smaller batch sizes support a lean operation, but if an organization is not prepared to rapidly respond to risks imposed by unexpected flow disruptions, any cost savings in internal flow improvement will be lost in external costs of quality to protect the customer from those disruptions. In short, when working to reduce batch size, also focus on reducing changeover time. Concurrently, look to improve process stability by increasing equipment reliability, material availability, individual capability and managing deviations from standard work instructions while striving to permanently eliminate defects.

In summary, continuous flow is considered one of the most efficient ways to produce. To move from batch to continuous flow requires a plan, discipline and persistence to reduce changeover time, batch size, non-value work, operator movements and material travel while improving equipment reliability (e.g. total productive maintenance [TPM]) and response time to downstream pull. Continuous flow is best served when product scheduling occurs at only one operation in production, considered the pacemaker process. The pacemaker process establishes the point beyond which continuous flow is expected for all subsequent downstream operations.

A focus on reducing changeover time at the pacemaker process will provide increased flexibility in response to shifting customer demands. The objective is to flow where possible by combining work areas to eliminate gaps between workstations and operators while employing smaller, simpler, dedicated equipment, where feasible. Supermarkets and FIFO can be used as a controlled form of batching to "pull" product where flow is not practical or possible upstream of the pace-setting process. Both supermarkets and FIFO are used to reduce and control inventories.

Successful transformation to a more flow-orientated line design requires people who understand and can effectively apply lean principles, methods and practices when needed to achieve specific improvement objectives. Remember, achieving flow requires the right environment, attitude and mindset driven by a

- Deep understanding of lean principles, practices and methods
- Management and employee commitment to continuous improvement
- Clear outline and understanding of roles, responsibilities and work routines

- Commitment to process control and continuous improvement
- Persistent follow-up and closure of prioritized actions
- Relentless pursuit of perfection

Value Stream Mapping (for Improvement)

As indicated previously, a value stream is a collection of cross-functional processes consisting of all necessary steps required to deliver value to the customer. According to the Shingo Institute, *Clearly understanding the entire value stream is the only way for an organization to improve the value delivered and/or improve the process by which it is delivered. Creating value for customers is ultimately accomplished through the effective alignment of every value stream in an organization.*

VSM is one of the few techniques that takes a holistic approach to improving the flow of material and information within a value stream with the objective of avoiding overproduction. A current state map visualizes flow relative to existing processes, procedures and facility layout, from receipt of raw materials to shipment of finished goods to the customer. It helps to see beyond a single process, highlighting sources of waste in the value stream while providing a common language and focus on issues impacting flow. A current state map can reveal opportunities for improving flow that can be visualized in a future state map in order to effect change. The future state map establishes a vision of how material and information can flow more efficiently while minimizing overproduction. It provides a roadmap for incremental improvement that can be used in planning a new production facility, designing a new manufacturing process or simply improving an existing line layout. By documenting the current state and visualizing a future state, a plan can be prepared to close the gap between the two existing states. Closing the gap should be an iterative process, often using simple tools and methods such as the plan-do-check-act (PDCA) cycle to identify, analyze and methodically eliminate each obstacle along the path to a more desired state, periodically employing a scientific approach of experimentation whenever one's threshold of knowledge is encountered.

Closing the gap is a journey, not a race since we are expected to continually redefine the future state as we enhance our knowledge from data and information acquired along the way to operational excellence. Value stream maps can be drawn at different points in time to raise awareness of opportunities for improvement. A current state determines current condition from order to delivery. A future state map establishes a reference for planning and deploying a plan to achieve a higher level of performance by visualizing opportunities for improvement.

In summary, one of the more fundamental notions that dominates process improvement today is the elimination of waste in the value stream, where a proactive effort exists to remove obstacles impeding process flow. To remain competitive, a relentless focus on waste removal must incorporate both a proactive as well as reactive effort reflective of behaviors consistent with the fundamental principles of operational excellence.

Improving process flow involves merging and optimizing workflows within a system, with the ultimate objective of achieving a continuous or "one-piece' flow. Breaking down process silos and integrating workflows is a strategy for enhancing flow with the aid of controlled but minimal buffers. Removal of barriers between people, products and equipment will most likely be required, followed by balancing workloads. Adopting a JIT approach and "pull" system is often required to facilitate continuous flow without overproduction. In addition, logistically tracking how much inventory needs to be replenished and the source of replenishment is crucial to reducing shortages that hinder the ability to maintain a smooth, steady flow. To institute continuous flow, stakeholders need to reduce variation by standardizing and stabilizing processes, followed by improving efficiency through waste reduction and removal of obstacles preventing flow.

Value stream improvement is a management responsibility that requires a vision of continuous efficiency improvement from receiving to shipping and a commitment to realize that vision. Improvements to flow should be part of the strategic planning process so lean projects can be financially supported in the annual budget, reviewed on a periodic basis, controlled for deviations from plan and verified effective upon completion. It's important to hold people accountable to project plans in order to increase their likelihood of success.

Sustainable process flow must be rooted in standardized procedures, monitored through daily work routines and controlled through deviation management using visual controls to facilitate the rapid identification and eradication of process anomalies and negative performance trends.

Key Points

- Continuous flow may not be practical or desirable for all products.
- A benefit of pursuing continuous process flow is the elimination of part congestion within and between processes.

- A predictable process flow will more easily reveal obstacles for elimination.
- Flow where you can, pull where you can't.
- Shorter changeover times and smaller batches will allow upstream processes to respond more quickly to downstream dynamics.
- A reduction in equipment setup time will facilitate a reduction in lot size.
- Stabilize and level the schedule; minimize material handling.
- Use pull signals (e.g. kanban) to replenish raw materials.
- FIFO provides material traceability for problem analysis.
- When it's difficult to find additional improvement opportunities, consider slowly reducing inventories.
- Changes to facility layout may provide the greatest opportunity for improvement but at a potentially significant cost and effort.
- VSM helps to visualize and understand the flow of information and material between work processes within a value stream.
- Building a leaner organization without a VSM is like building a house without a blueprint.
- VSM is used as a reference or baseline for developing improvement plans.
- We only get paid for what we do in the value stream.

References

1. Steven Spear and Kent Bowen. 1999. Decoding the DNA of the Toyota Production System. *Harvard Business Review.* https://hbr.org/1999/09/decoding-the-dna-of-the-toyota-production-system.
2. Mike Rother and John Shook. 1999. *Learning to See.* Cambridge, MA: Lean Enterprise Institute.

SUSTAINABLE IMPROVEMENTS

III

> Sustainable excellent results requires the transformation of a culture to one where every single person is engaged every day in making small, and from time-to-time large, changes.
>
> **The Shingo Institute**

Overview

Operational excellence is an idea; an idea of what an organization should be, an idea about how an organization should behave, an idea about how an organization can best serve its customers. It's an idea that starts with leadership; captured in the core principles and strategies of an enterprise; exercised through operational systems, procedures, tools and techniques; and displayed in the behaviors of every employee. It's an idea reflected in sustainable improvements, key performance metrics and long-term cultural change based on the pursuit of perfection in all areas of organizational operations.

The Shingo Model for Operational Excellence

The Shingo Institute, based at the Jon M. Huntsman School of Business at Utah State University, has developed *The Shingo Model for Operational Excellence.* The Shingo model introduces Shingo guiding principles that are intended to guide organizations in transforming their culture to achieve ideal results through operational excellence.

The Shingo model is based on the ideas of Dr. Shigeo Shingo who worked extensively with Toyota executives to apply and learn from these concepts through real-world experiences. He captured and shared his knowledge of these concepts through 17 published books. The model encourages use of the Shingo guiding principles to develop systems that influence behaviors to achieve ideal results through the application of tools and development of people. The institute believes, *Tools and systems alone do not operate a business. People do. Each person within an organization has a set of values and beliefs that influences the way he or she behaves. Ultimately, the aggregate of people's behaviors makes up organizational culture, and culture greatly influences the organization's results.*

The Shingo Institute has identified three important insights over the course of developing the Shingo model related to enterprise excellence:

1. Ideal results require ideal behaviors
2. Purpose and systems drive behavior
3. Principles inform ideal behaviors

The Shingo model describes the enabling role of improvement tools and systems influencing behaviors that lead to ideal results. Tools are expected to enable systems in achieving their intended purpose. The Shingo Institute further defines their 10 guiding principles as the basis for *building a lasting culture and achieving enterprise excellence* and divides these principles into four categories: cultural enablers, continuous improvement, enterprise alignment and results. These categories, guiding principles and supporting concepts are the basis for Chapter 10. Chapter 11 will put these concepts into the context of daily shop floor management as well as exploring the importance of structure, discipline and accountability in determining and sustaining quality and efficiency improvements. Chapter 12 will complete this discussion by reviewing the pillars upon which a lean enterprise is built. It will reinforce key points discussed in previous chapters and complement those with the task of leadership in linking these concepts together into a cohesive strategy for creating a sustainable environment for operational excellence.

Key Points

- Sustainability is achieved through a structured, disciplined approach to process control while holding people accountable to their commitments.
- Sustainable improvements can be achieved by putting the right systems in place and ensuring people execute those systems properly.
- It's often more difficult to sustain an improvement than to implement one. Discipline is required for long-term sustainability.

Bibliography

Shingo Institute, Utah State University. 2016. *The Shingo Model for Operational Excellence.* Logan, UT: Jon M. Huntsman, School of Business.

Chapter 10

Creating a Culture of Operational Excellence (Culture, Principles, Systems, Behaviors and Results)

> The only thing of real importance that leaders do is to create and manage culture. If you do not manage culture, it manages you, and you may not even be aware of the extent to which this is happening
>
> **Edgar Schein**
> *Professor MIT Sloan, School of Management*

Organizational Culture

Edgar Schein's model of organizational culture, originating in the 1980s, identified three distinct components of organizational culture: artifacts and behaviors, espoused values and assumptions. These three distinctions refer to the degree to which different cultural phenomena are visible to the observer.

Artifacts and behaviors are what we see. They are tangible, overt or verbally identifiable elements in an organization, such as architecture, furniture, dress code and office jokes. They are visible in a culture and recognized by people who are not part of the culture [1]. Espoused values include what is said. They comprise an organization's stated values and rules of behavior. Espoused values articulate how members represent the organization to themselves and others, as expressed in official philosophies and public statements of identity. Assumptions are what we actually believe; they are deeply embedded and unconscious behaviors that constitute the essence of culture. They are based on our closely held beliefs about cause and effect and about people. Assumptions are influenced by our understanding acquired through life experiences and are often so well integrated into our environment that they are hard to recognize. Figure 10.1 visualizes this model of organizational culture.

In essence, culture is defined by values, beliefs and behaviors. It's often difficult to recognize values and beliefs; however, we can observe behaviors as a window or a glimpse into an organization's culture. If we want to change culture, we must understand how values and beliefs are formed, and influence those factors in an impactful way by challenging the assumptions upon which they are based.

Changing culture also requires we observe behaviors as a way to monitor and control our effectiveness in doing so. Behaviors are a good visual indicator of our acceptance and commitment to changing cultural norms. Organizations that want to change and sustain different cultural norms must move beyond traditional monitoring and control of financial and operational performance indicators (e.g. key performance indicators) and start observing key behavioral indicators (KBI) so undesired behaviors can be adjusted and desirable behaviors reinforced. As an example, an organization that promotes a behavior of fear is likely to produce vastly different results than one that encourages behaviors rooted in trust and respect. Thus, if you want to achieve a culture of sustainable continuous improvements, you

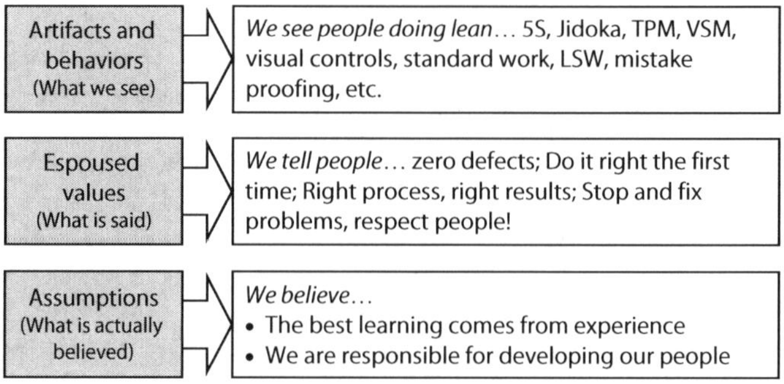

Figure 10.1 Edgar Schein's model of organizational culture.

must first challenge the values and beliefs upon which current culture is based and influence the factors that drive behaviors reflective of operational excellence.

SIDEBAR: OPERATIONAL EXCELLENCE ON DISPLAY

"Success not shared is a failure". Those are the words of the founder of one of the most successful tequila companies in Mexico. I had the rare opportunity to visit the Patron Tequila Company, recognized as one of the most trusted brands in their industry. At the time, they employed 17,000 employees in a truly handicraft-based process from the manufacturing of their glass bottles to the packing of their product for shipment. They shared a common vision of quality tequila that employees embraced and created value for the customer as evident in their continued growth over the years.

Although most of their manufacturing involved manually intensive process steps, their employees were proud to be part of the brand while blue agave plant growers yearned to be one of their chosen suppliers. They created a constancy of purpose among their people who work cooperatively to protect the brand's image in the eye of its customers and the world. Their guiding principles include a focus on maintaining consistent product quality by disciplined controls and batch traceability. Seeking perfection was integrated into their systems by blending lots and testing product to achieve a consistent, signature taste.

Value to the customer was demonstrated in their product as well as their production location, from the handmade bottles, the consistency of the product, the packaging and labeling of the tequila, to the décor of their guesthouse and the meticulous manicuring of the hacienda grounds. Even the reception guests received when they were invited to share in the Patron experience reflected the company's values and beliefs. This operation exhibited a clear commitment to the principles of operational excellence. If you were not a Patron Tequila fan before you entered the grounds, you became one before leaving.

Insights of Enterprise Excellence

In the Shingo Institute's quest to describe an excellent organizational culture, they attempted to understand what behaviors, results and fundamental characteristics help to define, influence and manage a sustainable culture.

In doing so, they identified three insights of enterprise excellence [2]. Let's consider the implications of each insight in creating a culture of excellence.

Insight #1: Ideal Results Require Ideal Behaviors

A mindset is a reflection of the ideas and attitudes with which a person approaches a situation, whereas behavior shapes how a person acts in response to a particular stimulus. If we want an organization to behave in a certain way, we must understand what drives behavior and make this the starting point for change. A framework for sustainable improvement emanates from a series of guiding principles recognized and embraced by the organization to facilitate a common mindset and culture.

Lean (gemba or management) walks can be used to observe operational behaviors and provide insight as to how an organization executes systems, follows procedures, tackles problems, makes decisions and interacts with each other as part of their daily work routines. Lean walks can be a valuable means of revealing employee behaviors in their natural environment.

Results hail from learned behaviors. The behavior of employees, observed and learned from their leaders, determine resulting outcomes. Management must mirror the behaviors required to produce the desired results and take the initiative to correct undesirable behaviors when observed. The sustainability of these behaviors hinges on the workforce's deep understanding of what the organization expects and the operating systems upon which the guiding principles are based. Behaviors reflect people's habits. One must form ideal habits to change and reinforce desired behaviors. In short, sustainable improvement practices must be deeply rooted in an organization's cultural norms.

For continuous improvement to truly become part of an enterprise's DNA, expected behaviors should be communicated in the roles and responsibilities of all employees and reinforced in the actions exhibited by an organization's hierarchy. Sustainable behaviors must be measured and desired behaviors verified. KBIs can be identified, monitored and controlled like any other process metric. Desired behaviors must be recognized, monitored, controlled and continuously reinforced to ensure sustainability. For example, an employee who repeatedly completes projects on time and within budget, while satisfying customer requirements, becomes an opportunity to reward a desired behavior. In the end, the value of influencing and developing ideal behaviors is proactive in nature since driving ideal behaviors often leads to predictable and desirable outcomes, especially if they are based on guiding principles. Every part of the business must start practicing and exhibiting principle-based behaviors, in every decision made and action taken, in order to establish and reinforce desired behaviors that eventually become unconscious routines embedded in the psyche and displayed in the intent of every employee.

Insight #2: Purpose and Systems Drive Behaviors

Systems are designed to produce a specific result by guiding people to behave in a deliberate way. In addition to people's beliefs, systems can also have a profound effect on behaviors. Managers have the responsibility of aligning organizational systems to drive ideal behavior and leadership has the ultimate responsibility to ensure meaningful and sustainable results are realized. Good outcomes are driven by good inputs, process activities and the right behaviors. According to the Shingo Institute, *Great results are the outcome of following the principles that govern the results. Ideal results require ideal behavior.*

As Gandhi once said, *Be the change you want to see in the world.* Thus, if you want to change behavior, it must start with you. If you want to change the attitudes and behaviors of your associates, you must ensure that management systems are aligned with the guiding principles recognized by organizational leadership.

A system is a set of related or interacting elements forming a complex entity or whole. In an organization, a system may consist of methods, processes or practices united to achieve a specific purpose, objective, activity or outcome. An example of a system designed to maintain process control may include visual controls, standard work routines, deviation management procedures, process audits and periodic performance reviews.

All work performed by an organization is the result of a system consisting of inputs and work activities intended to produce an expected outcome. In addition to producing outcomes, systems drive behaviors that affect those outcomes. The design and execution of a system can significantly influence behavior. Properly crafted and executed systems will promote good behaviors and deliver expected results, while poorly constructed systems can lead to unpredictable outcomes disruptive to business operations. Simply put, operational excellence is a reflection of properly created and controlled systems aligned with guiding principles reflective of an organization's core values and beliefs.

Business systems typically employ a collection of tools, working in concert, to accomplish a specific purpose or objective. The Shingo Institute™, in their publication *The Shingo Model for Operation Excellence*, states, *Perhaps the largest mistake made by corporations over the last three or four decades has been the inappropriate focus on a specific tool-set as the basis for their improvement efforts.* Simply implementing a tool, without just cause, brings little value to the long-term advancement of an organization. For example, implementing a kanban or load leveling system because that's what lean company's do, when no real justification exists, is simply waste.

The Shingo Institute™ defines a system as *a collection of tools or tasks that are highly integrated to accomplish an outcome.* They go on to define a tool as *a single device or item that accomplishes a specific task.* A system can be viewed as a collection of tools used in a coordinated way to achieve an objective or purpose. A tool can be anything that helps facilitate a particular function or achieves an objective or result. A tool should be implemented with purpose and enable a system to perform an intended function easier, faster, cheaper and/or safer.

Tools do not answer the question of "why", only the question of "how". The "why" can be better explained by a system that uses tools to accomplish a specific purpose or objective. One of the five fundamental paradigm shifts that Shingo teaches is that, *The tools of lean, TQM, JIT, Six Sigma, etc. are enablers and should be strategically and cautiously inserted into appropriate systems to better drive ideal behavior and excellent results.* In other words, a tool used without purpose or context is meaningless.

Systems are defined by procedures and tools that bring structure, consistency and efficiency to their execution. Systems require people to deploy procedures while interacting with materials, tools, equipment, machines and each other to make things happen. Operational excellence requires both managers and employees to hold themselves and others accountable to the highest standard of performance that systems allow. Peer pressure can be a very effective tool for maintaining employee accountability at all levels of the organization. Some of the most interesting examples of peer pressure can be observed in the behaviors of people from different cultures. For example, in Japan, people stop and wait for a light to change before crossing a deserted street. If a local or tourist breaks protocol, it's not unusual for someone to say something or a crowd of people to display auditory or facial expressions of disapproval. Peer pressure is often a powerful tool for establishing and maintaining accountability and can be especially effective in the workplace.

Insight #3: Principles Inform Ideal Behavior

The Shingo Institute™ believes that *Principles are foundational rules that govern the consequences of behaviors. The more deeply one understands principles, the more clearly they understand ideal behavior. The more clearly they understand ideal behavior, the better they can design systems to drive that behavior to achieve ideal results.*

The following excerpts, taken from *The Shingo Model for Operational Excellence*, captures this idea of principles as fundamental truths [3].

> *Stephen R. Covey described principles as fundamental truths. He defined a principle as a natural law that is universally understood, timeless in its meaning and fundamentally inarguable because it is self-evident.*
>
> *Principles govern the laws of science; they determine the consequences of human relationships; and ultimately, principles influence the successful outcome of every business endeavor.*

The Shingo model also prescribes that principles can predict performance, stated as follows:

> *One of the most powerful aspects of principles is their ability to predict outcomes. Principles govern the outcome or consequence of the behavioral choices we each make. The closer our actual behavior aligns with the ideal behavior that is linked to the principle, the greater the likelihood the outcomes of our behavior can be predicted.*

If principles can predict outcomes, as Covey suggests, one must identify the principles that best suit one's purpose, goals and objectives and align one's behaviors with the ideal behaviors of those principles to achieve desired results. For example, if an organization was interested in improving their problem-solving outcomes to achieve more permanent and sustainable solutions, they could embrace the principles of scientific thinking rooted in direct observation and repeated cycles of experimentation to constantly refine and improve their problem-solving aptitude.

Guiding Principles for Operational Excellence (The Shingo Model)

In addition to the three insights of enterprise excellence, the Shingo Institute™ has a mission to help organizations create a sustainable culture of operational excellence. In doing so, they promote five fundamental paradigm shifts to guide organizations toward a more robust and sustainable state of performance. These paradigm shifts are as follows:

1. Operational excellence requires a focus on both results and behaviors.
2. Ideal behaviors in an organization are those that flow from the principles that govern desired outcomes.
3. Principles construct the only foundation upon which a culture can be built, if it is to be sustained over the long term.
4. Creating ideal, principle-based behaviors requires the alignment of management systems that have the greatest impact on how people behave.
5. Tools of lean, total quality management (TQM), just-in-time (JIT), Six Sigma and so on, are enablers and should be strategically and cautiously inserted into appropriate systems to better drive ideal behavior and excellent results.

A paradigm shift is a fundamental change in one's approach or underlying assumptions. This change in approach or altering of assumptions requires an organization to reflect upon their current reality and consider realigning their operational practices with one or more of the foregoing statements, if they are accepted as valid truths.

If we accept the fundamental truth that system-based principles drive behaviors that produce ideal results and the notion that principles define systems, the following relationship establishes an approach for achieving desired results.

Principles → Systems → Tools → Behaviors → Results

Dr. Shingo, the inspiration for the institute, recognized that business results are the product of behaviors derived from an inherent relationship between principles, systems and tools. Principles answer the fundamental question of "why" we do, what we do. When people understand the "why" behind organizational expectations, they are more empowered to align their actions and behaviors with those expectations, resulting in less confusion, more harmonization and increased cooperation within the hierarchy. Knowing the "how" without understanding the "why" leaves people questioning the value of what they do and are often powerless to do anything about it. When people understand the "why" behind what they are doing, they share a common sense of purpose and direction that empowers them to make better decisions aligned with the initiatives of their organizations.

When employees and corresponding systems are aligned with organizationally accepted principles, appropriate behaviors become self-evident, leading individuals and teams to work more cooperatively toward a common purpose and goal. Clearly, it's much easier to manage people who share a common understanding and commitment to core principles than managing people who take a more "independent" view of work. Thus, organizations should consider which guiding principles best align with their collective vision and use these concepts to create systems and select tools to reinforce desired behaviors that lead to ideal results. Principles are not created or conceived but are realized through study and exploration. A principle is considered universal and timeless. This means that it can apply to anyone, anywhere at any moment with exact consequences.

The Shingo Model of Operational Excellence, as presented in Figure 10.2, has identified 10 guiding principles with supporting concepts, classified into four categories.

According to the Shingo Institute, these guiding principles were not created, they always existed. Dr. Steven Covey, as stated earlier, has described principles as "fundamental truths" or natural laws that are timeless in meaning and difficult to argue since they are "self-evident". In a similar context, the Shingo Institute stated:

> *Whether we acknowledge them or not, the principles of operational excellence always govern the consequence of our leadership and management behaviors.*

In *The Shingo Model for Operational Excellence,* cultural enablers focus on people; continuous improvement concerns process; enterprise alignment ensures purpose; and results support stakeholders. Let's dive into the four categorical principles in more detail.

Categorical principles	Guiding Principles	Supporting Concepts	Dimensions
Cultural Enablers	• Lead with humility	• Assure a safe environment • Develop people • Empower and involve everyone	People
	• Respect every individual		
Continuous Improvement	• Flow and pull value • Assure quality at the source • Focus on process • Embrace scientific thinking • Seek perfection	• Stabilize processes • Standardize processes • Insist on direct observation • Focus on value stream • Keep it simple and visual • Identify and eliminate waste • No defect passed forward • Integrate improvement with work • Rely on data and facts	Process
Enterprise Alignment	• Create constancy of purpose • Think systematically	• See reality • Focus on long term • Align systems and strategy • Standardize daily management	Purpose
Results	• Create value for the customer	• Measure what matters • Align behaviors with performance • Identify cause-and-effect relationships	Stakeholders

Figure 10.2 Shingo guiding principles and supporting concepts.

Cultural Enablers

The cultural enablers category, the foundation of the Shingo model, includes "Lead with Humility" and "Respect Every Individual". For most people, it's not hard to accept these two principles as fundamental truths since many of us recognize and understand their meaning and value as individuals and within organizations. Yet, understanding versus living these principles becomes one of the many challenges individuals and organizations face on the continuous improvement journey. Cultural enablers puts a focus on people. Let's explore the two guiding principles under this category.

SIDEBAR: THE UNDERUTILIZED RESOURCE

As most of us are aware, the world is becoming a more competitive place for conducting business every day. To remain competitive, companies must use all their available resources to drive efficiency improvements. One of the most available and flexible resources in organizations is people. The Shingo Institute stated it very well when they said: *For an organization to be competitive, the full potential of every single individual must be realized. People are the only organizational asset that has an infinite capacity to appreciate in value. The challenges of competing in global markets are so great that success can only be achieved when every person at every level of the organization is able to continuously innovate and improve.* Thus, if a company's greatest resource is its people and their untapped potential, before looking outside for help or support, consider the possibilities and potential within.

Lead with Humility

Leading with humility starts with creating a safe and healthy workplace for employees. It reflects an enterprise that cares about the environment and the surrounding communities it occupies and impacts. It's about developing people, allowing them to enhance their knowledge and explore new opportunities that broaden their thinking, influence their outlook and augment their behavior. It's about allowing each individual to achieve their full potential and releasing that potential in constructive, meaningful and beneficial ways for them and the company they support.

Lead with Humility can be both introspective and extrospective. From an internal perspective, it's about displaying vulnerability by acknowledging that you may not know everything and are willing to open your mind to the insights and ideas of others in order to continuously learn and adjust one's own behavior and actions in sync with the surrounding environment.

SIDEBAR: HUMILITY ON DISPLAY

Listening is a display of leadership. It's rare nowadays to see a leader take time to really listen to the people for whom they are responsible. I observed a rare display of this behavior when I did volunteer work in Honduras. A professor from a local university in Illinois was leading a group of 30 nursing students to perform charity work in low-income communities outside of Tegucigalpa city. The trip offered the students an exceptional experience to interact with local Hondurans while allowing them to exercise their medical training with the support of several certified nurses from the university and local Honduran doctors.

Each evening after dinner, the professor would gather her students together in a large room and ask each one to share their experiences from the day's activities. She listened intently, revealed a little of herself through her feedback, while making sure that every student shared a little about themselves through the insights they gathered during their day. It was a refreshing opportunity to see real leadership in action, as she took the time to listen and allow those she was leading to share their perspective among their colleagues, creating a collective experience for all. For many of the students, these daily experiences and evening discussions significantly changed their perspective on what community service was about and how their actions can make a difference in today's world.

From an external perspective, it's about seeking the input of others, valuing their ideas and trusting their judgment while understanding that sound logic leads to good decisions. Trust is one of the highest complements you can bestow upon someone, knowing their actions can impact your performance. Both individual and organizational growth occurs when people are trusted to do the right thing and are given the opportunity to make a difference.

Humility, in part, is about pushing decision-making to the lowest level of the organization possible, allowing those who are informed and closest to the problem influence the outcome. If done with humility and respect for others, the best of an organization starts to unfold.

Respect Every Individual

Respect for individuals comes in many different forms, starting with a safe and healthy work environment. Respect for every individual is reflected in the way organizations recognize, reward and develop their people. How leaders treat managers and managers treat their employees is observed by all and influences the way employees feel, behave and act toward each other and their work. Respect for every individual is a fundamental "law" that few can argue.

Developing a culture of mutual respect and humility starts at the top and must be reflected in the behaviors of the entire organization to ensure sustainability. Leaders, managers and supervisors must display the characteristics and behaviors they want their people to exhibit. When organizations treat their employees the way they expect their employees to treat their customers, mutual respect becomes evident.

Actionable improvement opportunities for cultural enablers include:

- Listen and learn from others
- Be open to new ideas and creative thinking

- Provide avenues for people to explore new opportunities
- Involve people in decisions that impact them

> *A leader's willingness to seek input, listen carefully and continuously learn creates an environment where associates feel respected and energized and give freely of their creative abilities.*
>
> **The Shingo Model for OE**

To facilitate the realization of each guiding principle, the Shingo Institute has identified supporting concepts to help establish the framework for a sustainable work atmosphere of respect, empowerment and creativity. Supporting concepts under the principle of "Lead with Humility" include "Assure a Safe Environment", "Develop People" and "Empower and Involve Everyone".

There is nothing more important than creating an environment in which people can work without fear for their safety or health. This is, without question, priority number one. Although this may seem obvious to some, there are many situations and places throughout the world where this basic need can be challenging and costly to realize. The idea of a safe atmosphere also extends to the external environment and communities touched by the reach of an organization's activities and interactions.

People development is a tenet of operational excellence since it can significantly influence and alter how people think, act and react. Expanding the knowledge and skills of those expected to drive change can accelerate the ability of an organization to achieve their lean transformation. People development is inexplicably linked to the third supporting concept of "Empower and Involve Everyone" by the idea that education and opportunity can release the untapped potential of people to grow and evolve in ways that can change the course of their lives and a company's future.

The business world of today is unlike anything ever experienced before, with global competition coming from all ends of the spectrum. Companies will be unable to compete unless they involve every employee and allow them to release their full potential to continuously innovate and elevate their level of performance. Organizational leadership must set the stage for continuous and sustainable improvements as demonstrated by their commitment to creating a safe, healthy, knowledgeable, skilled, empowered and involved workforce. Examples of supporting behaviors for guiding principles can be found in Figure 10.3.

Principles	Behaviors
Cultural Enablers	• Seek input of others • Listen for understanding • Learn through observation
Continuous Improvement	• People make improvements every day • Teams use scientific thinking to learn • Managers coach and mentor others • People go and see to solve problems
Enterprise Alignment	• Strategies are created and deployed • Employees ask "Why" to understand • Systems are developed to support people
Results	• Process stability and capability is maintained • Value is defined, understood and delivered • Systems are developed to create value

Figure 10.3 Behaviors supporting guiding principles.

Continuous Improvement

Continuous improvement focuses on process. Process encompasses many aspects of production from the receipt of raw material through product assembly to final goods staging for customer delivery. It involves selecting the right inputs and performing the correct activities to acquire the desired outputs. The mindset of continuous improvement is one of perfection with a behavior of everybody working to identify and make improvements, however minor, every day.

Several fundamental principles have been identified by the Shingo Institute™ for Continuous Improvement. These concepts including "Assure Quality at the Source", "Focus on Process", "Embrace Scientific Thinking" and "Seek Perfection", all four of which serve as a compass or direction for making process improvements while the fifth concept of "Flow and Pull Value" establishes a foundation upon which efficiency improvements are built. We will explore each of these topics in more detail.

Focus on Process

All too often, we focus on results and blame people when results don't meet expectations. Results are derived from process inputs and activities defined within a system. If we don't like the results, we should stop and evaluate the adequacy of the systems used to deliver those results before questioning the ability of people. Deep down, most people want to do a good job. Therefore, it's incumbent on management to take a step back and ask two fundamental questions: *Was the process designed to produce the desired results?* and, if so, *Was the process followed according to the method described?* Once you are convinced the process is capable of generating the desired outcome and it is being followed according to procedure, then consider the possibility of a personal performance issue. In short, question the integrity of a system before jumping to conclusions about a cause and have your facts straight before blaming those responsible for executing the process for its underperformance.

Management is responsible for the processes and systems that define how work is done; it's the employee's responsibility to ensure work, as defined by procedures, is done according to standards. There are plenty of opportunities to improve a process. In doing so, look to make a worker's job easier, faster and safer to perform so they are less likely to make mistakes. Focus on error proofing a process to prevent defects from occurring or reoccurring. Make it easier for an operator to do things right versus wrong. All too often, it's quicker to blame people than finding the real cause of a problem.

Embrace Scientific Thinking

Scientific thinking is about challenging the limits of our understanding and taking steps to push beyond those limits in order to validate ideas and acquire new knowledge. Performing root cause analysis and exploring new ideas through experimentation allow us to continuously refine our understanding of reality. Scientific thinking, applied to data collection and analysis, can help reconcile differences between predicted versus actual results, enhancing awareness. Repeated cycles of experimentation can also augment the knowledge and experience needed to make sound decisions and solve problems in a way that will prevent reoccurrences. Embrace scientific thinking through observation, experimentation and continuous learning.

Assure Quality at the Source

Quality is defined by conformance to requirements and fitness for use in a product's intended application. Quality can only be assured when systems to produce products and services are designed and executed with a clear understanding of expectations in mind. Assuring Quality at the Source includes identifying and correcting deviations from specification by stopping to fix problems immediately and using lessons learned to prevent reoccurrence for long-term stability.

Seek Perfection

Perfection is a utopian state. Although it's unrealistic to believe it can be achieved, the very act of seeking perfection creates a mindset of continuous improvement. It changes our thought process from "what can we do" to "what must we do" to eliminate a problem, remove an obstacle or achieve a strategic objective. Seeking perfection forces us to continuously look for problems to solve and obstacles to eliminate; it challenges the paradigms limiting our potential and pushes us to explore new ways to achieve the next level of performance.

Pull and Flow

If Toyota introduced anything new to the world of production, it's the value realized through pull and flow. Toyota disrupted the apple cart by starting to look at value from an internal process perspective as well as an external customer viewpoint. In doing so, they discovered vast improvement opportunities through cycle time reduction and waste elimination in an effort to deliver quality products on time and in quantities required by the customer with minimal waste. They broke the existing paradigm by moving beyond process optimization to optimizing a product's flow from incoming to shipping, realizing the plethora of opportunities existing in a product's "value stream". Once it became evident that customer value was linked to the continuous, uninterrupted flow of materials and information through a process, a new avenue for continuous improvement was introduced to the world.

The guiding principle of continuous improvement has a number of supporting concepts fundamental to good control practices and are essential for driving a sound improvement program. Most of these concepts have been discussed in previous chapters of this book, but they will be revisited and viewed in the context of operational excellence. The supporting concepts of continuous improvement, as presented by the Shingo Institute™, include:

- Stabilize processes
- Standardize processes
- Direct observation
- Value stream focus
- Keep it simple and visual
- Identify and eliminate waste

- No defect passed forward
- Integrate improvement with work
- Rely on data and facts

As is evident from the beginning of this book, *process stability* is a prerequisite for sustainable improvements. Without a consistent, repeatable process, improvements are elusive. The first step in any improvement program is to define process standards and methodically eliminate sources of instability through systematic removal of defects using proven tools of problem-solving.

Once stability is achieved, work documents must be updated to reflect and maintain current process performance. *Standardized processes* help retain improvement gains and further the ability to maintain process control through repetitive work tasks.

An important part of achieving and sustaining process stability is through deviation management. Often, this requires *direct observation* by going to the sources of variation to gather data and facts for decision-making. The value of direct observation is often not fully appreciated until you go and see for yourself. I have observed countless instances of managers sitting in meetings, listening to presentations, giving advice and providing direction without fully understanding the facts or complexity of the situation being discussed.

Insist on a go and see approach to understanding a problem or making a decision. It's difficult to challenge someone who presents factual information or argues a point based on facts. Engage in direction observation whenever possible. As stated by the Shingo Institute in the Shingo Model [2]:

> *All too frequently, perceptions, past experience, instincts and inaccurate standards are misconstrued as reality.*

A value stream perspective focuses on a broader scope, optimizing the interconnected processes from receiving to shipping versus simply improving the individual ones, independent of each other. A *value stream focus* requires we first understand what constitutes a product or service's value stream and incrementally remove obstacles disruptive to flow as we work to increase stakeholder satisfaction. Effective enhancement of the value stream requires a detailed understand of material and information flow and a genuine desire to make improvements. The key to increasing value is to optimize the interconnections between processes that deliver it.

In the world of lean, *keep it simple and visual!* It's generally believed better and cheaper outcomes result from simplification. Visualizing key information draws attention to problems, creating a target for waste elimination. It facilitates the rapid detection and response to deviations impacting process performance. One of the best ways to promote an atmosphere of control and improvement is to communicate data and information to those who need it to take action whenever a warning indicator or problem trigger is detected. If you want to know how to keep data and information simple and visual, ask those who need it!

It goes without saying the clear objective of lean is to identify and eliminate waste. This reaches beyond the simple idea of defect elimination; it involves the extra effort required to drive process changes to elevate and sustain improvements in performance. It's the desire to move beyond firefighting as a waste management program, recognizing that extinguishing fires is a prerequisite for the more serious improvement strategy of seeking out improvement opportunities every day, by everybody, everywhere.

Operational excellence requires a proactive mindset with the willingness to stop production long enough to determine root cause and implement a containment or corrective action to prevent reoccurrence. This is the idea behind *no defect passed forward*. Allowing defects to reach the next operation or a repair station is counterproductive as waste accumulates in process and increases the potential for non-conformances escaping to the customer.

Stopping to correct process deviations immediately goes to the heart of what is meant by *seeking perfection*. To successfully execute this type of response, clear work standards, reaction criteria and accountability must be established and executed in order to identify and resolve issues quickly and correctly with minimal impact to production. This supports the simple concept behind fixing problems at the source. It also extends into actively looking for and eradicating waste and obstacles to flow since excellence can only be achieved through the relentless pursuit of perfection.

As mentioned, we are hired to maintain and continuously improve the process. Thus, *integrating improvement with work* is not an idea, it's an expectation of anyone employed to perform work in a lean thinking enterprise; it's what we should be doing, every day and everywhere. Every associate should continuously challenge the status quo with the determination to find a better way of working, regardless of the obstacles. It's as much about attitude, as results. A simple methodology (e.g. plan-do-check-act [PDCA]) and a curious mind (e.g. scientific thinking) are often all it takes to integrate improvement into one's work habits.

As the saying goes, "in god we trust, all others bring data". Solving problems and sound decisions are more likely when we *rely on data and facts*. It should be the responsibility of every employee to seek and embrace reliable data and factual information in every decision they make and every problem they solve. At the same time, it's vital to understand the source of data and the origin of information before using it to influence future outcomes. Data-driven changes will ultimately lead to more predictable, successful and sustainable results.

Enterprise Alignment

Success in today's competitive global environment requires full alignment of all functions within an organization. Strategic planning is key to coalescing the organization toward a common vision and mission. Creating a unifying strategy to focus an enterprise is difficult enough; what becomes even more challenging is the ability to execute that strategy and stay on course while ignoring the plethora of distractions vying for attention. Success is significantly increased when deployment activities are defined in simple, comprehensible, actionable and standardized terms with the "why" and "how" clearly understood by all involved. Enterprise alignment focuses on two guiding principles, *create constancy of purpose* and *think systematically*.

Create Constancy of Purpose

As the saying goes, the only constant in life is change. Because we are continuously faced with change, it's only logical that we learn how to live and work in a world of constant challenges. This is even more relevant today than ever before. Survival requires companies recognize and adapt to changes quickly. The ability to respond rapidly and predictably starts with creating a unified vision, which provides a constancy of purpose so that no matter what issues or obstacles throw people off course, everyone knows how to get back on track. When everyone is clear on why the organization exists, where the organization is going and what actions are required to get there, people are empowered to move forward with confidence and purpose.

Thinking Systematically

Principles help establish systems that drive behaviors that produce results. These elements are all interconnected logically and purposefully. By understanding the connections between these relationships, the decisions we make and actions we take will facilitate system improvements that align with enterprise strategy and move operations closer to operational excellence. The idea of systematic thinking drives a constancy of purpose and helps unify an approach to continuous improvement.

There are several supporting concepts linked to "create constancy of purpose" and "thinking systematically". These concepts provide a more holistic perspective of what's behind the principle of enterprise alignment and include:

- See reality
- Focus on long term
- Align systems
- Align behaviors with performance
- Policy deployment
- Standardize daily management

Our busy lifestyles often distract us from seeing the interconnected reality around us. We tend to focus on a specific person, object or task without considering much else. To *see reality* is a lot more than just "seeing", it's about listening, touching, smelling and tasting in order to acquire a deep, more comprehensive perspective of the current situation than is considered usual. It's about understanding the scope of how decisions we make and actions we take affect us, our colleagues and our surroundings. Perhaps more importantly, it's about being aware of the lenses through which we view the world, and how this view often influences our experiences, opinions, expectations and mindset.

Organizations need to put systems in place that make it easy for people to see reality and share what they observe without filters. Only through the objective view of every employee will leadership receive a more accurate picture of reality and be better prepared to face it head-on.

A *focus on long term* allows corporations to avoid the ills associated with short-term actions taken to satisfy quarterly earnings reports. Creating a long-term strategy and sticking to it permits the achievement of more ambitious goals that one or two years of engagement will not allow. Strategy frequently looks to influence organizational culture, which is nearly impossible when only short-term goals and objectives are pursued.

Align systems plays to the constancy of purpose by allowing for a more coordinated and optimized approach to operations. When systems are aligned with the principles of operational excellence and management embraces these systems as demonstrated in their behavior, others within the organization will observe and start to follow a similar pattern of conduct. If aligned properly, individual and organizational performance should begin to reflect these changes in behavior and produce more desirable results over the long term. The goal is to *Align Behaviors with Performance* once the right systems are defined, put in place and executed.

According to the Shingo Institute, at a fundamental level, "*policy deployment* is a planning and implementation system, based on scientific thinking, employee involvement and respect for the individual". When viewed from a strategy perspective, policy deployment should reflect the principles of operational excellence in the form of policies, procedures, systems, tools and guidelines, at all levels of the organization, so as to deliver a common message and understanding while reinforcing desired behaviors and expected results.

When it comes down to managing daily business, every organization should have a set of periodic work routines, from the operator to the plant manager, which are designed to maintain process controls and drive continuous improvements in alignment with internal and customer expectations. It's these disciplined routines that are essential for driving and sustaining quality and efficiency improvements. The appropriate assigning and detailing of work standards at all levels of operations and management will ensure the proper balance of strategic and tactical work is being performed at every level, every day. This is the essence of *standardized daily management.*

Results

The end result is to *create value for the customer.* The challenge is to understand the wants, needs and expectations of key stakeholders and provide deliverables that meet those expectations in the quickest, most cost-effective way possible. Ultimate survival relies on a company's ability to consistently produce results that meet customer requirements at the lowest cost possible. This necessitates good systems, processes, organizational discipline and personal accountability. As stated by the Shingo Institute: *Great results are the outcome of following the principles that govern the results. Ideal results require ideal behavior. This is what we call operational excellence.*

CASE STUDY: OPERATIONAL EXCELLENCE IN ACTION

I once did volunteer work for a faith-based organization in Honduras. It's an organization that provides medical, social and faith-based support for struggling communities in the country. I found it to be an extremely rewarding experience, spending time helping others who welcomed and truly appreciated our engagement. The experience took on extra significance when I observed how well run this organization was, based on support by US donors in combination with skilled and passionate individuals on location. The ability to mobilize and set-up an ad hoc site (called a brigade) offering medical, dental, optical, pharmaceutical, children's hair lice treatment, the construction of cement floors and evangelism for 6 hours a day, 4 days a week, free of charge to the communities they served was impressive. The first day of my service with several paid doctors and 30 volunteer nurses and nurses in training, resulted in over 415 medical consultations, 41 dental procedures, 206 optical visits and 190 hair inspections with approximately 100 children treated for lice and on the side, 3 cement floors poured for families. The previous day (Sunday), this same team of medical volunteers packed over 70,000 pills of various types and prescriptions in preparation for this event, which totaled 4 days over a 5 day period, serving two different communities during this time. So why am I telling you this story? Because conducting an event of this type and magnitude, day after day, week after week, takes incredible commitment to process planning, execution, monitoring and control. Roles and responsibilities must be clearly defined, work routines established, equipment made available and materials procured before coordinating with the out-of-country volunteers and recipient communities. In addition to all this, skilled translators were required to allow this mostly English-speaking team to communicate with local community members.

In short, this service-orientated organization was highly efficient and successful due to their faith-based principles, augmented by clearly established systems and procedures that were communicated, understood and executed by passionate, skilled and dedicated individuals committed to their mission. This was a genuine display of constancy of purpose and a demonstration of operational excellence in action.

Create Value for the Customer

Value is defined by the customer and is captured in requirements obtained through two-way conversations, listening, clarifying questions and confirming understanding (through accurate and approved documentation). Regardless of the effort put forth to satisfy customers, if we do not get the requirements right, the results will not reflect the reality we seek.

To understand the topic of "create value for the customer", three supporting concepts are highlighted in the Shingo model. They are

- Measure what matters
- Who is the customer?
- Identify cause-and-effect relationships

Let's review these three concepts in the context of results, starting with "measure what matters".

There is so much data available today that it's often difficult to discern what's important to measure and monitor. At a minimum, measurements should help maintain control, facilitate improvements and serve as a window into an organization's progress toward meeting its strategic objectives. If you want to *measure what matters*, ask the customer for whom you are creating value. Value is the output of meaningful activities that transforms a product from one state to another (e.g. form, fit or function), creating something useful for the customer. To create value, a company must know and understand detailed customer requirements and, just as important, how those requirements, when realized, will satisfy actual customer needs. Only through satisfying both these conditions, conformance to requirements and fitness for use, at a competitive cost, will true value be achieved. Therefore, if you want to create value, *identify cause-and-effect relationships* that turn raw materials and components into products for which customers are willing to pay.

Once the right behaviors have been identified to transform process inputs and activities into outputs, standard work routines can be put in place to measure what matters and monitor what occurs so that non-conforming outcomes can be immediately recognized and addressed. In short, measurements should be clear, easy to collect and quick to visualize and communicate so that deviations from standard and opportunities for improvement are apparent and actionable.

A process should service one or more customers. If you can't identify the customers for whom a process is intended to serve, you need to seriously consider why you are doing it. Every process has inputs, activities and outputs and every output must serve a customer in some meaningful way. If you want to know who your customers are, look for who your process outputs are expected to serve.

Customers, or more broadly stakeholders, can be internal or external to an organization. Present-day stakeholders often encompass individuals and larger groups in society including policy makers, communities, governments and media, to highlight a few. Today, companies are expected to embrace a larger sense of purpose, positively contributing to the social and environmental well-being of humanity. A modern-day producer of goods and services must know all their stakeholders, articulate their expectations and satisfy their broad expectations.

In summary, if you want to create value for the customer, detail their wants, needs and expectations into a set of requirements and deliver on those requirements as agreed.

Ideal performance results from the attitude and actions of people. Attitude is influenced by the work environment and the interaction of people in it. If you want to affect results, look at the environment in which those results are produced. Good environment, good attitude, good behavior, good results.

Transforming a Culture

Cultural transformation starts with leadership understanding the current situation and future expectations prior to aligning with or reinforcing the guiding principles that will lead the company along the path to operational excellence. Once these principles have been recognized and accepted, they must be woven into the organizational fabric by first explaining the "why" behind these foundational concepts and integrating them into an organizational strategy that will assimilate them into the inner workings of the enterprise.

Strategic projects, which are mechanisms for deploying organizational strategy, should be selected and aligned with the enterprise's guiding principles. Operational systems should then be prepared or updated to reflect these principles, creating an unambiguous set of expectations for individual behaviors and process outcomes. Managers and supervisors must follow up by encouraging associates to embrace these fundamental principles in their attitudes, behaviors and work routines while continuously reinforcing their importance to the company.

SIDEBAR: WHAT ARE YOU TEACHING?

As a manager, ask yourself, what values are you demonstrating? What behaviors are you exhibiting? What skills and habits are you developing and reinforcing in people around you? As leaders within organizations, we exhibit habits and beliefs we consciously and often unconsciously display in our words and actions. We shape our corporate culture every time we interact with employees. Managers are teachers because people watch and learn by observing their leaders in action. What we do and how we do it, is what we teach every day! People are taught how to behave from the individuals who manage and lead them. If you want to change a culture and obtain different results, organizational leadership must practice and display the behaviors and habits they want others to exhibit. As a manager, if you do not like what you see within your own organization, look in the mirror and ask yourself, what am I teaching? If this is not what you expect, perhaps it's time to change.

Most would agree, transforming a culture is not easy and to be successful, must involve the integration of guiding principles into the values, beliefs and behaviors of organizational personnel. So how do you change a culture? One must start by creating a strategy that is deployed through projects that are focused on changing systems that drive desired behaviors to achieve ideal results. Thus, let's turn our attention to understanding strategy and how it can be used to influence and change culture.

Strategy Deployment

A good strategy translates leadership's vision into action. A strategy should provide a simple, understandable, identifiable and unifying statement, and a vision of the enterprise. It should clarify the products and services a facility provides, highlight core competencies needed to address anticipated risks and opportunities, identify activities required to transform the enterprise and justify facility infrastructure decisions. Once defined and developed, projects are identified and deployed to realize the strategy through structure, discipline and accountability.

SIDEBAR: DO YOU NEED A STRATEGIC PLAN?

If you have one or more of the following issues, you are likely to benefit from strategy planning and deployment:

- Too many bad projects in process
- Too many or too few projects
- Long lead time improvements
- Constantly missed budgets and forecasts
- Misalignment between organizational activities and the vision
- Disconnects between yearly plans
- A lack of identify or purpose
- A lack of employees' engagement

A strategy requires an awareness of the business landscape including internal strengths and weaknesses as well as external opportunities and threats. It should be created with the input of facility management, department heads and individuals in key roles throughout the organization. Strategy development typically includes the following:

1. *Self-assessment*: An assessment of enterprise strengths, weaknesses, opportunities and threats (e.g. SWOT analysis)
2. *Prioritization*: Important focuses and challenges (e.g. internal factors, stakeholder strategies, customer expectations and market conditions).
3. *Vision statement*: A simple statement or memorable phrase that everyone understands, can relate to and support.
4. *Strategy description (first-level strategy)*: A brief description of each strategy identified.
5. *Deployment plan (second-level strategy)*: A list of strategic projects (with targets, metrics and dates) needed to deploy each strategy.
6. *Communicate*: A sharing of the strategy roadmap with key stakeholders.
7. *Follow-up*: Periodic reviews of project performance; adjustments, corrections and updates to ensure progress to plan.

Let's follow up this method of strategy development by describing each step in more detail, starting with a situational assessment.

Situational Assessment

Facility staff should understand the current business climate including:

- Country conditions in which business is conducted (political, economic, social, universities, etc.)
- Current organizational mission, vision and values
- Relevant stakeholder strategies
- Facility planning
- Operational strategy
- Technology roadmap
- Key Performance Indicators s/KBIs
- Guiding principles and lean mindset
- Customer needs (and satisfaction criteria)
- Customer and supplier locations

Once relevant topics have been identified and corresponding information gathered, a discussion of the current situation and a more desirable state should occur among leadership to identify potential gaps and opportunities to move the organization forward.

SWOT Analysis

SWOT is an acronym for strengths, weaknesses, opportunities and threats. It's a subjective assessment of data and information used for understanding and decision-making, which considers both internal and external factors impacting an organization. An internal analysis explores organizational strengths and weaknesses. Strengths include the advantages a facility has in meeting target market needs, whereas weaknesses are obstacles a facility encounters in meeting those same needs. External analysis considers both opportunities and threats independent of the facility. Opportunities would be prospects with the potential to enhance company competitiveness and profitability, whereas threats would be trends or events that may negatively impact business outcomes. To differentiate between internal and external influences, ask the question: *Would this issue exist if the company did not exist?* If the answer is yes, it's an external issue.

When performing a SWOT analysis, some key topics to consider include:

✓ Organizational capabilities and resources
✓ Product portfolio (type and mix)
✓ Operational efficiency
✓ Current and future technologies
✓ Competitors (market analysis, current and future strategies, capabilities and resources)
✓ Strategy alignment with other departments and functions

Figure 10.4 provides a typical SWOT matrix for review. A final matrix would typically reflect broad inputs from organizational individuals and departments, which have been consolidated into key topics for consideration in strategy development.

Prioritization: *Focuses and Challenges*

Using the SWOT analysis, identify facility focuses and challenges by confronting each strength and weakness with corresponding opportunities and threats. Figure 10.5 can help facilitate this activity.

Vision Statement

A vision statement is a simple statement or memorable phrase that everyone understands. It's an image of the future we seek to create, a sentence or a short paragraph, a broad, positive image of a desired state. A good vision

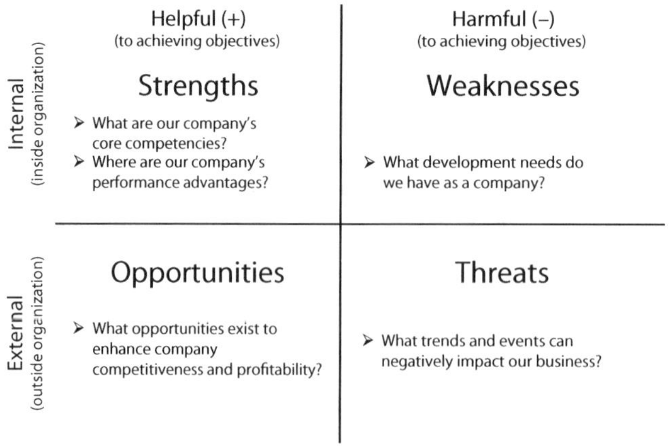

Figure 10.4 SWOT matrix.

	Opportunities	Threats
Strengths	How much does this strength help us to exploit this opportunity?	How much does this strength help us combat this threat?
Weaknesses	How much does this weakness hinder us to exploit this opportunity?	How much does this weakness hinder us in combating this threat?

Figure 10.5 Focuses and Challenges matrix.

should reflect the inputs of the entire organization and inspire everyone under its umbrella. Examples of famous visions statements include:

- *Google*: "To provide access to the world's information in one click"
- *Instagram*: "Capture and share the world's moments"
- *Khan Academy*: "To provide a free world-class education to anyone anywhere"
- *Microsoft*: "A computer on every desktop and in every home (using Microsoft software)"
- *Nike*: "To bring inspiration and innovation to every athlete in the world"

SIDEBAR: CREATING A VISION

- Take the strategic focuses and challenges
- Filter the strategic focuses and challenges
  - *Decide on what to do and what not to do!*
- Identify and prioritize the strategic topics (e.g. strategic goals)
  - *Lean methods, strategic indicators, etc.*
- Consider how these topics will transform the facility, if achieved, and … *write it down!*
- Describe the future state (destination) of the facility and function of the organization, once the strategic goals are implemented!
- Create a formal vision statement that answers the questions:
  - *Where do we want to be?*
  - *What will our business look like at some future time?*

Tip: Consider creating a *slogan* that complements, supports and communicates your vision. A slogan should have meaning to all employees.

Strategic Plan Development

When developing a strategic plan to transform a culture, consider some of the following questions:

- What outcomes do we want to achieve?
- What guiding principles does the organization believe and value?
- Do those guiding principles align with the results we want to achieve?
- Are the right systems in place and aligned to drive the organization to exhibit behaviors required to realize desired results?
- What changes in systems and behaviors are required to achieve operational excellence?

Strategy Development: First-Level Strategies

A vision must be transformed into individual strategies for deployment. These strategies should complement each other and reflect what's needed to realize the vision. Each strategy should have a brief statement containing the following:

- *Objective*: What is the strategy expected to achieve and when is it expected to be achieved?
- *Scope*: What are the boundaries or focus area in which the strategy will apply?
- *Expected improvement*: What strategic indicator or performance parameter will the strategy impact to achieve the vision?

A good strategy services to realign an organization along a new or modified path by identifying the actions needed to achieve the goals and objectives behind a clear and unified vision. The guiding principles of an organization must be in harmony with the vision and direction of the enterprise and create a foundation upon which to develop systems that influence behaviors in order to achieve expected outcomes.

Deployment Plan: Second-Level Strategies

To create a strategy deployment plan, list all individual strategies. Identify "strategic" projects for each strategy to realize their objectives. Confirm each project has a measurable goal statement and due date. It's good practice to link facility strategy development with the annual budgeting process so financial resources can be allocated where needed. It's also recommended that strategic projects be linked to annual employee compensation to create a sense of importance and priority in their timely execution. Figure 10.6 captures an organization's cascading vision of individual strategic projects for deployment.

After developing a strategy but prior to deployment, ask yourself a simple question:

Will the strategies and strategic projects identified move the organization closer to the vision?

Strategy deployment requires effective project management as a means to achieving targeted goals and objectives. This activity should include periodic reviews of project progress to plan, the identification and correction of plan deviations and regular plan updates based on the most recent data and information available. The following tools and activities will facilitate efficient and timely project execution, increasing the likelihood of realizing the strategy.

- *Project charter*: A project planning tool that provides a clear understanding and expectations for successful project execution and completion.
- *Project deployment plan*: A schedule of activities, their sequence and timing used to execute, monitor and control each strategic project plan.
- *A3 reporting*: A tool to facilitate, assess and communicate project performance (status) during project reviews. See Appendix XV for a typical A3 format.

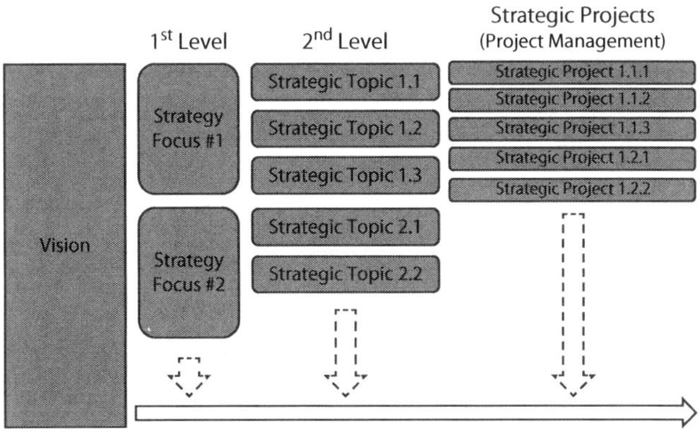

Figure 10.6 Cascading of an enterprise vision to strategic projects.

- *Performance reviews*: A periodic review of project progress to ensure deviations from plan are communicated and appropriate actions are taken to correct significant variances.

During project execution, project managers must ensure people and resources are being properly coordinated to satisfy stakeholder requirements, look for deviations from plan and take action to address significant variances from expectation. Follow-up actions will often be required to expedite timely project completion and closure.

When periodically reviewing the strategy for potential updates (e.g. a minimum of annually), consider the following:

✓ Has the business environment changed?
✓ Is the SWOT analysis still valid?
✓ Are current strategies working?
✓ Are the right things being measured?
✓ Is money being budgeted strategically?

Since strategies are long-term plans (3–5 years), a strategy roadmap can be an effective way to communicate deployment to departments and stakeholders throughout the organization. See Figure 10.7 for an example of a strategy roadmap.

Strategic planning is a process of defining projects to lead an organization in a different direction. It requires an organization to evaluate its current trajectory in light of existing and future business conditions, consider changes

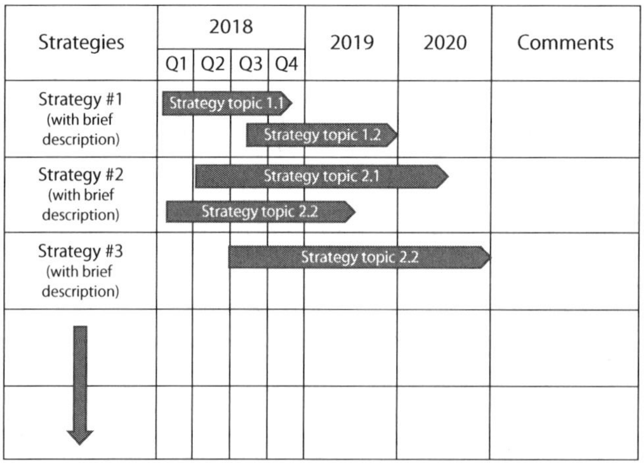

Figure 10.7 Example of a strategy roadmap.

to operational practices and the implementation of bold steps to navigate the challenges that lie ahead. Transforming a culture to align with the principles of operational excellence will stretch an organization beyond its comfort zone as multifunctional teams evaluate existing systems to modify and develop new ones, breaking current paradigms and engage the workforce in realizing a common vision.

The first-level strategy is where the vision of operational excellence is transformed into individual strategies concentrated on areas that require change to align with a new direction, while the second-level strategy breaks the first level into "strategic" topics and specific projects intended to realize an efficient and sustainable transformation.

Figure 10.8 presents a high-level overview of the strategy deployment process and can be used as a quick reference.

In summary, the concepts behind operational excellence can be used to construct a framework from which meaningful controls can be established and improvements achieved. To be effective, these core concepts must permeate an organization's DNA, most notably through the strategic planning and deployment process. Deployment requires the broad communication of a strategy through the enterprise's vision and mission as well as through projects. Projects are the mechanisms by which strategies are realized to drive changes outside of normal work conditions. This allows the development of systems to influence behaviors that align with a new direction.

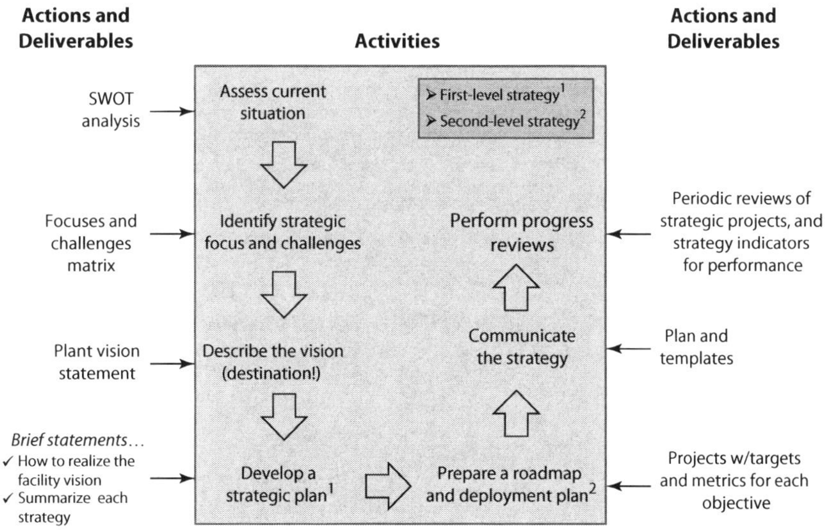

Figure 10.8 Strategy development and deployment overview.

SIDEBAR: BUSINESS STRATEGY SIMPLIFIED

A business strategy does not have to be complicated. In essence, four simple questions need to be answered:

- ✓ What are the key business objectives you want to realize?
- ✓ What metrics are needed to confirm the realization of these objectives?
- ✓ Who is responsible for what objectives (one person per objective) and when is each objective expected to be completed?
- ✓ What evidence is required to confirm the objectives have been achieved?

Key Points

- Know-why communicates purpose.
- Standards applied with discipline and accountability help establish culture.
- Changing culture starts with accepting a common set of guiding principles and a disciplined approach to organizational transformation.
- As stated by the Shingo Institute, "Ideal behavior drives long-term results. This happens when the systems are aligned with principles of operational excellence".
- Good inputs and properly executed activities supported by proper behaviors lead to expected outcomes.
- If we don't define behaviors, behaviors will define us!
- Results lag behaviors, therefore, be patient since results will reflect changing behaviors over time.
- As an organization matures, it needs more freedom to act.
- Getting people to behave in a particular way is one of the hardest challenges to embrace.
- Changing behavior starts with clearly defined, accepted and communicated principles and values.
- Remember, behavior that lasts the longest is behavior reinforced by random checks!
- Good processes = good results; Bad processes = bad results.
- Organizational principles should align with employee beliefs.
- Variation in behavior leads to variation in results.
- People's behavior can be strategically influenced toward the ideal when operational systems are aligned with principles of operational excellence.
- Continuous improvement requires learning from your mistakes and applying what you learn.

- Carefully defined work routines will facilitate desired behaviors and results.
- Pursuit of perfection is an "idea" with the purpose of bringing out the best in people and organizations.
- An operational excellence mindset does not flow down from the top. It must become an inherent part of what an organization believes and exhibits every day, in every action.
- It took years for employees to acquire the behaviors they exhibit today. If we expect to change behavior, it's going to take years to nurture behaviors of a more desirable state.

Strategic Planning and Deployment

- Strategic planning is only as good as the data and information used in determining your strategic objectives!
- Good strategic planning results from knowing the strengths and weaknesses of your organization as well as the opportunities and threats influencing it.
- Strategic planning is only a small percentage of the work; most of the effort is the execution, monitoring and control of plan deployment through projects!
- Projects identified to realize the strategic plan must be effectively managed (executed, monitored and controlled) to be successful!
- Successful completion of "strategic" projects = realization of an organizational strategy.
- Periodic reviews of "strategic" projects are essential to ensure that projects deliver the expected results on time and in budget!
- Project management will significantly influence the success of strategy deployment. Choose good project managers and guide them well!
- Suggested reading: *Beyond Strategic Vision* by Cowley & Domb (ISBN-13 978-0-7506-9843-6).

References

1. Wikipedia, October 2015. https://en.wikipedia.org/wiki/Edgar_Schein#Schein's_organizational_culture_model.
2. Shingo Institute, Utah State University. 2016. *The Shingo Model for Operational Excellence*. Logan, UT: Jon M. Huntsman, School of Business.
3. Shingo Institute, Utah State University. 2016. *The Shingo Model for Operational Excellence*. Logan, UT: Jon M. Huntsman, School of Business (pp. 9–10).

Chapter 11

Daily Shop Floor Management: Through Structure, Discipline and Accountability

> Greatness is not a function of circumstance. Greatness, it turns out, is largely a matter of conscious choice, and discipline.
>
> **James C. Collins**
> *Good to Great: Why Some Companies Make the Leap ... and Others Don't*

Preparing for Daily Shop Floor Management

Continuous improvement is not solely about the implementation of tools, techniques and methods; these are just conduits for enabling systems to drive desired behaviors that create the mindset and evolve an organizational culture of excellence. As previously stated, the Shingo model for operational excellence [1] believes that *The tools of lean, TQM, JIT, Six Sigma, etc. are enablers and should be strategically and cautiously inserted into appropriate systems to better drive ideal behavior and excellent results.*

The framework for a sustainable improvement program must emanate from a series of guiding concepts or principles recognized and embraced by an organization to facilitate a common mindset, culture and language. These principles must be translated into systems that drive desired behaviors to achieve excellent results. These systems must be maintained and managed in a coordinated way to create an efficient and effective long-term strategy for operational excellence. This is the value of daily shop floor management. Daily shop floor management plays a key role in achieving and maintaining an environment of operational excellence. However, before embarking directly on this topic, let's explore the idea of a sustainable culture and consider ways to facilitate it as a conduit for operational excellence.

Creating a culture of operational excellence requires having the right systems in place and developing or hiring the right people to execute those systems in meaningful and disciplined ways. Knowing who the right people are and adequately preparing them for what they are expected to do is a hallmark of good leadership. The following points will help facilitate the development of a sustainable culture based on trust and respect for people while preparing the enterprise for change.

- *Hire and prepare the right people*: Hire the best people possible. Orient people to the work expected; prepare them for what they will encounter (e.g. work environment, standardized procedures, safety practices). Train them on enterprise systems so they know how to properly and instinctively execute them. Set expectations, stress the importance of exhibiting the right attitude and reinforce the need to follow standard work routines at all levels of the hierarchy. Clarify the "why" and "how" of work standards so individuals are able to provide quality parts and services to customers, on time and in the amount requested.
- *Expect people to leave*: Not everyone can do the required work, but communicate and demonstrate job expectations up front, before the hiring process is complete. Expose potential hires to actual work conditions or simulate the work environment before offering employment. Observe them in action; ask how they felt. Have company team leaders and employees talk to and educate potential recruits on expected roles and responsibilities. Clearly communicate requirements for work quality and productivity.
- *Allow teams to self-manage*: Encourage job rotation during a work shift to provide ergonomic relief and share the burdens of work tasks. It's difficult for people to complain when they all share equally in work activities. Empower people and teams to "re-design" their work to make it easier, faster, cheaper and safer to perform. Permit an acceptable level of peer pressure to regulate the work environment and allow people to take responsibility for their work and support each other for the benefit

of the team, company and customers they serve. Promote an environment of trust and respect.

- *Production is king*: Focus on continuously improving production work by making it cheaper, easier, faster and safer to perform. Establish visual indicators displaying the status of safety, quality, productivity and delivery performance so issues can be identified immediately and actions taken to address deviations and implement improvements. Help front-line workers be successful. Their work is likely to be the first thing the customer will see.

Effective management and leadership in great companies evolve around the treatment of people and dignity displayed at all levels of the hierarchy, including individuals working in production who have the most direct influence on product quality as goods make their way to customers.

In addition to the right people, organizations need structure, discipline and accountability to maintain focus on what's important, drive prioritized work routines and ensure closure of actions to sustain and advance operations. Structure establishes boundaries or limits within which work can be accomplished. A properly defined and executed organizational structure can lead to greater operational efficiency. The structure an organization puts in place and the discipline exhibited to ensure its effective execution will influence behaviors that will determine the level of success achievable.

Operational Structure

Lean management can be defined, in part, by the daily, weekly and monthly work routines expected to be completed by every level of the enterprise. These routines are performed on a regular basis to look for deviations from expectation and opportunities for improvement. Deviations are good indicators of potential process instability. By identifying and managing deviations, a process is likely to remain stable and continue to operate at a desirable level of performance. A structured approach to process control ensures that critical operational activities are executed, monitored and controlled on a regular basis to maintain a stable and predictable output while building on improvements.

Operational structure, defined by systems, methods and procedures, can address known weaknesses, reinforce desired strengths and exploit the benefits of lessons learned. Structured methods and other practical tools can be weaved into an organization through disciplines like project management, process control, problem-solving, change management and standardized work. These disciplines are critical to an organization's ability to minimize variation while regulating performance and stimulating business growth. Many of these disciplines help create a framework for how to behave and act within the workplace.

A structured, analytical approach to problem-solving can lead to faster, more efficient and permanent solutions. Methods help define the operational structure needed to create a more effective workplace. Methods used to shape an organization's actions may be defined to a level of detail necessary to ensure consistent and predictable outcomes. Generally speaking, the more detail a method provides, the less variation expected in the final results. However, there is a balance between methods that provide too much structure but not enough flexibility. Methods should be implemented to the degree they provide sufficient value without compromising innovation or creativity needed to drive continuous improvements.

Methods also need discipline to be effective. While methods define a structured approach for execution, discipline ensures compliance to their intended purpose. Discipline in the workplace is reflected in the practice of executing work systems, activities and tasks as defined or prescribed in documents such as project plans, procedures, processes and work instructions.

One unique characteristic of the Toyota Production System is Toyota's rigorous adherence to standardized work while driving continuous improvements. The key to this apparent dichotomy is in their disciplined and scientific approach to deviation and change management [1]. *Toyota expects a clear understanding of the current and desired state as part of a scientific approach to planning and comprehensively evaluating a potential change in state. They use data and facts generated from scientific thinking and evaluations for decision-making and problem-solving. Nothing is left to chance; there is structure and discipline in every improvement Toyota makes. Toyota's way of continuous improvement expects every employee follow a structured and disciplined method of improvement that is both engaging and effective while respecting the current state, until a new operating state is proven effective.*

People also need structure, discipline and accountability. Structure in one's personal approach to work and life can facilitate significant achievement. For many people, the structure of a morning routine helps get the kids to school and themselves to work on time. In the workplace, clarity and competence, combined with structure and discipline, can lead to personal recognition and reward. As demands on our personal and professional time increase, injecting more structure into our lives helps us become more efficient by accomplishing more within the limited time available each day.

Structure can be applied to how we make decisions, solve problems, manage deviations, make changes and drive continuous improvements. A structured approach generally provides a more efficient and effective way to engage in activities necessary to control and improve processes by reducing variation and increasing consistency in how work is performed.

Discipline

Discipline can be viewed as an attitude or behavior. When we talk about discipline, it's often discussed from the perspective of self-discipline or organizational discipline. Self-discipline is concerned with an individual's ability to control and motivate oneself, to stay focused or on track, to follow the rules or respect the code of conduct. It's the ability to get things done correctly and in a timely manner. An example of self-discipline for a leader is taking the first 30 minutes upon arriving to work each day to connect with employees while coming up to speed on the current state of operations. Self-discipline is a learned behavior; it emanates from good habits that can lead to targeted accomplishments. Without personal drive and persistence, self-discipline would be elusive.

Organizational discipline, or lack thereof, can be viewed from many perspectives including punitive in nature where an employee, lacking the skills or desire to complete a job assignment, is subjected to coaching, training, reprimand or even termination. Another view can be of a team with the appropriate skills and desire to perform a work assignment failing to achieve a successful outcome or employees following a structured approach to business, where a conscious effort is made to follow procedure and perform their duties as outlined in their job requirements.

Organizational discipline and self-discipline can be desirable traits for corporate teams and employees given the responsibility to execute work assignments and strategic initiatives. Organizational discipline must be exhibited by all levels of management as a way to demonstrate and reinforce expected behavior. If roles, responsibilities, business systems and work routines are clearly defined, discipline in completing work assignments can be reinforced through the actions and behaviors of others. Holding people accountable for timely execution and efficient task completion (e.g. reinforcing expected discipline) can be accomplished through casual communication between employees or more formally through planned reviews. Promoting discipline within an enterprise can be facilitated through the following actions:

- Hire the right people
- Define clear roles, responsibilities and expectations
- Demonstrate expectations through leadership's actions
- Implement systems and procedures that reinforce discipline (e.g. work routines)
- Perform layered process audits (LPAs) to confirm and reinforce expected behaviors
- Create boundaries and time lines within which to work
- Reward desired behaviors

Culture is built on the shoulders of self-disciplined individuals with clear direction and a passion to achieve sustainable results. In his book, *Good to Great* [2], Jim Collins talks about enterprise-wide discipline as being essential to achieve great results. These results come from people whose patterns of behavior are consistent with the direction of the leadership they support. He goes on to say that bureaucracies form to compensate for incompetence and lack of discipline when the wrong people are hired.

A culture steeped in discipline will most likely yield consistent and predictable results. To realize a continuously improving yet sustainable culture of discipline, it must be rooted in principle-based systems defined by clear constraints within which individuals have the freedom and flexibility to act. Self-disciplined people don't need to be managed, they need direction. In great organizations with a well-defined and consistent path forward, managers manage systems, not people.

An enduring culture of discipline comes from hiring the right people who have demonstrated an ability to perform within a framework of clearly established goals, objectives and systems while working with the best interest of the company in mind. As Jim Collins would say, disciplined people, disciplined thought and disciplined action.

SIDEBAR: DISCIPLINE MATTERS

Management by email does not work well. Case in point, I once worked for a large global company that had difficulty changing procedures, not because we were large but because the process was "complicated". So, to work around this problem, management from the central office would effect change through emails. Plants would periodically receive an email from the central office stating a change in procedure. These emails, which could be written by anyone from a project manager to senior leader, might "eliminate" an approved requirement, request a change in procedure or add a new control on operational activities. The plants were frustrated because they were being held to an industry standard of following approved procedures in order to demonstrate compliance while the central function expected them to follow the latest email with little regard for the formal change process. In lieu of improving (e.g. simplifying or "leaning-out") the current change control process, the central function chose to circumvent it by issuing email "changes", making the process confusing and difficult to control. In the middle were the plants struggling to follow their documented systems while trying to satisfy central management's "need for speed". Management believed it was easier and faster to drive their agenda via email and common directories than to use the documented change management system to institute changes. Clearly, the wrong mindset for a lean thinking organization.

Systems drive behaviors. A good system may be no better than a bad system, if not followed. Discipline must accompany systems to influence behavior and drive desired results. Structure without discipline is meaningless. If people do not like the existing system, instead of working around it, they should target it for improvement.

Accountability

Individual behavior is influenced by organizational values and beliefs as well as existing policies, procedures and systems. Desirable performance, which is the outcome of ideal behaviors, reflects the interaction, encouragement and reinforcement that individuals receive from leaders, managers and their peers. Good organizational discipline requires process owners hold responsible employees accountable to following process standards. Accountability is assigning responsibility to complete an activity or task and ensuring the assignment is completed to specified quality, cost and time requirements. Transparent accountability should be established for key activities to ensure the status of tasks is visual and easily determined. Effective accountability can be as simple as conducting daily meetings and performing periodic reviews to ensure work assignments are progressing to schedule and are completed in a timely manner.

Accountability is not only about following work standards, it also encompasses a mindset that stops processes from producing defects, investigates root cause for permanent corrective action, engages teams in waste elimination to reduce cycle time and works to remove obstacles to flow. Accountability requires periodic checks to confirm critical process activities are being performed as prescribed in standards and procedures. These checks must be integrated into work routines to ensure employees, at all levels of the organization, perform the work for which they were hired to do and confirm systems continue to function as intended. Desired behaviors that last the longest are behaviors reinforced by random checks.

Project planning, documented work routines and action item lists are ways to establish and maintain accountability. To ensure accountability, these activities must be consciously managed as part of an organization's daily operations. If accountability is ignored, it's unlikely an organization can maintain process stability and capability or sustain efficiency improvements long term.

In part, accountability is about responding to deviations and improvement ideas by prioritizing actions, escalating issues to appropriate levels and ensuring all relevant items are addressed and closed. With self-motivated and disciplined people on board, the issue of accountability significantly diminishes, leaving leadership to focus on improving systems, not people.

Enterprise structure, discipline and accountability must create a mindset that aligns with the principles of operational excellence. It's leadership's job to define the guiding principles and practices of the organization. It's management's job to ensure these principles and practices are integrated into the methods, systems and procedures of the organization and it's everyone's responsibility to ensure compliance with and drive continuous improvement of these directives. Most important, leadership and management must demonstrate the actions and behaviors they want others to display; only through "walking the talk" will an organizational culture start to change. People often mimic what leaders do, not what they say.

We have discussed structure, discipline and accountability in reference to culture. Let's now turn our attention to how these ideas can be applied to create a more effective approach to daily shop floor management.

Daily Shop Floor Management

Daily shop floor management (which will often be referred to as "Shop Floor Management") is a holistic management endeavor that involves the planning, execution, monitoring and control of manufacturing processes. It requires understanding and managing the interaction of man, machines, methods, materials and the surrounding environment. It requires coordination of information and material flow through the facility from order entry to receipt of raw materials, and on to shipment of finished goods. In short, it's about the daily, weekly, monthly or essentially periodic work activities essential to maintaining a well-run operation; one in which every individual knows what to do and why. Motivation in doing their work routines, as prescribed, is knowing the consequences of what happens when work is not completed as planned. Typical daily shop floor management activities, consisting of two primary work responsibilities of process control and continuous improvement, can be found in Figure 11.1.

Effective shop floor management facilitates the quick identification of and reaction to deviations, drives structured problem-solving, enables the efficient use of resources, proactively responds to negative trends in data and ensures sustainable improvements while encouraging people to scientifically think through issues in order to identify creative and innovative solutions that continuously enhance stakeholder value.

Shop floor management should be defined through a set of management guiding principles outlining the role and responsibilities of managers, supervisors, shift and manufacturing line leaders. These responsibilities should be further detailed in a series of work routines performed on a periodic basis to maintain process control and drive productivity improvements. When engaging in process control and continuous improvement activities, it's important not to spend a disproportionate amount of time on one at the expense of the other. Although control is a clear priority and a prerequisite for sustainable improvements, an adequate amount of time must be allocated

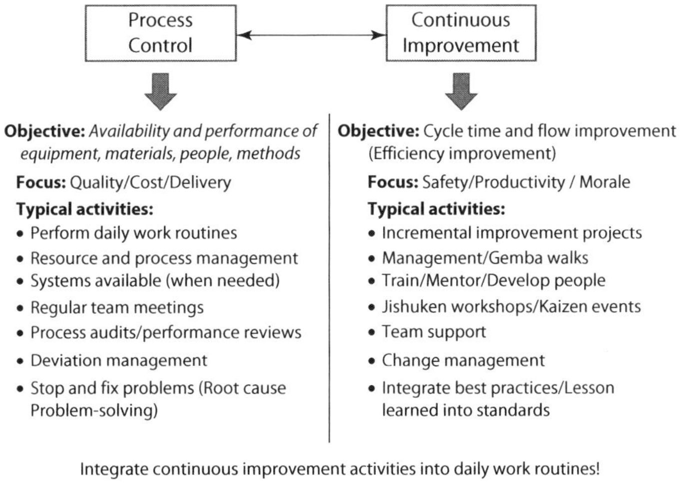

Figure 11.1 Daily shop floor management: Process control and continuous improvement.

to improvements in order to avoid the spiral of doom where firefighting becomes the dominant mode of operation.

Modern-day shop floor management focuses on process as well as results, leverages underutilized workforce resources, emphasizes prevention and empowers multidisciplinary teams to solve problems at the lowest possible level of the organization. In addition to an increased focus on process, prevention and empowerment, shop floor management must integrate organizational guiding principles into its systems to promote behaviors that generate anticipated results. It must also set up the expectation that managers are present on the floor, reviewing operational performance, understanding critical issues, removing barriers to problem resolution, coaching employees and discussing ways to make work faster, easier, cheaper and safer. Supervisors must also work with shop floor personnel to improve standards in order to enhance operational efficiency.

Lean management has moved organizations from being reactive to placing more emphasis on control and efficiency where the bulk of improvement opportunities exist. However, companies don't just leap to a proactive state of performance; they often start by improving their problem-solving acumen in reaction to quality issues plaguing production. Eventually, they move up the maturity curve to managing deviations from standards and procedures, recognizing the value of process stability and the importance of maintaining control. Seasoned companies focus on operational efficiency, reaping the benefits of a proactive mode of operation. Let's review three levels of shop floor management maturity (Figure 11.2), classified as reactive, control and proactive, respectively, and the behaviors required for each.

Level 1: Reactive (Stability through Problem-Solving)

Basic daily shop floor management involves reactive root cause problem-solving at the source aimed at minimizing defects upon detection and implementing countermeasures to avoid problem reoccurrence. At this fundamental level of operations, immediate identification and reaction to problems must occur to prevent additional problems and defects from generating waste and disrupting continuous flow. Unfortunately, many firms remain in this mode of operation, continuing to solve problems with no clear objective in sight. For those who are serious about improvement, the road to operational excellence is clear – eradicate defects causing process instability using the tools of problem-solving. Once the goal of stability is reached, an operation can move into the second phase of shop floor management maturity – process control through deviation management.

Maturity level	State	Primary Activities	Objectives
Level I	Reactive	Problem-solving • Problem statement/definition • Containment • Root cause analysis/Verification • Identify and implement solution • Verify effectiveness	• Eliminate defects • Process stability
Level II	Control	Deviation Management • Implement visual controls • Identify deviations • Analyze cause • Contain/Corrective action • Monitor for reoccurrence	• Process control (Stability and capability achieved and maintained)
Level III	Proactive	Waste Elimination – Achieve Deviation management – Sustain • Propose change • Validate change (prove-out) • Confirm/Reject change • Implement/Confirm effectiveness	• Operational efficiency

Figure 11.2 Shop floor management maturity: Three fundamental levels.

Level 2: Control (Process Control through Deviation Management)

Level 2 reflects a robust deviation management process focused on maintaining process control through active use of visual control to identify and eliminate non-conformances to process standards, tolerances and critical parameters. This requires continuous monitoring for warning signs indicating a change in process input or activity has occurred that may negatively impact output results, if ignored. When chronic problems occur, consider preparing a rapid response plan for each type of event, employing tools such as fault tree analysis or decision trees for individuals to reference. This will help keep known issues under control while teams look for permanent solutions to problems.

Once control is demonstrated and becomes an instinctive part of shop floor management, the organization is likely exhibiting behaviors reflective of the third maturity level.

Level 3: Proactive (Efficiency Improvement through Waste Elimination)

Efficiency improvements are proactive in nature. Coach-based improvement projects using scientific thinking and structured methods (e.g. plan-do-check-act [PDCA]) often facilitate the implementation of innovative, creative and sustainable improvements. Opportunities for improved efficiency typically focus on process capability and manufacturing capacity improvements through the continuous, incremental elimination of waste. Kaizen events, Jishuken workshops and value stream mapping (VSM) can be effective techniques for identifying, analyzing, prioritizing and targeting additional opportunities for improvement. Once an enterprise starts exhibiting behaviors indicative of a proactive environment, an increased effort will likely be required to maintain the existing level of performance. This is when a renewed interest in structure, discipline and accountability can make a difference between good and great shop floor management. Along with the levels of maturity just discussed, the following activities can also serve as a pretext for supporting a leaner shop floor management system.

Systems Definition

Every organization must have defined systems with integrated methods and tools to operate effectively. Good systems reduce process variation by bringing structure and discipline to functional areas. Management must display and reinforce the behaviors and attitudes required to follow systems and work with individuals executing these systems to continuously improve them.

Standardized Processes

The development of process standards for repetitive and critical work activities helps to optimize product quality, delivery and overall efficiency, driving consistency and predictability in process outputs. Processes should be standardized within a clearly defined scope of requirements while allowing continuous improvements within established boundaries. Standardized processes establish the foundation upon which shop floor management is built.

Daily Work Routines

Work routines, defined at all levels of management, are executed on a daily, weekly and sometimes monthly basis to maintain process control and drive efficiency improvements through structured methods, discipline and accountability. Work routines establish the framework within which daily shop floor management is executed.

Communication

Efficient communication is the ability to disseminate clear data and information throughout the organizational hierarchy in the shortest possible time. Accurate and rapid communication is essential to a robust shop floor management system. The ability to solve problems, escalate issues and make quick decisions requires timely, reliable data and information facilitated by daily meetings, standardized agendas, electronic media and observation. Communication facilitates the integration of systems within the shop floor management domain so they can be coordinated and exploited in the most efficient way possible.

Knowledge Sharing

Best practices and lessons learned must become an integral part of a robust shop floor management system. Sharing knowledge among teams, departments and facilities to prevent problem reoccurrence and promote improvements is a hallmark of organizational excellence. A review of best practices and lessons learned can become a periodic agenda item at regular meetings to ensure vital information is distributed to key individuals and groups who can benefit from it the most.

One element of modern-day shop floor management that should not be overlooked is the continuously changing external environment that challenges workforce systems and behaviors. The development of a strategic plan, deployed through projects, offers an organization the opportunity to adapt their systems and operations in response to industry trends, allowing the enterprise to remain competitive in the face of changing business dynamics. Periodic reviews and updates to organizational strategy are required to pursue new opportunities and capabilities in defense of evolving business threats.

Let's continue exploring the world of daily shop floor management by reviewing the role of process management in supporting lean efficiency improvements and the activities of process planning, execution, monitoring and control, all of which help establish the framework for continuous and sustainable improvements.

William Thom, in his 2009 publication [3], defined process management as "the application of knowledge, skills, tools, techniques and systems to define, visualize, measure, control, report and improve processes with the goal to meet customer requirements profitably". Simply put, process management supports the fundamental activities and routines that are required for process control, which is a prerequisite for sustainable lean improvements. Let's dig deeper into process management.

Process Management

Rapid problem-solving and deviation management work in concert under the umbrella of process management to establish and maintain process control through planning, execution and process monitoring. Process-orientated management supports the concept of driving results by spending time monitoring and controlling process inputs and activities to proactively influence outcomes versus monitoring outcomes in anticipation of good results. Switching focus from results-orientated management to process-orientated management often requires a change in behavior from passively waiting for results to occur, to proactively looking for warning signs that trigger a reaction leading to a predictable outcome.

Process management is about planning, executing and monitoring the systems, methods and tools to establish and maintain process control in support of continuous improvement. It's about continuously refining those systems, methods and tools with the objective of optimizing process performance from a process-centric and value stream perspective. It involves the management of systems working in concert to generate desired outcomes. More specifically, process management consists of

- Planning, executing and monitoring process activities
- Identifying and driving process improvements
- Communicating reasons and benefits for process changes
- Recognizing and rewarding employees for desired behaviors
- Monitoring and maintaining conformance to requirements
- Influencing process inputs and activities for desired results
- Tracking and evaluating improvements for effectiveness
- Maintaining a stable, capable and efficient process through discipline and accountability

Process management is rooted in method- and tool-based systems. It's unrealistic to think the deployment of quality and efficiency tools alone can define, drive and sustain a lean culture. Both require the execution of daily work routines by various levels of management to ensure that control and improvement actions are identified and executed in a timely manner. Work routines must include mandatory activities required to reinforce the behaviors expected of a lean thinking and acting organization.

Functional routines will vary depending on the roles and responsibilities of individuals in the organizational hierarchy. As one's level of responsibility increases, routines generally shift from a process control focus to one of continuous improvement.

In an *Industry Week* article titled "Wanna Sabotage Your Lean Implementation Effort? Try This" [4], the author states that "the most common cause of failure has more to do with the existing weaknesses businesses have in their own management systems rather than issues brought about by implementing the new items that represent the difference between their existing system and elements of a lean manufacturing system". This is true now more than ever. As we try to do more with less, we tend to overlook some of the fundamentals required to keep a process healthy enough to support the changing dynamics of a "leaner" manufacturing environment.

As with many great buildings, products or even software development projects, there is a solid foundation, platform or base code upon which they are built. This foundation serves as an anchor and support for long-term sustainability. And so it goes for building, maintaining and improving reliable processes. Every well-performing process starts with a robust design and work standards to maintain its stability and disciplined monitoring and control to ensure its long-term capability. Once a process has been established and proven effective, it's the responsibility of each owner to maintain and continuously improve their processes over time. This is not necessarily an easy task since process control and improvement activities are competing with many other operational priorities.

In today's environment, it's not sufficient to simply maintain process performance. To remain competitive, organizations must continuously increase efficiency through the elimination of waste and improve the flow of information and materials through the value stream. Consequently, the implementation of lean methods has become an essential part of today's corporate survival strategy. Unfortunately, we can't simply start implementing lean principles and practices and expect them to take root. To realize the benefits of lean, we must first understand the current state of an existing process and ensure it's ready to support the building blocks of lean. Once these conditions are met, we must confirm the appropriate structure, discipline and accountability are in place to sustain current levels of performance and continuously improve upon process efficiency.

Process management must define the activities required to establish and maintain process control and enforce the disciplines required for continuous improvements. It's an essential management practice to keep organizations profitable, competitive and growing. Let's review some of the activities necessary to support process management including planning, execution, monitoring and control.

Process Planning

Good process planning leads to good process execution, monitoring and control. The planning phase sets the stage for how the shop floor will be managed. The need to define roles and responsibilities, standardize processes, establish visual controls, schedule product line walks, conduct audits and perform periodic reviews are essential activities for effective shop floor management. The documentation of work routines helps standardize these practices by identifying critical daily, weekly and monthly activities necessary to ensure consistent and predictable outcomes with time.

Work routines are essential activities for maintaining and improving work efficiency at every level of management and within key organizational functions. These routines help clarify and detail the roles and responsibilities of individuals and teams who are expected to perform work tasks as part of ongoing operations. Periodic work routines, often referred to as leader standard work (LSW), typically start one level up from standardized work instructions used by operators to perform highly repetitive work. The work referred to as LSW is daily and weekly routines required of supervisors and managers whose primary responsibility is to audit and maintain operations. As we move up the ladder of responsibility, the focus of work routines shifts from tactical control to one of strategic in nature (Figure 11.3).

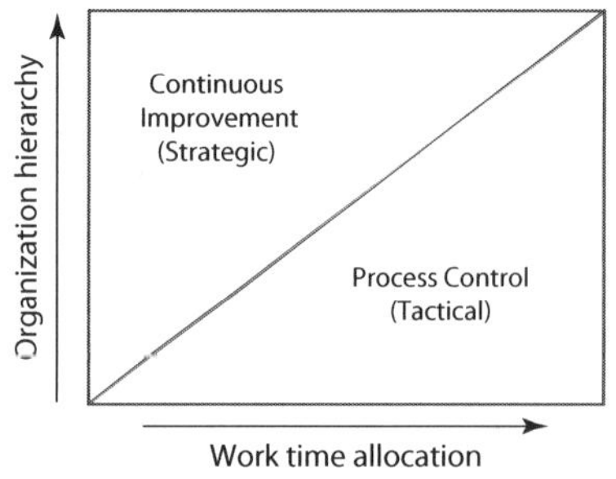

Figure 11.3 Organizational hierarchy work routine focus.

Operational structure defined, in part, by work routines, can offer significant benefits to an organization if executed properly. These benefits include but are not limited to

- Clearly defined work activities necessary to maintain process control
- Continuous and sustainable improvements
- Reinforcement of desired behaviors and practices
- Verification of completed routines
- Clearly defined expectations of what's important to maintain operations
- Stable work activities that do not change when people leave; operations are system driven, not people dependent
- More stable and predictable processes outcomes
- Employee engagement in continuous improvements
- Employees spend time on what's important for maintaining operations
- Clear ownership of problems for resolution
- Enhanced information flow throughout the management chain

As evident from the preceding list, work routines can play a vital role in outlining a plan of action to manage critical shop floor activities required to ensure uninterrupted process stability and flow. How this plan of action is executed is our next topic.

Process Execution

Process execution typically involves implementing standard work and performing the daily routines expected to "run the business". Work routines are performed on a prescribed basis to look for deviations from targets or standards. They can sometimes be executed as a "checklist" of activities to help people organize, prioritize and complete their daily, weekly and monthly tasks on time. While performing these routines, there may be a need to clarify product and process specifications, coordinate people and resources, manage internal and external stakeholders and complete additional activities to satisfy unanticipated expectations. The execution of work routines may also include activities such as production line walks, LPAs, communication meetings and performance reviews scheduled to occur at periodic intervals to confirm that planned activities are being completed and critical process parameters are in compliance with specifications.

The personal and organizational discipline required to perform work routines can be reinforced through the verification of completed routines by the next level of management. A manager's routines should include verification that their subordinates' routines have been completed since the routines defined for each level of management are considered fundamental for effective operational performance. Any incomplete routines should be treated as a deviation, understood and addressed through appropriate countermeasures. The verification of completed work routines helps maintain accountability and reinforces desired behaviors. Typical work routines carried out by organizations to control operations and drive improvements are highlighted in Figure 11.4. Spot checks and reviews should be performed to ensure that daily work routines are being performed and incomplete routines are addressed.

Daily meetings are an important part of process execution since they provide an opportunity for comparing actual versus planned performance, revealing deviations with the potential for process disruption. These meetings are an opportunity to escalate issues, make decisions, solve problems, discuss improvements and follow through on open actions. Actions to drive countermeasures and initiate changes should be assigned an owner for review and follow-up at subsequent meetings. As a general rule, an action should not be placed on a list for follow-up if it can be corrected immediately or within a specified time period (e.g. within a shift). Daily meetings should start on the shop floor with critical information escalated to subsequent levels of management for consideration.

Accountability can be facilitated by interconnected meetings held between various levels of the facility hierarchy. A typical organization might hold three daily accountability meetings, first at the lowest level between a production team leader and team members. A first-level meeting can be a brief discussion among team members at the line information board to

Perform Work/Verify Compliance

Process Control	Continuous Improvement
✓ Standard work compliance	✓ Go and see problems; Ask why
✓ Layered process audits	✓ Mistake proofing
✓ Workplace 5s	✓ Kaizen events
✓ Review Jidoka stops	✓ A3 review/Coaching
✓ Line walks/Line board reviews	✓ Jishuken workshop actions
✓ Monitor visual controls	✓ Update standardized work
✓ Review scrap	✓ Update work routines
✓ Review deviation management	✓ Changes management
✓ Review problem-solving	✓ Idea management
✓ Review capability	

Work routine accountability = Sustainability

Figure 11.4 Typical shop floor work routines topics.

review relevant data, information and concerns gathered during the shift. Team leaders would then represent their teams at a second-level meeting with the shift leader or supervisor, making sure to highlight critical issues or problems that require awareness and potentially further escalation. The third meeting would occur between supervisors and shop floor management in the presence of key support staff to discuss and prioritize issues needing immediate attention. It's important to prioritize actions at all levels since time and resources are limited. Depending on the organizational structure, additional meetings may occur to delegate responsibility and maintain accountability throughout the various departments and functions supporting operations.

Employees, team leaders, supervisors and managers should be prepared to discuss any noteworthy abnormalities that occurred during their shift, communicate what steps are being taken to address open concerns within their span of control and highlight any additional support required to close due or overdue issues.

Relevant topics likely to be covered during shop floor meetings include safety, quality, delivery, costs, productivity and attendance as well as risks related to man, machines, materials and methods. Delivery schedules and line stops are common topics at most production meetings. The depth of detail may vary at each level. Topics concerning strategic project execution and human resources may be discussed at greater length during upper tier meetings. Figure 11.5 outlines the common topics for discussion at various levels. It's recommended that each organization identifies standard topics to cover at its meeting so that responsible owners of key issues can acquire the data and information needed to prepare for brief yet meaningful discussions.

Level I – Line Meetings **Team Members/Leader**	**Level II – Unit Meetings** **Team Leaders/Supervisor**	**Level III – Plant Management** **Supervisors/Managers/Staff**
Safety • Personal protection • Injuries Attendance • Absenteeism • Cross-training Delivery • Daily requirements • Delinquencies • Production Line issues Issues/Concerns • Materials • Process/Methods • Equipment/tools	Safety • Current and past issues Attendance • Plan • Issues Delivery • Schedule • Actual versus Plan • Production Line issues Issues/Concerns • Quality • Project status	Safety • Current and past issues Delivery • Schedule • Actual versus Plan • Delinquencies Productivity • Quality (first pass yield, scrap) • Overall equipment effectiveness • Systemic issues • Risks • Challenges

Figure 11.5 Typical content of daily accountability meetings.

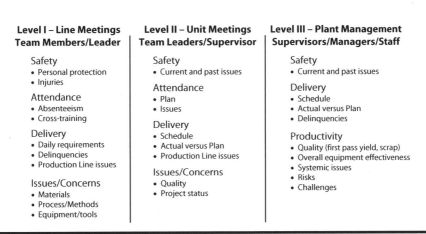

It's best to set a specific time, location and agenda for daily meetings to create a habit of communicating. If made part of daily routines, short, focused, stand-up meetings can be an efficient way to quickly disseminate information throughout the chain of command while prompting action. Meetings scheduled with clear objectives in mind will allow participants to arrive prepared to discuss key issues. Generally speaking, the flatter the hierarchy, the quicker the escalation and response to urgent issues. It's important to note that these are the meetings where the attitudes and behaviors of employees are formed and reinforced. Thus, if you want to influence behavior, start by teaching and coaching the leaders of these gatherings on how to behave so that they set the tone for others to follow. Management's words and actions instruct others on how to behave in the workplace.

Managing deviations can help maintain process accountability. Since many issues arise during daily meetings, all issues should be captured and prioritized so available resources and time are spent addressing the most significant topics. Deviations should be documented and prioritized before being assigned to their respective owners with corresponding due dates. The documentation of actions, owners and due dates helps establish a baseline for individual accountability. However, management must exhibit the discipline to follow up in order to effectively maintain accountability. Lack of timely follow-up on actions promotes an attitude of indifference and erodes the trust and integrity of the organization and specifically leadership's ability to manage operations effectively.

Figure 11.6 is an example of a template that is used to maintain transparent accountability of actions, assess their timely completion, monitor for issue reoccurrences and determine the effectiveness of the implemented countermeasures. An action list can be used to track timely closure of issues while monitoring the effectiveness of countermeasures by checking for reoccurrence.

ID	Item	Action	Owner	Open date	Due date	Complete date	Days w/o reoccurrence					Close date
							1	2	3	4	5	

Figure 11.6 Action item template (with reoccurrence monitoring).

The execution of process activities is likely to reveal deviations and defects requiring detailed analysis and development of countermeasures such as changes to the type and frequency of routines, updates to work instructions, resource adjustments and employee development. Prepare to respond accordingly.

Executing process work routines encompasses a wide range of activities, many of which include the following:

- ✓ Implement planned methods and standards
- ✓ Perform planned activities to accomplish process objectives
- ✓ Satisfy required deliverables
- ✓ Verify work is properly completed
- ✓ Identify the need for training, coaching and mentoring required to complete assigned tasks
- ✓ Manage available resources; obtain what you need but don't have
- ✓ Distribute communications required to complete work activities
- ✓ Generate work performance data for review and response
- ✓ Evaluate change requests and implement approved changes
- ✓ Manage risks and implement risk response activities when triggers occur
- ✓ Document best practices and lessons learned for continuous improvement
- ✓ Manage key stakeholders

There is no silver bullet to daily shop floor management, it takes structured routines and a disciplined approach to ensure responsible individuals are held accountable for their assigned tasks, and actions are taken to correct significant deviations as described in process monitoring and control.

Process Monitoring

Process monitoring is concerned with comparing planned versus actual performance, looking for abnormalities or deviations from expectation. It involves tracking, reviewing and reporting significant deviations from expected work performance and critical process parameters from specification.

Work routines outline which controls and activities to monitor for abnormalities while observations may prompt an investigation as to why certain deviations occurred. Anomalies often require analysis and follow-up actions to eliminate their causes. While performing work routines and monitoring for deviations, look for improvement opportunities. Unfortunately, conducting repeated routines can be boring but add value when problems are prevented and opportunities leading to improved performance are realized.

During process monitoring, if you are not finding deviations, you are not looking hard enough since there are always issues to be uncovered. Look a little harder, probe a little deeper and ask a few specific questions. Stress the system by increasing output requirements, reducing in-process buffers or introducing a different operator to see what a new set of eyes will reveal. The objective is the relentless pursuit of perfection through problem elimination and performance enhancements.

Process monitoring also requires frequent reviews of key performance indicators to facilitate a fast response to questionable outputs and concerning trends. Planning ensures that critical performance indicators are visualized while periodic monitoring checks for significant variances. This is where methods, tools and techniques such as 5S, visual controls, LPAs and line (information) board reviews can help facilitate actions required to maintain control. The following is a brief overview of commonly used tools and techniques for process monitoring.

Visual Controls

Visual controls are essential for monitoring operational performance and triggering deviation management. Effective visual controls make monitoring for deviations easy and quick to detect and facilitate prompt reaction to problems in the workplace. A good example of visual controls would be a hospital patient's vital signs (e.g. body temperature, pulse rate, respiration rate and blood pressure), which provide critical information required for life-saving decisions; or a traffic light where deviations from protocol can have significant consequences. Simple and visual is better than elegant and complex. The frequency at which visual controls are updated will determine their usefulness in monitoring and managing the process.

Visual controls are the foundation for good deviation management and continuous improvement. Visuals should be chosen carefully since too much data and information may result in sensory overload while too little may be insufficient for effective process control. Every visual should have a clear owner as well as user and deliver key information with impact. Upon implementation, visuals should quickly identify even small abnormalities for fast containment and permanent corrective action. Properly selected, placed and maintained visual controls will reduce the cycle time of reviews including production line walks and process audits.

Production Information Boards

Production (line) information boards are intended to provide a quick and easy way to visually display data and information necessary to manage processes in real time and drive improvements. The board can be a meeting point for production teams, supervisors and management to stop, review data and discuss daily issues, actions and problems specific to production. They can be used to facilitate shift changeovers where key information is shared among transitioning team members.

Line boards should display data and information that line operators and team leaders need to monitor and control their operations. Simple lines with little or no automation may benefit from a manual board since data is typically easy to collect and update. Highly or fully automated lines may benefit from a digital solution where data is collected automatically from a system and updated in real time.

It's important to remember that line information boards are not for management to discipline poor performance or a showcase for customers. They are owned by the Line Leaner and used by team members as a tool for managing production performance. Quality, in cooperation with line personnel, should determine the information and layout best suited to help the production team efficiently and effectively manage the line based on expectations communicated by management.

4M's Risk Awareness

Toyota has been known to use a 4M's display chart on their production line boards to communicate recent process changes or risks. Whenever there is a production line change to man, machine, materials or methods, the event is documented under the relevant display topic and a color change is made as an indication of potential risk. This visual will remain in place until the risk has subsided or has been mitigated. This tool is a way to notify key stakeholders of a production risk due to recent issues in one or more of these process categories. An example of a 4M display is shown in Figure 11.7.

Process Layered Audits

LPAs are process audits performed by multiple management levels within an organization to confirm system functionality and identify deviation in process so undesirable behaviors and outcomes can be corrected. LPAs are

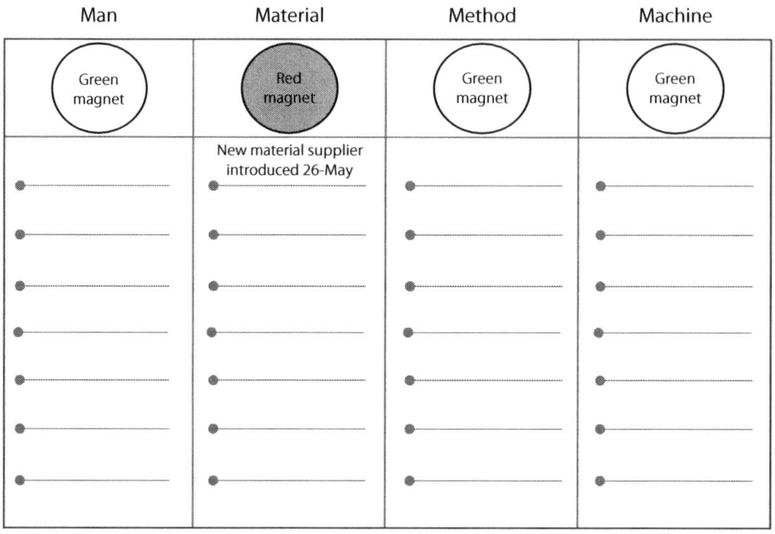

Figure 11.7 4M's line risk indicator.

a management tool for verifying process and system compliance while elevating management awareness of shop floor activities and performance. They also provide employees with the opportunity to see what's important to operations while reinforcing behaviors expected of the workforce.

LPAs allow management to review operations while looking for deviations from work standards, product specifications and critical process tolerances. If significant deviations are noted, issue owners are assigned to perform causal analysis and take action to bring the process back on track. LPAs are expected to monitor process inputs and corresponding outputs in real time while facilitating a rapid response to non-conformances. An LPA should be a structured, independent method used to objectively determine if process activities are being executed according to organizational guidelines, procedures and work instructions. Production parameters (tolerances) can often be validated by a checklist, whereas system functionality may require a more in-depth assessment.

As an alternative, process audits can be performed as a three-step process to accelerate a response to deviations. The three steps are verify, clarify and amplify. Verify conformance to standards through on-site observation or documented evidence. Clarify any deviations from requirements, confirm understanding and obtain agreement. Amplify by reinforcing expectations for gap closure and, if necessary, clarify actions to ensure full compliance to standards and procedures within a specified time period.

Line Walks

Line walks, also called lean, gemba, management or go and see walks, are about going to the place of work looking to learn and understand what's happening by talking to people, asking questions and collecting information through interaction and direct observation. Direct observation allows individuals to obtain a deep grasp of the process or issue being studied. These types of shop floor interactions are intended to expose management to the work environment, provide an opportunity to talk with employees and learn about problems affecting performance. Go and see is about using an individual's five senses to evaluate an existing situation or problem under review. Consider the medical intern following the doctor on their daily rounds. It's a "real-time" learning experience as the doctor asks the intern: What do you see? What would you do? What would you expect?

During line walks, leaders should review visuals, scan for warning signs and triggers, initiate proactive responses to concerns and hold people accountable for follow-up actions. In short, communicate, gain consensus, delegate actions, obtain commitment, clarify accountability and follow-up.

When limited time is available to go and see, focus attention on a specific item or topic. Lean walks are most effective when you focus on one process element at a time. For example, a review of 5S, visual controls, total productive maintenance (TPM) or Jidoka may be the topic of interest for a walk. Through this approach, potential trends or patterns observed may be complemented by an in-depth discussion of the issues. Covering multiple topics in one walk may not provide sufficient time to obtain the data and information required for adequate understanding or meaningful action. Next time you go to the shop floor, go with a purpose or objective in mind. Plan to do a lot of listening and observe with big eyes and ears. Listen to understand, not to respond. Plan to provide help in whatever capacity required.

Line walks can be an effective tool for changing and reinforcing desired behaviors. As managers walk around, they observe, ask questions and interact with people to understand how value is created. In doing so, they can enrich their own knowledge of the organization while developing a deeper sense of what's required for long-term sustainability. As Albert Einstein once said, "True knowledge comes with deep understanding of a topic and its inner workings".

SIDEBAR: LINE WALKS

Manufacturing line walks can be a very effective way to change the culture of an organization. They bring management to the frontlines of operations to review real-time performance, identify critical issues, discuss problems and reflect on pending risks. While reviewing operations, management should ask questions, explore improvement opportunities and teach/coach employees by reinforcing desired behaviors. It's an occasion for management to interact with organizational employees, promote an environment of respect and listen while sharing their views, concerns and insights with others. It provides an opportunity to exhibit discipline, emphasize the importance of organizational structure, hold people accountable as well as reinforce the sustainability of performance improvements. It provides employees with a good opportunity to engage with management, escalate issues and ask questions of key individuals. Line walks heighten awareness of current activities for all involved.

If you are skeptical about the impact of line walks on changing culture, simply try it. Pick a line and visit it every day or at least twice a week for several weeks. Review the lines output performance, ask questions about issues and enquire as to what you can do to make their work easier, faster or safer. Take a minute to mentor or coach employees on an improvement opportunity. Engage in conversation, ask them if they have any improvement ideas and make an effort to do something of value for the line.

Performance Reviews/Reporting

Performance reviews involve the periodic collection and analysis of baseline versus actual data to understand and convey work progress, performance and forecasted results. It provides an opportunity for management to review the "health" of a process by evaluating key performance metrics for expected results while scanning data for significant patterns, spikes and trends. Any unusual or undesirable behavior in operational performance should prompt discussion as to why it occurred and initiate countermeasures to address negative outcomes. Performance reviews allow organizations to assess the effectiveness of existing process controls and the sustainability of implemented improvements. Relevant data needs to be readily available (visualized) and presented in a form that quickly communicates the information needed for problem-solving and decision-making.

Performance reporting is the act of collecting and disseminating performance data and information to appropriate stakeholders as needed. Reports can include:

- Overview of past performance
- Analysis of schedule forecasts
- Status of current issues and risks
- Work completed since the last review
- Work planned for completion before the next review
- Summary of changes pending and approved
- Open and overdue issues needing attention

To be effective, performance reporting needs to be timely and relevant to the audience for which it's intended.

To summarize, process monitoring is a way to ensure accountability through the review of visual controls, performance metrics and completion of work routines. Daily shop floor walks allow management to monitor current performance, discuss issues of concern with employees and become familiar with the overall state of operations.

Process Controls

Process control is one of the most overlooked steps in shop floor management. It's intended to maintain a stable, capable and efficient process, sustain process improvements, communicate reasons and benefits for changes, recognize training opportunities, evaluate and reward employees for desired behavior, highlight key measures to monitor and manage process performance over time, react when process outcomes no longer conform to requirements as well as track and evaluate process improvements for effectiveness. Control also involves managing deviations through preventive and corrective measures, while making changes to policies, procedures and work instructions required to elevate operational performance. Control should influence the factors that could circumvent integrated change control so only approved changes are implemented. Helpful tips for process monitoring and control include:

✓ Hold periodic status (performance) reviews
✓ Continuously prioritize actions based on new data and information
✓ Focus on what's important

- ✓ Verify key deliverables are being completed on time and correctly
- ✓ Monitor and control for potential problem triggers and risks
- ✓ Maintain execution of scheduled tasks
- ✓ Monitor standardized work
- ✓ Perform periodic audits looking for process deviations
- ✓ Walk around and talk to employees about their activities
- ✓ Solicit feedback from team members and employees
- ✓ Look for ways to make work easier, faster, cheaper, safer
- ✓ Monitor data for patterns, trends and spikes
- ✓ Correct deviations from process or procedure quickly
- ✓ Confirm the effectiveness of preventive and corrective actions
- ✓ Manage deviations and changes to specifications, processes and procedures
- ✓ Review the sustainability of implemented changes
- ✓ Use best practices and lessons learned for improvement
- ✓ Allocate time for process improvement

A structured approach to process control helps ensure these and other activities are performed on a regular basis as a way to monitor and maintain harmony within the work environment. Leadership work routines, in combination with proven operating methods and tools, can create a structured way to monitor and control key process indicators (KPIs) and critical parameters.

Process control is important for two key reasons: it's a way to confirm process outputs are meeting desired performance expectations and prompts action whenever significant deviations from process standards occur. Controls can be instituted in many different ways such as operator work instructions, automatic equipment stops and management work routines. Some of the more common methods for process control are included in the following sections.

Standard Work

Work standards are used to standardize the way work is performed. This helps reduce process variation and drives a more consistent, predictable output. Standardized work also serves as a baseline from which process performance and improvements can be measured. Good standards contain work activities, work sequence and expected cycle time as well as assisting in process control by

- Highlighting critical steps required to ensure quality
- Heightening awareness of safety, quality, productivity and delivery issues
- Providing customers with more predictable outcomes
- Facilitating the on-boarding of new employees
- Minimizing operator fatigue

Work standards must be clear, unambiguous, accessible and highlight critical activities to be effective. They should include the who, what, when, where, why and how for performing repetitive work to ensure uniformity, consistency and quality of output (Figure 11.8). Standard work routines should include periodic monitoring and control of key metrics to ensure they are being continuously implemented as intended.

Control Plans

Control plans provide a structured approach for documenting the functional elements of quality control used to minimize process and product variation while maintaining compliance with standards. It's a tool to highlight the specific process and product parameters to be maintained within specification to ensure a state of control. Control methods, tolerances, measurement techniques, sample size, sample frequency and reaction plans are documented with the purpose of keeping key product and process characteristics within tolerance.

Control plans focus on controlling a process's significant parameters and provide a way to standardize and replicate product and process characteristics among product lines and between organizational facilities by

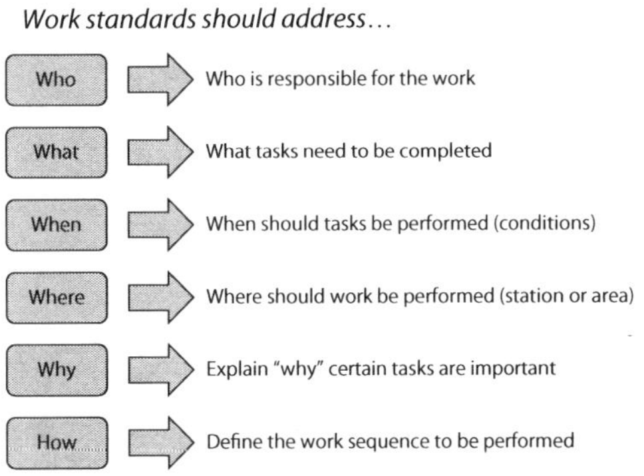

Figure 11.8 Work standards for process control.

communicating process priorities and performance standards. Control plans help highlight deviations from specification and provide a method for data collection while documenting process performance targets for customer and engineering requirements. A typical control plan, published by Chrysler, Ford and GM [5], is shown in Figure 11.9.

Control Charts

Control charts plot process output over time, revealing anomalies with the potential of causing process instability. They are an effective process monitoring tool for revealing non-random behavior displayed as patterns, trends and spikes in output data. Unusual behavior in output data should trigger actions to avoid defect generation. Control charts exist for continuous and variable data and can be generated manually as well as automatically, depending on equipment and software available to support data collection and analysis.

Statistical process control (SPC) charts use statistical techniques to analyze process output. They are trend charts with data-based control limits used to assess if a process is in statistical control (e.g. stable) and aid in maintaining control over time. Control limits generated from process data are used to judge process stability. Variation beyond a control limit is evidence that special cause is affecting process output and likely contributing to instability. SPC aids in eliminating uncontrolled process variation and serves to maintain process control.

Checklists

A checklist consists of a list of tasks that you "check off" as you complete each item or activity on the list. It can be a practical tool for remembering to complete work routines, especially if completing tasks in a specific sequence is important. Checklists can reduce stress and human error while improving individual and group discipline. It's one way to standardize a process and can be used to define shift start-up procedures, layered process audits and change control requirements to highlight a few applications.

Deviation Management

Two types of deviations are commonly observed in production: a nonconformance to specification or target (data) such as a material specification and a deviation from a process or procedure such as the omission of a step in a work instruction or performing work out of sequence. Deviations from

Advanced Product Quality Planning (APQP) and
Control Plan Reference Manual

Process Control Plan

CONTROL PLAN NUMBER	KEY CONTACT/PHONE	DATE (ORIG)	DATE (REV.)
LATEST CHANGE LEVEL	CORE TEAM	ENGINEERING APPROVAL/DATE (IF REQ'D)	
PROCESS NAME/DESCRIPTION	APPROVAL/DATE	QUALITY APPROVAL / DATE (IF REQ'D)	

					METHODS					
							SAMPLE			
PART/ PROCESS NUMBER	PROCESS NAME/ OPERATION DESCRIPTION	MACHINE, DEVICE, JIG, TOOLS FOR MFG.	PRODUCT	PROCESS	PRODUCT / PROCESS SPECIFICATION/ TOLERANCE	EVALUATION / MEASUREMENT TECHNIQUE	SIZE	FREQUENCY	CONTROL METHOD	REACTION PLAN

Figure 11.9 Example of a process control plan template.

procedures or specifications can cause an increase in cycle time, disrupt workflow or cause a defect with the potential of escaping to a customer. Deviations, if not managed, can contribute to process inefficiencies.

Deviation management requires visual controls (e.g. triggers) to highlight variances, regular monitoring to recognize anomalies and good problem-solving skills to facilitate corrective action. Visual controls can play a key role in deviation management by displaying warning signs that activate a response, without which deviations may continue undetected.

During routine production line walks, LPAs and performance reviews, leaders are expected to review data, information and corresponding visuals for unacceptable variances. Deviations may not necessarily lead to defects but increase the likelihood for defects to occur. Leadership must assess the possible impact of each deviation on process performance and prioritize their reaction to ensure process integrity is maintained. If follow-up action is required, an owner should be assigned to work the issue until a suitable countermeasure has been implemented and confirmed effective. A transparent method for closed loop handling of deviations will reinforce process ownership and accountability.

Problem-Solving

Problem-solving is critical to maintaining the stability and capability of a process. If action is not taken to correct significant process or product deviations, control is quickly lost and problems start mounting. As you become "leaner", the urgency to solve problems quickly becomes more prevalent since reductions in material buffers and finished goods inventory decrease the available time to respond.

Problem-solving tools and methods can range widely from the more basic 5 Why's and fishbone analysis to a more structured approach such as define, measure, analyze, improve and control (DMAIC), 8 Disciplines and A3. Problem-solving must be a core competency of all those who have process responsibility. It's a fundamental skill set for everyone to have, develop and continuously exercise.

Issue Escalation

Issue escalation is usually a predetermined sequence of actions initiated to effectively manage process abnormalities at the most appropriate level of the hierarchy. The objective is to rapidly raise awareness and a sense of urgency once a problem or issue has been identified and prioritized for upper management attention. If a corrective action to a problem impacting production can't be immediately addressed, a containment should be put in place to allow the continuation of production with minimal risk. Escalation should also be used when a problem or issues has occurred and communication to the appropriate individuals without any follow-up action occurring within a timely manner.

In summary, structure is introduced into organizations in different ways to help reduce variation and improve the efficiency of work performed. Methods for product development, project management, material handling and product manufacturing are integrated into systems and work activities to create a disciplined approach to conducting business.

If we don't maintain a healthy dose of discipline, by holding people accountable for their daily work routines, organizational discipline starts to erode and internal systems start to break down, leading to inefficient operations and unacceptable results.

Although structure provides a framework within which an organization builds and grows its business, discipline and accountability help to maintain the advances achieved while reinforcing the mindset of continuous incremental improvement. Daily shop floor management requires structure, discipline, accountability, creativity and transparency from all functions and levels within operations, to deliver on the promise of maintaining a stable, capable and continuously improving workplace where operational excellence is a journey, not a goal. At this point, let's turn our attention from process management to process improvement, the second key focus of shop floor management.

Process Improvement

Daily shop floor management must ensure process stability, capability and control before spending valuable resources on process improvement. Similar to process management, systems can also provide a structured and disciplined approach to process improvement, with the goal of institutionalizing the activities of continuous improvement into the unconscious mind of employees. Let's view process improvement from this perspective as we move into a more proactive phase on our road to operational excellence.

Continuous improvement must become a core competency of every lean thinking and acting organization. It has been well documented in recent literature that successful improvement programs can't be solely defined by the application of tools; they require an integration of methods, tools and expertise into a principled-based system that leverages the right behaviors to produce predictable results. Policy (strategy) deployment is an example of a system combining a series of tools, methods and techniques to create a set of projects targeted to achieve an organization's strategic vision and objectives.

Systems, formed with the right tools, methods and techniques, executed in a structured and disciplined manner, guide an organization along the path to operational excellence. Structure, in the form of a PDCA cycle approach to improvements, reinforced by a discipline of scientific thinking and experimentation to remove obstacles, will eventually lead organizations to a higher level of performance. Disciplined execution of these systems will eventually produce a critical mass of knowledge, experience and momentum that pushes employees beyond a threshold of resistance, changing the behaviors, habits and mindset of organizations to drive improvements through daily work routines.

Some people see a thin line between process control and continuous improvement. This line is defined by documented process standards. If the team is addressing a deviation to specification, standard or procedure, they are engaged in process control as they realign work activities back to the current level of expected performance. Since quality is conformance to requirements, and process control is the act of bringing deviations back into conformance with requirements, process control is equivalent to quality improvement since both are pursuing the same goal. However, when requirements must change to reflect a new, improved standard of performance, the act of process control does not change but the standard to which the process is controlled does, realizing true improvement.

Continuous improvement is reflected in teams working to elevate the current standard of performance (refer to Figure I.2). This change from a quality to an efficiency view of process turns a team's attention from focusing on stability and capability to waste reduction and continuous flow. When this occurs, there is a shift from root cause analysis to experimentation as we encounter our threshold of knowledge and engage in scientific thinking to determine the next steps for eliminating obstacles in pursuit of perfection.

Change Management

True continuous improvement is evident when a change is made to elevate an existing process standard to a new, higher level of performance. This differs from a quality improvement, where a deviation from an existing standard triggers an action to correct the deficiency. Good continuous improvement practice requires a change to be thoroughly evaluated to fully understand its potential risks since high-quality improvement opportunities do not guarantee risk-free implementation. As a matter of fact, poorly managed change is one of the primary causes of quality issues in many manufacturing operations.

The execution of improvements often involves changes to the methods, procedures, standards and behavior of people expected to implement them. Change may result in altering people's work habits. Therefore, change needs to be addressed on two levels: physical and mental. The "physical" involves all documents that need to be updated, coordinated, approved and distributed to reflect the latest state of operational performance. The "mental" is about obtaining genuine commitment from people to accept and implement a change. People are an integral part of change control since making a change not only involves updating documents but also requires employees to understand, accept and often change their work routines. People are more receptive to change when it benefits them directly, not necessarily the company as a whole. The question on most people's mind, but not often expressed, when introducing a change is "how will the change affect me?".

Implementing change is often difficult. If people are not convinced that a change will positively impact them, making it happen is likely to become more difficult and sustaining it more challenging. When little is known about a change, people's initial reaction is often one of resistance. Resistance to change can provide a wealth of information as to why people may be defending the status quo. A lack of communication about a change will often facilitate opposition. Not being open, honest or forthcoming about a change may also fuel its disapproval. One way to minimize resistance is to prepare a plan on how best to deploy change with those who will be most affected by it.

People experience change in many ways and have been found to undergo four distinct stages of change. These stages, based on the Kübler-Ross model (five stages of grief), are denial, resistance, exploration and commitment. See Figure 11.10 and the Sidebar: "Stages of Change" for more information on this topic.

To manage change properly, a change facilitator, sometimes called a change "agent", is recommended to help navigate individuals and teams through various stages of change in order to realize and accept it. Preparing

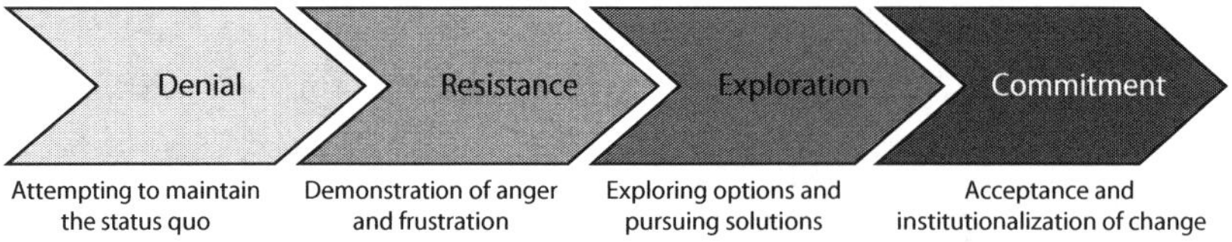

Figure 11.10 Stages of change.

answers to the following questions will help people to identify and process relevant information when a change is introduced.

- Why change? Why change now?
- What does the new change look like? What are its benefits?
- What's the rational for change (data)?
- What is the change plan (who, what, when, where and how)?
- How will the change plan be communicated?
- What will happen if we don't change?

When asking people to change, consider the following factors:

- *Commitment*: Obtain individual and team commitment to change; create a "can do" atmosphere!
- *Control*: Allow individuals to exercise some degree of control over the change; allow them to feel they can influence outcomes.
- *Challenge*: Use change to create a positive atmosphere of opportunity, growth and development.
- *Communicate*: Keep people informed of change activities throughout the process.

Success is the long-term sustainability of a proven change. People who see the benefit of change will more likely accept, support and commit to change by following the revised process, procedure or method, effectively institutionalizing it. Guidelines for managing change include:

- Don't consider change as negative; embrace the process of change
- Lead by example; control your attitude
- Look at change versus reality
- Keep a sense of humor
- Practice good stress management techniques
- Look toward the future; let go of the past

- Be part of the solution by supporting change, not the problem by fighting it
- If the company is changing, so should you

One other perspective to consider is that process changes can be planned or unplanned, sudden or gradual. For example, unplanned changes due to a switch in material supplier or unexpected machine breakdown are disruptive and, if not fully vetted, pose a risk to production. Gradual change is more difficult to identify since it occurs over time and can subtly affect man, machine, methods and materials. Situations in which change occurs gradually need to be periodically monitored for patterns or trends in output data. Examples of changes occurring over time include operator performance due to fatigue or non-conformance to dimensional tolerances of an injected part due to die wear caused by material friction.

Change is an essential component of shop floor management. The challenge of making a change is to thoroughly evaluate its impact on product quality and process performance before approval. Once approval is granted, the real work of implementation and sustainability begins.

Improvement Systems and Activities

Techniques such as Toyota Kata, Jishuken workshops, Kaizen events, Yamazumi charts and VSM are commonly used methods to facilitate efficiency improvements with the help of a coach or experienced facilitator. A structured, disciplined approach to efficiency improvements, with the guidance of experienced lean coaches, will help to develop the mindset and reinforce desirable habits of employees in a continuously learning and improving organization.

Jishuken workshops are undertaken to answer the question "What needs to change to achieve a specified target condition?" and become the engine for Kaizen events that determine how change will occur. VSM combined with value stream design (VSD) can provide an improvement path facilitated by repetitive PDCA cycles employed to methodically eliminate obstacles on the path to an improved state of material and information flow.

When combined into a system, various lean methods and tools create a more efficient approach to improvement. The following examples show how methods and tools can be joined into a system that promotes a continuous improvement mindset.

- **Strategy realization** = Strategic Plan + Strategic Projects + Project Management
- **Waste elimination** = Jishuken Workshops + Kaizen Events
- **Continuous flow improvement** = VSM + VSD + PDCA cycles + Lean Coaching

We must first approach every improvement effort with clear and quantifiable expectations. KPIs can be identified for critical output requirements as a way to measure progress and verify achievement. A detailed analysis of the current process state can then be performed and documented through a layout drawing, time and motion studies, machine times, cycle time calculations, output rates and production staffing requirements. In addition, supporting data such as equipment reliability, available working time and changeover times can also be collected. When performing time studies on standard work, look for non-standard or periodic work routines that may contribute to unacceptable process fluctuation and constrain the line's ability to meet takt time. Time studies can reveal the lowest repeatable time under stable conditions, providing a view of process capability.

Once data and factual information have been gathered and reviewed, a baseline picture of current performance is established and improvement targets can be defined. An action plan can then be prepared to determine the subsequent steps needed to reach each target. For example, if increasing line capacity by 15% is the target condition, individual activities to improve key input parameters affecting cycle time, equipment reliability and scrap rate may be initiated to achieve this challenge within a specified time frame.

The execution of improvement projects must be prioritized and integrated into each team member's work routines to realize timely completion of actions and overall improvement objectives. If continuous improvement is an expectation of every employee, it should become part of their work routines by reserving time each day, week or month for this purpose. Gains from improvements must be translated into procedures and work standards through change control and made part of ongoing process control activities to guarantee sustainable benefits. It's wise to verify the stability of revised standards by tracking performance over time. Once an improvement's effectiveness has been confirmed, consider how best to standardize and replicate it across the business. In doing so, determine the actions needed to properly deploy improvements in other departments and facilities across the company to effectively leverage best practices.

Idea Management

Idea management is a way to leverage the collective knowledge and creativity of an organization by encouraging all employees to submit improvement ideas that have the potential to enhance business and customer value. Employees are often the best source of improvement ideas within their work areas. Companies flourish from the creativity, innovation and engagement of their employees. When embraced, employee knowledge, experience and skills can drive safer, more productive operations while enhancing a company's competitive advantage. Key elements behind an idea management program include the following:

Submission of Ideas

Everyone in the company should be encouraged to submit ideas for evaluation with the expectation that value-added ideas will be accepted and implemented. Upon evaluation and acceptance, an owner should be assigned responsibility for implementing the idea, confirming its effectiveness and communicating results to other areas that may also benefit from its application.

It's recommended that a formal process be established for submission, assessment, selection, implementation and tracking of ideas. Ideas are typically submitted via paper format to a direct supervisor, an idea box or electronically via an intranet sites. Regardless of the method, all employees should have the ability to easily submit an idea for consideration. Reflect on the potential attributes for anonymous submissions. Ideas should be submitted prior to implementation to avoid the issue of "ownership" rights. All submissions should be confirmed with the employee along with the date received. Incentives may be used to encourage employees to submit ideas.

Disposition of Ideas

A formal, clearly documented process should be in place to manage idea submission and disposition within a reasonable time period. This process should be transparent to all eligible employees. Upon submission, ideas may be classified into different categories to aid in the efficacy of assessment. Typical categories may include safety, productivity, quality, cost or environmental. Consider the following evaluation criteria:

- Cost of implementation
- Time required for implementation
- Resources required for implementation (material, equipment, people, etc.)
- Individuals or groups expected to benefit
- Value of idea to the company
- Conflicts with similar ideas

All ideas under consideration should be reviewed by a knowledgeable individual or group within the function or department likely to be impacted by the improvement. Ideas can be rejected for different reasons including:

- Non-compliance with program requirements
- Lack of technical, practical or economic feasibility
- Conflict with existing laws or regulatory requirements
- Proposal is within the submitter's expected work responsibility
- Existence or submission of a similar idea prior to the one under review

Consideration should also be given to the possible application of proposals outside the department or company for which it's being recommended.

Acknowledgment

All employees who submitted ideas should be formally notified of the final decision. Rejection of an idea should be communicated to the employee with justification. It's recommended that a procedure for handling decision disagreements be available.

Appropriate recognition or reward should be extended to those whose ideas were accepted, implemented and confirmed effective in delivering expected results. Appreciation may be suitable for ideas submitted but not selected or implemented.

Trust Curve

When ideas for continuous improvements are submitted, it's important to document them. Although some ideas may never be implemented due to technical difficulty, limited value, time constraints or resource availability, it's important to acknowledge all ideas and provide feedback on the disposition of each idea to the submitter. One way to visualize the performance of a process is through a "trust curve" designed to graphically display the disposition of all ideas received relative to those rejected and accepted for implementation. The trust curve is intended to provide process transparency and build a sense of "trust" within the organization by showing a continuously updated status of all ideas submitted.

A trust curve visually displays the implementation of ideas relative to the number of ideas submitted. It's a way to hold management accountable for the review and disposition of ideas while revealing the impact ideas have on the organization. A trust curve plot can be used to display the number of ideas submitted, accepted, implemented and rejected to show the transparency of the idea management process. See Figure 11.11 for an example of a trust curve.

Lessons Learned

Lessons learned is about capturing and leveraging knowledge gained from past experiences and outcomes to improve the way work is performed. It can provide valuable insight into an organization's continuous improvement efforts. By considering things gone right and things gone wrong,

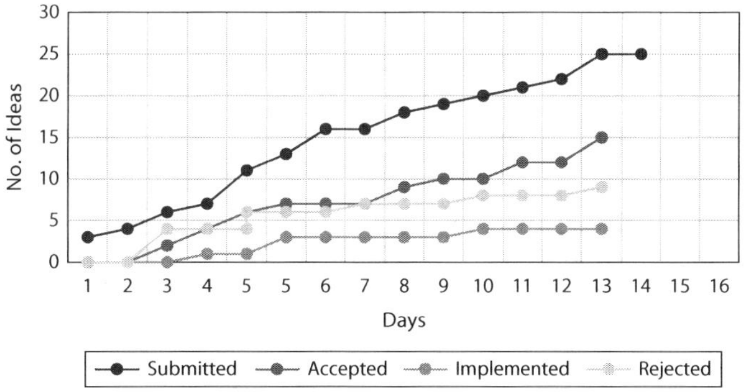

Figure 11.11 Trust curve of ideas.

companies can build on their strengths and recognize opportunities to address weaknesses. Although documenting these attributes for future reference may be challenging, a learning organization is one that does this well and uses knowledge from experiences to improve their management systems and results. If managed effectively, the entire organization can benefit from lessons learned, captured from some of the following sources:

- Customer preferences and complaints
- Product returns
- Completed projects
- Performance reports
- Process mistakes and product defects
- Focus groups

Lessons learned may also serve as a source for identifying potential risks when considering future projects and new business opportunities.

As organizations grow and develop, methods, tools and techniques are introduced to bring structure, discipline and accountability to the way work is performed. A well-run and maintained shop floor management system produces predictable results that satisfy stakeholders. By defining appropriate work routines and holding people accountable to their routines on a continuous basis, behaviors are reinforced and habits form that seamlessly maintain process control and unconsciously drive continuous improvements, both of which are essential for remaining competitive for long-term survival.

The objective of this chapter was to review and highlight the importance of a well-defined and executed shop floor management system. Clearly, an unstable process is unpredictable. An unpredictable process can never be capable or efficient. Thus, before starting any efficiency improvements, we must first ensure process stability and capability. Once confirmed, structure, discipline and accountability must be in place to maintain long-term stability and capability through process control. These activities are defined, executed and sustained through effective daily shop floor management. Once these basic practices are in place, we should have the confidence to implement efficiency improvements as we build a more efficient, competitive and sustainable lean enterprise focused on operational excellence.

Key Points

- Successful people and organizations recognize that structure, discipline and accountability are core competencies of excellent organizations.
- Discipline is the conduit between goals and accomplishment.
- Daily meetings should reduce the response time for issue escalation and standardize the way escalations occur.
- Implementing change to elevate performance enables a culture of continuous and sustainable improvements.
- Visual controls must communicate actionable information at a glance.
- Line walks bring management to the place where value is created to observe and learn.
- Convergent thinking leads us to "how", while divergent thinking leads us to "why".
- Control strives to institutionalize process disciplines that prevent the process from reverting to its previous state!
- LPAs help ensure standards are being followed and processes are delivering desired outcomes.
- Standard work routines add value when actions taken to address deviations result in process improvements.
- Process Management = Standard Work + Daily Work Routines + Layered Process Audits + Deviation Management + Problem-Solving + Change Management + ….
- Use checklists when monitoring the process to ensure critical parameters are not overlooked.
- If an activity is everyone's responsibility, it becomes nobody's responsibility (by default).
- Change in a manual process can often be accomplished immediately whereas change in an electronic or automated one can take more time.
- Visualization without action is waste!

References

1. Jeffrey K. Liker. 2004. *The Toyota Way*. New York: McGraw-Hill.
2. Jim Collins. 2001. *Good to Great: Why Some Companies Make the Leap and Others Don't*. New York: HarperCollins.

3. William Thom. 2009. People, Process, and Performance Management in Project Management. https:/pmhut.com/people-process-and-performance-management-in-project-management (Process Management, Wikipedia. June 28, 2017).
4. Lonnie Wilson. 2013. "Wanna Sabotage Your Lean Implementation Effort? Try This" *IndustryWeek*. http://www.industryweek.com/continuous-improvement/wanna-sabotage-your-lean-implementation-effort-try (March 5, 2013).
5. Chrysler Corporation. 1994. *Advanced Product Quality Planning (APQP) and Control Plan Reference Manua*l. State College, PA: Pennsylvania State University Press.

Chapter 12

Building a Sustainable Lean Enterprise

> The pursuit of perfection reveals that there are always opportunities for improvement.
>
> **The Shingo Institute**

The Lean Enterprise

The ultimate goal of any lean enterprise is to deliver value to the customer in the form of quality products, services and results. The internal goal is to eliminate waste and remove obstacles to achieve a continuous flow. One key to developing lean management systems is the rapid identification and permanent elimination of waste. A way to achieve this objective is for everyone in the organization to engage in problem-solving and participate in activities to improve organizational processes, products and services as an integral part of their daily work routines (DWR).

Building a lean enterprise starts with a lean management system that is rooted in a set of core principles used to guide the enterprise on a journey of efficiency improvement. These principles must align with the organization's strategic direction; be visible and understood by all employees; provide a simple, clear message of intent; and become a way of thinking, behaving and acting. These guiding principles set the tone and direction of the organization, but may require the intervention of knowledgeable and experienced individuals to help coach, mentor and lead the organization through a lean transformation. If this expertise does not exist internally, organizations must hire or develop lean practitioners within their own ranks who are passionate, capable and resourced to lead a transformation. These people, considered enterprise change agents, must encourage and motivate others to apply lean principles, practices, methods and tools, forging a new path along the road to operational excellence (OE). As individuals and teams move along this path, the successful deployment of lean will become evident with increasing productivity and customer satisfaction as defects, inventories and cycle times decrease.

One of the fundamental principles of lean is pull-based flow driven by customer demand. Migrating to a pull system begins with understanding the current state of material and information flow. From this point, organizational leadership can visualize and prepare a future state, identify the gaps between "what is" and "what should be" and devise a plan to incrementally move from one state to the next, employing the tools and techniques of lean in an intentional, efficient and productive manner. This is the objective of using value stream mapping (VSM) and value stream design (VSD) in combination with plan-do-check-act (PDCA) cycles to facilitate incremental improvement (Figure 12.1).

Pull-induced material flow is one of the truly unique aspects of a lean management system since it's a fundamental change from a traditional batch-orientated push production system. It shifts the thought process from focusing on people and equipment efficiency to one of continuous material and information flow through a value stream. This is significant since the methods, tools and techniques rooted in batch and push processing do

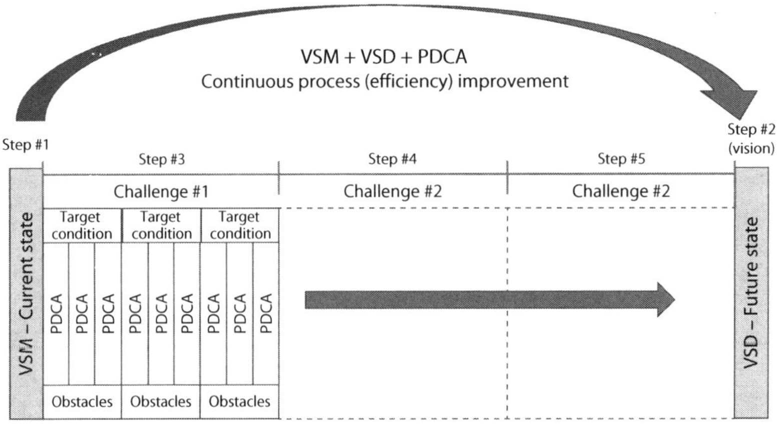

Figure 12.1 Example of an incremental system of continuous improvement.

not always translate well for improving continuous flow. Two core competencies that don't change when transforming the enterprise are problem-solving and decision-making. In a lean enterprise, problems are expected to be solved at the lowest possible level of the organization, closest to where the problems occur since escalating problems and decisions up the chain of command adds to their resolution time. Engaging people to solve problems and make decision at the lowest levels of the organization will facilitate waste reduction while creating an environment of trust and empowerment. Employees know their processes and can directly contribute to improving their efficiency.

On a similar note, good processes, products and services emerge from good design and development activities, especially when simplicity and lean concepts are kept in mind. Customer feedback is important during the initial stages of product design in order to clarify requirements and verify the capability of meeting them within the guidelines of good lean practices. In fact, building a lean enterprise starts at the point of design. Design teams need to be familiar with lean concepts for plant layout, material flow, equipment design and product line configuration in order to minimize the movement of materials and people during production. It takes an entire workforce, from design and development to material receiving and finished goods shipping, to understand and apply the fundamentals of lean when preparing a new line or simply making improvements to an existing one. Lean is a team effort and takes the collective knowledge and effort of able and passionate individuals creatively collaborating to build a lean enterprise, one facility, one value stream, one production line or one workstation at a time.

SIDEBAR: ATTRIBUTES OF A LEAN ENTERPRISE

- Continuous improvement; every one, every day
- Problems solved at the lowest possible level of the organization
- Continuous employee development
- Taking actions to improve customer value and support business prosperity
- An atmosphere of mutual trust and respect
- Development of robust products and processes
- Understanding of the "why" and "how" of what people are doing
- Hold people accountable for the work they do
- Systems and visuals to identify and solve problems quickly
- Value stream improvement through the removal of obstacles
- A controlled process before driving process improvements

- Engage in change control to elevate performance standards
- Employees who define their standard work and suggest ideas for their continuous improvement
- Leaders who work on improving systems while managers work on executing, controlling and improving processes
- Employee empowerment to experiment and learn (under the guidance of a lean coach)
- Leadership that coaches and mentors others
- Employees who define, execute and improve their DWR
- Employees who exhibit tenacity, patience, focus, commitment and persistence
- Acquiring knowledge through scientific thinking
- A mindset of driving change in the workplace, not in meeting rooms
- A relentless focus on process and results
- A short-term (DWR) and long-term (strategy deployment) view of improvement
- Continuous development of next generation lean coaches and leaders
- Addressing underperformance by seeking out the cause (precursor) leading to undesirable behavior
- Management frequently visits the work area to confirm understanding, increase awareness and look for opportunities to add value
- Continuously identifies lessons learned and shares best practices
- Stop to fix and eliminate problems

Although not comprehensive, the following short topics establish an entry point for building a lean enterprise. Awareness of these and other subjects will help change agents prepare for the application of lean methods, tools and techniques in anticipation of the long journey ahead.

Know What Constitutes Customer Value

Value is defined by the customer. Know your customer, talk to them, ask questions and confirm understanding by clarifying what they want, need and expect from your products and services. This does not mean you need to satisfy every requirement immediately, but it's a starting point for discussions on what constitutes value and what key deliverables must be met, by when, to ensure satisfaction. Remember, defining customer value starts at contract negotiation and continues throughout the product life cycle.

Embrace customer feedback; it's your window into understanding how they think and what they expect from their suppliers.

Engage in Strategic Planning

Decisive leadership is essential when starting a lean journey. A clear and common vision unites an organization, giving it direction and purpose. Strategic planning requires a collective group of experienced people from key functions within the enterprise working together to establish a plan and identifying corresponding projects to exploit company strengths and augment inherent weaknesses to stimulate growth and prepare for future challenges. A lean enterprise engages in long-term strategic thinking, planning and strategy deployment.

Develop Lean Coaches

Every organization needs change agents. These are the people who know what to do and how to do it. They command respect from others and influence the organization by explaining the why and how of change. They are coaches, mentors and teachers who help their organizations prepare for and embark on the long journey to OE. These individuals must be the best and the brightest a company has to offer since they will shape, mold and transform the enterprise's future. The talents of a lean coach must eventually spread upstream to develop suppliers who are key stakeholders and an integral part of a lean transformation since they are expected to provide a steady stream of quality materials on time and in the quantities required to maintain a predictable flow of finished goods to expecting customers.

Be a Learning Organization

Organizations must develop an ability to learn quickly and use this new knowledge as a competitive advantage. Learning is about developing new patterns of thinking to enhance creativity, drive innovation, acquire new skills and enhance existing capabilities. Organizations must develop employees and suppliers, learn from problem-solving and adapt this knowledge to compete in a dynamic business environment. Learning organizations standardize what works, practice what works well, learn from what they practice and identify improvements for implementation. In short, learning organizations continuously standardize, practice, learn and improve.

Measure Lean Progress

As is often said, a process can't be improved if it can't be measured. We measure for three reasons: justify a rationale, make a comparison and imply a performance level. During a lean transformation, periodically assessing our performance relative to where we were, where we are and where we want to be, allows us to assess our lean maturity. It affords us the opportunity to assess our progress to plan, course correct when necessary and ensure steady advancement toward stated objectives. This activity can be facilitated by monitoring one or more key performance indicator that can help determine the next steps and direct our continuing activities in the meaningful pursuit of OE. Reference Appendix XIV for a tool to assess Process Maturity and Operational Excellence.

Reinforce Desired Behaviors

Systems drive behaviors and the right behaviors should be recognized and rewarded to reinforce good habits. Organizations must ensure proper systems are in place to drive desired behaviors, producing expected results and creating the right habits. Be aware and prepared to reward favorable conduct while taking swift action to correct poor behaviors leading to undesirable habits.

Continuous Improvement

Continuous improvement is about everybody making improvements every day. World-class continuous improvement is rooted in scientific thinking and the unwavering pursuit of perfection, knowing perfection is a fictitious state of existence. It's concerned with making small, medium and large, continuous, incremental process changes targeted at waste elimination and the removal of obstacles to flow.

Continuous improvement can be made a habit by teaching, coaching and mentoring employees to repeatedly think, work and act while developing and applying their knowledge in creative and innovative ways. Employees should be encouraged to expand their threshold of knowledge through exploration and experimentation, leveraging newly acquired knowledge to move the organization further along the path to excellence.

Value Stream Improvement

One of the most effective methods to see, understand and optimize the flow of *material and information* through the value stream is VSM. The preparation of a current state and future state map will reveal the gap or obstacles between the two levels of performance, which can be used to develop an incremental flow improvement plan. Kaizen events can then be employed to target specific waste and flow disruptors in the value stream for elimination. This is lean improvement in action (Figure 12.1).

Start Simple, Small, Slow and Steady

There is no rush to "become" lean. It's not a race. Lean is a journey of continuous "incremental" improvement that works to change the culture of an organization; something that does not happen overnight. It takes time to develop people, have those people experiment and put what they have learned into action. It takes time to understand, through trial and error, how lean methods and tools can be effectively integrated into local operations in meaningful ways to make work easier, cheaper, faster and safer. A good approach to implementing a lean management system is to start simple, small, slow and steady, allowing people to PDCA as they build a solid and sustainable future, one improvement at a time.

Project Management

Projects are a mechanism by which organizations can implement activities outside their normal mode of operation. They can be used to implement business strategies or to realize a strategic plan.

If you are looking to change a system, implement a new method or develop a new capability, project management can be employed to inject structure, discipline and accountability into these unique endeavors. Project management is a business discipline that establishes clear ownership and accountability to an individual who becomes the focal point for all project activities. It can be an effective instrument for changing the infrastructure needed to create and support a lean management system.

A lean enterprise uses the principles and practices of lean, made popular by Toyota, to change the way people think and create value. Fundamentally, there are five principles of lean manufacturing originally described by James Womack and Daniel Jones in their book, *Lean Thinking* [1], which include the concepts of value, value stream, flow, pull and perfection. A lean enterprise, first and foremost, must understand what constitutes value as defined by product and service requirements. Value is then realized through a series of activities within the value stream through real-time pull and flow of material and information consistent with customer demand. While this is happening, a lean enterprise continuously makes sustainable improvements in process and product quality, cost and delivery as they pursue perfection. This high-level view of a lean enterprise, when complemented with an efficient lean management system, can provide a holistic approach to developing a sustainable culture of continuous improvement.

A Lean Management System

It's hard to argue the benefits of a lean system; achieving those benefits requires a significant commitment to changing the mindset, attitudes and fundamental operational activities of most organizations. It took Toyota over 40 years to do just that. For a majority of companies, implementing a lean management system is a daunting task. It's a significant departure from how operations are fundamentally run, and if you consider all the prerequisites required to obtain the significant benefits of a lean management system, such as just-in-time (JIT) inventory control, pull systems, Jidoka, standardized work, visual controls, kanbans and supermarkets, the implementation of a lean system will take time, patience, unwavering management commitment and execution of a good, long-term strategic plan to change the way business is conducted.

There is no question that existing lean methods, tools and techniques, rooted in more traditional management systems, can be helpful in achieving various degrees of efficiency; however, a true lean management system that strives to eliminate waste with the goal of continuous flow, must focus on methods, tools and techniques specifically developed for this purpose. In the following sections, we will examine the concepts of a lean management system, explore the fundamental building blocks leading to OE and consider how supporting methods, tools and techniques can be integrated in meaningful ways to create systems and subsystems that work in concert as functional elements. As stated by the Shingo Institute in their 2017 publication describing the Shingo Model™: *Think of a system as a collection of tools working together to accomplish an intended outcome. A successful enterprise is usually made up of complex systems that can be divided into layers of subsystems, each containing the necessary tools to enable the successful outcome of the system.*

There are many variations in systems and subsystems that can be created to support a management system. What's important is to consider what needs to be accomplished and selecting the best combination of methods, tools and techniques that achieves the objectives for which a system was intended to deliver. Examples of methods combined with tools used for lean management include:

- Deviation Management (DM) = Visual Controls + Problem-Solving + Action Plans + Follow-up
- Pull System = Pacemaker Process + Supermarkets + FIFO + Kanban
- Change Management (CM) = Proposal + Evaluation + Decision + Change Control
- Idea Management (IM) = Ideas + Review + Disposition + Implementation
- Problem-Solving (PS) = Problem Statement + Root Cause Analysis + Root Cause Verification + Solution Implementation
- Quality Assurance = Standards + Deliverables + Verification + Control
- Process Control = Standards + Stability + Capability
- Efficiency Improvement = Waste Elimination + Continuous Flow
- Daily Work Routines (DWR) = Activities + Frequency + Owners + Follow-up

Clearly, these are combinations of methods and tools brought together to create systems to achieve specific objective. They can also trigger the opportunity to consider other combinations of methods, tools and techniques that work together effectively to create systems and subsystems to achieve desired behaviors and ideal results.

Roadmap for Efficiency and Operational Excellence

To create a truly sustainable lean management system, a fundamental set of building blocks, presented in logical sequence, will help organizations evaluate their level of maturity, strengthen their existing operational base and drive sustainable improvements through needed structure, discipline and accountability. These fundamental building blocks represent levels of organizational and process maturity required for OE. Organizational personnel must display the right skill sets, competence and discipline to work at increasingly higher levels of efficiency, functionality and maturity over time while the process is kept in control, continuously improving and delivering anticipated results as confirmation of its advancing state of performance.

These building blocks represent a logical, natural evolution of a process's life cycle, starting with standardized work and continuing until characteristics of OE are displayed. The objective is to achieve, maintain and build upon each block, using existing methods, tools and techniques in various system and subsystem combinations to facilitate and guide the journey to OE. A roadmap for efficiency and OE, based on these building blocks, was first presented at the beginning of this text and will be discussed further in the following pages (see Figure 12.2).

Although the fundamental building blocks are universal and do not change, the subsystems can and do change based on how an organization chooses to pursue lean. Let's briefly review the building blocks of a lean management system and consider typical systems and subsystems used to support and help drive organizations to achieve higher levels of maturity with time and experience.

Quality Improvement

Quality improvement is the act of bringing deviations from a target, specification or procedure back into compliance with established standards. Standards define the requirements for control. Work routines monitor and control process activities established to maintain stability and ensure capability. Quality improvement is about returning underperforming processes back into a state of acceptable performance. Standardized work is one of the first stops on the road to OE.

Process Standardization

Standardized work controls the vital tasks performed at the lowest level of the organization. It defines the activities, sequence and timing of highly repetitive work intended to drive consistent and predictable process

Figure 12.2 Operational Excellence Maturity; building blocks for quality and efficiency improvement.

outcomes. It serves process stability, helps maintain process capability and creates a baseline for continuous improvement. Examples of subsystems to support standardized work include:

- Standardized Work = Standard Work Instructions + Audits + Deviation Management
- Standardized Work = Standard Work Instructions + Idea Management + Change Management

Standard work subsystems are intended to maintain consistency and compliance to repetitive work routines through audits and deviation management. Change control is required to continuously evaluate the efficacy of proposed improvements for implementation. Standardized work contributes to process stability, capability and efficiency as well as being an essential component of OE.

Process Stability

Process stability is a fundamental requirement for all processes expected to produce consistently capable results. It's a hallmark of a structured and disciplined work environment. Stability must be continuously monitored since significant fluctuations from targets can quickly erode process integrity and destabilize output performance. Corresponding subsystems for process stability may look like the following:

- Process Stability = Daily Work Routines + Layered Process Audits (LPAs) + DM
- Process Stability = SW + Control Charts + Trend Analysis + DM

A stable process will produce consistent results. A capable process will produce consistently good results. The right process will produce the right results. Once a process is demonstrated to produce the desired outputs, it's the responsibility of management to ensure systems are in place and executed to maintain stability and capability over time.

Process Capability

Process stability can be monitored via control limits (process data), whereas capability by specifications (customer) limits. Although there is no direct relationship between these two characteristics, capability is dependent on stability. If process stability can't be maintained, there is no way to guarantee a process will consistently produce output within customer requirements. The subsystem for process capability is clearly linked with process stability.

- Process Capability = Process Stability + Capability Analysis + Variation Reduction

Capability is built upon a standardized and stable process. Documenting and executing work instructions allows for targeting and eliminating process anomalies. A stable process (e.g. free of defects) allows a comparison of natural process variation to imposed tolerances in order to assess a process's ability to deliver consistently good results. If required, process capability can be improved by aligning the mean output with the target value and reducing process variation.

Process Control

Process control is the act of maintaining continuous process stability and capability through process monitoring and control. We use activities such as line walks, LPA and performance reviews as part of our DWR to identify significant process deviations and engage in deviation management. There are many ways to exercise process control. The following subroutines combine typical tools and techniques to do so.

- Process Control = DWR + Visual Controls + LPA + DM
- Process Control = DWR + Control Plans + Control Charts + DM
- Process Control = Performance Reviews + KPI Trend Analysis + Action Items

A standardized process that consistently exhibits a stable and capable output establishes the operational framework for sustainable efficiency improvement. Systems create the structure while DWR drive the discipline and accountability for process monitoring of visual controls used to recognize deviations requiring action to maintain control.

Efficiency Improvement

Quality assurance, through standards and control, will move us along the road to our next stop of efficiency improvement. Efficiency improvement embraces the lean methodology to minimize non-value-added activities with an emphasis on a steady flow of material and information through the value stream. Tools and techniques such as Jishuken workshops and Yamazumi charts have been specifically developed by Toyota to acquire a deep and fundamental understanding of interactions between man, machine, material and methods to clarify the next logical steps for efficiency improvement. The following building blocks and corresponding subsystems combine some of these lean instruments in order to strengthen the foundation for operational excellence.

Waste Elimination: Process

There are many opportunities to eliminate waste within a working environment. Some are obvious, but spotting improvement opportunities, once the low-hanging fruit is gone, becomes more challenging as time marches on. Jishuken workshops can reveal clear and targeted process improvement opportunities by prompting a detailed study of production line operations, highlighting problematic areas such as capacity constraints, excess motion and workload imbalances. When a structured approach to process analysis is paired with high priority improvement events, significant advances in process efficiency can be realized. Examples of the effective pairings of tools and techniques include:

- Waste Elimination = Jishuken Workshops + Kaizen Events
- Waste Elimination = Yamazumi Charts + Kata/PDCA
- Waste Elimination = Lean (Line) Walks + Action Items
- Waste Elimination = LPA + Kaizen Events
- Waste Elimination = Process Mapping + Value Analysis + PDCA

Look to eliminate waste within and between operations. If you can't find waste, you are not looking hard enough. Waste exists everywhere. In addition, think creatively when looking for ways to reduce waste. Simple and cheap approaches to waste reduction are often the best.

Waste Elimination: People

The development and utilization of untapped talent can lead to a more knowledgeable, skilled and engaged workforce willing and able to make improvements at all levels of the organization. The utilization of available human talent can open a vast potential of resources for the company and opportunities for employees willing to embrace them. However, a company must acknowledge, develop and promote this internal potential by preparing management and supervisors to recognize, cultivate and engage individuals as well as teams in the pursuit of perfection. Every opportunity for improvement realized, regardless of its magnitude, edges the organization closer to the idea of OE. Subsystems that promote people development for the benefit of the organization include:

- Employee Development = Training + Mentors
- Employee Development = PDCA + Scientific Thinking + Lean Coaching (Kata)
- Employee Development = Certification = Knowledge Demonstration + Knowledge Application (e.g. Six Sigma belts, project management, lean practitioner)

Process improvement is not only about the production floor. It requires the total elimination of waste in every aspect of process, product and service systems used to support production and customers. The more people engaged in waste removal, the more "real" OE becomes.

Continuous Flow

Improving process flow starts with establishing a smooth, steady, uninterrupted movement of information and material through the value stream followed by reducing the batch size to an ideal one-piece. VSM (current state map) and VSD (future state map) shows the link between information and material flow and is a valuable tool for identifying obstacles to achieving a more desirable state.

- Continuous Flow = Material Flow + Information Flow + Line Layout + Buffers
- Continuous Flow = Takt Time + Pull Systems (Supermarkets and FIFO) + Kanban + Pacemaker Process + Production Leveling (mix and volume)
- Continuous Flow = VSM + Improvement Plan + Plan Execution (Kaizen Events/Kata/PDCA)
- Continuous Flow = VSM + VSD + PDCA + Lean Coaching

VSM/VSD visualizes the current and future state of a product family's value stream, revealing a path for improvement. When a clear path is revealed, an action plan can be developed to move operations from the current to future state through incremental removal of obstacles using PDCA cycles and lean coaching. This systemic approach to improvement can establish a behavior and mindset reflective of a lean enterprise.

Sustainability

Process control establishes the foundation upon which continuous improvements and sustainable productivity are achieved. A lean management system, rooted in process control and continuous improvement, requires structure, discipline and accountability to reinforce desired behaviors and create a mindset for OE. The ability of an organization to achieve a sustainable work environment starts with clearly defined work routines, assigned to employees, executed without compromise and transparent to all. DWR, reflected in the habits of enterprise employees, sets the stage for stable, capable, improving and sustainable operations. These organizational building blocks must be evident in the systems and subsystems designed to realize and sustain an environment of OE.

- Sustainability = Structure/Discipline/Accountability + Audits + DWR
- Sustainability = Guidelines and Procedures + Lessons Learned + Best Practices

A sustainable work environment is one in which work expectations are clearly defined, measurable, achieved and maintained. In addition, adequate resources and skilled employees are assigned to do the work of the organization with the right behavior and commitment reflected by output results.

Operational Excellence

OE can only be achieved when it's an inherent part of leadership's mindset, articulated through the organization's strategy and reflected in the systems and behaviors of employees. This mindset must be pervasive in the strategy, principles, systems and behaviors of an enterprise and realized through sustainable and continuously improving key performance and behavioral metrics. Fundamental changes to an organization's behavior can be driven through strategic projects designed to reinforce process controls, drive continuous improvements and sustain productivity gains. This can be accomplished through subsystems such as the following:

- OE = Process Control + Continuous Improvements + Structure/Discipline/Accountability
- OE = Mindset + Principles + Systems (and Tools) + Behaviors + Results (KPIs and KBIs)
- OE = Strategy + Strategic Projects + Project Management

Leadership is essential in establishing the organizational structure, discipline and accountability that will lead to OE. Leadership creates the vision, mission and strategy with which the organization will align systems, procedures and behaviors. They must also allocate the time, proper tools and training while facilitating open discussion to find the best way to structure and exploit the lean management system in realizing OE.

Operational Excellence: The Secret of Success

I once encountered a story about the secret to success and it went something like this: a young man asked Socrates, an ancient Greek philosopher, the secret of success. Socrates told the young man to meet him near the river the next morning. They met. Socrates asked the young man to walk with him toward the river. They entered the water together and walked until the water was neck high. Suddenly, without warning, Socrates took the young man by surprise and dunked him into the water. The man struggled to get out, but Socrates was strong and kept him under until he started turning blue. The young man struggled and managed to get up. The first thing he did was gasp and take a deep breath.

At that point, Socrates asked, "What did you want most when you were under water?" The man replied "air". Socrates said: "That's the secret to success. When you want success as badly as you want air, you will get it. There is no other secret". In reflection, a burning desire is the starting point for all accomplishments. However, just like a small fire cannot give much heat, a weak desire cannot produce great results.

In the book *Good to Great*, author Jim Collins [2] highlighted three things that are needed for success: passion, ability and resources. One of the secrets to achieving OE is to look for people who understand and believe in OE and demonstrate the passion to pursue it. Passion is reflected in the interest and desire of an individual who is ready and willing to make a difference. Passion, properly placed, is contagious. However, steering a culture toward the guiding principles of OE takes more than just passion, it takes ability. The right people, in the right places, at the right time with the essential mindset, influence and authority can create a movement that changes the way people think and act. Ability is rooted in people's knowledge, experience and demonstrated actions along with the desire to make a difference.

Unfortunately, passion and ability alone can't keep an initiative alive without the resources to maintain the momentum of change with the passage of time. Resources, including people, equipment, materials and methods, must be available to address problems and make changes to update and create innovative systems that can drive an organization in new directions. People, as a resource, must demonstrate commitment to change. People who understand the "*why*" of change and believe it's the right thing to do, will likely accept and support it. Upon observing the benefits of change, these same people may begin to display the passion and influence to nudge even more people in a common direction, setting the larger organization in motion toward the critical mass needed to institutionalize the mindset of excellence.

$$\text{Success} = \text{Passion} + \text{Ability} + \text{Resources}$$

In 1983, Toyota and GM entered a joint venture (called New United Motors Manufacturing, Inc. or NUMMI) to produce a small car named "Nova" [3]. They used a former GM automotive assembly plant located in Fremont, California, which was closed in 1978 due to an unusually hostile work environment, fueled by abysmal relations between management and the union, resulting in some of the poorest quality vehicles produced by GM at that time.

As part of the agreement, Toyota accepted responsibility for all plant operations including product design, engineering, marketing, sales and service for Toyota's version of the vehicle, the *Corolla*. GM agreed to marketing, sales and service for the Chevy *Nova*. Eighty-five percent or approximately 2200 people of the startup workforce were hired from the original GM employees laid off during the 1978 closing. In the first year of production, the facility produced nearly 65,000 vehicles rated by consumer reports as one of the highest quality small car worldwide. The goals of the facility were to continually improve quality and safety while reducing vehicle cost. The NUMMI plant was recognized as one of the most efficient producers of quality automobiles compared to the rest of GM. One of the primary reasons cited for the plant's success was an alignment of operational and business processes with the interests of workers and managers, which empowered and focused the workforce on what was important to achieving their goals.

NUMMI management created an environment in which over 90% of workers indicated that they were proud of the cars they built. Three principles identified as key to their success:

1. Management and the employee union recognized their futures were dependent on working together toward a common vision.
2. A respectful working relationship was required for mutual cooperation.
3. An effective production system required teamwork and trust among all employees.

To prepare the workforce for working within a Toyota Production System, 400 Japanese trainers were sent to NUMMI while 600 NUMMI employees were sent to Japan for on-the-job training, working side by side with their Japanese counterparts.

Toyota believes that a company is only as good as its people, individually and collectively. Thus, respect for people is core to the success of its production system, and support of production and its people is paramount. The NUMMI human resource group established a philosophy to realize their commitment to building quality automobiles at the lowest possible cost:

- Recognize our worth and dignity
- Develop individual performance
- Develop team performance
- Improve the work environment

This commitment focused on their desire to establish a work environment for success.

Team members were expected to take responsibility for their work and rotate between jobs to establish cross-function capability. Employees took ownership for process control and continuous improvement. First-level managers (group leaders) within the NUMMI plant were responsible for team leader training and support of continuous improvement activities. They were the first responders to line-related process and people issues beyond the scope of team members with the added responsibility to step in and work on the line, if needed. Second-level managers retained a similar responsibility for process but were expected to seek out and resolve problems at the lowest appropriate levels. This organizational structure demands cooperation, trust and respect for people at all levels of the hierarchy and recognizes that everyone benefits when team members are properly supported in their quest to deliver quality product to the customer.

This next story is a well-documented one about the Canada Post Corporation (CPC). Similar to the United Postal Service [4], the CPC is a government-owned corporation run like a private company. Their 2017 vision is to be "a world leader in providing innovative physical and electronic delivery solutions, creating value for our customers, employees and all Canadians". According to Wikipedia, "the Canada Post provided service to more than 15.8 million addresses and delivered almost 9 billion items in 2015 and consolidated revenue from operations reached $8 billion". They have 25,000 letter carriers, a 13,000 vehicle fleet, over 6,200 post offices across Canada in various forms, nearly 843,000 rural residential mail delivery locations (as of 2004) and employs approximately 64,000 people as part of the Canada Post Group.

In the mid-1990s, when the CPC first started working with lean methods, their situation was dire. At the time, the CPC operated 22 main sorting and distribution plants that served as the nerve centers for their operations. They functioned like automated warehouses with high-speed sorting equipment used to process large batches of material. During this period, facilities struggled with excess storage, material transport and long lead times. Although material moved quickly through sorting machines, it had to be stored, disrupting flow to the distribution points.

As an initial approach to efficiency improvement, the CPC started to apply lean methods in a trial-and-error approach. In doing so, significant gains were realized. As expressed by Jeff Liker in telling this story [4]: *At its Ottawa sorting facility, CPC mapped the current state of the value stream for the facility on a wall, showing how letters, advertisements, and parcels went all over the place in the facility. They discovered that from the moment an incoming letter entered the facility to when it left the facility it traveled 167 meters, was stored and removed eight times, took 26 hours of total lead time to process, and the value-added time sorting (actual work) was only 12 seconds.* According to Steve Withers, CPC's senior advisor of lean, "Mail was sorted in seconds, transported in minutes, staged in hours, and delivered in days. The plant was a warehouse". In response to this new found understanding, in 1997, they reduced inventory and rearranged their facility layout and equipment to accommodate a more continuous process flow, resulting in a 28% reduction in mail travel time, a 37% reduction in lead time and a 27% reduction in storage.

What was the secret to their success? Admitting they had a problem, gathering data and information required to understand the problem, analyzing it to recognize the source of the problem, using tools and techniques in a trial-and-error approach to learn what would eliminate the problem and applying effective solutions that resulted in sustainable improvements. In short, there is no secret; it's doing what's necessary to fully understand the complexities of an issue or problem and discovering what works to address or eliminate it.

Lean Leadership

One of the icons of Toyota, former chairman Fujio Cho, highlighted three keys to lean leadership:

- Go see; spend time on the plant floor
- Ask why; continuously ask "*why*" to seek understanding
- Show respect; respect your people

Leadership needs to engage people in the practice of go and see by setting the example they want others to follow. At every opportunity, leadership, management and employees should ask "why" to facilitate a deep understanding of a situation while continuously showing compassion and respect for others by remaining humble, listening and learning from those who hold a unique perspective on the topic under discussion. Leaders must help those around them be successful by showing respect and reflecting on how their decisions impact others.

SIDEBAR: I DON'T KNOW

Fear of appearing incompetent in front of a group has probably deterred many of us from saying "I don't know". However, acknowledging your own threshold of knowledge allows you to pause and open yourself up to new ideas and possibilities before taking that next step or making that critical decision.

When was the last time you felt comfortable saying, "I don't know" to yourself or others? Have you ever felt uneasy asking for help? Why does it seem difficult to admit that we don't understand something? Could it appear as though we are incompetent? Being unable to say "I don't know" for any reason, becomes a barrier to effective leadership and must be overcome before an organization can move forward in developing a truly effective improvement culture.

If you can't say "I don't know", and fail to delegate certain actions and decisions to others, you may be closing the door to seeking a broader knowledge base from which issues and obstacles can be resolved quickly, efficiently and permanently. Thus, next time you find yourself trying to formulate a response to a question you don't know the answer to, stop and think, is this the right way to react or should I simply stop and ask others what they think. Recognizing that you don't know, opens the door to discovery and learning that can lead an organization to a higher level of performance by empowering others to explore a broader scope of possibilities while expanding their own viewpoint.

No one person has all the answers. When faced with a situation in which the direction or next steps are not clear, get the right people in a room and challenge them. Ask questions, consider options, engage in debate and recognize the current threshold of knowledge so as to explore the best opportunities for solving problems and making decision in pursuit of perfection. If you don't know the answer, start the discussion!

Leadership must define guiding principles that will help shape the culture they want the organization to embrace and establish systems within which individuals are expected to work while displaying behaviors they want others to follow. In addition, they must encourage and support people by providing the time, training and resources necessary to implement a lean management system.

Perfection is the ultimate goal of a lean culture. Perfection, considered the fifth lean principle of Womack and Jones in their book *Lean Thinking* [3], was defined by them as "complete elimination of muda (waste) so that all activities along the value stream create value". This understanding sets the stage for reinforcing a lean mindset of continuous incremental improvement. Clearly, perfection is not an achievable goal, but it does create a vision and direction that everyone can understand, embrace and engage.

To be realized, lean must be an inherent part of an organization's business strategy. A strong sense of purpose can be instilled in people when a clear vision and mission are established as to where the organization is going and how it plans to get there. Lean leadership creates that vision, sets the direction, molds the culture and monitors progress for continuous improvements. Reflecting on its current state can help an organization understand its weaknesses and reveal opportunities for improvement when developing a strategy.

It's also leadership's job to motivate people, challenge the status quo, go and see what's happening at the hub of activity, continuously ask "why" to clarify understanding and engage everyone in scientific thinking when solving problems or exploring improvement opportunities. Perhaps just as important is to reinforce the disciplines of performing DWR to maintain the foundation upon which improvements are built. Change is driven from the top, meaning that upper management must verbalize as well as demonstrate the behavior they expect to see from others. It's about "walking the talk" while traveling the road to OE. Remember, leadership actions should mirror spoken words.

SIDEBAR: AN ATTRIBUTE TO GOOD LEADERSHIP

Knowing your audience is a key attribute of good leadership. I once attended a lean convention at a major automotive supplier and listened as the leadership spent a full day lecturing lean coaches from 25 different global locations on the tools, techniques and benefits of lean. Leadership did not recognize or care to acknowledge that most of the 50–60 attendees were lean experts who understood lean and were more interested in discussing the "how" and not "what" of lean.

Leadership did what they were comfortable doing, talk about what they knew instead of what their management team really needed. They failed to recognize that the value of their contribution was to facilitate a discussion on the topic of "how" without the expectation of having all the "answers". If leadership had realized that value was in facilitating a focused discussion versus delivering a lecture, their contribution to the cause and those they serve would have been recognized and appreciated. Instead, leadership's credibility eroded as attendees sat patiently and respectfully listening to their words while contemplating what to do next. If you want to add value, know what your audience needs by asking them and delivering on their expectations; it may be easier than you think.

It's important for leadership to recognize that they are on stage 24/7 and, as such, must embrace and display many of the traits that are valued in lean leadership. Some of those traits and practices are captured in the following points.

- *Go and see; question why*: Leaders continually ask why to acquire a deep and fundamental understanding of issues, frequently going to the place where value is created to see for themselves and gather facts. It's important to understand *why* as well as *how* work is accomplished.
- *Show respect*: Arrogance or indifference toward people has no place in a lean environment. How you want to be treated should be no different to how you treat others. You will be remembered by how you made people feel.
- *Challenge assumptions*: Don't accept the status quo. Assumptions are considered true, real or certain, but are just opinions until proven otherwise. Base problem-solving and decision-making on data and facts; challenge assumptions.
- *Decision-making*: Decisions should be deliberate, never habitual. Leaders do not have all the answers and should seek input from others. Decisions are best made at the lowest possible level of the organization closest to where value is created.
- *Don't direct. Coach and mentor*: Knowledge is power but it must be exercised and shared to be meaningful. Leaders use knowledge to develop others. Coaching involves listening and leading others to think and make decisions on their own using facts, data and experimentation.
- *Take deliberate, meaningful actions*: Every action taken is an example for others to follow. Leaders should model the behavior they want others to display. When taking action, understand its impact and identify lessons learned for continuous improvement.
- *Look for simple solutions*: The most effective solutions are often the simplest. Steve Jobs once said: "When you first start off trying to solve a problem, the first solutions you come up with are very complex, and most people stop there. But, if you keep going, and live with the problem and peel more layers of the onion off, you can often times arrive at some very elegant and simple solutions".
- *Communicate, communicate, communicate*: It's important to communicate clearly and frequently. Keep the organization informed and communicate the "why" and "how". People want to know about the decisions and actions that affect their lives.
- *Enable problem-solving*: Discuss problems openly; use lessons learned from things gone right and be aware of why certain things went wrong. Leaders must support the frontlines by helping people solve their problems, quickly!

- *Provide engaging feedback*: Learn to provide meaningful feedback. Strike a balance between complementing and correcting people. Complements should outweigh corrections and reinforce desired behaviors.
- *Build trust*: Organizational integrity is built on mutual trust. Leaders must foster trust. Trust is good for relationships and business. A lack of trust undermines organizations.
- *Facilitate cross-functional interaction*: Leaders, managers and supervisors should engage people to solve problems with multidisciplinary, cross-functional teams. Diverse teams generate creative ideas leading to more choices for solutions.
- *Challenge people*: Lean leadership challenges people to think and plan before acting by asking probing questions and listening to confirm understanding and agreement. Challenge people to do better, work smarter, probe deeper and take calculated risks.
- *Learn by doing*: Leadership needs to encourage teams to learn by doing through experimentation. Experimentation confirms and creates knowledge. If you try something and fail, figure out what went wrong, why it went wrong and try again until you succeed. A persistent, open-minded, scientific approach to improvement will eventually yield the desired results. When learning to ride a bike, if you stopped trying after falling the first time, would you ever learn to ride?

Lean leadership consists of many attributes and characteristics, only some of which have been highlighted. The truth about lean leadership is simple: learn by doing. Consider what others have to say, then take time to develop a strategy with a select group of individuals. Plot a course, deploy the plan, learn by going and make course corrections along the way from lessons learned. There is no better teacher than experience.

SIDEBAR: DATA OR EXPERIENCE?

Source (rewritten): https://www.inc.com/minda-zetlin/1-big-mistake-smart-people-always-make-according-to-the-bestelling-author-of-mon.html?

The bestselling author of *Moneyball,* Michael Lewis, observed that experienced people have a tendency to rely more on their judgment and experience than on data. In his latest book, *The Undoing Project,* Lewis talks about a study that discovered people are less rational than they believe. He goes on to highlight several points as to why data is better than human judgment.

First, people are always looking for patterns or connections in data. These patterns may be real or appear real. It's best to look at data as objectively as possible and use statistics to determine if a true pattern or correlation exists. Secondly, data is not influenced by physical appearance. Good data objectively reflects what it was intended to represent and does not carry the bias that humans often don't see in themselves. The third point, unlike humans, data does not have an ego. Experts did not get to where they are without sacrifice in one form or another. As such, they put a high value on their knowledge, experience and instincts. In many instances, this has likely served them well. However, according to Lewis, it's not unusual for human experts to ignore overwhelming evidence when it contradicts their instincts.

The Lean Journey

The lean journey is your journey. It's a unique, customized adventure, experienced through trial and error, advanced through learning and achieved through tailored application of lean methods, tools and techniques to solve problems, improve processes and deliver increasing value to stakeholders. There is no cookbook or 10-step process. It's a one-of-a-kind experience impassioned by organizational leadership and guided by those who know where to go but not always how to get there.

It's an endless journey of seeking perfection through continuous improvements. It requires in-depth process knowledge acquired through experience, education, scientific thinking and experimentation. It's learning by doing, continuously asking questions and going to the source for answers. A successful journey often starts with a roadmap; a document that sets the direction and pace and outlines progress toward achieving specific objectives. When preparing your own unique roadmap, consider the following approach of study, plan, execute and navigate, before setting off on your journey to OE. Prepare yourself for the journey ahead.

Study

What does an operationally excellent organization look like? Where are we now? What changes are needed to improve performance? What obstacles stand in the way of change? The road to a leaner enterprise begins with understanding where you are and a vision of where you want to be. This can be accomplished through strategy deployment that starts with an understanding of the following:

- *Value*: What constitutes customer and business value? Talk to your customer.
- *Vision*: Create a short, simple, easy-to-remember vision for your organization.
- *Mission statement*: Provide a practical definition focused on the aims and values of the enterprise. The mission should articulate the core purpose behind the vision.
- *Situational assessment*: Assess organizational strengths, weaknesses, opportunities and threats (SWOT) analysis. Understand their impacts on current and future operational performance. Perform a gap assessment between your current and desired state.
- *Strategy definition*: Identify strategic focus issues and areas; define first-level strategies.
- *Lean awareness*: Create lean awareness by providing overview training to organizational personnel.

At the beginning of a lean journey, it may be helpful for some corporations to set up a lean governance structure for making strategic decisions and overseeing the initial direction, activities and projects supporting the lean initiative. This governance team may also benefit from performing periodic reviews to elevate their awareness of deployment progress and effectiveness. A structured approach can be used to solidify the importance and commitment of the organization to this new or changing direction. A governance board of steering committee senior leaders can reinforce this commitment by serving to guide the enterprise through the initial phase of a lean transformation. The concept of governance would eventually be faded out, once the building blocks of lean have been institutionalized and lean thinking is pervasive throughout the enterprise.

Plan

It has often been said that if you fail to plan, you plan to fail. Planning helps prepare the enterprise for the long journey ahead. It requires you think about the activities, resources and specific objectives to be achieved, in addition to the time required to accomplish pending challenges. It brings people together to contemplate, engage in conversation, share insights, explore possibilities and plot a preliminary course of action likely to change as knowledge, experience and information are acquired.

Embarking on a lean journey requires a plan and organizational awareness of what lean is, why it's important, the expected benefits, methods, tools and techniques that will be employed to help facilitate its realization. During awareness training, a learning/action model to lean implementation is recommended so people in training immediately put into practice what they have learned. The assignment of each course participant to a lean project will allow individuals to learn by doing with the support of a lean coach available to mentor individuals and teams through the ups and downs of project deployment.

In the course of planning for a lean journey, consider some of the following methods, systems, tools, techniques and building blocks required for navigating obstacles likely to be encountered along the way.

- *Foundational activities*: 5S, standard work, Jidoka
- *Pull system attributes*: JIT, supermarkets, first-in-first-out (FIFO), kanbans
- *Management systems*: Visual controls, deviation management, change management, DWR
- *Process control*: Standardization, stability, capability, capacity
- *Waste elimination*: Jishuken workshops, Kaizen events, Yamazumi charts, Toyota kata improvement projects
- *Continuous flow*: VSM/VSD, buffer management
- *Sustainability*: Culture, structure, discipline, accountability, transparency
- *Strategy deployment*: Strategic projects, key process indicator (KPI) metrics, performance reviews

There are certain questions to ask and answer during the planning process. Consider some of the following questions when planning your journey.

- Who are the enterprise change agents? What will their role and responsibilities be during the journey ahead?
- How will customer value be determined?
- How will value streams be defined? Who will take responsibility for them?
- Will a change to facility layout be required?
- Does material and information flow need to be improved?
- Are current line configurations sufficient?

- What lean techniques will need to be exercised to obtain the data and information needed to achieve efficiency goals (Jishuken workshops, VSM, etc.)?
- What resources, skill sets and training will be required to support lean?
- Will an allocation of funds be required in the annual budget to support lean activities in the coming year?

Execute

When setting out on a lean journey, the ebb and flow of life's ups and downs will become apparent. The idea of failure should be expected during implementation since deployment requires experimentation, often through trial and error, to learn and evolve lean thinking and modify concepts to suit the existing environment. At the same time, once you start this journey, it's difficult to return since the place you once occupied continues to change with every action taken. If done in a thoughtful and intentional way, lean thinking and acting will lead the enterprise forward and start to reveal what's possible while altering your view of its potential.

One key to lean execution is ensuring that teams have the skills, support and time to execute methods and tools while minimizing disruptions to production. Expect a continuous learning process as you tailor each approach to meet specific operational needs. Lean coaches should coordinate individuals and teams in the execution of planned activities, keeping the project goals and objectives in mind. Sharing best practices and lessons learned within the lean community also falls within the scope of a lean coach. Execution and support of ongoing activities are likely to include those outlined in Figure 12.3.

Navigate

As the old adage goes, an ounce of prevention is worth a pound of cure. This is the idea behind navigating your way through lean deployment. By continuously monitoring process controls and historical trends, deviations can be identified and timely adjustments made, preventing major disruptions to process outcomes. This minimizes a reactionary mode, caused by indifference to process abnormalities, which leads to the deterioration of process performance and firefighting versus time better spent on process improvement. The following activities must become an integral part of DWR in order

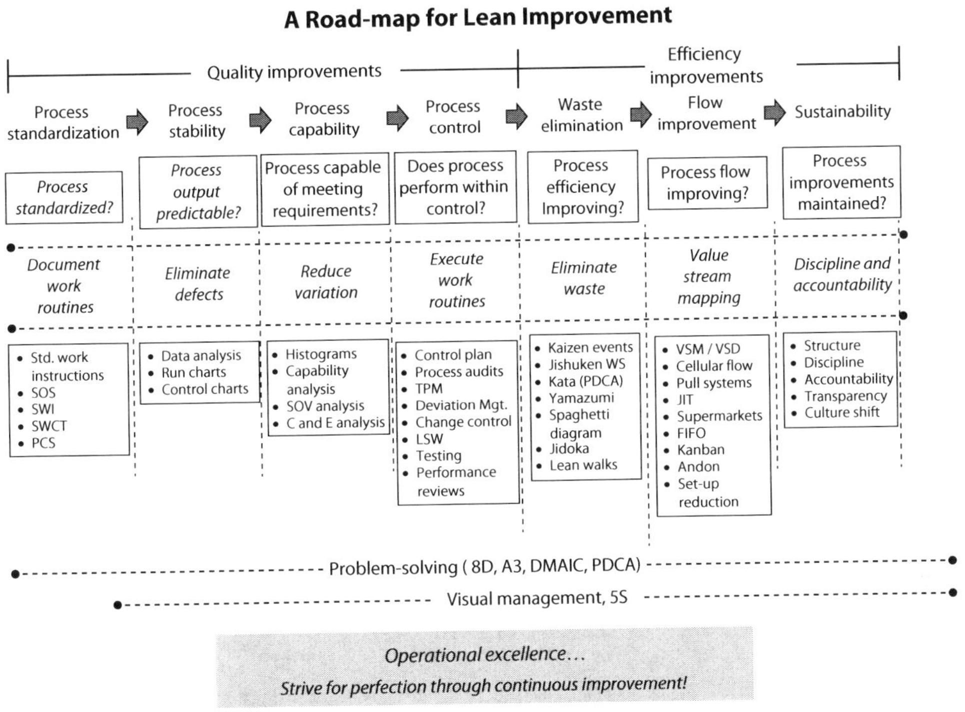

Figure 12.3 Lean journey method, tools and techniques.

to maintain process control and facilitate sustainable improvements throughout the process life cycle.

- Monitor visual controls for deviations
- Identify issues requiring escalation
- Perform LPA
- Apply error proofing
- Perform root cause analysis and corrective action
- Review KPIs for patterns and trends
- Conduct performance reviews
- Engage in deviation/change management

After the application of lean tools and projects, significant improvements in quality, reliability, safety, cost and employee morale should start to emerge. In the end, you reap what you sew. Good planning, proper execution, diligent monitoring and disciplined control will be reflected in process reliability, consistency, capability and efficiency performance. Finally, maintain process transparency whenever possible, as it facilitates understanding, reinforces accountability and promotes trust.

Lean Maturity

Lean is not easy to implement and people are slow to change. Developing a lean culture will take time and patience. You will be asking people to change the way they work, which is not a simple request, especially for those who have been doing the same job in the same way for years, if not decades. People must be willing and able to change. In preparing for the lean transition, a clear time line of change activities should be established and communicated to all stakeholders. It's not unusual for a cultural change to take time, lots of time. Figure 12.4 outlines a way to recognize lean progress as you make your way along the road to OE.

Time is missing from the pyramid since it's relative to the culture and environmental dynamics that each organization experiences on their lean journey. As stated in the *Shingo Model for Operational Excellence* handbook [5]: "Lasting change is only possible when timeless principles of operational excellence are understood and deeply embedded into culture. The focus of leaders must change to become more oriented toward driving principles and culture while the manager's focus should be on designing and aligning systems to drive ideal principle-based behavior".

Building a lean enterprise will require a radical change in the way organizations think, operate and engage their people. A real commitment to change needs to be reflected in the systems, behaviors and actions of management before true buy-in and acceptance becomes evident. It's important to remember; lean is a journey with many challenges and obstacles along

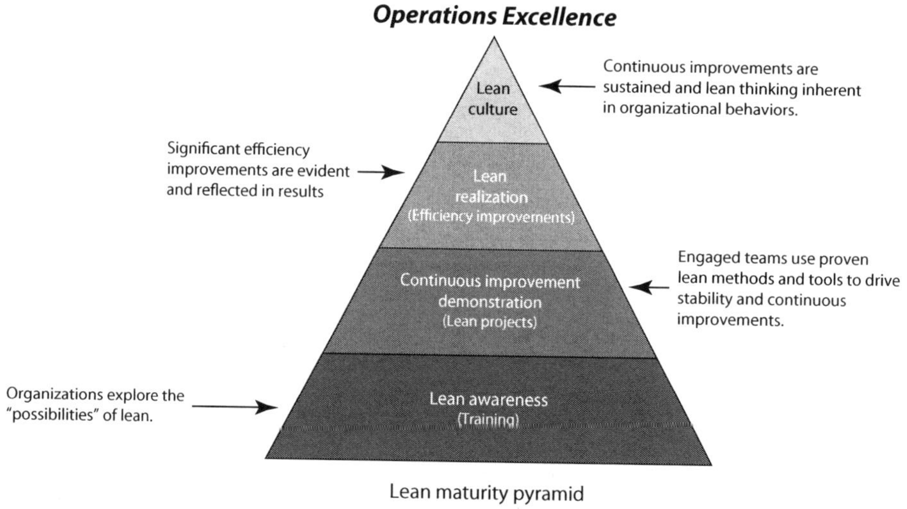

Figure 12.4 Indicators of lean maturity.

the path to OE. In organizations with structure, discipline and accountability in place, complemented by strong lean coaches, ready to lead the effort, are the enterprises best suited to tackle the challenges of tomorrow and advance their agenda toward a more efficient state of performance on the never-ending quest for excellence.

SIDEBAR: PUSH OR PULL LEAN MATURITY

The concept of push versus pull works just as well for support operations as it does for manufacturing. Case in point, I worked for a central function in a large global automotive company. Management in the central function believed that they could effect change by "pushing" lean tools and methods to the plant, and then request monthly reporting targets to monitor and control progress. Since each plant was at a different level of maturity and already understood what they needed to do, corporate simply ended up micromanaging the plants and creating a lot of non-value-added activity.

A more effective approach would have been for corporate to establish a lean maturity roadmap and a set of guidelines that the plants could use to assess their maturity and request the support they needed from corporate to help close the maturity gaps. This would have created a "pull" system, keeping ownership of improvement with the plants while supporting their need for change with expert resources to help them achieve their plant-specific maturity targets. This demonstrates leading with humility, trusting in others as well as maintaining accountability where it belongs. In essence, people are more committed when asked, versus told, what to do.

Key Points

- Visibility leads to transparency, which facilitates trust and accountability.
- Accountability reinforces the importance of timely adhering to commitments.
- Lean tools and methods are important but behaviors determine final results!
- DWR for all organizational levels should provide the structure, discipline and accountability required to effectively maintain your lean management system.
- Focus on what you want to do as a company, not what you want to be!
- Continuous improvement requires constant re-evaluation of the value stream for ways to eliminate waste and improve flow.

- Lean leaders work to improve themselves as well as their organizations.
- The pursuit of perfection involves the notion that everything can be made better.
- Lean involves simplification. Keep processes simple; focus on what's important.
- A lean manager manages by going to the source, not PowerPoint.
- Avoid mindless execution; understand why you are doing what you are doing.
- Significant variation creates a burden on people and equipment, leading to waste. Decreased variation = decreased burden = less waste.
- Leaders decide the outcomes they want and design processes to make those outcomes a reality.
- Time spent on designing and aligning systems with guiding principles rooted in OE is time well spent.
- "Vision without action is a daydream. Action without vision is a nightmare". (Japanese proverb)

References

1. James P. Womack and Daniel T. Jones. 1996, 2003. *Lean Thinking: Banish Waste and Create Wealth in Your Corporation.* New York: Free Press.
2. Jim Collins. 2001. *Good to Great: Why Some Companies Make the Leap and Others Don't.* New York: HarperCollins.
3. Modified from Stanford Graduate School of Business, New United Motors Manufacturing, Inc. (NUMMI); Case HR-11, Date 12/2/1998 (Rev'd 11/19/04).
4. J.K. Liker. 2004. *The Toyota Way: 14 Management Principles from the World's Greatest Manufacturer.* New York: McGraw-Hill (*Using Toyota Way to Transform Technical and Service Organizations:* Canada Post Corporation: Lean in Repetitive Service Operation; 272–275).
5. Shingo Institute, Utah State University. 2016. *The Shingo Model for Operational Excellence.* Logan, UT: Jon M. Huntsman, School of Business.

Appendix I: Lean Process Improvement – Overview

A culture of process improvement is composed of two critical activities: *process control* and *continuous improvement*. Process control establishes the foundation upon which continuous improvements are rooted. A process must be stable and capable (in control) before improvements can be sustained. A controlled process permits an organization to deliver products and provide services that meet customer requirements on time and within budget. Continuous improvement allows a business to reduce costs and remain competitive by incrementally enhancing its operational efficiency.

Process Control

Process control is the act of monitoring and controlling a process for stability and capability. A process is *stable* when its output is consistent and predictable over time, and *capable* when process output consistently meets customer requirements. *Process capability can't exist without process stability.* Process control is achieved by performing daily and weekly work routines intended to monitor the process for anomalies and deviations to standard practices and implementing countermeasures to maintain process performance to established standards. Process control is *reactive* and requires *deviation management* to ensure process stability and capability are maintained.

Continuous Improvement

Continuous improvement is the act of improving process efficiency by eliminating waste and removing obstacles preventing the continuous, uninterrupted flow of materials and information through the value stream. Observation is used to identify improvement opportunities while experiments are conducted to evaluate and validate process changes implemented to elevate process performance standards. Continuous improvement *proactively* looks for potential problems and waste for elimination and requires countermeasures to prevent these issues from impacting process performance. *Whereas deviation management is required for process control, change management is required for continuous improvements.* The continuous process improvement graph visualizes the relationship between process control and continuous improvement:

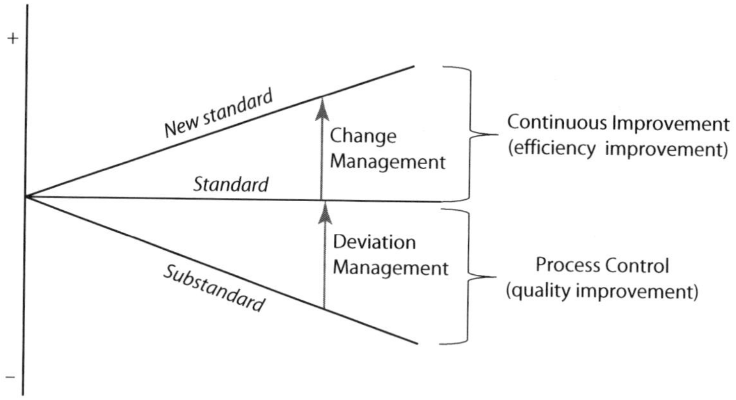

Deviation Management

Deviation management requires monitoring the process for deviations from standards such as machine setup parameters, material specifications and work standards. Significant deviations cause process instability and often require corrective actions to bring the process back into a stable state. Process monitoring for deviations can be accomplished through standard work routines (e.g. leader standard work), including layered process audits, gemba (management) walks and performance reviews. Process control involves the discipline of systematic problem-solving to identify and eliminate deviation root causes and track implemented solutions for effectiveness and reoccurrence. *5S* and *visual controls* can help facilitate easy and rapid detection of abnormalities for correction and prevention.

Change Management

Continuous improvement is rooted in process control and is driven by change management. A process can only be improved if the standard to which it's being monitored and controlled is stable and process changes have been implemented to elevate its level of performance. Ideas for improvement can come from many sources including employee suggestions, observation, experimentation and lessons learned. Due to limited time and resources, all ideas should be considered, prioritized and validated effective, prior to implementation using a variety of methods such as PDCA (plan, do, check and act or adjust), 8D/A3 thinking and DMAIC (define, measure, analyze, improve and control). The incremental and continuous validation and implementation of value-added process changes creates a culture of *sustainable process improvements.*

In summary, *process control* and *continuous improvement* are two interdependent activities essential to *lean process improvement* and require *deviation* and *change management*, respectively, in *pursuit of operational excellence.*

Appendix II: Process Quality and Efficiency Improvement through Macro and Micro Variation Reduction

A fundamental objective of shop floor management is to achieve process stability through the elimination of defects and realize process capability by methodically reducing sources of variation until process output consistently meets process targets. Process stability is achieved when process performance becomes predictable and process capability becomes evident when process output is consistently within process tolerances. Process control, using daily work routines, is then employed to maintain process stability and capability while establishing the foundation for sustainable process efficiency improvements.

Macro Variation Reduction

To achieve process control, we must first manage macro variations before focusing on efficiency improvements (e.g. cycle time reduction). *Macro variations* are deviations from the production *output target* when the actual number of units produced per time period is inconsistent with expectations. Inconsistent output requires the elimination of process defects to achieve stability. A run chart or statistical process control (SPC) chart, prepared with corresponding observations of events, can be used to identify *defects* and their contribution to process instability. Root cause analysis and corrective actions are implemented to remove process defects, leading to process stability (see Problem-Solving Flow in Appendix III).

Stability does not guarantee capability but it is a prerequisite for achieving capability. If process stability does not result in a capable process, ensure output performance aligns with the target mean and, if necessary, reduce one or more major sources of variation to the point where process output is consistently within acceptable process specification limits. In essence, macro variation reduction focuses on the elimination of process defects to achieve stability followed by reducing major sources of systemic variation until process capability is demonstrated. Both stability and capability are maintained through process control activities.

Micro Variations Reduction

Efficiency (productivity) improvement focuses on reducing process *anomalies and fluctuations*. Anomalies are deviations *from* standard work (SW) routines while fluctuations are variations *within* SW routines. When auditing SW cycle times for compliance with work instructions, if a deviation from the SW cycle time target is observed, the line leader can use the *abnormality tracker* (see Abnormality Tracker in Appendix X) to identify and record the frequency of process anomalies occurring at a workstation or work area over time. A Pareto chart of abnormalities (e.g. anomalies and fluctuations) can be used to document and prioritize the occurrence of deviations from within and outside SW to target excess micro variation for elimination, further improving stability and productivity. A production line leader or line operator can record fluctuations and anomalies for their workstation or area.

Further improvements in process performance (variation reduction) can come from Jishuken workshops and Kaizen events targeted at specific improvement objectives.

Appendix III: Problem-Solving Flow

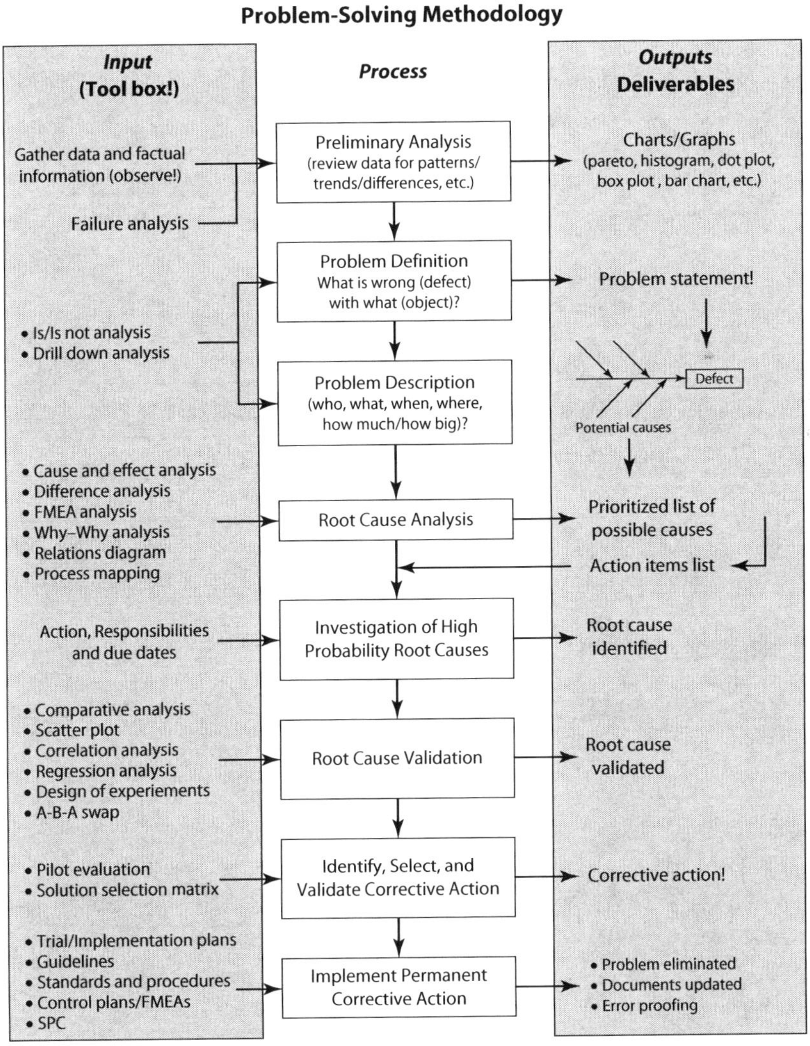
Problem-Solving Methodology
Input
(Tool box!)
Process
Outputs
Deliverables
Gather data and factual information (observe!)
Failure analysis
Preliminary Analysis
(review data for patterns/trends/differences, etc.)
Charts/Graphs
(pareto, histogram, dot plot, box plot, bar chart, etc.)
Problem Definition
What is wrong (defect) with what (object)?
Problem statement!
• Is/Is not analysis
• Drill down analysis
Problem Description
(who, what, when, where, how much/how big)?
Defect
Potential causes
• Cause and effect analysis
• Difference analysis
• FMEA analysis
• Why–Why analysis
• Relations diagram
• Process mapping
Root Cause Analysis
Prioritized list of possible causes
Action items list
Action, Responsibilities and due dates
Investigation of High Probability Root Causes
Root cause identified
• Comparative analysis
• Scatter plot
• Correlation analysis
• Regression analysis
• Design of experiements
• A-B-A swap
Root Cause Validation
Root cause validated
• Pilot evaluation
• Solution selection matrix
Identify, Select, and Validate Corrective Action
Corrective action!
• Trial/Implementation plans
• Guidelines
• Standards and procedures
• Control plans/FMEAs
• SPC
Implement Permanent Corrective Action
• Problem eliminated
• Documents updated
• Error proofing

Appendix IV: Process Quality Improvement Flow

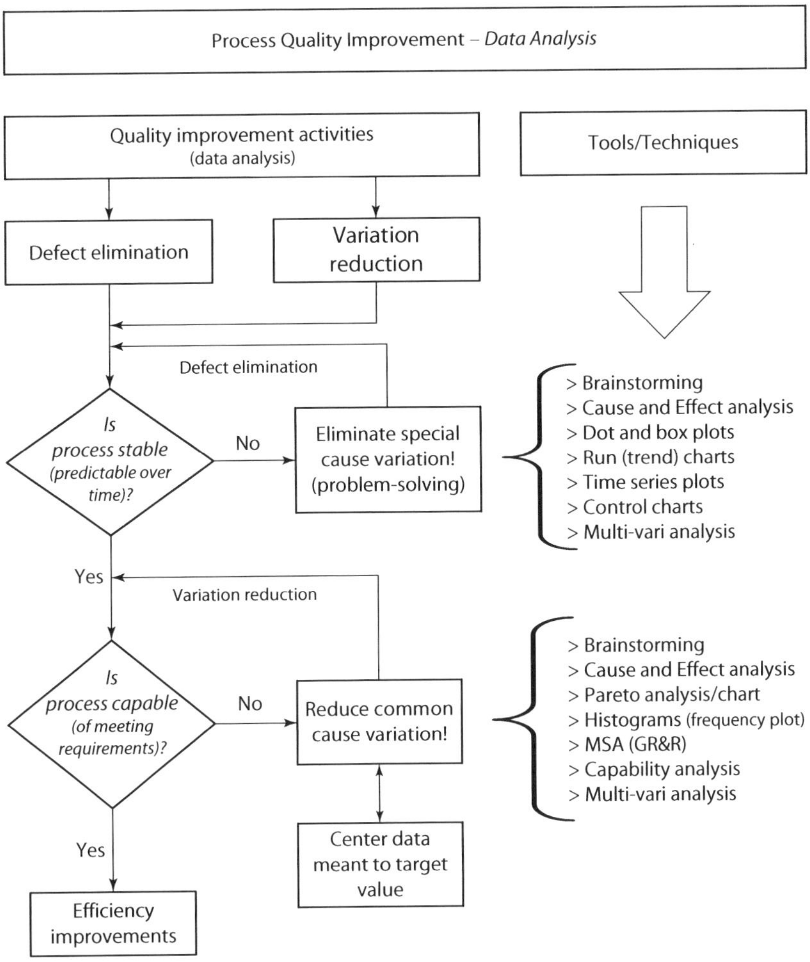

Process Quality Improvement – *Data Analysis*
Quality improvement activities
(data analysis)
Tools/Techniques
Defect elimination
Variation reduction
Defect elimination
Is process stable (predictable over time)?
No
Eliminate special cause variation! (problem-solving)
> Brainstorming
> Cause and Effect analysis
> Dot and box plots
> Run (trend) charts
> Time series plots
> Control charts
> Multi-vari analysis
Yes
Variation reduction
Is process capable (of meeting requirements)?
No
Reduce common cause variation!
> Brainstorming
> Cause and Effect analysis
> Pareto analysis/chart
> Histograms (frequency plot)
> MSA (GR&R)
> Capability analysis
> Multi-vari analysis
Center data meant to target value
Yes
Efficiency improvements

Appendix V: Layered Process Audit (LPA) Checklist

Layered process audits - Checklist - Questions

Date:	Auditor:							
Time:	Job title:							
Comments:								
Layered Audits - Are layer audits being performed per schedule by all management levels?	Reference	Shift team leader	Daily supervisor	Weekly level II Mgr.	Monthly level I Mgr.	Quarterly plant Mgr.	Yes / No	Audit comments
5S	Reference?							
>> Compliance - Is the area meeting their 5S standards?								
>> Audits - Are regular 5S audits being performed?								
>> Findings - Are non-compliances being documented?								
>> Actions - Are corrective actions being closed in a timely manor?								
Health, safety and environmental	Reference?							
>> Standards - Are there any health, safety, or environmental standards/guidelines available? Are they visible?								
>> Action - Do any health, safety, environmental concerns exist? Are they being addressed?								
Performance and Capacity								
>> Metrics - Are mandatory performance metrics up-to-date? Are targets visual and challenging?								
>> Deviations - Are actions on deviations defined?								
>> Line Capacity - Is the line capacity visible?								
Jidoka (line information board)								
>> Application - Is the line being stopped according to the Jidoka guidelines?								
>> Documentation - Are Jidoka stops documented, including the reason for stopping the line?								
>> Stop Root Cause - Is the root cause known and the effectiveness of each countermeasure documented?								
>> Reaction time - Is the reaction time acceptable, escalation process followed, and the results effective?								
>> Operators involvement - Are operators involved in the Jidoka meetings? Is their participation visible?								
>> Metrics - Are problems monitored for reoccurrence?								
>> Continuous improvement - Are Jidoka intervention limits regularly reviewed and targets set appropriately?								
Visual management								
>> CBS line certification - Is the status of the stickers up-to-date?								
>> Andon board - Is the display clear and understandable and does it provide current data? Are targets visual and challenging? Does Andon prompt production staff to quickly react to deviations?								
>> Andon Board - Are the color codes and status consistent with line performance?								
>> Andon lights - Are the lights working and is the team responding to the color codes?								
>> Standard work - Are workers following standard work?								
>> Is work being done in the proper sequence?								
>> Does a smooth and steady work flow exist?								
>> Visual controls - Are production line boards/visual controls updated properly and timely?								
Standard work								
>> Leader standard work - Is LSW being performed per schedule? Does evidence exist to support this activity?								
>> Actions - Are improvement actions being identified and closed in a timely manner?								
Employee Involvement								
>> Suggestions - Are improvement suggestions of operators considered and followed-up (e.g. CIM, TPM, or Responsibility programs, etc.)?								
>> Communication - Are operators informed about current topics (e.g. customer complaints, plant strategy, product changes, etc.)?								
Total productive maintenance								
>> Schedule - Is preventive maintenance done according to the planned schedule?								
>> Execution - are the different maintenance levels defined and is maintenance done accordingly?								
Scrap								
>> Target - Is the scrap target defined and being maintained?								
>> Top Issues - Are the top 3 process issues causing scrap identified and are corrective actions being taken?								
Other topics (optional)								
>> Line boards - Are line board records up-to-date?								
>> Equipment calibration - Is equipment calibration within their due dates?								
>> Central (public) areas - Are documents in the central (public) areas up-to-date?								
>> Work clothing - proper and consistent use of work clothing (e.g. coats, jackets, hair nets, gloves, ESD straps,								

Pre-conditions

>> 5S standards / guidelines are documented and available.

>> Jidoka standards are documented and available.

>> Standard work is implemented for the entire production line.

>> All operators are trained on implementation of standard work.

Notes:

White boxes are suggested questions for various levels.

Appendix VI: Standardized Work Recording Chart

Updated 8/21/2017	Standardized Work Recording Chart	GL-B	GL-R	TL-B	TL-R

Process:	Operator #1	Model:		Observer:	Team

Clear sheet:		1	2	3	4	5	6	7	8	9	10	Min	Max	Fluctuation
	Filename	00385.mts												
	Start time	0:00:31												
A	Pick up assembly from fixture (both)	00:33.2												
	Assembly lifted	00:01.8												
B	Flip assembly	00:33.8												
	Assembly scanned	00:00.6												
C	Scan assembly barcode left h	00:34.7												
	Assembly placed on fixture	00:00.9												
D	Flip assembly	00:34.8												
		00:00.1												
E	Load assembly on fixture (both	00:38.0												
		00:03.1												
F	Take housing from left hand	00:39.8												
		00:01.8												
G	Move housing to chamber for	00:41.3												
		00:01.5												

Note: The SWRC is used to record the work elements (break points) and corresponding times taken from a video of an operator performing their work cycle (5 –10 times).

Appendix VII: Source of Variation (SOV) and Variation Reduction

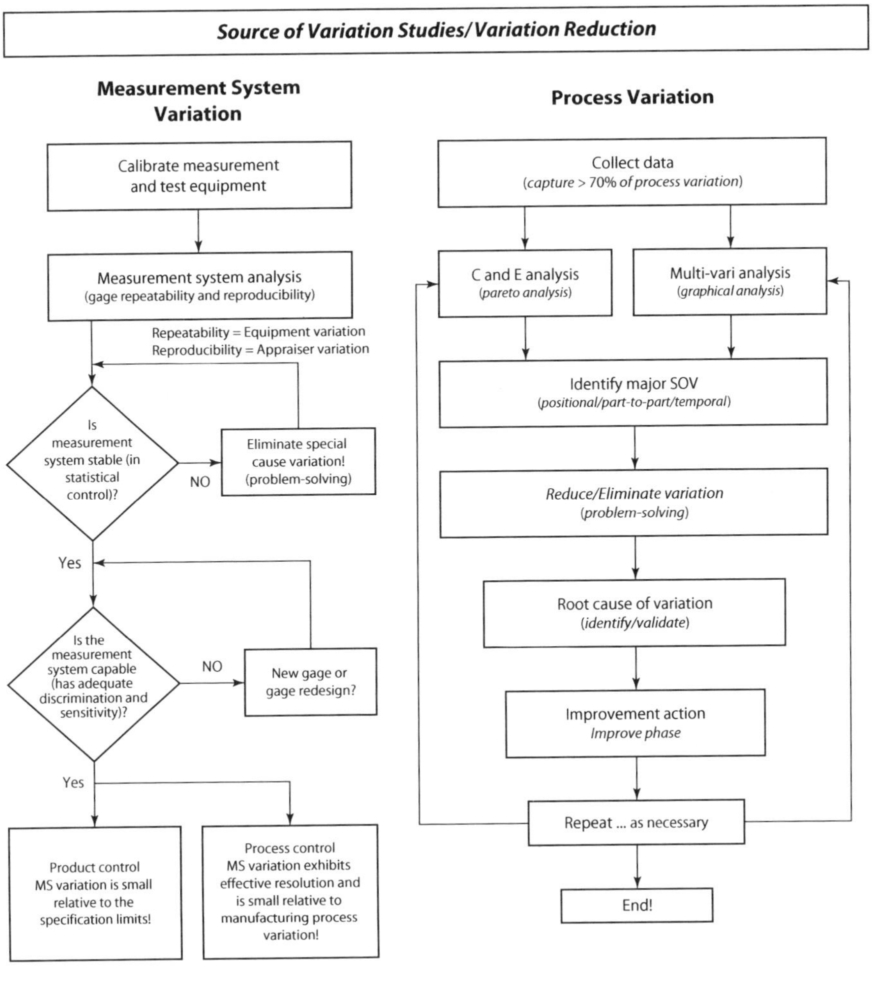

Source of Variation Studies/Variation Reduction
Measurement System Variation
Calibrate measurement and test equipment
Measurement system analysis (gage repeatability and reproducibility)
Repeatability = Equipment variation
Reproducibility = Appraiser variation
Is measurement system stable (in statistical control)?
NO
Eliminate special cause variation! (problem-solving)
Yes
Is the measurement system capable (has adequate discrimination and sensitivity)?
NO
New gage or gage redesign?
Yes
Product control MS variation is small relative to the specification limits!
Process control MS variation exhibits effective resolution and is small relative to manufacturing process variation!
Process Variation
Collect data (capture > 70% of process variation)
C and E analysis (pareto analysis)
Multi-vari analysis (graphical analysis)
Identify major SOV (positional/part-to-part/temporal)
Reduce/Eliminate variation (problem-solving)
Root cause of variation (identify/validate)
Improvement action Improve phase
Repeat ... as necessary
End!

Appendix VIII: Efficiency Improvement

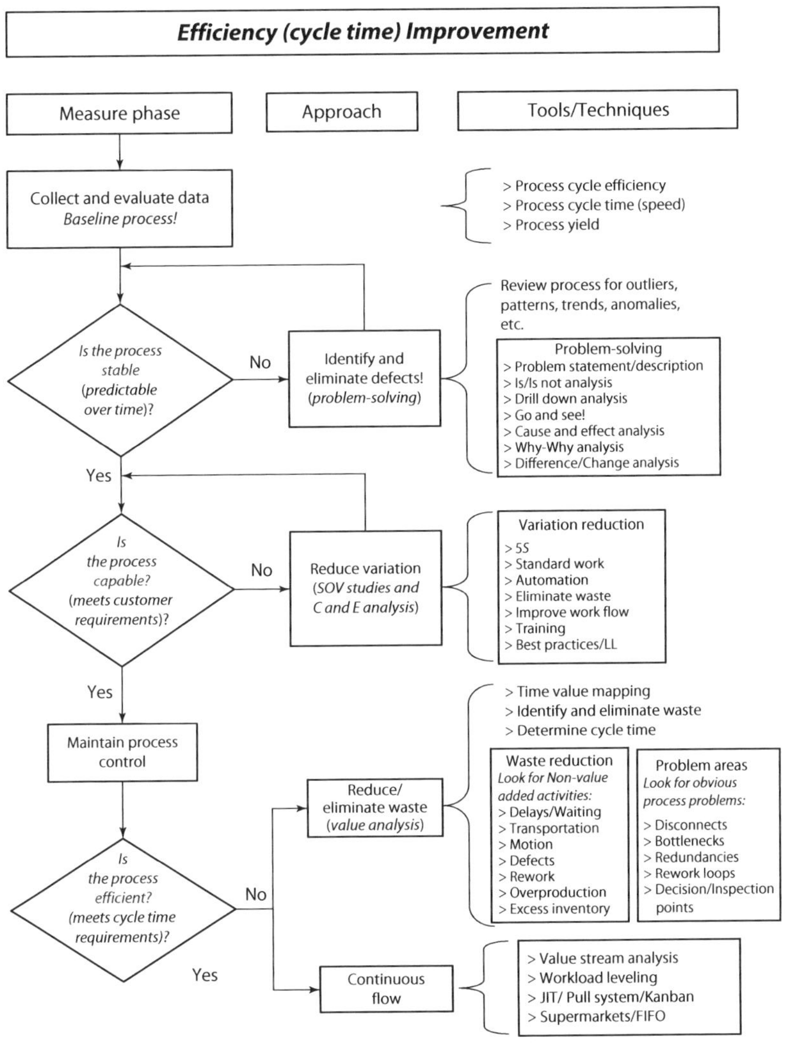
Efficiency (cycle time) Improvement
Measure phase
Approach
Tools/Techniques
Collect and evaluate data
Baseline process!
> Process cycle efficiency
> Process cycle time (speed)
> Process yield
Is the process stable (predictable over time)?
No
Identify and eliminate defects! (problem-solving)
Review process for outliers, patterns, trends, anomalies, etc.
Problem-solving
> Problem statement/description
> Is/Is not analysis
> Drill down analysis
> Go and see!
> Cause and effect analysis
> Why-Why analysis
> Difference/Change analysis
Yes
Is the process capable? (meets customer requirements)?
No
Reduce variation (SOV studies and C and E analysis)
Variation reduction
> 5S
> Standard work
> Automation
> Eliminate waste
> Improve work flow
> Training
> Best practices/LL
Yes
Maintain process control
> Time value mapping
> Identify and eliminate waste
> Determine cycle time
Reduce/ eliminate waste (value analysis)
Waste reduction
Look for Non-value added activities:
> Delays/Waiting
> Transportation
> Motion
> Defects
> Rework
> Overproduction
> Excess inventory
Problem areas
Look for obvious process problems:
> Disconnects
> Bottlenecks
> Redundancies
> Rework loops
> Decision/Inspection points
Is the process efficient? (meets cycle time requirements)?
No
Yes
Continuous flow
> Value stream analysis
> Workload leveling
> JIT/ Pull system/Kanban
> Supermarkets/FIFO

Appendix IX: Operations versus Lean Management

Operations Management (Business) → Lean Management

- Manage complexity → Reduce complexity
- Systemic thinking → Systematic and scientific thinking
- Top-down communication → Two-way communication
- Focus on results → Focus on results and process
- React to problems → Prevent problems
- Think logically → Think logically and creatively
- Capture lessons learned → Apply lessons learned
- Target-based management → Long-term strategy
- Tool-based systems → Principle-based systems
- Do it → Learn by doing (PDCA)

Operations Management (Shop Floor) → Lean Management

- Work instructions → Standardized work
- Follow the standards → Continuously improve the standards
- Push systems → Pull systems
- Reactive maintenance → Preventive maintenance
- Eliminate problems → Eliminate waste
- Systems drive results → Systems drive behaviors
- Performance metrics → Process input parameters
- Process control → Process control + continuous improvement
- Batch processing → Continuous flow processing

Operations Management (People) → Lean Management

- Roles and responsibilities → Work routines
- Experts solve problems → Everyone solves problems
- Managing people → Coaching and mentoring people

Appendix X: Abnormality Tracker

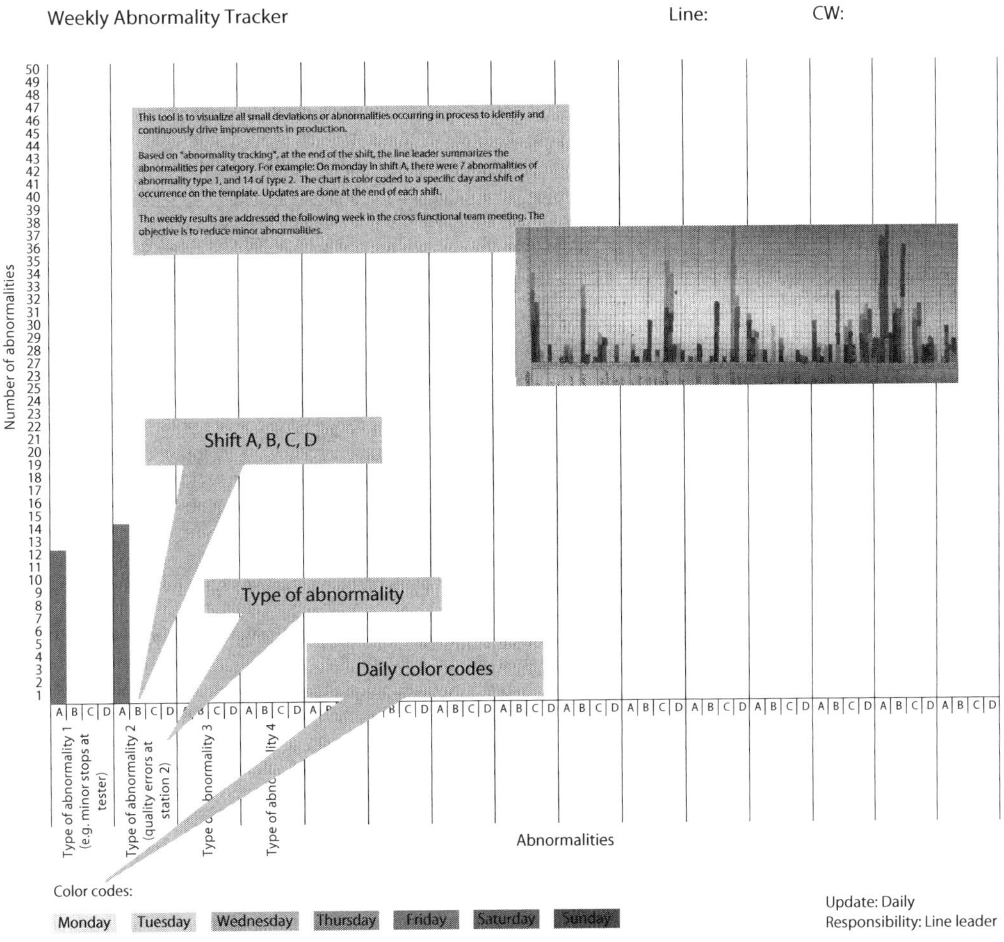

Weekly Abnormality Tracker
Line:
CW:
Number of abnormalities
This tool is to visualize all small deviations or abnormalities occurring in process to identify and continuously drive improvements in production.
Based on "abnormality tracking", at the end of the shift, the line leader summarizes the abnormalities per category. For example: On monday in shift A, there were 7 abnormalities of abnormality type 1, and 14 of type 2. The chart is color coded to a specific day and shift of occurrence on the template. Updates are done at the end of each shift.
The weekly results are addressed the following week in the cross functional team meeting. The objective is to reduce minor abnormalities.
Shift A, B, C, D
Type of abnormality
Daily color codes
Type of abnormality 1 (e.g. minor stops at tester)
Type of abnormality 2 (quality errors at station 2)
Abnormalities
Color codes:
Monday
Tuesday
Wednesday
Thursday
Friday
Saturday
Sunday
Update: Daily
Responsibility: Line leader

Appendix XI: Daily Shop Floor Management Flow

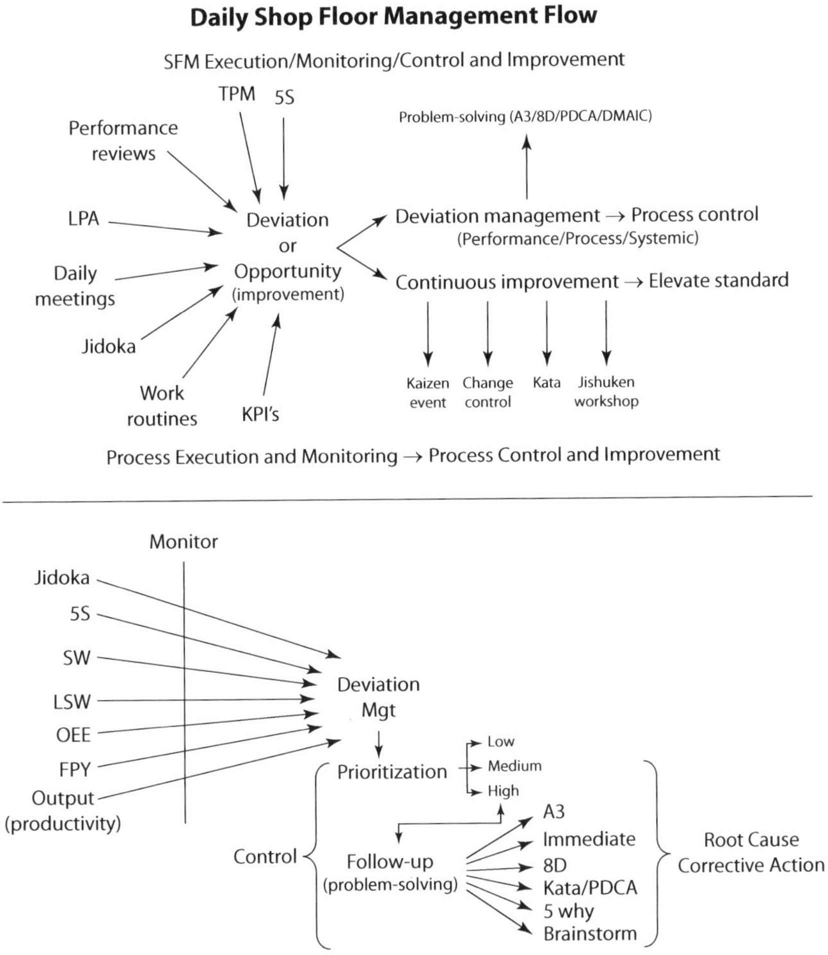

Appendix XII: Daily Shop Floor Management Tools and Techniques

Fundamental Tools and Techniques

Process Control *Daily Management*	*Process Improvement* *Continuous*
Standardize/Stabilize/Capability/Control	**Efficiency/Sustainability/Excellence**
Standardize • Workplace organization (5S) • Standard work instructions ***Stabilize*** • Key performance indicators • Daily work routines • Work standards • Run/control charts ***Capability*** • Histogram/Cpk analysis ***Control*** • Visual controls • Shop floor walks • Daily communication meetings • Layered process audits • Problem-solving 8D/A3 • TPM • Deviation management	***Waste elimination*** • Process mapping • Value analysis • Toyota Kata/PDCA • A3 thinking/reporting • Jishuken workshops • Yamazumi charts • Kaizen events • Standardized work ***Continuous flow*** • Value stream mapping • Just-in-time/Jidoka • Pull system • Supermarket/FIFO • Workload balancing ***Sustainability*** • Principles/systems • Change management • Structure, Discipline accountability

Appendix XIII: Work Routine Management

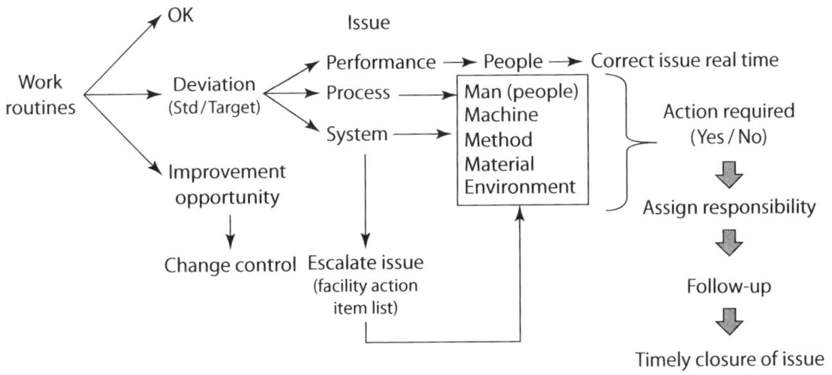

Appendix XIV: Process Maturity and Operational Excellence Assessment

This Process Maturity and Operational Excellence self-assessment is a tool for evaluating an organization's lean management system maturity and serves to provide a baseline from which next steps along the road to operational excellence can be identified. It should be tailored to meet the needs of an enterprise. Each level (Immature, Starting, Developing, Maturing and Excellence) has an assessment value (0 to 4). Upon reading each question, select the level which best describes your current state and place the corresponding score in the score column next to the question.

Total the scores of each question in a section. For example, the "Process Standardization" section has 9 questions. If questions 1 to 9 received the following scores: 3, 3, 1, 2, 3, 4, 3, 4, 0, the scores would be averaged as follows 23/ 9 questions=2.6. Thus, the score for *Process Standardization* would be 2.6. Once a score is determined for each section, a spider chart can be created to visualize your score and used to identify areas for improvement, actions and follow-up. Visualization of an assessment score is provided in the following Spider chart.

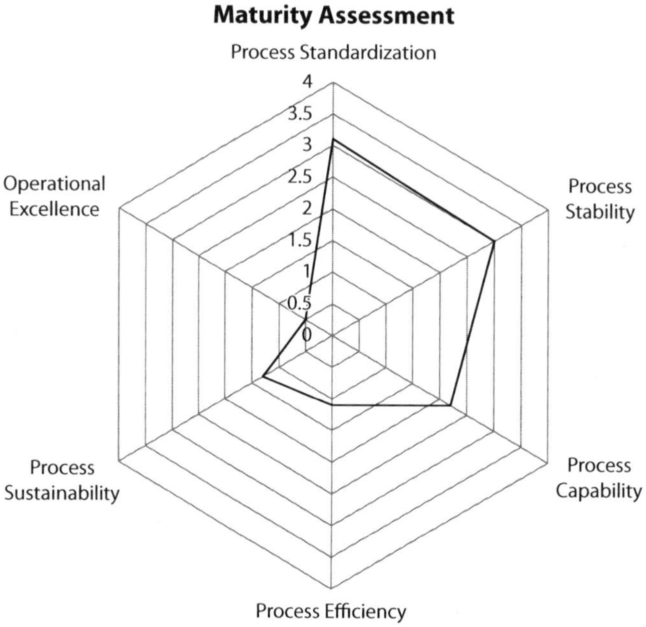

Section	Score		
	Assessment #1	Ass #2	Ass #3
Process Standardization	3.1		
Process Stability	3		
Process Capability	2.2		
Process Efficiency	1.1		
Process Sustainability	1.3		
Operational Excellence	0.5		

Expectation	*Score*	*Immature*	*Starting*	*Developing*	*Maturing*	*Excellence*
Value:		0	1	2	3	4
Process Standardization						
Are procedures and work instructions documented to minimize variation?	1	No (<20%)	Some (20%–40%)	Many (40%–60%)	Most (60%–80%)	Yes (>80%)
Are procedures and work instructions available and used?	1	Rarely (<20% of time)	Sometimes (20%–40% of time)	Often (40%–60% of time)	Mostly (60%–80% of time)	Always (>80% of time)
Are procedures and work instructions continuously improved?	1	Rarely (<20% of time)	Sometimes (20%–40% of time)	Often (40%–60% of time)	Mostly (60%–80% of time)	Always (>80% of time)
Do standards exist for repetitive work routines?	1	No (<20%)	Some (20%–40%)	Many (40%–60%)	Most (60%–80%)	Yes (>80%)
Are standards appropriate? If you follow the standard, will you achieve the target?	1	No (<20%)	Some (20%–40%)	Many (40%–60%)	Most (60%–80%)	Yes (>80%)
Are employees aware of their standards? *(e.g. members can tell/show you where their standards are)*	1	No (<20%)	Some (20%–40%)	Many (40%–60%)	Most (60%–80%)	Yes (>80%)

(Continued)

(Continued)

Expectation	*Score*	*Immature*	*Starting*	*Developing*	*Maturing*	*Excellence*
Are the standards understood? *All employees understand their standards, continuously improve them and cross-train others*	1	Rarely (<20% of time)	Sometimes (20%–40% of time)	Often (40%–60% of time)	Mostly (60%–80% of time)	Always (>80% of time)
Do employees follow the standards?	1	No (<20%)	Some (20%–40%)	Many (40%–60%)	Most (60%–80%)	Yes (>80%)
Are standards confirmed? *Audits are performed to ensure compliance to standards*	1	Rarely (<20% of time)	Sometimes (20%–40% of time)	Often (40%–60% of time)	Mostly (60%–80% of time)	Always (>80% of time)
Section score	1					
Process Stability						
Measures are in place to monitor stability (output consistency)	1	No (<20%)	Some (20%–40%)	Many (40%–60%)	Most (60%–80%)	Yes (>80%)
Stability and how to measure it is understood by employees	1	No (<20%)	Some (20%–40%)	Many (40%–60%)	Most (60%–80%)	Yes (>80%)
Process stability is being measured and monitored for deviations	1	Rarely (<20% of time)	Sometimes (20%–40% of time)	Often (40%–60% of time)	Mostly (60%–80% of time)	Always (>80% of time)

(Continued)

(Continued)

Expectation	*Score*	*Immature*	*Starting*	*Developing*	*Maturing*	*Excellence*
Actions are taken when deviations from control limits occur. *Actions are documented and the root cause of deviations determined*	1	Rarely (<20% of time)	Sometimes (20%–40% of time)	Often (40%–60% of time)	Mostly (60%–80% of time)	Always (>80% of time)
Actions taken to maintain stability are completed in a timely manner. *Root cause is identified and countermeasures implemented by the specified due date*	1	Rarely (<20% of time)	Sometimes (20%–40% of time)	Often (40%–60% of time)	Mostly (60%–80% of time)	Always (>80% of time)
Actions taken to maintain stability are effective and permanent. *Countermeasures eliminate root cause and prevent reoccurrence*	1	Rarely (<20% of time)	Sometimes (20%–40% of time)	Often (40%–60% of time)	Mostly (60%–80% of time)	Always (>80% of time)
Processes are stable. *All processes remain within their control limits*	1	No (<20%)	Some (20%–40%)	Many (40%–60%)	Most (60%–80%)	Yes (>80%)
Section score	1					

(Continued)

(Continued)

Expectation	*Score*	*Immature*	*Starting*	*Developing*	*Maturing*	*Excellence*
Process Capability						
Measures are in place to monitor capability (key process indicators [KPIs] within specifications)	1	No (<20%)	Some (20%–40%)	Many (40%–60%)	Most (60%–80%)	Yes (>80%)
Capability and how to measure it, is understood by employees	1	No (<20%)	Some (20%–40%)	Many (40%–60%)	Most (60%–80%)	Yes (>80%)
Process capability is being measured and monitored for deviations	1	Rarely (<20% of time)	Sometimes (20%–40% of time)	Often (40%–60% of time)	Mostly (60%–80% of time)	Always (>80% of time)
Actions are taken when KPIs exceeds specifications. *Clear triggers initiate actions needed to address deviations from specification*	1	Rarely (<20% of time)	Sometimes (20%–40% of time)	Often (40%–60% of time)	Mostly (60%–80% of time)	Always (>80% of time)
Actions taken to maintain capability are completed in a timely manner. *Root cause is identified and countermeasures implemented by the specified due date*	1	No (<20%)	Some (20%–40%)	Many (40%–60%)	Most (60%–80%)	Yes (>80%)

(Continued)

(Continued)

Expectation	*Score*	*Immature*	*Starting*	*Developing*	*Maturing*	*Excellence*
Actions taken to maintain capability are effective and permanent. *Countermeasures eliminate root causes and prevent reoccurrence*	1	No (<20%)	Some (20%–40%)	Many (40%–60%)	Most (60%–80%)	Yes (>80%)
Processes are capable (e.g. are maintained within their specification limits)	1	No (<20%)	Some (20%–40%)	Many (40%–60%)	Most (60%–80%)	Yes (>80%)
Section score	1					
Process Control						
Standard work routines (SWR) are defined for maintaining process control (stability and capability)	1	No (<20%)	Some (20%–40%)	Many (40%–60%)	Most (60%–80%)	Yes (>80%)
Critical metrics (KPIs) have been defined for monitoring and controlling process stability and capability	1	No (<20%)	Some (20%–40%)	Many (40%–60%)	Most (60%–80%)	Yes (>80%)
DM: Visuals are available (e.g. charts, graphs, templates) and quickly communicate deviations from control limits and specifications	1	No (<20%)	Some (20%–40%)	Many (40%–60%)	Most (60%–80%)	Yes (>80%)

(Continued)

(Continued)

Expectation	*Score*	*Immature*	*Starting*	*Developing*	*Maturing*	*Excellence*
DM: Appropriate triggers (e.g. limits) are defined for effective deviation management	1	No (<20%)	Some (20%–40%)	Many (40%–60%)	Most (60%–80%)	Yes (>80%)
Actions are taken and closed in a timely manner when triggers occur	1	No (<20%)	Some (20%–40%)	Many (40%–60%)	Most (60%–80%)	Yes (>80%)
PS: All employees are trained and engaged in problem-solving. Root cause is identified, permanent corrective actions implemented and problems reoccurrence prevented	1	Rarely (<20% of time)	Sometimes (20%–40% of time)	Often (40%–60% of time)	Mostly (60%–80% of time)	Always (>80% of time)
Processes are stable and capable. Output trends are consistent, within target or improving	1	Rarely (<20% of time)	Sometimes (20%–40% of time)	Often (40%–60% of time)	Mostly (60%–80% of time)	Always (>80% of time)
Section score	1					

(*Continued*)

(Continued)

Expectation	*Score*	*Immature*	*Starting*	*Developing*	*Maturing*	*Excellence*
Operational Efficiency						
The organization understands and continuously applies the concepts, tools and techniques required for (lean) efficiency improvement	1	Rarely (<20% of time)	Sometimes (20%–40% of time)	Often (40%–60% of time)	Mostly (60%–80% of time)	Always (>80% of time)
Methods, tools and techniques (e.g. value analysis, Jishuken and Kaizen) are defined and continuously used to eliminate waste	1	No (<20%)	Some (20%–40%)	Many (40%–60%)	Most (60%–80%)	Yes (>80%)
Systems and methods (e.g. JIT, Jidoka, supermarkets, FIFO, VSM) are understood and effectively used to improve flow	1	No (<20%)	Some (20%–40%)	Many (40%–60%)	Most (60%–80%)	Yes (>80%)
Score	1					

(*Continued*)

(Continued)

Expectation	*Score*	*Immature*	*Starting*	*Developing*	*Maturing*	*Excellence*
Operational Sustainability						
Organizational structure: Systems, methods and tools are effective in maintaining process control and driving efficient improvements	1	Rarely (<20% of time)	Sometimes (20%–40% of time)	Often (40%–60% of time)	Mostly (60%–80% of time)	Always (>80% of time)
Organizational structure: Systems, methods and tools are updated to reflect lessons learned and best practices	1	Rarely (<20% of time)	Sometimes (20%–40% of time)	Often (40%–60% of time)	Mostly (60%–80% of time)	Always (>80% of time)
Discipline: Employees understand organizational policies, systems and procedures and follow them as intended and completely	1	No (<20%)	Some (20%–40%)	Many (40%–60%)	Most (60%–80%)	Yes (>80%)
Accountability: Employees take ownership of their assigned actions, complete them correctly and close them on time	1	Rarely (<20% of time)	Sometimes (20%–40% of time)	Often (40%–60% of time)	Mostly (60%–80% of time)	Always (>80% of time)
Change management: A system is documented, approved and effective in implementing and institutionalizing changes	1	Rarely (<20% of time)	Sometimes (20%–40% of time)	Often (40%–60% of time)	Mostly (60%–80% of time)	Always (>80% of time)
Score	1					

(*Continued*)

(Continued)

Expectation	*Score*	*Immature*	*Starting*	*Developing*	*Maturing*	*Excellence*
Operational Excellence						
Guiding **principles and practices** are defined, used as the basis for developing systems, communicated to the organization and understood by all	1	No (<20%)	Some (20%–40%)	Many (40%–60%)	Most (60%–80% of time)	Always (>80% of time)
Systems, methods, tools and techniques are defined, understood and used to drive desired behavior and produce ideal results	1	Rarely (<20% of time)	Sometimes (20%–40% of time)	Often (40%–60% of time)	Mostly (60%–80% of time)	Always (>80% of time)
Desired behaviors: Employee behavior is aligned with enterprise principles and practices. Expected results reflect desirable employee behaviors	1	Rarely (<20% of time)	Sometimes (20%–40% of time)	Often (40%–60% of time)	Mostly (60%–80% of time)	Always (>80% of time)
Expected results: KPIs are stable or improving	1	No (<20%)	Some (20%–40%)	Many (40%–60%)	Most (60%–80%)	Yes (>80%)
Score	1					

DM: deviation management; PS, problem-solving.

Appendix XV: A3 Reporting Template and Description

A3 Reporting

Location	Dept.	1 – Title/ ID Number	Date	Author	Sponsor

2 – Problem Description and Background

Background – Why is this topic relevant to the organizational objectives? Provide historical data and information, if available.

Problem Statement – Define what is wrong with what.

Problem Description – Define the who, what, when, where and how much of the problem.

Presentation tools: Graph, Chart, Photographs

3 – Current Condition

Current State – Quantify the facts related to the current state of the situation (e.g. Process map, Pareto analysis, gap analysis). Provide quantitative data.

Presentation tools: Tally Sheet, Pareto Diagram, Sketch, Current-State Map, Histogram, Scatter Diagram, Control Chart, Graph, Photographs

4 – Target Condition/Goal

Target Condition – Quantify the goal you want to achieve relative to the current condition. Include a date you expect to achieve the goal.

Presentation tools: Graph, Chart, Photographs

5 – Root Cause Analysis/Gap Analysis

Root Cause – Are all the relevant factors considered (Man, Machine, Material, Method, Environment)? Does the data and information provided clearly lead to and justify root causes? Describe the analytical tools used to identify root cause.

Presentation tools: Control Chart, Cause-and-Effect Fishbone, Relation Diagram, Histogram, Tree Diagram, Pareto Diagram, Graph, Scatter Diagram, Photographs

6 – Corrective Action/Countermeasure

What will be done, by whom and when to achieve the target or eliminate the problem.

Presentation tools: Diagrams, Charts, Future-State Map, Evaluation Matrix, Photographs

7 – Confirm Results

How will you measure the effectiveness of the counter-measures? Qualitative comparison of actual result to the goal.

Presentation tools: Graph, Chart, Photographs

8 – Follow-up Actions

Updating documentation, communication, identifying best practices and capturing lessons learned.

What is necessary to prevent recurrence of the problem? What remains to be accomplished?

Presentation tools: Graph, Chart, Photographs

Index

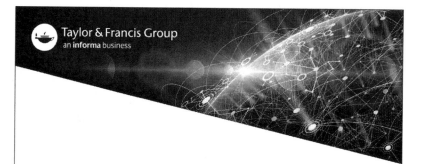